Improving the Legal Process

Improving the Legal Process

Effects of Alternatives

Stuart S. Nagel
University of Illinois

Lexington Books
D.C. Heath and Company
Lexington, Massachusetts
Toronto London

Library of Congress Cataloging in Publication Data

Nagel, Stuart S. 1934-
Improving the legal process.

Includes index.
1. Justice, Administration of—United States. 2 Law reform —United States. I. Title.
KF384.N3 347'.73 74-29481
ISBN 0-669-97824-8

Published simultaneously in Canada.

Printed in the United States of America.

International Standard Book Number: 0-669-97824-8

Library of Congress Catalog Card Number: 74-29481

To the people from whom I have learned, including my teachers and students

Table of Contents

List of Figures

List of Tables

Introduction

The purpose of this book is to bring together a series of studies all of which involve applying social science method, theory, and substance to controversial issues regarding the effects of alternative legal policies designed in some way to improve the legal process. Some of the included studies have previously appeared in diverse law and social science journals. But only by making them and the previously unpublished ones accessible between two covers can their integrated nature be perceived. When most of the studies were originally being written, their role in such an integrated volume was taken into consideration. It has thus been unnecessary to do a large amount of editing in order to provide a coherent whole.

In the context of this book "the legal process" refers mainly to the procedures whereby courts arrive (1) at decisions affecting the immediate parties before the court and (2) at decisions having the prospective effect on others of legal policy-making. The concept also refers to procedures whereby legislative bodies as well as administrative agencies, arrive at decisions. The concept of "improving" in the context of this book refers to maximizing or moving toward the achievement of given goals which have been offered by commentators and others as goals which the legal process should be seeking to achieve.

The book is primarily concerned with six problems involved in applying social science to improving the legal process. The six problems correspond to the parts into which the book is divided, namely (1) developing a basic conceptual and methodological scheme which can be used for testing effects of alternative legal policies, (2) decreasing discrimination against weak litigants, (3) improving judicial personnel, (4) improving procedural efficiency, (5) increasing compliance with the law, and (6) developing new research and teaching approaches that will facilitate the application of social science to improving the legal process.

The basic *conceptual* scheme proposed is one which views the legal process mainly as a stimulus to subsequent effects and also as a response from prior stimuli, rather than as a set of rules to be learned by law students and applied by lawyers. The effects may be considered desirable or undesirable, and they may relate to goals or unintended consequences. The *methodology* proposed for analyzing the effects of alternative legal policies differs depending on whether the policy is one of (1) should something be legalized or authorized, as contrasted to: (2) how scarce resources should be allocated to alternative possibilities. Where legalization is the issue, the methodology emphasizes the use of simple percentage comparisons and other sociological correlation techniques. Where resource allocation is the issue, the methodology emphasizes the use of simple graphical analysis and other econometric programming techniques.

Decreasing *discrimination* against weak litigants involves studies which deal with testing the effects of various procedural devices deisgned to have the outcomes of court cases depend more on the law and the evidentiary facts and less on who the parties are. The types of parties who may be discriminated against include persons who are poor, members of minority ethnic groups, socially deviant personalities, women, residents of malapportioned geographical areas, and members of minority political parties. The kinds of procedural and related devices discussed include matters relating to providing attorneys for those who can not afford them, facilitating the willingness of attorneys to represent unpopular clients, having more demographically balanced representation on juries, and using bipartisan computer-aided redistricting. The general social consequences of providing basic civil liberties for weak litigants are also discussed.

The attempt to improve judicial *personnel* may benefit from our knowing something about the characteristics that have been associated with being a highly regarded judge. The method whereby judges are selected for the bench has also often been discussed as being relevant to the quality of the judges chosen. One particularly important chapter in this section of the book deals with the methodology and findings involved in comparing elected and appointed judicial systems. Another chapter presents material relevant to the problem of decreasing the relation between judges background characteristics and their decisions, so that the outcome of future cases will depend less on who the judges are.

The improvement of procedural *efficiency* is treated mainly from the point of view of minimizing time and money costs within the system, while maximizing the satisfaction of whatever groups one is interested in serving or one considers to be important or representative. This section particularly makes use of such econometric technques as linear programming to allocate scarce system resources. The section also deals with some of the problems involved in measuring costs and benefits as steps in the design of research directed toward improving procedural efficiency.

The fifth part of the book deals with procedural means for increasing *compliance* with law. It discusses, in a general way, why some constitutional precedents are more complied with than others. A varicty of incentives for compliance with the law are presented in the context of violations of environmental protection standards. Without high compliance, it makes little difference how desirable the effects of substantive legal policies might be in the abstract.

The last part of the book attempts to describe recent trends and *needs* in research related to testing the effects of alternative legal policies. It is especially concerned with presenting and justifying the need for (1) a legal data repository, (2) empirical readings to supplement traditional casebooks in basic law school courses, and (3) a conference of law professors and social scientists designed to inventory the past, present, and future empirical research on socio-legal procedural and substantive problems.

This book builds on the author's previous book, *The Legal Process from a Behavioral Perspective* (Dorsey, 1969), which was mainly designed to describe the stimuli elements which determine both law-making and adjudication responses. These elements included prior legal and judicial precedents, cultural patterns, litigant characteristics, evidentiary and other facts, and the nature of the policymakers and policy-appliers. To a lesser extent that book dealt with law-making and adjudication as stimuli to subsequent responses which is the main focus of this present book, and which was emphasized in the concluding chapter and epilogue of the prior book.

The present book is partly designed to lead in two directions with regard to the author's subsequent research and publication. One direction is toward applying a similar conceptual and methodological orientation toward testing the effects of alternative substantive, rather than procedural, policies. Controversial policy issues in that regard will include such matters as anti-discrimination legislation, divorce laws, abortion reform, inheritance and state taxes, federal housing programs, and public employee strikes.

The other future direction is toward further developing the econometric methods which are presented here for allocating scarce resources to alternative possibilities. Examples of specific studies planned include allocating OEO legal services funds between rural and urban areas, allocating public housing expenditures between clustered and scattered site housing, applying game theory to plea bargaining and settlement negotiations in court cases, applying queuing theory to allocating personnel for processing incoming cases, applying PERT analysis to the optimum sequencing of legal processes, and allocating school aid funds between integration and compensatory education.

The contributions of various people to specific chapters are acknowledged in the footnotes, but there are some people and institutions who have contributed substantially to the whole book and to whom I am extremely grateful. These include my research assistants, namely Allan Wichelman, David Calfee, and Secil Tuncalp. They also include my sources of research funds, namely the LEAA National Institute of Law Enforcement and Criminal Justice, the National Science Foundation (grant GS-2875), the Russell Sage Foundation, the Yale Law and Social Science Program, and the University of Illinois Research Board. They further include my extracurricular employers who provided enriching insights from the nonacademic world, namely the Champaign County Legal Services Program of the Office of Economic Opportunity, the Lawyers Constitutional Defense Committee in Mississippi, and the United States Senate Subcommittee on Administrative Practice and Procedure. I also greatly appreciate the help provided to me by Marian Neef (of the Illinois and Harvard Ph.D. programs) in putting my thoughts for this book into words, and especially the help provided by my wife Joyce in the logistics involved in efficiently pulling this research together.

I am also indebted to those University of Illinois graduate students who collaborated with me in writing certain chapters, namely, David Neubauer (chapter 4), Anthony Champage and Marian Neef (5), and William Cantrall (8). Lenore Weitzman, of the University of California at Berkeley, and I collaborated on Chapter 7. I also acknowledge the generosity of the following journals and publishers for allowing me to reprint portions of my articles: Sage Publications, *Current History,* Jay Stewart Publications, *Indiana Law Journal, Chicago Daily Law Bulletin, Hastings Law Journal,* New York Academy of Sciences, *Polity, American Bar Association Journal, Policy Sciences,* Atherton Press, *Law and Society Review*, and *Journal of Legal Education*. None of the above persons, organizations, agencies, journals, or publishers should be considered responsible (unless otherwise credited) for any of the ideas advocated in this book on *Improving the Legal Process: Effects of Alternatives*.

Part I
Basic Concepts and Methods

The basic conceptual scheme for this book involves thinking of law and the legal process *not* as something to be studied in itself, the way a lawyer would who desires to learn (1) the law in his field of specialty and (2) the procedures designed to maximize the chances of victory for his clients. Instead, law and the legal process are viewed here mainly as phenomena which produce various kinds of effects.

Different legal alternatives generally produce different effects, although legal alternatives over which there may be great controversy may sometimes produce surprisingly similar effects. Some effects are considered socially desirable and some are not. Making such a distinction often involves determining the effects of the effects of the legal alternatives. Such a distinction also ultimately involves determining how the effects are evaluated by the general public, by legislators, or by some other relevant group of people.

Although the emphasis in this book is on the effects of alternative legal policies, mention is frequently made of the social forces and other causal factors responsible for why a society adopts one legal policy alternative rather than another. Having such knowledge may be quite useful in making realistic policy recommendations with regard to what alternative legal policy one should seek to have adopted. In other words, realistic policy recommendations need to consider the likelihood of adoption (based on casual analysis of alternative legal policies) rather than just the desirable or undesirable effects of alternative legal policies.

This combined perspective of viewing legal policies as producing various effects and as being produced by various causes lends itself to a clarifying flow chart like that shown in figure I-1. The central concept in the flow chart is legal policies, which can be defined as rules supported by governmental or societal authority which specify the rights and obligations of (1) persons whether human or corporate and (2) governmental agencies. Legal policies can be either substantive or procedural. Substantive policies define the legal rights and obligations of persons (or governments) to governments (i.e., public law), or the legal rights and obligations of persons to other persons (i.e., private law). Procedural policies describe the steps or routines one has to go through in order to establish or enforce one's legal rights or another's legal obligations.

Procedural policies can be judicial, administrative, or legislative de-

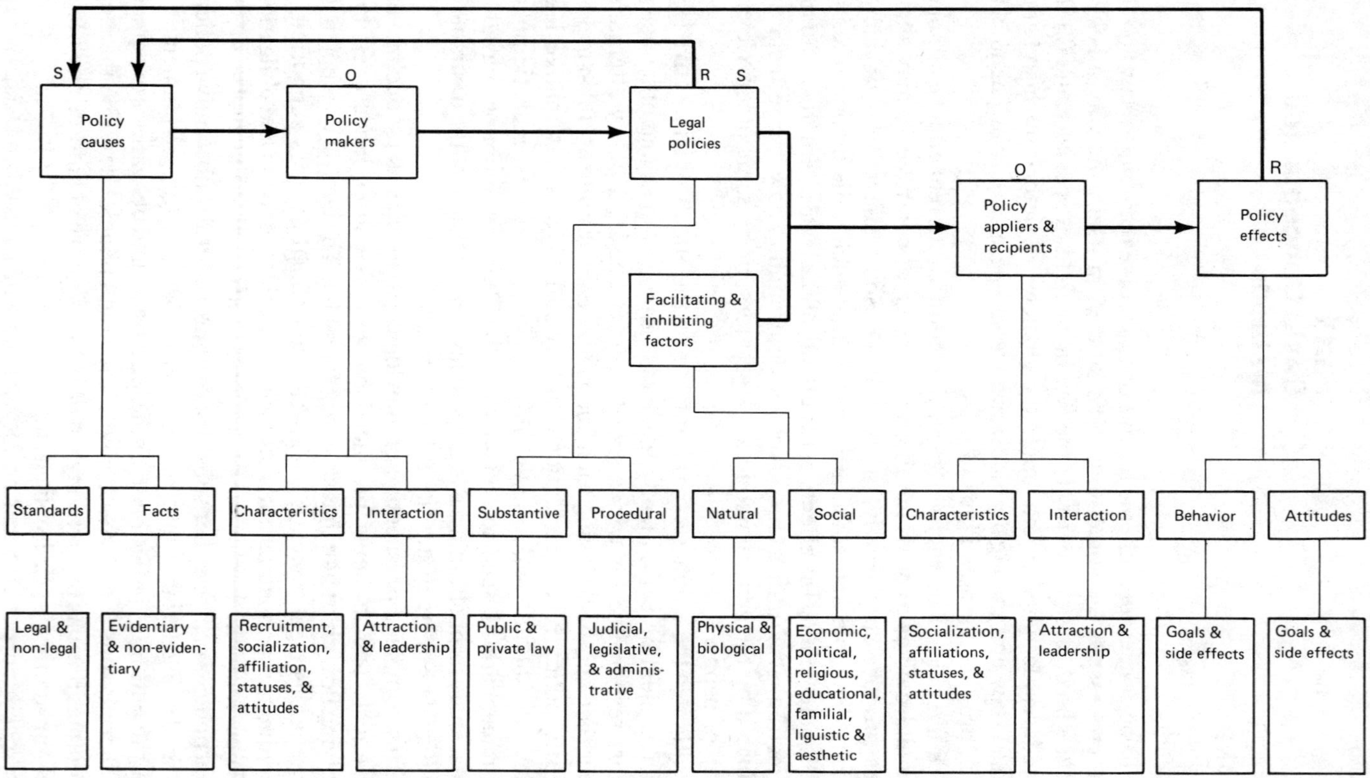

Figure I-1. A Conceptual Scheme of the Legal Process

pending on the governmental unit responsible for the establishment or enforcement. Extra-legal procedures may also exist for establishing or enforcing rights and obligations such as employment grievance procedures, vigilante justice, and direct-action consumer boycotts. This book will concentrate on the legal process and on effects of alternative legal *procedural* policies in the judicial, legislative, and administrative realms, although primarily the judicial. A future book by this writer is planned which will concentrate on the effects of alternative substantive policies.

To the far right of the concept of legal policies in the flow chart are the policy effects which can manifest themselves in changed attitudes and changed behavior, and can also manifest themselves with regard to the goals of the policies or unintended side effects. Between the legal policies and the policy effects are intervening variables that relate to (1) facilitating and inhibiting factors and also to (2) the nature of the policy-appliers and the policy-recipients. Facilitating and inhibiting factors are mainly social (such as economic, political, religious, educational, familial, linguistic, and aesthetic factors), but may also be natural (such as physical and biological factors). These intervening factors can determine the degree and kinds of policy effects which the legal policies produce. Also determinative are the characteristics of the policymakers and the policy-recipients (including their socialization, group affiliations, statutes, and attitudes), and the interaction among the policymakers or policy-recipients (especially with regard to matters of leadership and who attracts whom).

To the far left of the concept of legal policies in the flow chart are the policy causes which take the form of empirical facts or normative standards. The empirical facts may be legally admissible evidence or may be legally irrelevant items particularly those relating to the relative power of the contesting groups or forces. The normative standards may also be legal in the sense they have been promulgated by governmental bodies, or they may be non-legal in the sense they only manifest themselves in customs, scholarly commentaries, and philosophical notions of justice. Between the policy causes and the legal policies are intervening variables that relate to the characteristics and interaction of the policymakers, roughly comparable to the characteristics and interactions of the policy-appliers and policy-recipients. Facilitating and inhibiting factors may also intervene to influence the relation between the policy causes and the policy effects.

In addition, the flow chart has feedback loops in that newly created legal policies become normative policy causes for future legal policies. Likewise, policy effects feed back to become empirical policy causes for future legal policies. The whole flow chart with its concepts and subconcepts helps to provide pigeonholes for categorizing and integrating legal process findings and helps to provide prods for stimulating legal process hypotheses.

The diagram shown in figure I-1 could be made more complicated although more accurate if it were divided into three sections (relating to policymakers, policy-appliers, and policy-recipients) rather than two sections (in which policy-appliers and policy-recipients are grouped together). A three-section diagram would show that the responses or output from the policymakers becomes the stimuli or input to the policy-appliers, and that the responses from the policy-appliers becomes the stimuli to the policy-recipients. The diagram would also show that the responses or output at each of the three stages can feed back on the input of that stage and on the input of the one or two previous stages.

Chapter 1 of this section on basic concepts and methods provides the methodology that is used throughout the book. It basically consists of using a system of correlation analysis to choose among conflicting legal policies that are primarily regulatory rather than subsidizing policies, and using a system of linear programming for choosing among conflicting legal policies that primarily involve allocating scarce governmental resources.

The book mainly deals with legal policy problems in which the policymakers or policy-appliers need to choose among conflicting non-expenditure policies, such as whether to encourage more female representation on juries, whether to prohibit malapportionment of legislatures, and whether to elect or appoint judges. To a lesser extent, it deals with legal policy problems involving the allocation of scarce governmental resources such as the ideal mix of OEO Legal Services funds between routine case handling and broader law reform work. Some legal policy problems can be viewed as both expenditure and non-expenditure problems, such as (1) whether to adopt a public defender system rather than an assigned counsel system, or (2) how to try to apportion county funds between (a) the public defender's salary and (b) fees for simultaneously-operating assigned counsel.

In recent years there has been a trend away from the emphasis on policy problems involving regulation, legalization, or whether something should be adopted over to policy problems involving subsidization, expenditures, or how money should be spent. This trend is partly responsible for the reduction in the role of lawyers in high governmental administrative positions, and the increase in economists, management specialists, and operations research consultants. A future book by this writer is planned which will concentrate more on the applications of operations research techniques like linear programming to legal policy problems.

Chapter 2 of this section provides a brief discussion of the need for a judicial reform. In doing so, it provides a set of legal process problems to which the methodology in Chapter 1 can possibly be fruitfully applied. Chapter 2 emphasizes seven legal process problems about which there is a great deal of literature expressing discontent with the presently prevailing or recently prevailing procedures for handling criminal and civil cases. The seven problems relate to: (1) bail reform, (2) legal counsel for the poor in criminal and civil cases, (3) delay in civil and criminal cases, (4) mass media reporting on pending cases, (5) judicial selection, (6) the jury system, and (7) judicial nullification of legislative and administrative acts.

These problems were the ones emphasized in the intercollegiate and high school debates of 1971-72. They are also emphasized at many points in this book, especially the problem of legal counsel for the poor, but also the problem of judicial selection, delay in adjudicative proceedings, and the need for more female representation on juries. There are also other important legal process problems that do not so heavily involve the judicial process. For example, Chapters 8 and 9 deal with the need to improve those aspects of the legal process which relate to how to reapportion legislative bodies. Likewise, Chapters 15 and 16 deal with the need to improve those aspects of the legal process which particularly relate to more effective legal administration so as to increase compliance with the law.

1 Choosing Among Alternative Public Policies

The purpose of this chapter is to provide an introduction to a basic methodology which is used throughout this book for testing the effects of alternative legal or public policies. The testing methodology depends mainly on whether the legal policies involve (1) making legal or illegal some activity like capital punishment or (2) deciding how to allocate governmental funds to alternative activities like subsidizing low-rent public housing versus home ownership for the poor.

Other examples of controversial legal policies involving the issue of whether something should be made legal or illegal include legalizing marijuana, prohibiting malapportioned legislatures, legalizing medical abortions, or providing for elected rather than appointed judges. Other examples of controversial legal policies involving the allocation of scarce governmental resources include allocating funds between busing versus compensatory education in improving educational opportunities for poor children, between anti-pollution water enforcement programs versus water clean-up facilities, and allocating funds between fair employment enforcement activities versus manpower training to provide better employment opportunities to minorities.[1]

Choosing Among Non-Expenditure Policies

The General Problem and the Illustrative Data

Table 1-1 summarizes the decision rules involved for adopting or preferring non-expenditure policies. Each row in the table illustrates a different problem situation. The first situation involves one policy and one goal, and the problem is to decide whether or not to adopt the policy in light of its relation to the one goal. The second situation involves two policies and one goal, and the problem is to decide which policy to prefer if they both cannot be adopted. Situation three involves one policy and two goals, and the problem (like the first problem) is to decide whether or not to adopt the policy in light of its relation to the two goals. Situation four involves two policies and two goals, and the problem there (like the second problem) is to decide which policy to prefer if they both cannot be adopted.

Table 1-1
Decision Rules for Adopting or Preferring Non-Expenditure Policies

Problem Situation	*Policies or Means (X's)*	*Goals or Ends (Y's)*	*Adopt X_1 (where there is only one policy under consideration) if:*	*Prefer X_1 over X_2 if:*
One	X_1	Y_a	$R_{X_1Y_a \cdot z}$ is greater than zero.	
Two	X_1 and X_2	Y_a		$R_{X_1Y_a \cdot z}$ is greater than $R_{X2Ya \cdot z}$.
Three	X_1	Y_a and Y_b	[($R_{X_1Y_a \cdot z}$ times W_{Y_a}) plus ($R_{X_1Y_b \cdot z}$ times W_{Y_b})] is greater than zero.	
Four	X_1 and X_2	Y_a and Y_b		U_{X_1} is greater than U_{X2}. where U_{X_1} = the expression in brackets under situation three.

Meaning of Symbols:

$R_{X_1Y_a \cdot z}$ = the correlation or slope between X_1 and Y_a holding constant intervening variables Z.
W_{Y_a} = the value weight of goal a.
U_{X_1} = the rank-order utility of policy 1.
X, Y, and Z can be dichotomous attributes or interval-measured variables.
X, Y, and Z can be static (i.e., one point in time) or dynamic (i.e., ΔX, ΔY, and ΔZ, where Δ = change in).
Numbered subscripts differentiate policies, and alphabetic subscripts differentiate goals.

In order to better understand the decision rules, it is helpful to have a concrete example. One concrete example that can be used is the problem situation of deciding what to do to decrease the occurrence of illegal searches by the police. One alternative that the courts have adopted is to exclude or throw out illegally obtained evidence from courtroom proceedings in criminal cases on the theory that doing so will deter the police from using illegal methods to obtain evidence. Prior to 1961 the United States Supreme Court allowed the state courts and legislatures to decide themselves whether to adopt this exclusionary rule. In 1961 the Supreme Court in the case of *Mapp v. Ohio* declared that the fourth amendment required that illegally seized evidence be inadmissible in all American criminal cases, at least when objected to by defense counsel.

In 1963 a mailed-questionnaire survey was made of one randomly selected police chief, prosecuting attorney, judge, defense attorney, and ACLU official in each of the fifty states to determine among other things their perceptions of changes in police behavior before and after *Mapp v. Ohio*. The experiment was aided by virtue of the fact that twenty-four of the fifty states had already adopted the exclusionary rule before *Mapp v. Ohio*. and respondents from those states could thus serve as a control group; twenty-three were newly forced to adopt the rule at that time, and respondents from those states could thus serve as an experimental group; and three states which were not used in the analysis had partially adopted it.

Table 1-2 shows that 57 percent of the respondents from the control group of states reported an increase in police adherence to legality in making searches since 1961; whereas 75 percent of the respondents from the experimental group of newly-adopting states reported an increase. This 18 percentage points difference (or, roughly speaking, a correlation of +.18) cannot be readily attributed to a chance fluke in the sample of respondents since there is less than a five out of 100 probability that one could distribute 104 respondents over the six cells in table 1-2 purely by chance and come out with a +.18 correlation. This +.18 correlation is also not readily attributable to a misperception of the reality on the part of the respondents since there was such a high correlation among the different kinds of respondents from the same state or type of states on the empirical question of police adherence to legality, even though there was great disagreement on the normative question of the desirability of the exclusionary rule.

The +.18 correlation between newly adopting the exclusionary rule and increased police adherence to legality in searches seems to be largely attributable to the fact that the states that newly adopted the exclusionary rule also disproportionately reported an increase in programs designed to educate the police as to search and seizure law, which in turn correlates highly with increased police adherence to legality. States that already had

Table 1-2
The Relation Between Adopting the Exclusionary Rule and Increased Police Adherence to Legality in Making Searches

		Exclusionary Rule		
		Had All Along (Control Group)	*Newly Adopted (Experimental Group)*	
Police Adherence to Legality	*Increase since 1961*	57%	75%	+18 percentage points difference
	No change	34%	21%	
	Decrease	9%	4%	
	Number of Respondents	48	56	104

the exclusionary rule also often underwent an increase in police adherence to legality possibly because of the stimulus of the publicity given in *Mapp v. Ohio,* and because of long-term public opinion trends demanding higher standards of police behavior.[2]

The Four Decision Situations

Figure 1-1 shows the relation between alternative policies and alternative goals involved in the problem of increasing police adherence to legality in making searches, and can be nicely used to illustrate the decision rules in table 1-1. The top part of figure 1-2 shows that the exclusionary rule (X_1) should be adopted (in light of the decision rule for problem situation one) if increased police adherence to legality (Y_a) is one's only goal since there is a positive correlation between X_1 and Y_a.

Many judges and others (including Felix Frankfurter in his dissenting opinion in *Mapp v. Ohio)* have argued that tort or criminal actions against the police are far more effective than adopting the exclusionary rule as a means of increasing police adherence to legality. The questionnaire asked the respondents how often tort or criminal actions had occurred against the police in their communities for making illegal searches. If one divides the respondents into those relatively few who said there had been at least one such action in recent years versus those who said there had been none, then there is only a +.05 correlation between the occurrence of such actions and increased police adherence to police legality. The low correlation and the low occurrence of such actions may be attributable to the fact that pros-

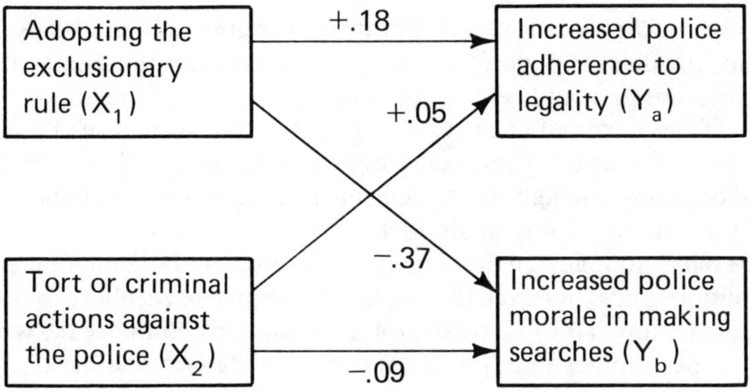

Figure 1-1. Alternative Policies and Goals Involved in Increasing Police Adherence to Legality in Making Searches

ecutors are reluctant to prosecute the police who have been aiding them, and searched individuals are reluctant to sue because of the time, cost, embarrassment, unsympathetic juries, police discretion, and difficulty of assessing collectible damages. Thus, the exclusionary rule (X_1) should be preferred (in light of the decision rule for problem situtation two) over tort or criminal actions (X_2) if increased adherence to legality (Y_a) is one's only goal (and the decisionmaker cannot adopt both policies) since there is a greater positive correlation between X_1 and Y_a than there is between X_2 and Y_a.

An additional goal one might have in dealing with the problem of increasing police adherence to legality in making searches is the goal of simultaneously increasing police morale, or at least not decreasing it. The mailed questionnaire asked the respondents about changes in police morale before and after *Mapp v. Ohio*. The correlation between being a respondent from a state that had newly adopted the exclusionary rule (X_1) and reporting increased police morale (Y_b) in making searches was a −.37. The negative correlation may be attributable to the fact that when evidence is thrown out which the police have worked hard to obtain through what they may have considered a lawful search, this is demoralizing to their enthusiasm for making future searches. If the correlation between X_1 and Y_b had been positive like the correlation between X_1 and Y_a, then it would be easy to decide in favor of adopting X_1. However, since the correlation between X_1 and Y_b is negative, one must decide whether that negative correlation is enough to offset the positive correlation between X_1 and Y_a. The matter is not resolved simply by noting that the X_1 and Y_b correlation is greater than the X_1 and Y_a correlation. This is so because it is unlikely that one would weight the Y_a and Y_b equally. If the Y_a goal has a weight 3 times or more the Y_b goal, then the −.37 correlation would not be enough to offset the +.18

correlation in view of the fact that 3 times .18 is greater than 1 times .37. On the other hand, if the Y_a goal has a weight 2 times or less the Y_b goal, then the −.37 correlation would be enough to offset the +.18 correlation. In other words, if the correlation of X_1 and Y_a (times the weight of Y_a) plus the correlation of X_1 and Y_b (times the weight of Y_b) is greater than zero, then X_1 should be adopted in light of the decision rule for problem situation three if Y_a and Y_b are one's only goals.[3]

The most complicated problem situation involves both multiple policies and multiple goals, but even this situation is simple to resolve conceptually after going through the first three problem situations. Suppose the weight of Y_a is 3 times greater than the weight of Y_b as determined by a scientific psychological survey of public, legislative, or judicial opinions. Note also that the correlation between the occasional occurrence of tort or criminal actions against the police and increased police morale was a negative −.09. Thus the exclusionary rule (X_1) should be preferred (in light of the decision rule for problem situation four) over tort or criminal actions (X_2) if increased adherence to legality (Y_a) and increased police morale (Y_b) are one's only goals (and the decisionmaker cannot adopt both policies) since in figure 1-1: $+.18 \times 3$ plus $-.37 \times 1$ is greater than $+.05 \times 3$ plus $-.09 \times 1$. In other words, .54 plus −.37 is greater than −.15 plus −.09.

Variations and Alternatives to the Basic Rules

Instead of using the correlation coefficients between the variables shown in figure 1-1 in order to make the policy choices shown in table 1-1, one could use the regression slopes between the policy and goal variables when a line is fitted to the dots on a graph of the variables. The dots are generated by plotting the positions of the communities of the respondents. Whether regression or correlation measures are more meaningful is a somewhat disputed issue among social scientists.[4] Correlation coefficients are simpler and not influenced by the units of measurement used, but unlike regression coefficients they are not capable of being used to predict how many additional units of Y can be obtained by an increase in units of X. Correlation coefficients should be favored in this decision-making context because each one can be used to indicate the amount of variation on Y_a and Y_b accounted for by X_1 and X_2 respectively. Regression weights cannot be used in this comparative context because they can be increased or decreased by changing the units of measurement (e.g., from dollars to pennies) without changing how closely the variables vary together.[5]

The decision rules in table 1-1 can be logically extended to cover more policies. For example, three or more policies and one goal is analogous to situation two. One policy and three or more goals is analogous to situation three. Likewise, analogous to situation four is (1) two policies and three or more goals, (2) three or more policies and two goals, or (3) three or more policies and three or more goals. Additional policies concerning the problem of illegal police searches might relate to police training and police selection practices. Additional goals might relate to decreasing the crime rate and decreasing the unsuccessful prosecution rate.

The methodology can also be extended to other areas of controversy like marijuana, malapportionment, abortion, and judicial selection, provided that one can obtain data on the relations between adoption of the controversial policy (and alternative policies) and the goals (on which there are some mutual agreement). In the American federal system where states and cities do experiment with alternative approaches to given social problems, these kind of data can often be obtained provided one has (1) some financial support and (2) some cooperation from knowledgeable persons. Even if solid data cannot always be fully obtained, use of the conceptual approach outlined can often be helpful in clarifying and making more effective governmental policy analysis.[6]

The correlation approach just presented is closely related to benefit-cost analysis in that for each situation, benefit-cost analysis says make the following decisions:[7]

Situation one. Adopt X_1 if the benefits of X_1 are greater than the costs of X_1.

Situation two. Prefer X_1 if the B-C of X_1 is greater than the B-C of X_2.

Situation three. Adopt X_1 if B of X_1 is greater than C of X_1, where $B = B_{Ya} + B_{Yb}$ and $C = C_{X1} + C_{X2}$.

Situation four. Prefer X_1 if the B-C of X_1 is greater than the B-C of X_2, where B and C are figured as in situation three.

Determining such benefit minus cost differences is often less meaningful than the correlation approach for three reasons. First, the B-C approach does not consider the correlation or probability that X will achieve Y, unless one resorts to a complicated system of probability calculations.[8] Second, the B-C approach does not measure X in interval units but just as present or absent, unless one resorts to a complicated system of marginal analysis. Third, the B-C approach requires B and C to be measured in the same units, unless one resorts to a complicated system of exponent weights.[9]

The correlation approach can also be distinguished from the matrix decision theory approach for choosing among non-expenditure policies. In the matrix decision approach to the problem of increasing police adherence to legality, there is one state of nature or Z variable, unless one wants to distinguish between rural and urban police or some other possibly significant intervening variable. There are four alternative policies since there are two positions on X_1 and two positions on X_2. There are nine possible payoff alternatives since there are three positions on Y_a and three positions on Y_b. This yields a matrix with one column and four rows. In each cell of the matrix, one shows the average payoff score (with ranks from 1 to 9) for each of the four alternative strategies. The strategy to choose using this approach is simply the one with the highest payoff score.[10]

This matrix decision approach, however, won't work relative to the correlation approach if one X or means variable is measured on a continuum, rather than broken into a few discrete sub-positions. If an X variable is continuous, then theoretically there are an infinity of alternatives. If the X variables yields a manageable 10 to 15 alternative strategies, then the drawback exists that the strategy with the highest payoff may be one that exists in only a few communities; but by small-sample coincidence, those few communities may have undergone an increase in both police adherence and police morale. In other words, the decision matrix approach can lead to faulty decisions if the sample size is not substantial for the empirical occurrences of each alternative strategy, whereas the correlation approach mainly requires a substantial sample only for the overall sample size.[11]

One of the goals that can be included (in the correlation analysis) is to keep costs down. However, when trying to decide how to allocate scarce financial resources among diverse policy activities, it may be more meaningful to use a kind of linear programming approach about to be described rather than the correlation approach which we have just presented.[12]

Choosing Among Expenditure Policies

The General Problem and the Illustrative Data

To illustrate on a very simple level what is involved in applying linear programming concepts to choosing among alternative expenditure policies, let's take the problem of allocating \$10 in campaign expenditure money to media dollars and precinct organization dollars. Suppose we are in a congressional district in which thirty-nine votes are expected to be cast among the two candidates running, which means our candidate needs twenty votes to win.[13]

There may be some combination of media and precinct dollars that will enable us to get our twenty votes while spending substantially less than the

$10 we have available. Finding that combination is the cost minimization problem. Likewise, there may be some combination of media and precinct dollars that will enable us to get as many votes as possible above twenty votes while spending no more than the $10 we have available. This is the benefit maximization problem. Linear programming is an excellent method for determining what combination of expenditures will minimize costs while achieving at least a minimum benefit level or determining what combination will maximize benefits while keeping within a maximum cost level.

Linear programming or optimizing can be defined as a procedure whereby one finds the optimum allocation of funds or some other scarce resource between two or more alternatives in light of a given minimizing or maximizing goal and in light of given constraints or conditions. In order to be linear rather than non-linear programming, the relations between the resources and the goals must be straight-line or constant-return relations rather than curved-line or diminishing-return relations.

Suppose that we have obtained (1) data from the Federal Communications Commission showing how much money was spent by each of the approximately 800 congressional candidates in 1972 on television and radio, (2) data from the General Accounting Office showing how much money was spent in total by each of the candidates, and (3) data from the *Congressional Quarterly* showing how many votes were obtained. If we subtract the FCC media expenditures from the GAO total expenditures, we should have a rough estimate of precinct organization expenditures for each candidate. If we then do a regression analysis with media dollars (M) and precinct dollars (P) as the independent variables and votes obtained as the dependent variable, we should be able to come up with a roughly accurate empirical equation between these variables, which might read something like Votes Obtained $= 5 + 2M + 1P$. The 5 in this equation indicates the number of votes likely to be obtained without any expenditure of funds. The 2 and the 1 indicate the relative weights of media dollars and precinct dollars in determining the number of votes obtained.[14]

In our illustration there are basically only two constraints. One relates costs to our two activity variables; the other relates benefits to our two activity variables. The first says the sum of media dollars and precinct organization dollars must be less than or equal to $10. This is our maximum cost constraint. The second constraint says 20 Votes $= 5 + 2M + 1P$. This is our minimum benefits constraint.

Graphing the Solution

To understand better what is involved in finding optimum expenditure combinations through linear programming, it is helpful to make a graph depicting our constraints. Figure 1-2 shows the maximum cost line as a straight line connecting (1) the point at which \$0 is spent for precinct organization and \$10 is spent for media to (2) the point where \$0 is spent for media and \$10 is spent for precinct organization. Every point on that line involves a combination of *M* and *P* that adds up to \$10 which is why it is also called an equal cost line.

Figure 1-2 also shows the minimum benefits line as a straight line connecting (1) the point at which \$0 is spent for precinct organization and \$7.50 therefore has to be spent for media (in order for $5 + 2M + 1P$ to add up to 20) to (2) the point at which \$0 is spent for media and \$15 therefore has to be spent for precinct organization (in order for $5 + 2M + 1P$ to add up to 20). Every point on that line involves a combination of *M* and *P* that produces twenty votes, which is why it is also called an equal benefit line or an indifference line.

Regardless of whether we want to minimize costs or maximize benefits, the ideal combination has to be below the maximum cost line. Likewise, it has to be above the minimum benefit line. This means the ideal combination has to be a point somewhere in figure 1-2 within the area marked "feasible region" since that is the only area where both constraints are satisfied simultaneously.

Point A (where M = \$7.50, and P = \$0) is the point where total cost is minimized while providing at least twenty votes. This is so because that is the point furthest away from the maximum cost line that is still within the feasible region. By only spending \$7.50, we save \$2.50 for the next election or for other worthwhile causes. Point B (where M = \$10 and P = \$0) is the point where votes are maximized while not spending more than \$10. This is so because that is the point furthest away from the maximim benefit line that is still within the feasible region. At that point, twenty-five votes will be obtained since the number of votes obtained equals $5 + 2M + 1P$. One may wish to obtain these extra votes as insurance against miscalculation or in order to claim a mandate for an aggressive political program or for ego gratification.[15]

Note that the minimum benefits line represents a binding constraint on cost minimization in the sense that if we did not need to get at least twenty votes we could save additional money. The money we are not saving by virtue of that constraint can be considered an opportunity cost. Also note that the maximum cost line represents a binding constraint on benefit maximization in the sense that if we did not need to limit ourselves to \$10 we could obtain additional votes up to thirty-nine votes. The votes we are not obtaining by virtue of that constraint can also be considered an opportunity cost.

An alternative way of interpreting the optimizing in figure 1-2 is to use

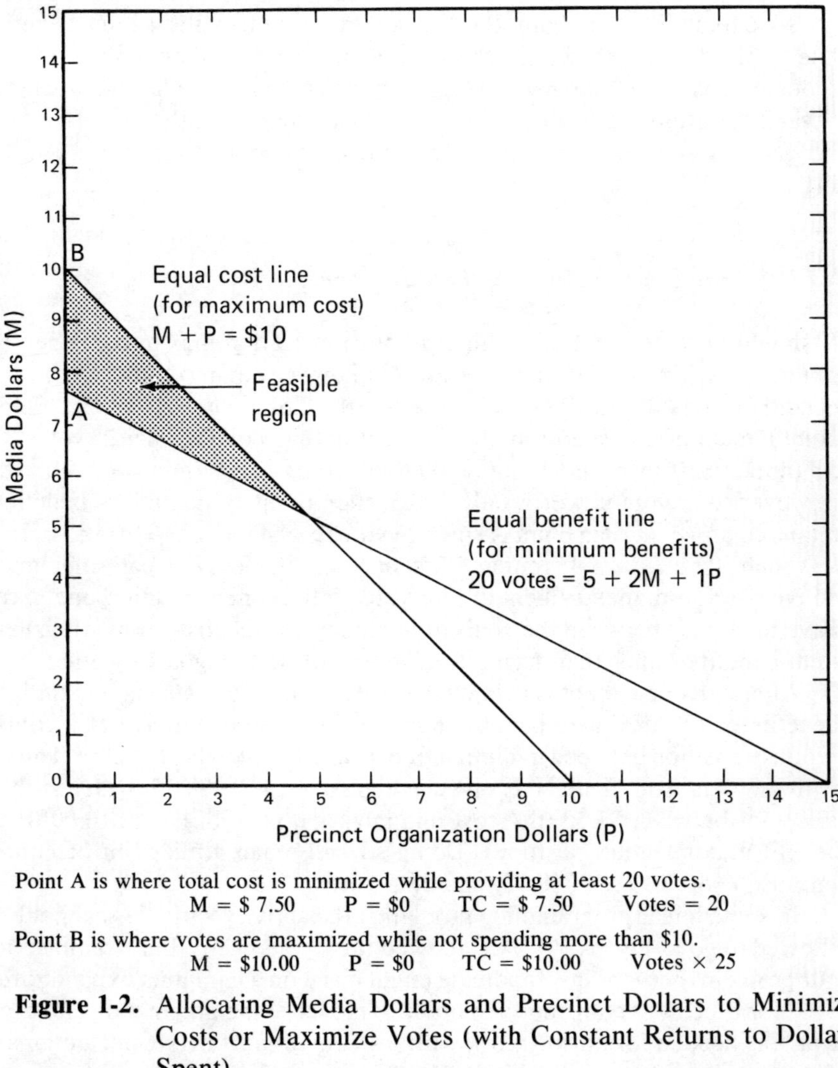

Point A is where total cost is minimized while providing at least 20 votes.
M = \$ 7.50 P = \$0 TC = \$ 7.50 Votes = 20

Point B is where votes are maximized while not spending more than \$10.
M = \$10.00 P = \$0 TC = \$10.00 Votes × 25

Figure 1-2. Allocating Media Dollars and Precinct Dollars to Minimize Costs or Maximize Votes (with Constant Returns to Dollars Spent)

concepts from production and consumption economics. With those concepts one recognizes that point A is the cost minimization point because there is a family of parallel equal cost lines for every possible total cost, and point A is the point where the lowest equal cost line is at which just touches the minimum benefit line. This point can be thought of as the point where the producer of votes minimizes his total costs in allocating his budget to two factors of production, namely media dollars and precinct organization dollars, analogous to labor and capital. Likewise, point B is the benefit maximization point because there is a family of equal benefit lines for every possible total vote, and point B is the point where the highest equal benefit line is at which just touches the maximum cost line. This point can be thought of as the point where the consumer purchasing media and precinct organization units maximizes his total utility by optimally allocating his budget between these two consumer goods, analogous to food and clothing.

Variations and Alternatives to the Basic Scheme

It should be noted that one cannot in our illustration maximize: benefits minus costs. This is so because we do not know how many dollars we or our candidate considers a given vote to be worth. If one vote is worth \$1, then point B maximizes benefits minus costs better than point A since 25 votes × \$1 (minus \$10 in costs) is more than 20 votes × \$1 (minus \$7.50). If, however, one vote is worth only \$0.45, then point B maximizes benefits minus costs *worse* than point A since 25 votes × \$.45 (minus \$10 in costs) is *less* than 20 votes × \$.45 (minus \$7.50 in costs). Unless one can somehow convert a non-monetary benefit like votes into monetary units, one may have to choose between the goals of minimizing total costs or maximizing total benefits rather than trying to combine these two goals together.

Although one cannot (1) simultaneously minimize costs and maximize benefits or (2) maximize benefits minus costs, one can arrive at a compromise position between minimizing costs and maximizing benefits. Thus, with the data from figure 1-2, one can choose an *M* of \$8.75, which is the midpoint between \$7.50 (the cost minimization position) and \$10.00 (the benefit maximization position). Doing so will mean a midpoint or compromise *P* of \$0, *TC* of \$8.75, and 22.5 votes.

In some linear programming problems, the activity variables cannot be allowed to go as low as \$0 as we allowed them to do here. For example, in our problem, perhaps our candidate might insist on a minimum expenditure of \$2 for precinct organization in order to preserve the precinct machinery which is needed for liaison work with his constituents between elections. This would mean drawing a vertical line in figure 1-2 up from the \$2 precinct organization point to the top of the graph, thereby narrowing the feasible region and shifting it to the right. If such a constraint existed in our problem, then the new cost minimization point would be to spend \$2 for precinct organization and \$6.50 for media. The \$6.50 is needed to bring the total expenditure up high enough to obtain twenty votes in light of the equation 20 votes $= 5 + 2M + 1P$. Likewise, if such a constraint existed in our problem, the new benefit maximization point would be to spend \$2 for precinct organization and \$8 for media. Such a combination will mean spending our full \$10 in order to obtain twenty-three votes in light of the equation, votes obtained $= 5 + 2M + 1P$.

An alternative way of expressing the same ideas shown in figure 1-2 (that is more like the non-expenditure correlation analysis model previously presented) is to plot four separate graphs for the two goal variables and the two policy variables.[16] The first graph would show total cost as a goal or dependent variable on the vertical axis and precinct dollars as a policy or independent variable on the horizontal axis. One would then plot the relation $TC = 7.5 + .5P$, which follows from the fact that $TC = M + P$ and $M = (20 - 5 - P)/2$. Doing so indicates total cost is at a minimum at \$7.50 with twenty votes where $P = \$0$. The second graph would show total cost against media dollars by plotting the relation $TC = 15 - M$, which follows from $TC = M + P$ and $P = 20 - 5 - 2M$. Doing so also indicates that total cost is at a minimum at \$7.50 where $M = \$7.50$, provided neither P nor M can be negative. The third graph would show total votes against precinct dollars by plotting votes $= 25 - P$, which follows from votes $= 5 + 2M + 1P$ and $M = 10 - P$. Doing so indicates that total votes are at a twenty-five-vote maximum when \$0 are spent for P which means the whole \$10 is being spent for M. The fourth graph would show total votes against media dollars by plotting votes $= 15 + M$, which follows from votes $= 5 + 2M + 1P$ and $P = 10 - M$. Doing that also indicates total votes are at a maximum of twenty-five when $M = \$10$.

To make our expenditure allocation problem somewhat more realistic although somewhat more complicated, we could change the minimum benefit line to reflect the fact that incremental expenditures of either media or precinct organization dollars do not bring equally incremental votes. Instead, additional dollars spent tend to produce additional votes at a decreasing rate by virtue of the fact that additional votes, at least beyond a certain point, become harder to get.[17] A minimum benefit equation reflecting this phenomena (and at the same time indicating that media dollars are more potent vote getters than precinct organization dollars) would be 20 votes $= 5 \cdot \sqrt[2]{M} \cdot \sqrt[3]{P}$.

Figure 1-3 shows this new diminishing-returns minimum-benefit line as a straight line because it is drawn on logarithmic interval paper rather than equal interval paper. The \$10 maximum-cost line comes out to be a curved line rather than a straight line on logarithmic interval paper. Logarithmic interval paper is used because it converts the equation $20 = 5 \cdot \sqrt[2]{M} \cdot \sqrt[3]{P}$ into a straight line which makes it much easier to plot. Note that there is no point on the \$10 maximum cost line which touches the minimum benefit line, and therefore, there is no combination of M and P adding up to less than \$10 which will achieve twenty votes with this new minimum benefit line.

In order to create a feasible region, a \$12 maximum cost line is also shown. The feasible region is then logically at or beneath the \$12 maximum-cost line and also at or above the twenty-vote minimum benefit line. The cost-minimization point A is at the point on the minimum benefit

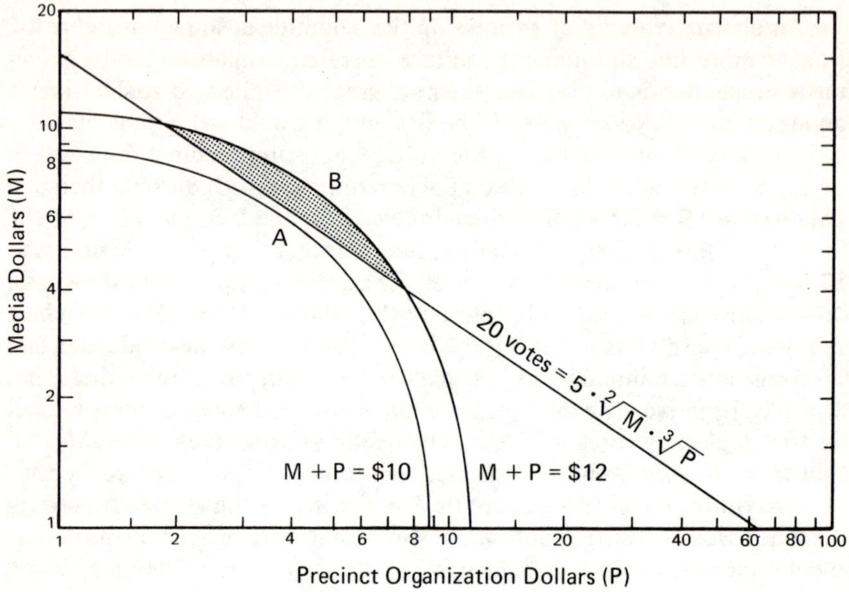

Point A is where total cost is minimized while providing at least 20 votes.
M = $6.20 P = $4.15 TC = $10.35 Votes = 20

Point B is where votes are maximized while not spending more than $12.
M = $7.23 P = $4.77 TC = $12.00 Votes = 23

Figure 1-3. Allocating Media Dollars and Precinct Dollars to Minimize Costs or Maximize Votes (with Diminishing Returns to Dollars Spent)

line furthest away from the $12 cost line or closest to the $10 cost line. It just so happens that this is the point where $6.20 is spent for media and $4.15 is spent for precinct organization. This exact allocation was determined by using simple differential calculus, but one can make an accurate enough estimate by carefully examining the graph especially if more detailed one-cycle logarithmic graph paper is used. The benefit maximization point B is at the point on the maximum cost line furthest away from the minimum benefit line. This is the point where $7.23 is spent for media and $4.77 is spent for precinct organization. This exact allocation was also determined by using differential calculus, but again, one can make a reasonably accurate estimate from the graph or a more detailed version of it.[18]

To ease the work involved in linear programming, there are now available many canned computer routines that only require a simple statement of the constraints to satisfy and the goals to optimize in order to calculate the optimum allocation points for two or more expenditure alternatives. Unfortunately, such computer routines are not so readily available for the diminishing returns or non-linear programming problem, but it can often be handled either graphically or with the aid of an electronic calculator for doing the calculus arithmetic involved. Computer routines for doing linear and non-linear regression analysis are helpful for determining the benefit constraint equations.[19]

The Need for Refinements and Applications

In many expenditure-policy problems, the goal or benefits variable is not as easy to measure as votes are. Nevertheless there are a number of imaginative ways to measure psychological satisfaction or other goal variables.[20] Goal measurement problems are involved in both expenditure and non-expenditure policies. They are generally not as difficult to handle as the broader problem which this article has emphasized of relating means or policies to goals in making policy choices.

Many further refinements can be developed on the basic methodological techniques presented here for choosing among non-expenditure and expenditure policies. What is especially needed, however, is not so much additional methodological refinements, but rather the application of these existing methodologies to more public policy controversies by social scientists, policy appliers, and policymakers.

Notes

This research is one of a series of policy science studies on measuring and achieving effects of alternative legal policies partly financed by the National Science Foundation grant GS-2875. The writer also thanks Duncan MacRae for his suggestive ideas.

1. The distinction between legalization policies and expenditure policies made in this article is closely related to the distinction between regulatory and distributive policies made by Theodore Lowi, "American Business, Public Policy, Case Studies, and Political Theory," 16 *World Politics* 677-715 (1964) and the distinction between legal and economic policies made by Peter Szanton, "Public Policy, Public Good, and the Law," *Journal of Antitrust Law and Economics* (1973). This distinction is also partly one between policies that are primarily dichotomous versus those that are measured on a continuous interval scale.

2. For further discussion of the problem of increasing police adherence to legality in making searches, see Dallin Oaks, "Studying the Exclusionary Rule in Search and Seizure," 37 *University of Chicago Law Review* 665-757 (1970); Wayne LeFave, "Improving Police Performance

Through the Exclusionary Rule,'' 30 *Missouri Law Review* 391 (1965); and Stuart Nagel, ''Testing the Effects of Excluding Illegally Seized Evidence,'' *Wisconsin Law Review,* 283-310 (1965), reproduced as Chapter 23 in Nagel, *The Legal Process from a Behavioral Perspective* (Dorsey, 1969).

3. On the methodology of weighting goals, see J.P. Guilford, *Psychometric Methods* (McGraw-Hill, 1954), 154-301; and Churchman, Ackoff, & Arnoff, *Introduction to Operations Research* (Wiley, 1957), 136-154.

4. Hubert Blalock, *Causal Models in the Social Sciences* (Aldine, 1972), 73-152; and Hubert Blalock, *Causal Inferences in Nonexperimental Research* (U. of North Carolina Press, 1964), 50-52.

5. Hubert Blalock, *Social Statistics* (McGraw-Hill, 1972), 361-385, especially 383-385. Unstandardized regression weights statistically hold constant the influence of other variables, but so do partial correlation coefficients and standardized regression weights. *Ibid.* 429-458. The difference between the two upper percentages in table 1-2 is closer to the regression weight of X (as the independent variable) and Y (as the dependent variable) in the table, then the correlation coefficient of X and Y. *Ibid.* 294, 385. The correlation coefficient equals the regression weight if both variables have the same spread or dispersion. *Ibid.* 384. The closer the standard deviations of the two variables, the more useful the *correlation* is for predicting Y from X, but not the *correlation squared* although it more accurately indicates the percent of variation on Y accounted for by X. Mueller, et al., *Statistical Reasoning in Sociology* (Houghton Mifflin, 1970), 315-319.

6. For another more concrete, less abstract example of the use of the correlation approach in making non-expenditure policy choices, see Stuart Nagel, *Comparing Elected and Appointed Judicial Systems* (Sage Publications Series on American Politics, 1973).

7. Wherever the equations use B − C, one can substitute B/C if the benefit and costs are not measured in the same units. The B − C calculation, however, is more meaningful if the same units are used since one is more interested in maximizing total profits (i.e., B − C) than in maximizing the profit rate (i.e., B/C). See Roland McKean, *Efficiency in Government through Systems Analysis* (Wiley, 1966), p. 35-37, 46-47.

8. The correlation coefficients or regression weights can be treated roughly as probabilities are in decision theory under risk. In the regression approach, $Y = a + bX$ where a linear relation is present, and $\text{Log } Y = \text{Log } a + b\text{Log}X$ where a non-linear relation is present. In the probability approach, EU or expected utility equals the probability of the occurrence (or non-occurrence) of some crucial intervening Z event times the $+X$

payoff (or $-X$ payoff). *EU* is like Y, probability like b, and the X payoff is like X.

9. For further discussion of benefit-cost analysis, see A.R. Prest and R. Turvey, "Cost-Benefit Analysis: A Survey," 75 *The Economic Journal* 683-735 (1965); Guy Black, *The Application of Systems Analysis to Government Operations* (Praeger, 1968), 37-118; and David Miller and Martin Starr, *Executive Decisions and Operations Research* (Prentice-Hall, 1960), 33-102.

10. In situation 1, our decision choices are to choose $+X_1$ or $-X_1$. If the percentage of $+X_1$ places which are $+Y_a$ is greater than the percentage of $-X_1$ places which are $+Y_a$, then choose $+X_1$. Those percentages stated as decimals can be considered the payoffs. In situation 2, the choices are $+X_1$ $+X_2$; $+X_1$ $-X_2$; $-X_1$ $+X_2$; and $-X_1$ $-X_2$. Choose whichever one of those four choices gives the highest percentage of $+Y_a$. Alternative one, however, is impossible if we cannot have both X_1 and X_2. Alternative four is also impossible if we cannot reject both X_1 and X_2. Alternative two says prefer X_1, and alternative three says prefer X_2. In situation 3 we have to choose between $+X_1$ and $-X_1$ as in situation 1. Choose $+X_1$ if the $+X_1$ places have a higher average score on $W_a \cdot Y_a + W_b \cdot Y_b$ or on $Y_a^{Wa} \cdot Y_b^{Wb}$ than the average score of the $-X_1$ places on those same dependent variable measures. The same payoff approach is used in situation 4 as in situation 3 except the decision choices are the same as those in situation 2.

11. For further discussion of matrix decision theory, see Samuel Richmond, *Operations Research for Management Decisions* (Ronald Press, 1968), 3-39, 501-560; and David Miller and Martin Starr, *Executive Decisions and Operations Research* (Prentice-Hall, 1960), 55-100.

12. For further discussion of some important aspects of the correlation approach to making non-expenditure policy choices, see Donald Campbell, "Reforms as Experiments," 24 *American Psychologist* 409-429 (1969); Hubert Blalock, *Causal Inferences in Nonexperimental Research* (U. of North Carolina Press, 1964); and Stuart Nagel; "Optimizing Legal Policy," 18 *University of Florida Law Review,* 577-590 (1966), reproduced as Chapter 25 in Nagel, *op. cit.,* note 1. The Nagel article mainly deals with the statistical manipulation of dichotomous policy and goal variables that have been coded 1 for present and 0 for absent.

13. For further discussion of the problem of rationally allocating campaign expenditures, see Gerald Kramer, "A Decision-Theoretic Analysis of a Problem in Political Campaigning," *Mathematical Applications in Political Science,* (Arnold Foundation, 1966), 137-160; Robert Agranoff, *The New Style in Election Campaigns* (Holbrook Press, 1972); and Stuart Nagel, "Rationally Allocating Campaign and Governmental Expenditures

among Geographical Districts,'' (mimeographed paper available from the writer).

14. On doing a regression analysis between policy alternatives and goals, see Hubert Blalock, *Social Statistics* (McGraw Hill, 1960), 273-285; and N.R. Draper and H. Smith, *Applied Regression Analysis* (Wiley, 1966).

15. If the regression weight of P were greater than the regression weight of M, then the minimum benefits line would intersect the vertical axis above the maximum cost line rather than below it. In other words, the minimum benefits line would be substantially steeper thereby showing just a little change in P is needed to offset a relatively big change in M to hold votes constant. In figure 1-2, however, just a little change in M is needed to offset a relatively big change in P to hold votes constant. The consequences of such a shift in the relative slopes and positions of the linear constraints are to (1) shift the feasible region to the lower portion of the hour glass figure, (2) shift minimization point A to the intersection of the P axis with the minimum benefits line, and (3) shift the benefits maximization point B to the intersection of the P axis with the maximum TC line.

16. Graphing a goal variable against a policy variable (rather than graphing the policy variables against each other as in linear programming) is what Richmond refers to as a deterministic model. Samuel Richmond, *Operations Research for Management Decisions* (Ronald Press, 1968), pages 87-124. The deterministic approach especially lends itself to the use of differential calculus (where curved line relations are involved) for finding the slope of the goal variable with respect to the policy variable, setting this slope equal to zero, and then algebraically solving to find the optimum position on the policy variable.

17. For an analysis of some aspects of curvilinear correlation, see Nagel, ''Simplified Curvilinear Correlation'' (mimeographed paper available from the writer).

18. To make a calculus determination of M at the cost minimization point, find the slope of the equation $TC = M + P$, with $(20/(5 \cdot \sqrt[2]{M}))^3$ substituted for P. Then set the expression for the slope equal to zero, and solve for M. To make a calculus determination of M at the votes maximization point, find the slope of the equation $V = 5 \cdot \sqrt[2]{M} \cdot \sqrt[3]{P}$, with $10 - M$ substituted for P. Then set the expression for the slope equal to zero, and solve for M. Richmond, *op cit.* note 11, at 40-66 and 577.

19. For further discussion of the linear programming approach to making expenditure policy choices, see Charles Laidlaw, *Linear Programming for Urban Development Plan Evaluation* (Praeger, 1972); William Baumol, *Economic Theory and Operations Analysis* (Prentice-Hall, 1965), 70-102; and Stuart Nagel, *Minimizing Costs and Maximizing Benefits in Providing*

Legal Services to the Poor, (Sage Publications Series on Administrative and Policy Studies, 1973).

20. On measuring benefits and costs of public policies, see Guy Black, *The Application of Systems Analysis to Government Operations* (Praeger, 1968), 37-89; R. Dorfman, *Measuring Benefits in Government Investments* (Brookings, 1964); David Alberts, *A Plan for Measuring the Performance of Social Programs; The Application of Operations Research Methodology* (Praeger, 1970); and J.P. Guilford, *Psychometric Methods* (McGraw-Hill, 1954), 154-301.

2 The Need For Judicial Reform

There are seven judicial reform problems which tend to be felt in criminal and civil cases: (1) bail reform, (2) legal counsel for the poor in criminal and civil cases, (3) delay in civil and criminal cases, (4) mass media reporting on pending cases, (5) judicial selection, (6) the jury system, and (7) judicial nullification of legislative and administrative acts.

Pretrial Release

One of the first stages in criminal proceedings which seems to call for judicial reform is the stage at which a decision is made about an arrested suspect prior to his trial. The basic alternatives involve releasing or not releasing him prior to trial depending on (1) whether he can offer a sufficient money deposit to serve as a guarantee or incentive that he will return for trial, or (2) whether his characteristics are such that he is likely to return for his trial rather than risk being prosecuted as a trial jumper. The first alternative is referred to as the traditional bail bond system, and the second alternative as release on one's own recognizance or the ROR system.

In past years, the bail system was by far the dominant method. This was so partly because of the belief that individuals were economically motivated and partly because the system favored middle class people whose interests tended to dominate legal rulemaking. The reform trend is increasingly toward a more objective and scientific ROR system for a number of reasons.

Studies by the Vera Institute in New York City have shown that by carefully screening arrested suspects into good risks and bad risks (largely on the basis of their roots in the community and the seriousness of their crimes), one can obtain at least as low a percentage of trial jumpers as one does with the traditional money-deposit system.[1] Trial-day mail or phone reminders also help reduce trial jumping. These studies have further shown that, with the screening and notification system, a far higher percentage of arrested suspects can be released from jail pending their trial than under the money-deposit system. Such release means these good risks can (1) continue their jobs, (2) better prepare their cases to establish their innocence, (3) save the taxpayer money by not occupying jail space, and (4) be less bitter than if they spent time in jail and were then acquitted. The money-deposit system so inherently discriminates against the poor that the United States Supreme Court may someday declare it to be in violation of the equal protection clause of the Constitution.[2]

One objection to the ROR system is that it might result in releasing a number of arrested suspects who will commit crimes while awaiting trial. One response to this objection is that truly dangerous persons should be kept in jail pending a speedy trial regardless of how able they are to offer a large money deposit. Another response is to point out that pretrial crimes are more often due to long delays prior to trial than to poor screening or the lack of a bail bond requirement. The delay problem however, is a separate area of judicial reform.[3]

Legal Counsel for the Poor

In the 1962 case of *Gideon v. Wainwright*, the Supreme Court declared that criminal defendants who could not afford to hire an attorney to represent them should be provided with a free attorney by the prosecuting government at least for crimes involving more than a possible six-month jail sentence.[4] Prior to 1962, some states already provided counsel to indigent defendants before the Supreme Court required it, although many states felt that free counsel to the poor was too expensive, or socialistic, or unnecessary.

The big problem now is how, not whether, to provide counsel. The basic alternatives are either (1) relying on unpaid or paid volunteer attorneys, (2) having the courts assign attorneys to represent indigent defendants, or (3) using full-time public defenders who receive a salary from the government to which they are attached.

The unpaid volunteer system has the disadvantage that it too often attracts young attorneys who are seeking experience at the possible expense of a client whose liberty might be jeopardized. The paid volunteer system, however, works well at the federal level, where only well qualified attorneys are allowed to volunteer, and where they are fully compensated for their services. In smaller communities, where assigned counsel is often used, clients are frequently represented by reluctant attorneys or by attorneys who have had little or no crininal case experience.

The full-time public defender system is being increasingly used, although many public defender offices are under-financed and under-staffed and thus cannot investigate and defend their cases as vigorously as they otherwise should. To make the public defender applicable to smaller communities, states like Minnesota are beginning to experiment with regional public defenders who cover a number of rural counties.

Although the Supreme Court has not yet required free counsel for the poor in housing eviction, auto repossession, or other civil cases, the federal

Office of Economic Opportunity and most local communities have sought to provide some form of civil legal aid. Their efforts are justified on the grounds that legal aid can promote respect for the law, protect the innocent, encourage orderly law reform, and educate the poor to their legal rights and obligations.

The basic alternatives for civil legal aid are similar to those for criminal legal aid. The traditional system has involved volunteer attorneys whose availability is generally limited and little known. In recent years, the O.E.O. has provided many cities with full-time civil legal services programs similar to public defender offices. Some attorneys have proposed the judicare system for civil legal aid whereby poor clients go to the attorney of their choice, and the government pays the attorney's fee as in medicare. The judicare system has been criticized as lacking visibility, specialists in poverty law, preventative education, and law reform; it is also criticized for an excess of bookkeeping, potential federal regulation and expensiveness.

To provide legal service to middle class people, proposals have been made for various kinds of legal insurance and various plans whereby attorneys for unions or other organizations can represent individual members. Such plans have, however, been opposed by bar associations who fear that organization attorneys will lack a close attorney-client relationship and who also fear the economic competition which such a system would represent to traditional law practice. Certain organizational schemes, however, have been declared by the Supreme Court to be protected by the freedom of assembly clause of the Constitution, and will probably increasingly be established.[5]

Delay in the Court

Increased industrialization and urbanization have indirectly produced undesirable delays in both civil and criminal cases. Automobile accidents mainly explain the long delays in civil cases, often extending to five years in the larger cities. Urbanization and the accompanying increased crime rates have significantly added to criminal court congestion.

In a delayed personal injury case, the injured party may be unable to collect what he is entitled to because of the forgetfulness and loss of witnesses and the pressure to settle for quicker, although reduced, damage payments. Although the delays are shorter in criminal cases, they can be especially harmful if the arrested suspect must wait in jail pending his trial and then receives an acquittal or a sentence shorter than the time he has already waited in jail. Criminal case delays are also harmful if the arrested suspect is released pending trial and commits further crimes during the long waiting period.

To reduce delay in civil cases, various reforms have been attempted or proposed. Some reforms are designed to encourage out-of-court settlements by providing for impartial medical experts, pretrial settlement conferences, interest charges beginning with the day of the accident, and pretrial proceedings to enable the parties to know where they stand with regard to each other's evidence. Other reforms are designed to remove personal injury cases from the courts by shifting them to administrative agencies, or by providing that injured parties automatically collect from their own insurance company regardless of their negligence as with fire insurance.

The time consumed by the jury trial stage can be reduced by having high jury fees, providing earlier trial for non-jury cases, randomly picking 12 jurors without lengthy selection, and by separating the liability and damage issues (so there is no need to discuss damages if the defendant is found non-liable, and so settlement can be facilitated if liability is established). Reformers have also recommended that delay be reduced by having more judges, making them work more days per year and more hours per day, shifting judges from low to high congestion courts, and decreasing wasted judge-time due to poor scheduling of the same attorney in two different courts.

Reforms designed to reduce delay in criminal cases are similar to those in civil cases. There can be better screening of complaints, more encouragement of guilty pleas where merited, more criminal court personnel, less use of grand jury indictment, more pretrial proceedings to narrow the issues, random jury selection, and release of the defendant within a specified period of time if he is not tried. The Supreme Court has recently made speedy trial in criminal cases a constitutional right at both the state and federal levels.[6]

Reporting on Pending Cases

How to handle the problem of mass media reporting on criminal cases involves an interesting conflict between two civil liberties. On the one side is freedom of speech and freedom of the press which includes the right to report on pending cases. On the other side is the constitutional right to a fair trial which should not be prejudiced by distorted reporting or by reporting evidence that is not admissible in court.

The United States Supreme Court has been more sensitive to the fair trial interest than to the free press interest in cases where the two have conflicted. This was especially so in the 1966 Sam Sheppard case where the Cleveland newspapers published front page editorials demanding Sheppard's conviction, created near chaos outside the courtroom with their numerous photographers, and published unsubstantiated damaging statements by Walter Winchell and the Cleveland police chief that were never testified to at the trial.[7] The Supreme Court declared that in future sensational cases the trial should be held away from the community where the crime was committed; attorneys should be reprimanded for gossiping to reporters; jurors and sometimes witnesses should be kept from seeing newspapers; reporters should be held in contempt for printing gossip while a trial is still in process; and the number of reporters in the courtroom should be severely limited. After many years in prison, Sam Sheppard was eventually retried without prejudicial press publicity, and in that trial he was acquitted.

Since the Sam Sheppard case, many newspapers and newspaper associations have established various rules providing for voluntary press restraints. The American Bar Association has likewise established a set of rules restraining attorneys in criminal cases from communicating prejudicial information to the press. Because these restraints have not been sufficiently effective, some reformers have proposed more use of the British system whereby newspapers are readily held in contempt of court for publishing almost anything other than the barest facts about criminal trials until the trial is completed.[8]

Judicial Selection

How should judges be chosen? Basically, they are either (1) appointed by the President, governor, or mayor with or without the approval of a bipartisan nominating commission or legislature, or (2) elected by the general public with partisan or non-partisan election procedures. Originally nearly all United States judges were appointed, but during the period of Jacksonian democracy a shift toward electing state and local judges began. Federal judges have always been appointed as specified in the Constitution. In the last few decades, there has been a shift back to gubernatorial appointment of state and local judges.

Those who argue in favor of elected judges point out that judicial decision-making frequently involves subjective value judgments. In a democracy, these values should probably reflect general public opinion. The electoral advocates also point out that elected judges will come closer in their backgrounds to the general public than appointed judges, especially if the nominating commission tends to be dominated by the state bar association. These and other differences in the attitudes and background of elected and appointed judges can be tested[9] by comparing elected judges with judges who have been appointed on appointed courts or on elected courts as interim judges to complete the unexpired terms of dead, retired or resigned judges.

Those who argue in favor of appointed judges seek to establish that appointed judges are less partisan in their judicial voting behavior. This may, however, be due more to the bipartisan approval that is needed for appointment, to appointment across party lines by some governors, and to the differences in how appointed judges view their roles, rather than directly to the selection process. The advocates of appointment also argue that appointed judges are technically more competent because they tend to come from the better law schools and colleges than elected judges, but the empirical evidence does not support this point.

Closely related to the method of judicial selection is the length of judicial tenure, since judicial reform movements usually advocate both appointive selection and longer judicial terms. Longer terms give a judge more independence from political party pressures. Such terms, however, are likely to make judges less responsive to public opinion although possibly more sensitive to minority rights.

Because of the somewhat evenly divided controversy over elected versus appointed judges, various compronises have developed. Illinois, for instance, has provided for regular elections for vacant judgeships (with provision for opposition candidates) to be followed periodically by retention elections (whereby each sitting judge runs against his record with the voters being able to vote only yes or no on his retention). Such compromises will probably become increasingly prevalent.[10]

The Jury System

Jurors in medieval England were originally persons from the community who were witnesses to the facts in dispute. Eventually the jury evolved into a group of community representatives who resolved factual disputes in cases, while the judge determined the applicable law. Traditionally the jury has consisted of 12 people chosen by both sides from a list of voters, and they have determined guilt in criminal cases and liability civil cases by unanimous decision. In recent years, the idea of having juries to supplement the work of judges has come under attack.

It is argued that jury trials consume too much time or that juries lack competence. It is also charged that juries sometimes ignore the legal instructions given them, such as when they are told that plaintiffs in auto accident cases should not collect anything if the plaintiff has been partially negligent regardless of how negligent the defendant may have been. One can counter this criticism by saying that if an old law is unjust, as this rule of contributory negligence may be, the jury system often softens its harsh effects by applying a more contemporary community sense of justice.

The defenders of the jury system point out that a jury trial is more likely to free the innocent than a bench trial because all approximately 12 jury members must agree to convict and because jurors tend to be more like defendants than judges are. Judges and juries agree approximately 83 percent of the time in criminal cases, but when they disagree the jury is nearly always pro-defendant and the judge pro-prosecutor. This and other findings about jury behavior have been developed as part of the research of the University of Chicago Jury Project.

Defenders also argue that the jury system by providing public participation encourages respect for the law. It has, for instance, been found in before-and-after tests that being a juror does improve one's attitude toward the legal system. This public participation also enables ambiguities in the facts or law to be resolved in the direction of general public opinion.

As a compromise between the attackers and the defenders of the jury system, the trend seems to be in the direction of juries smaller than twelve men deciding by less than unanimous vote. This trend has been especially present in civil cases, and the Supreme Court has recently held it to be constitutional for criminal cases.[11]

Judicial Review

After pretrial release, appointment of counsel, possible delay, newspaper reporting, picking of a judge and the jury's decision, there comes the stage of a possible appeal to a higher court. The most controversial aspect of appellate-court decision-making, although it can also occur at the trial court levels, is the potential nullification by the court of a state or federal statute or administrative regulation. This process of judicial review is peculiar to countries whose constitutions are embodied in a single written document (unlike Great Britain) and is partly attributable to the personality of John Marshall as manifested in his *Marbury v. Madison* decision.[12]

Many arguments favor giving the courts the power of judicial review rather than leaving it to Congress and the people to determine the constitutionality of legislative acts. It is argued that Congress cannot be trusted to police itself since it has a vested interest in its own legislation. Another strong point is that unpopular minority viewpoints need the courts to protect them. It is also said that constitutional interpretation requires technical legal training which the courts have, and that the courts have less political bias than legislatures do.

Arguments against judicial review emphasize that Congress is more responsive to public opinion, although in the long run the courts are also somewhat responsive, at least via personnel changes. Attacks in the past on judicial review have also stressed the conservatism of the courts, particularly with regard to economic regulation. It is further noted that the lack of preciseness in the Constitution makes it more a political than a legal document, and that there have often been substantial differences between Democratic and Republican judges in constitutional interpretation.

Between the positions of complete judicial review over all types of statutes and no judicial review at all, there are many intermediate positions. It could be made more difficult for the courts to exercise judicial review by (1) requiring more than a simple majority of judicial votes or (2) allowing for congressional overruling, as with presidential vetoes. Other intermediate positions seek to make the Supreme Court more responsive by having it (1) composed of representatives from all three branches of government as in some West European systems, (2) an elected or shorter-term court, or (3) composed of representatives from all 50 states (a suggestion proposed in a constitutional amendment which many states have passed).

Further intermediate positions involve judicial review only over legislation relating to (1) the judiciary where the court has a special protective interest, (2) state legislation, in order to preserve American federalism, or (3) civil liberties matters where ideological, ethnic, or other minority interests need protection. The trend is decidedly toward the latter position of a civil liberties-oriented judicial review. Big business, which received so many of the benefits of judicial review in the past, can more adequately protect itself in the legislative process.[13]

There are other fields of reform in the American system of justice. For example, prior to the bail stage there is considerable controversy over how to make the police more efficient in apprehending criminals while at the same time complying with constitutional requirements relating to searches and interrogation.[14] Likewise subsequent to the appeal and judicial review stage, there is considerable controversy over how to make prisons more rehabilitative while at the same time providing a negative deterrence to criminality.[15]

A Changing Environment

The fact that reform is needed does not necessarily indicate that the American system of justice has been inefficient or discriminatory as measured by past standards. It does indicate that the American environment is changing with regard to urbanization which affects efficiency, and that middle class Americans are becoming more sensitive to discriminatory injustices that were formerly tolerated. It is certainly encouraging to note that in recent years the courts and other policy-making bodies have instituted numerous innovations to attempt to resolve the problems raised by pretrial release, legal aid, court delay, pretrial reporting, judicial selection, the jury system and judicial review, although more still remains to be done.[16]

Notes

1. C. Ares, A. Rankin, and H. Sturz, "*The Manhattan Bail Project: An Interim Report on the Use of Pre-Trial Parole*," 38 N.Y.U. LAW REVIEW 67-95 (1963).

2. *Bandy v. United States*, 364 U.S. 477 (1960).

3. For further detail on bail reform, see D. Freed and P. Wald, BAIL IN THE UNITED STATES (Washington, D.C.: Govt. Printing Office, 1964) and R. Goldfarb, RANSOM: A CRITIQUE OF THE AMERICAN BAIL SYSTEM (New York: Harper & Row, 1965). See also the article by R. Pious in the July, 1971, CURRENT HISTORY.

4. *Gideon v. Wainwright*, 372 U.S. 335 (1963).

5. For further detail on legal aid programs, see P. Wald, LAW & POVERTY (Washington, D.C.: Govt. Printing Office, 1965) and L. Silverstein, DEFENSE OF THE POOR (Boston: Little Brown, 1966).

6. *Klopfer v. North Carolina*, 386 U.S. 213 (1967). For further detail on court delay, see H. Zeisel, H. Kalven, and B. Buchholz, DELAY IN THE COURT (Boston: Little Brown, 1959); H. Jones, THE COURTS, THE PUBLIC, AND THE LAW EXPLOSION (Englewood Cliffs, N.J.: Prentice Hall, 1965); and other articles in this symposium.

7. *Sheppard v. Maxwell*, 384 U.S. 333 (1966).

8. For further detail on pretrial publicity, see A. Friendly and R. Goldfarb, CRIME AND PUBLICITY (New York: Twentieth Century Fund, 1967); D. M. Gillmor, FREE PRESS AND FAIR TRIAL (Washington, D.C.: Public Affairs Press, 1966); and other articles in this symposium.

9. H. Jacob, "*The Effect of Institutional Differences in the Recruitment Process: The Case of State Judges*," 13 JOURNAL OF PUBLIC LAW 104-119 (1964) and S. Nagel, THE LEGAL PROCESS FROM A BEHAVIORAL PERSPECTIVE (Homewood, Ill.: Dorsey Press, 1969), pp. 173-197.

10. For further detail on judicial election, see R. Watson and R. Downing, THE POLITICS OF THE BENCH AND THE BAR: JUDICIAL SELECTION UNDER THE MISSOURI NONPARTISAN COURT PLAN (New York: John Wiley, 1969) and E. Haynes, THE SELECTION AND TENURE OF JUDGES (New York: National Conference of Judicial Councils, 1944).

11. *Williams v. Florida*, 399 U.S. 78 (1970). For further details on the jury system, see H. Kalven and H. Zeisel, THE AMERICAN JURY (Boston: Little Brown, 1966); C. Joiner, CIVIL JUSTICE AND THE JURY (Englewood Cliffs, N.J.: Prentice-Hall, 1962).

12. *Marbury v. Madison*, 1 *Cranch* 137 (1803).

13. For further detail on judicial review, see H. Dean, JUDICIAL REVIEW AND DEMOCRACY (New York: Random House, 1966) and R. Carr, THE SUPREME COURT AND JUDICIAL REVIEW (New York: Rinehart, 1942).

14. For further detail on police efficiency, see O. W. Wilson, POLICE ADMINISTRATION (New York: McGraw Hill, 1963); J. Skolnick, JUSTICE WITHOUT TRIAL: LAW ENFORCEMENT IN A DEMOCRATIC SOCIETY (New York: John Wiley, 1967).

15. For further detail on prison reform, see D. Glaser, THE EFFECTIVENESS OF A PRISON AND PAROLE SYSTEM (Indianapolis: Bobbs-Merrill, 1964); P. Tappan, CRIME, JUSTICE, AND CORRECTION (New York: McGraw-Hill, 1960).

16. For further detail on judicial or justice reform in general, see H. James, CRISIS IN THE COURTS (New York: McKay, 1968); A. Vanderbilt, MINIMUM STANDARDS OF JUDICIAL ADMINISTRATION (New York: National Conference of Judicial Councils, 1949); American Bar Association, MINIMUM STANDARDS FOR CRIMINAL JUSTICE (Inst. of Judicial Administration, a series of booklets published from 1967 on).

Part II
Decreasing Discrimination Against Weak Litigants

The legal process problem that many people consider to be most in need of improvement is the problem of decreasing discrimination against weak litigants in the judicial process and weak interest groups in the legislative process. Weak litigants mainly refers to persons who because of economic class do not have the financial ability to hire a good lawyer to represent their interests against prosecutors, landlords, merchants, government administrators, and others having greater power to win in a conflicting adversary situation.

Weak litigants can also refer to blacks who may suffer from racial prejudice as well as their disproportionate association with being poor. Likewise, weak litigants can include unpopular or socially deviant clients whose unconventionality may decrease their chances of having their legal rights adequately recognized. Women, too, may suffer from some forms of discrimination in the judicial process although they may simultaneously receive some forms of favoritism. Urban or rural people in some situations may find themselves discriminated against, as may Democrats or Republicans, particularly in legislative representation.

The problems of these sometimes weak litigants are discussed in this section of the book, with particular emphasis on alternative legal policies for reducing the extent to which discrimination may be occurring. Given the diversity of the types of weak litigants, this is the longest section in the book.

The section begins with an analysis in Chapter 3 of the social consequences of basic legal rights which are particularly designed to protect weak litigants. The rights include freedom of speech and religion which may be especially helpful to socially deviant speakers or minority religions. The consequences emphasized, however, are those which can be considered beneficial to the majority of the population. The rights also include equal treatment under the law, especially for minority ethnic groups, although the consequences to the majority ethnic group is also emphasized here. The rights further include safeguards for the innocent from conviction and harassment and the right to basic economic security.

In order to make these rights meaningful, the most important device may be to provide attorneys for those weak litigants who cannot otherwise afford them or who are shunned because of their social deviancy even if they can afford the normal attorney's fee. Chapter 4 deals with the effects of alternative types of counsel on criminal procedure treatment. The kinds of counsel being compared consist of (1) counsel versus no counsel, (2) hired counsel versus provided counsel, (3) public defender versus assigned counsel, and (4) early-obtained counsel versus late-obtained counsel.

Merely recognizing the need for counsel and establishing institutional devices to provide attorneys for those who might otherwise lack them is not enough if attorneys have unfavorable attitudes toward representing the poor and the unpopular. Such attitudes may result in those litigants either going without attorneys or in those litigants having reluctant, less effective attorneys. Chapter 5 deals with the attitudes of attorneys toward the unpopular and the poor. It attempts to show what causes some attorneys to have more favorable attitudes toward the unpopular and the poor and to be more likely to have represented them. From the findings, some policy recommendations are drawn designed for increasing these relevant attitudes and behaviors.

While Chapters 4 and 5 mainly deal with *criminal* proceedings and with having *attorneys* as a move toward enforcing the legal rights of the poor, Chapter 6 deals mainly with the lack of enforcement of the legal rights of the poor in *non-criminal* proceedings, and with having *ombudsmen* as a move toward enforcing those legal rights. Since this chapter was written, there has been more law and order where the legal rights of the poor are involved than was the situation prior to the late 1960s. There has also been a consequent reduction in the demand and need for ombudsmen among the poor. Nevertheless, there is still a substantial lack of housing code compliance, open housing enforcement, and objectivity in bureaucratic processing of poverty law adjudications. Thus, there still seems to be a substantial need for an expanded OEO Legal Services Program, even if a lessened need for an ombudsman program. More about efficient legal services for the poor is provided in Chapter 14.

Unlike low income and black litigants, at least in criminal cases, women do *not* seem to suffer from a discriminatory pattern involving harsher sentences than men for the same crimes and less safeguards for the innocent. On the contrary, although it may be a manifestation of paternalism, Chapter 7 shows women tend to receive lighter sentences and almost the same safeguards for the innocent. In personal injury cases, however, women (like blacks and children) tend to receive lower damage awards even controlling for the nature of the injuries, although they are almost as likely as men to be able to establish liability. In divorce cases, women receive most of the judgments, but their former husbands tend to be the overall winners through noncompliance and nonenforcement of divorce judgments. Further data in Chapter 7 show a substantial portion of the discrimination against women litigants might be reduced by providing more equal representation for women on juries.

In recent years much has been written in the law review literature describing the court cases and the political process relating to reapportionment of legislative bodies. These cases helped to reduce the lack of representation which had previously been granted to urban and suburban geographical areas. To some extent, although indirectly, these cases also helped to reduce the lack of representation which had previously been accorded to minority political parties or less powerful factions within the dominant political party. Before-and-after studies have been made of effects of reapportionment on changes in geographical and partisan representation. Such studies have also been made of the effects of reapportionment on the changing nature of state expenditures. Chapter 8 deals with the effects of reapportionment on such non-expenditure matters as anti-discrimination legislation, capital punishment, minimum wages, public employee rights, and welfare regulations.

Regardless of what one thinks of the desirability of reapportionment and regardless of what goals one has in carrying out the reapportionment orders of the courts, it might be quite helpful to make use of computers in doing the redistricting in order to be able to maximize simultaneously various goals while satisfying certain constraints. Chapter 9 analyzes the role of computers in achieving reapportionment goals. The chapter particularly emphasizes how computers can arrive at bipartisan solutions which will provide fair or proportional representation to the political parties and also to the diverse geographical areas within the state. It further deals with using computers to provide more equitable representation to blacks and other minority ethnic groups while still satisfying the requirements of equal population per district, contiguity, political realism, and computer feasibility.

3

A. GENERAL

The Social Consequences Of Basic Legal Rights

Basic Concepts

The purpose of this chapter is to describe some of the consequences to a society of providing various controversial basic legal rights. A "right" can be defined as (1) a behavior which a society tolerates a person to engage in without subjecting him to an injunction or penalty for doing so, or a (2) benefit which a society affirmatively confers upon a person that cannot be withdrawn unless there is a change in the societal rules. Rights can thus be "tolerated rights" which a society allows or "affirmative rights" which relate to benefits that a society grants.

Rights can also be controversial or noncontroversial depending on whether their exercise arouses much or little dissension within the society. Thus the tolerated right to breathe is generally non-controversial, but the tolerated right to advocate radical ideas often raises controversy. Likewise the affirmative right to receive mail from the post office is generally non-controversial, but the affirmative right to receive a minimum income as provided for in welfare legislation often raises controversy.

Rights can be legal or human rights. Legal ones are found in statements promulgated by government bodies with regard to how people (including government officials) ought to behave toward each other or be subject to sanctions. These statements manifest themselves in constitutions, statutes, judicial precedents, or in administrative regulations or adjudications. Human rights represent statements similar in content to those found in legal rights but which philosophers find present in religious literature, in the inherent nature of man, or in an inductive analysis of the legal rights present in a variety of societies. This chapter will only explicitly deal with the consequences of legal rights, although what is said is applicable to human rights to the extent they overlap in content.

Legal rights can be basic or non-basic. Basic legal rights are those embodied in a society's governmental constitution or in statutes that can be supplemented although they are unlikely to be repealed. This chapter will emphasize the consequences of controversial basic legal rights in an American context although what is said is generally applicable to other societies as well.[1] The rights that will be particularly discussed are those that relate to (1) freedom of speech and religion, (2) equality of treatment, (3) safeguarding the innocent from conviction and harassment, and (4) the right to basic economic security. The consequences to be discussed are not so much the effects on the individuals who exercise these rights, but rather the effects on the total society. Available behavioral science or empirical research relating to these effects will be cited wherever appropriate.[2]

Freedom of Speech and Religion

The right of free speech in the American context can be defined as allowing without penalty both popular and unpopular viewpoints to be advocated or communicated in any media of communication so long as the communication does not involve hard core pornography, untruthful defamation, obtaining money under false pretenses, invasion of privacy, or the likely promotion of bodily injury. In the United States this is a tolerated right rather than an affirmative right in that it does not include providing free access to the communication media with the exception of the narrow FCC equal-time rules.

What are the effects on a total society of providing the right of free speech? There are three basic effects which philosophers have tended to emphasize.[3] First, in matters of empirical science, free speech allows the truth to have a better chance of getting accepted. The suppression of Galileo and his observation that the earth revolves around the sun rather than vice versa is a case in point.

Second, in matters of normative policy, free speech allows the most effective means toward given ends to have a better chance of getting accepted. For example, suppression of the slavery abolitionists delayed the improved labor productivity per labor expense and the improved capital equipment which free labor promoted.

Third, free speech provides a check on corrupt and inefficient leadership and administrative personnel. Even dictatorships recognize the value of encouraging critics of administrative inefficiency even though they do not encourage criticism of top national officials or fundamental government policy.

Free speech is indirectly responsible for higher standards of living to the extent that free speech promotes scientific discovery and dissemination, more effective means toward given societal goals, and more efficient governmental personnel. This partly explains why table 3-1 shows a positive correlation between the level of free speech permissiveness and the level of modernity in the 84-country sample used.[4] Some of the positive correlation is also due to the reciprocal fact that higher standards of living create a more tolerant middle class which allows still more freedom of speech.

Some critics of free speech argue that it leads to political instability and revolution. The empirical data tend to show just the opposite relation.

Table 3-1
Relationship Between Permissiveness and Modernity in 84 Countries, 1948-1960

Level of Modernity	*Level of Permissiveness*			
	Coercive	*Mid-level permissive*	*Permissive*	*Total*
Modern	Argentina East Germany Czechoslovakia USSR (4)	Austria France (2)	Australia Canada Belgium Denmark Finland Iceland Ireland Israel Luxembourg Netherlands New Zealand Norway Sweden Switzerland Un. Kingdom Un. States Uruguay West Germany (18)	24
Transitional	Albania Bulgaria Cuba Dom. Repub. Egypt Korea Nicaragua Paraguay Poland Portugal Romania U. S. Africa Venezuala Yugoslavia (16)	Brazil Ceylon Chile Columbia Cyprus Ecuador El. Salv. Guatamala Greece Honduras Japan Lebanon Panama Peru Syria Thailand Turkey Tunisia (18)	Costa Rica Italy Mexico (3)	37
Traditional	Afghanistan China Ethiopia Haiti Morocco Saudi Arabia Taiwan (17)	Bolivia Burma Cambodia Ghana Indonesia India Iraq Jordan Laos Liberia Libya Malaya Pakistan Philippines Sudan (16)	(0)	23
Total	27	36	21	84

Table 3-2 shows a positive correlation between being a country that has a permissive free speech policy and being a country that has a high degree of stability. This relation is partly attributable to the fact that free speech facilitates non-violent change, particularly by providing more peaceful outlets through which potential revolutionaries can make themselves heard and win converts without resorting to revolution. The positive relation between free speech and non-violent change is also partly attributable to the fact that free speech and non-violent change are partly co-effects of having a large tolerant middle class. The correlation between permissiveness and stability is, however, not as high as the correlation between permissiveness and modernity.

Freedom of religion is a legal right that has two aspects. One aspect says there shall be no governmental interference with religion and the other aspect says there shall be no governmental aid to religion. The American version allows exceptions to the no interference principle for dangerous religious practices like rattlesnake ceremonies, and exceptions to the no aid principle for indirect or minor aid like bus fare reimbursement to parochial school children.[5]

The effects of the no interference right are similar to the effects of the free speech right since religious activity is a form of communication. In the field of religious speech, it may be even more important to let all viewpoints be heard since truth and effectiveness are so much more difficult to determine in this field. The field of religion also tends to be more highly emotional and small interferences can lead to strong resentments and to severe social conflict especially in a religiously heterogeneous society. Indeed, the Thirty Years War of the Protestant Reformation represented a greater per capita loss of life to the nations involved than any political war in European history.

Violations of the right to have the government give no aid to religion can produce many effects that even members of the aided or dominant religion might consider socially disfunctional. First, aid can lead to interference toward the religion aided. This is why the Catholic hierarchy in the past opposed federal aid to parochial schools for fear that such aid would lead to restrictions on religious teaching in the parochial schools. Second, aid can easily lead to real or perceived favoritism since it is almost impossible to allocate aid equally among religions, partly because there is not likely to be agreement on whether equality should be measured by population, need, or some other criteria. Third, government aid can have the effect of decreasing church and home initiatives as John F. Kennedy noted in supporting the Supreme Court's ban on school prayers. Fourth, in a country that has many religious denominations, being in the safe majority in one place does not guarantee that one will be in the safe majority in other places, and thus what may be viewed as beneficial aid to religion in one part of the country may be

Table 3-2
Relationship Between Permissiveness and Political Stability 1955-1961

Degree of Political Stability	*Level of Permissiveness*			
	Coercive	*Mid-Level Permissive*	*Permissive*	*Total*
Stability	Czechoslovakia East Germany Ethiopia Portugal Romania Saudi Arabia Taiwan (7)	Austria Cambodia Libya Philippines Tunisia (5)	Australia, Canada, Costa Rica, Denmark, Finland, Iceland, Ireland, Israel, Luxembourg, Netherlands, New Zealand, Norway, Sweden, Switzerland, Un. Kingdom, Un. States, Uruguay, West Germany (18)	30
Mid-Level Instability	Afghan., Albania, Bulgaria, China, Dom. Repub., Egypt, Haiti, Morocco, Nicaragua, Paraguay, Poland, Spain, Un. S. Africa, USSR, Yugoslavia (15)	Burma, Ceylon, Chile, Ecuador, El. Salv., France, Ghana, Greece, Iran, Japan, Liberia, Malaya, Pakistan, Panama, Jordan, Sudan, Thailand (17)	Belgium Italy Mexico (3)	35
Instability	Argentina Cuba Hungary Korea Venezuela (5)	Bolivia, Brazil, Colombia, Cyprus, Guatemala, Honduras, Indonesia, India, Iraq, Laos, Lebanon, Peru, Syria, Turkey (14)	(0)	19
Total	27	36	21	84

viewed by the same religion as detrimental aid in other places. Fifth, aid like interference can also generate strong resentments and severe social conflicts as is shown by the repeated anti-clerical conflict in France over French government aid to the Catholic church.

Equality of Treatment

Equal treatment under the law in the American context mainly relates to prohibitions on ethnic group discrimination, particularly discrimination against blacks. Discrimination refers to denying someone because of his race various opportunities for which he would otherwise be qualified. Discrimination can take many forms including (1) governmental discrimination with regard to criminal procedure, school access, and voting; or (2) private discrimination with regard to housing, public accommodations, and employment.[6] A form of discrimination exists when the dominant group forces segregation or involuntary separation on the minority group, but not when minority group members voluntarily choose to live together or to be distinctive. What are the effects of discrimination on the total society particularly the dominant racial group, not just the group discriminated against?[7]

Discrimination probably has a substantial effect on decreasing the gross national product by failing to make full use of the actual and potential skills that blacks have. Long established discrimination by the building trade unions is a good example. Likewise housing discrimination may prevent qualified blacks from living near suburban job openings to which they might otherwise lack meaningful access. Past school discrimination and inferior black school facilities might greatly lessen the chances that potential black lawyers or doctors will achieve their potentiality.

Another kind of societal economic effect comes from segregated school and housing facilities. Segregated school systems may involve duplicate costs like the special Texas black law school or the Tennessee black medical school which were established with only a few students to avoid integrating white southern universities, although these two schools may have recently become economically viable institutions. Segregated housing patterns combined with employment discrimination can lead to ghetto slums with their disproportionately high costs for police, fire protection, and welfare recipients. These unnecessarily high costs of segregation should especially trouble conservative taxpayers.

Discrimination against a minority group frequently has a depressive effect on weaker members of the majority group. Thus low wages paid to blacks tend to keep down the wages of whites in occupations that blacks might enter. Black strike-breaking labor can also deter more aggressiveness on the part of white unions. Likewise depressed standards of police behavior in dealing with blacks are sometimes hard to change when the police deal with whites especially poor whites.

Psychologically speaking, discrimination against blacks can create a false sense of superiority on the part of some whites. This may partly account for the lack of education and occupational ambition of many white southerners who have their race to fall back on to compensate for their lack of education and job status. Discrimination can also cause guilt feelings and anxieties on the part of whites, especially if their behavior and attitudes toward blacks conflict with democratic ideals which are preached in their society, thereby creating the American Dilemma. Discrimination can, of course, have severe psychologically disturbing effects on blacks, but the emphasis in this impact analysis is on the effects on the total society in general and the majority whites in particular.

With regard to American foreign and military policy, domestic discrimination decreases the ability of the United States to win influence in Africa, Asia, and Latin America. Domestic discrimination may also decrease the morale of blacks in the armed forces, especially in a war against non-Caucasian people, and it may increase interracial friction within the armed forces as indicated by numerous clashes in the late 1960s.

An especially important effect of discrimination is the antagonism and hatred that it generates on the part of blacks toward whites, which emotional incidents can spark into intra-ghetto riots and possibly eventually into inter-neighborhood riots. Discrimination also divides whites themselves between those who advocate faster removal of discriminatory barriers and those who advocate retention or slower removal. This intra-white hostility sometimes manifests itself in student and other youthful protest activities.

Miscellaneous effects of discrimination include the loss of new manufacturing developments by discriminatory communities, which business executives consider to have an undesirable environment for raising their families. Discrimination by reducing black income can also reduce black consumer purchasing power thereby hurting white business concerns. Finally, the presence of discrimination often deters non-discriminatory behavior on the part of whites who do not want to discriminate, but who feel compelled to comply with what they perceive to be the dominant viewpoint unless the dominant viewpoint is made illegal by anti-discrimination legislation.

In addition to mentioning various phenomena that behavioral scientists tend to agree are effects of discrimination, some alleged effects that have no scientific acceptance should also be mentioned. For example, the absence of discrimination may indeed lead to increased intermarriage, but no accepted biological study has shown that the children of a racially mixed marriage are in any sense biologically defective. In fact, by lessening the purity of the races, there may be a lessening of friction between the races. In addition, the children of a racially mixed marriage are likely to have access to more societal opportunities than children with a wholly black background.

It is sometimes alleged that integrating schools will have the effect of lowering the learning level of white students without necessarily raising the level of black students. The Coleman Report, however, tends to show that economic class integration or racial integration along class lines (i.e., poor blacks with middle class whites, poor whites with middle class blacks, poor blacks with middle class blacks, or poor whites with middle class whites) does not generally lower the learning level of middle class children, but does raise the learning level of the poorer children.

Some whites in more frank moments correctly allege that their jobs would be in jeopardy if discrimination barriers were dropped. In this regard, dropping discrimination against blacks is like dropping tariff discrimination against foreign products. It might mean a temporary relocation of marginal less-efficient persons, but the total national economy benefits from the lowered consumer prices and from the more efficient use of its labor. Likewise in the long run, removing inefficient racial discrimination can raise the gross national product, decrease governmental costs attributable to slums and duplicative facilities, increase depressed wages, make for more efficient geographical allocation of industry, and increase consumer purchasing power as have been previously mentioned.

Although this discussion of equal protection under the law has emphasized racial discrimination, many of the same social consequences described would apply to much of the discrimination which is based on sex, religion, ancestral nationality, economic class, or other characteristics which usually lack sufficient correlation with ability to be meaningful criteria for allocating employment and other social opportunities.

Safeguarding the Innocent from Conviction and Harassment

In the American context, the basic legal rights designed to safeguard the innocent from conviction and harassment include approximately ten different rights. They relate to all the stages of criminal procedure from the legislative process passing criminal laws through arrest, trial, and sentencing. They include the right to (1) no retroactive or vague criminal statutes or statutes declaring named persons to be guilty of wrongdoing, (2) arrest or search only where there is substantial likelihood of guilt, (3) no involuntary confessions or self-incrimination, (4) release pending speedy trial,

(5) hired or provided counsel at trial and before, (6) formal notice of charges, (7) unanimous decision by a group of one's peers, (8) questioning adverse witnesses and calling one's own witnesses, (9) no excessive punishment, and (10) no repeated prosecution for the same matter.[8]

The effect of these rights, where they are applied, is to lessen the likelihood that an innocent person will be convicted or harassed. This effect can be easily supported by people who are unlikely to commit crimes, but who recognize the possibility that they or other innocent people might find themselves in a situation or business practice where they could be falsely suspected or accused of some kind of wrongdoing. These rights also decrease the likelihood that a guilty person will be convicted of a greater crime than he committed, or that he will receive punishment or treatment disproportionate to his crime. This effect can also be easily supported by most people who recognize that if the guilty are over-convicted or over-sentenced, this breeds unnecessary bitterness and general disrespect for the law rather than rehabilitation or deterrence. These rights also make it more difficult to convict the guilty, but most people probably recognize that it is more detrimental to their self-interest and the orderly functioning of society for one innocent person to be convicted than for one or even a few guilty persons to go uncaught for a specific crime. In general there would be no need to have these rights if there was some accurate automatic way of separating the innocent from the guilty.

In regard to specific rights, the right to a hired or provided lawyer is probably the most important for preventing wrongful convictions and harassment.[9] Having a lawyer aids the investigation of the facts, negotiation with the prosecutor, examination of witnesses, presentation of legal and factual arguments to the judge and jury, and the preparation of an appeal. A lawyer also provides psychological support to the defendant and an air of objectivity which the defendant himself could not provide. All the other procedural rights become less meaningful without an attorney to inform the defendant of his rights and to call violations to the attention of the courts, including violations that might occur at the police interrogation stage. Of the basic legal rights, only free speech may be more important, because without free speech violations of rights could not be readily called to the attention of a larger public.

Right to counsel has some important effects on the legal system besides protecting the innocent. The American adversary system presumes that both sides will be vigorously represented so that the neutral judge can arrive at the truth somewhere between the adverse positions; but if only one side is represented, the system may not function effectively. If the poor generally lack lawyers in prosecutions, evictions, repossessions, or other cases, their respect for the law will decrease although right to counsel currently extends only to criminal, not civil cases. Counsel for the poor and other alienated groups can also help to bring orderly reform of the law as an alternative to disorderly or violent change. In addition, widespread availability of counsel can serve to educate those who otherwise would be without counsel, and such education may prevent them from getting into legal trouble with creditors, landlords, and other people with whom they deal.

While it is generally agreed that brutal or random arrests, searches, and confession-obtaining techniques have adverse social effects (by creating an unduly fearful population and disrespect for the police), there has been some controversy over how to deter such police tactics. One cannot expect the prosecutor to be very vigorous in prosecuting police who have been zealously trying to help him. Likewise private damage suits are costly, time-consuming, embarrassing to the plaintiff, unlikely to result in victory because of police discretion and generally unsympathetic juries, and if victorious unlikely to result in a deterring damage judgment because of the officer's lack of money, the difficulty of assessing damages, and a tendency of the city to pay the judgment. Internal police administration in these matters tends to be more protective than disciplinary. As a result of the lack of more effective alternatives, the courts have chosen to exclude illegally obtained evidence from the courtroom in hopes that doing so will encourage the police to operate more within the law when making arrests or searches and when obtaining confessions. Behavioral studies have shown this exclusionary rule has changed some police behavior.[10]

Some important behavioral research has recently shown that regardless of the nature of the crime or the defendant's prior record, he is more likely to be convicted if he is not released pending trial.[11] His conviction chances are increased because (1) being in jail awaiting trial decreases his ability to investigate and prepare his defense, and because (2) he makes a relatively bad impression on the judge and jury when he is brought for each trial session from the prisoners lockup area, rather than on his own through the regular courtroom entrance. Denying pre-trial release for want of bail money also has the effect of discriminating against the poor, increasing jail costs, promoting loss of jobs, and increasing the likelihood that the innocent will spend time in jail and that the guilty will spend more time than their sentence or the law provides. Studies have shown that careful screening of defendants to determine their roots in the community followed by reminders of their court dates has the effect of producing a higher percentage of pre-trial releases and a lower percentage of those who do not show up in court than the traditional money bond system does.[12] Other behavioral studies have provided useful information with regard to how court congestion can be reduced so that released and failed defendants can be tried and convicted or acquitted sooner.[13]

There has been more behavioral research on the consequences of criminal procedure rights than on any of the other basic legal rights. The effects of criminal jury trials rather than bench trials has been well researched revealing that juries are more likely to acquit in 17 per cent of the cases, although there is agreement in 75 per cent, and the judge is more likely to acquit in 2 per cent, with the jury being undecided in 6 per cent.[14] The unanimity requirement, the multiple decision-makers, and the less upper-class composition of juries probably accounts for their lesser propensity to convict compared to judges. Studies have also been made of the effect of various punishments especially capital punishment, although the right to be free from capital punishment has not yet been established in American legal rights.[15]

Although no behavioral research has been done on some of the other procedural rights, the effects of their presence or absence can be readily hypothesized. Vague or retroactive criminal statutes obviously cannot have a meaningful deterrent effect if the statute does not clearly refer to future behavior. Likewise it is common sense that if a prosecutor could repeatedly prosecute a defendant for the same matter, he might eventually get a conviction of an innocent person or an over-conviction of a guilty person, to say nothing of the obvious harassment involved. Without clear notice of the charges against him and right to call his own witnesses and to question opposition witnesses, an innocent defendant would clearly tend to have a much more difficult time establishing his innocence.

The Right to Basic Economic Security

The right to basic economic security is a relatively modern right at least in the American context. It is embodied in statutes rather than in the Constitution. To the extent it is provided, however, there can constitutionally be no arbitrary classifications of recipients, or the equal-treatment right will be violated. Likewise there can be no deprivation of government economic benefits unless the recipient is provided with due process to give him an opportunity to show the illegality of the deprivation.

Relevant statutes in American law include (1) the National Labor Relations Act of 1935 which provides the right to join labor unions which can aid in providing economic security; (2) the Fair Labor Standards Act of 1938 which provides for the right to a minimum wage, maximum hours, safe working conditions, and freedom from child labor; (3) the Social Security Act of 1935 which provides for aid to the aged, disabled, unemployed, and to dependant children; and (4) the Employment Act of 1946 which declared that the American people have the right to expect the federal government to provide maximum employment, production, and purchasing power.[16]

Sometimes critics of these rights talk in terms of a conflict between freedom and economic security. On the contrary though, freedom of speech was very important in revealing the harm that was being done to society by the absence of these economic rights. Likewise basic economic security is necessary to make freedom of speech meaningful, because those lacking economic security are generally not in a financial position to take advantage of expensive forms of communication, and economic insecurity also makes one less tolerant of deviant ideas and less adaptable to social change except change that will mean personal economic benefits. There is clearly a close relation between economic security and equal treatment with regard to race relations, since (1) being black and being poor are positively correlated, and because (2) those who discriminate often do so out of economic insecurity, and (3) being poor makes one more subject to discrimination.

An important general effect of increased economic security is to lessen economic anxieties that workers might have. Such anxieties can interfere with morale and efficiency and thereby lower the gross national product. Too much security, however, might cause a worker to lessen attempts to improve himself.

All four of the key New Deal statutes mentioned above have had important specific consequences for American society, just as related statutes have in other countries. Statistics show a substantial increase in union membership subsequent to the passage of the National Labor Relations Act, and a substantial decrease in strikes for union recognition as contrasted to strikes for more favorable contract terms. Other statistical studies have shown that unions do produce higher wages, shorter hours, and safer conditions at least for union members. For non-union members, the Fair Labor Standards Act has provided similar although lower benefits. These economic effects have directly benefited a large segment of the population and indirectly benefited the total economy, particularly by virtue of the more efficient use of capital and labor which raising the price of labor has encouraged, and also by the economic stimulus stemming from increased purchasing power to the extent wages have increased more than prices. Strengthening unions has also had political effects by increasing the likelihood that legislation will be passed favoring union interests.

The Social Security Act has encouraged earlier retirement for the aged and therefore earlier advancement for the young. The aid to dependent children provisions have spawned a tremendous bureaucratic apparatus, and in that regard may soon be replaced by the Family Assistance Bill of 1971. The Employment Act has not eliminated unemployment or price inflation, but its encouragement of greater government spending and lower taxes in time of unemployment and the reverse in time of inflation (combined with other governmental regulatory devices) has dampened the business cycle to some extent. Provisions in the Social Security Act that provide payments to the unemployed, dependent children, and the retired also help to level off business cycles because these payments increase in times of recession and decrease in times of prosperity.

In general, this chapter has attempted to describe and footnote some of the broad consequences of providing various basic legal rights. There is clearly a need for more behavioral research on the impact of rights. Such social science research is needed to supplement the more philosophical discussion of the definitions, justifications, identifications, and relations of both human rights and legal rights. Such research will also help to build further bridges between philosophy and the behavioral sciences. It is hoped that this chapter has pulled together some of the relevant ideas and literature for others to build upon.

Notes

1. For empirical studies of basic legal rights in a non-American context see D. Bayley, PUBLIC LIBERTIES IN THE NEW STATES (Rand McNally, 1964); and references under Constitutional Law in C. Szladits, A BIBLIOGRAPHY ON FOREIGN AND COMPARATIVE LAW BOOKS AND ARTICLES IN ENGLISH (Oceana Publishers, 1955 to present).

2. Behavioral materials that deal with the social consequences of general legal rights include S. Wasby, THE IMPACT OF THE UNITED STATES SUPREME COURT: SOME PERSPECTIVES (Dorsey Press, 1970); T. Becker, THE IMPACT OF SUPREME COURT DECISIONS: EMPIRICAL STUDIES (Oxford, 1969); and J. Levine, "*Methodological Concerns in Studying Supreme Court Efficacy*," 4 LAW & SOCIETY REVIEW 583-611 (1970).

3. For a summary and bibliography of the philosophical, non-behavioral aspects of free speech see T. Emerson *et al.*, POLITICAL AND CIVIL RIGHTS IN THE UNITED STATES 1-28 (Little Brown, 1967), and the 1969 SUPPLEMENT. The rest of Emerson's Volume 1 clarifies what free speech covers.

4. The free speech, modernity, and political stability data come from I. Feierband and R. Feierband, "*The Relationship of Systematic Frustration, Political Coercion, International Tension, and Political Instability: A Cross-National Study*" (Paper presented at the annual meeting of the American Psychological Association, 1966). See their paper for further details on the criteria for categorizing the countries. Other empirical studies in the free speech area include J. Levine, "*The Bookseller and the Law of Obscenity: Toward an Empirical Theory of Free Expression*"

(Northwestern U. Ph.D. Dissertation, 1967); and S. Stouffer, COMMUNISM, CONFORMITY, AND CIVIL LIBERTIES (Doubleday, 1955).

5. Studies dealing with the impact of decreasing government aid to and interference with religion as manifested in prayers in the public schools include W. Muir, PRAYER IN THE PUBLIC SCHOOLS: LAW AND ATTITUDE CHANGE (U. of Chicago Press, 1967) and R. Johnson, THE DYNAMICS OF COMPLIANCE: SUPREME COURT DECISION-MAKING FROM A NEW PERSPECTIVE (Northwestern U. Press, 1967).

6. A detailed description of the right to be free of discrimination is provided in Volume 2 of T. Emerson *et al.*, POLITICAL AND CIVIL RIGHTS IN THE UNITED STATES (Little Brown, 1967) and the 1969 SUPPLEMENT.

7. For behavioral science approaches to the effects of racial discrimination, see "*The Effects of Segregation and the Consequences of Desegregation*," 37 MINN. L. REV. 427 (1953), and G. Grier and E. Grier, EQUALITY AND BEYOND (Quadrangle, 1966). For the effects of anti-discrimination legislation, see M. Berger, EQUALITY BY STATUTE (Doubleday, 1967), and L. Mayhew, LAW AND EQUAL OPPORTUNITY, (Harvard U. Press, 1967). For the effects of school integration, see J. Coleman *et al.*, EQUALITY OF EDUCATION OPPORTUNITY, (Office of Education, 1966) (Also known as the Coleman Report); and on housing integration, see Wilner, HUMAN RELATIONS IN INTERRACIAL HOUSING (U. Minnesota Press, 1955).

8. A description of the nature of the safeguards to protect the innocent from conviction and harassment is given in D. Fellman, THE DEFENDANTS RIGHTS (Rinehart, 1958) and W. Lockhart *et al.*, CONSTITUTIONAL RIGHTS AND LIBERTIES (West, 1970).

9. Behavioral studies of the consequences of having counsel include L. Silverstein, DEFENSE OF THE POOR (Little Brown, 1966); N. Lefstein and V. Stapleton, COUNSEL IN JUVENILE COURTS (National Council of Juvenile Court Judges, 1967); and D. Wenger and C. Fletcher, "*The Effect of Legal Counsel on Admissions to a State Mental Hospital: A Confrontation of Professions*" (Paper presented at the annual meeting of the American Sociological Association, 1967).

10. Empirical research on protecting the right to be free from unreasonable arrests, searches, and interrogation techniques include R. Medalie *et al.*, "*Custodial Police Interrogation in our Nation's Capital: The Attempt to Implement Miranda*," 66 MICHIGAN LAW REVIEW 1347-1422 (1968); S. Nagel, "*Testing the Effects of Excluding Illegally Seized Evidence*," WISCONSIN LAW REVIEW 283-310 (1965); and E. Green, "*Race, Social Status, and Criminal Arrest*," 35 AMERICAN SOCIOLOGICAL REVIEW 476-490 (1970).

11. A. Rankin, "*The Effect of Pretrial Detention*," 39 N.Y.U. LAW REVIEW 641-55 (1964).

12. C. Ares *et al.*, "*The Manhattan Bail Project: An Interim Report on the Use of Pretrial Parole*," 38 N.Y.U. LAW REVIEW 67-95 (1963).

13. H. Zeisel *et al.*, DELAY IN THE COURT (Little Brown, 1959); and J. Navarro and J. Taylor, DATA ANALYSIS AND SIMULATION OF A COURT SYSTEM FOR THE PROCESSING OF CRIMINAL CASES (Institute for Defense Analysis, 1967).

14. H. Kalven and H. Zeisel, THE AMERICAN JURY (Little Brown, 1966), p. 56.

15. H. Bedau, THE DEATH PENALTY IN AMERICA (Anchor, 1967).

16. Empirical studies of the statutes relating to the right to basic economic security are described in H. Koontz and R. Gable, PUBLIC CONTROL OF ECONOMIC ENTERPRISE (McGraw-Hill, 1956), 487-590, 758-794; G. Bloom and H. Northrup, ECONOMICS OF LABOR RELATIONS (Irwin, 1954); M. Lee, ECONOMIC FLUCTUATIONS (Irwin, 1955) 421-538; and G. Steiner, SOCIAL INSECURITY: THE POLITICS OF WELFARE (Rand McNally, 1966).

4

B. CLASS, RACE, AND SOCIAL DEVIANCY

Effects of Alternative Types of Counsel on Criminal Procedure Treatment

The purpose of this chapter is to present some findings with regard to how defendants having certain types of counsel differ in their criminal procedure treatment from defendants who have opposite or other types of counsel. The kinds of counsel being compared consist of (1) counsel versus no counsel, (2) hired counsel versus provided counsel, (3) public defender versus assigned counsel, and (4) early-obtained counsel versus late-obtained counsel.

The data on which the findings are based consist of the 1,101 state grand larceny cases compiled by Lee Silverstein of the American Bar Foundation for the year 1962 from a sample of 194 counties located in all 50 states. The total sample consisted of 11,258 felony cases.[1] Only the grand larceny cases, however, were used in order to control for the type of crime committed in comparing the above-mentioned types of counsel.[2] Such a control is necessary because the more severe the crime is, the more likely the defendant will have a good hired attorney; and the more severe the crime is, the longer the sentence is likely to be. Thus, unless one holds constant the type of crime committed, having a hired attorney will correlate positively with receiving a long sentence, which makes having a hired attorney falsely appear to be worse than no attorney or a provided one. For related reasons, which will be clarified in discussing the tables, the urbanism and economic class of the defendants may also have to be controlled for in order to make meaningful comparisons between types of counsel.

Other articles have been written relevant to the effects of alternative types of counsel on criminal procedure treatment, but they tend to be (1) non-quantitative or (2) quantitative studies of specific communities, or (3) studies which fail to control for crime severity, urbanism, economic class, or other variables which disrupt the comparisons between types of counsel in criminal procedure treatment. Other studies also tend to concentrate on fewer stages of criminal justice treatment than the approximately a dozen stages included in the tables and footnotes of this chapter.[3]

Counsel Versus No Counsel

Table 4-1 shows how defendants who have attorneys differ in their criminal procedure treatment from those who lack attorneys. Criminal procedure

Table 4-1
How Defendants Who Have Attorneys Differ in Their Criminal Procedure Treatment from Those Who Lack Attorneys (Using a Nationwide Sample of 1,101 State Grand Larceny Cases)

Fraction in Sample	*Criminal Procedure Treatment*	*All Cases*			*Urban Cases*			*Non-Indigent Cases*		
		Counsel		*No Counsel*	*Counsel*		*No Counsel*	*Counsel*		*No Counsel*
$\frac{376}{576}$	% who received preliminary hearing	57	⊕	44	59	⊕	41	64	⊕	38
$\frac{458}{873}$	% who were released on bail	53	⊕	36	54	⊕	39	74	⊕	37
$\frac{165}{245}$	% who had short delay of two months or *less* from arrest to disposition or trial while in jail	60	⊖	89	64	⊖	89	57	⊖	96

76/242	% who had jury trial of those tried	31	+	30	29	+	20	34	+	33
138/957	% who were *not* found guilty	11	+	7	10	+	5	12	+	10
320/734	% who received a suspended sentence or probation rather than a prison sentence	47	+	37	45	+	39	58	⊕	38
118/266	% who received short prison terms of one year or *less* of those imprisoned	48	⊕	22	48	+	40	37	–	46
1101	Number in Sample	769		109	590		50	363		58

+ means defendants who *had* lawyers received better treatment.

– means defendants who *lacked* lawyers received better treatment.

The sign is circled where the difference is greater than ten.

treatment refers mainly to receiving (1) a preliminary hearing, (2) being released on bail, (3) having a relatively short delay from arrest to disposition if one is in jail pending trial, (4) receiving a jury trial if one is tried, (5) not being found guilty, (6) receiving a suspended sentence or probation if one is convicted, and (7) receiving a relatively short prison term if one is imprisoned.

The column "fraction in sample" shows (1) in the denominator how many of the 1,101 state grand larceny cases had applicable information available with regard to each treatment stage, and shows (2) in the numerator how many of those (for which applicable information was available) received favorable treatment. For example, 676 of the 1,101 cases had information available on whether or not the defendants received a preliminary hearing in counties that provide preliminary hearings, and 376 of those 676 defendants did receive one. The lowness of the numerator with regard to the percentage who had a jury trial of those tried (242 cases) reflects the fact that all defendants who were not tried are excluded from the numerator and those cases are thus not applicable.

If one divides the 1,101 cases into those in which the defendant did have counsel (769 cases) and those in which he did not (109 cases), and disregards the ones for which information on the presence of counsel was unavailable (223 cases), then some interesting percentages are revealed with regard to the relation between having or not having counsel and criminal procedure treatment. These percentages, like most of the others in this chapter, are generally based on large enough denominations to be statistically reliable although the denominators vary depending on which treatment stage is involved since different treatment stages have different degrees of completeness of applicable information (i.e., different ratios between the denominator in the "fraction in sample" and the 1,101 total).

In the Total Sample of Cases

The first row shows that 57 percent of the defendants with counsel received a preliminary hearing, whereas only 44 percent of the defendants without counsel did so. Those who did not receive a preliminary hearing were either recorded as having waived it without realizing its importance or they were recorded as having "no preliminary hearing, reason unknown." The preliminary hearing is important for obtaining release of the defendant on bond, filtering out the innocent if a lack of probable cause can be shown, establishing inconsistencies in the testimony of the prosecution witnesses between the preliminary hearing and the trial, and obtaining knowledge of the prosecutor's evidence.[4] Defendants without counsel, however, may not realize the importance of a preliminary hearing, and they may therefore by more willing to waive it or at least not to request it.

The defendant with counsel was also substantially more likely to be released on bail. This is so in spite of the fact that defendants with counsel were more likely to be indigent and thus less capable of putting up bail money. Indigent defendants are more likely to have counsel since in most counties (even as of the early 1960s) indigent defendants could obtain court-appointed counsel, but non-indigent defendants had to pay for their own counsel and therefore often went unrepresented. What may be happening is that attorneys representing indigents are able to get the bond sufficiently reduced so that even the indigent defendants can be released, but the unrepresented non-indigent defendant has his bond set at an unreduced figure beyond even his greater ability to pay.[5] One might also argue that indigent defendants tend to commit less severe crimes than middle-class defendants and their bond is therefore set lower, regardless of whether they are represented by counsel. This explanation seems faulty, however, in view of the fact that all 1,101 cases in table 4-1 involve the same crime, namely grand larceny, although one could argue there are empirical degrees of grand larceny which are not recorded in the docket data but are known to the judge in setting bond at the preliminary hearing.

The next row reveals one possible disadvantage of having counsel, namely that if a defendant is not released on bond, then he is more likely to have a relatively long delay in jail if he has counsel than if he has no counsel. This may be due to the fact that the presence of defense counsel may delay the defendant from coming to trial because his attorney has to investigate and prepare, and may have to ask for one or more postponements. Part of the explanation may also lie in the fact that defendants who hire attorneys have more complicated or more severe cases than those who do not, even if one is holding constant both the crime and the fact that all the defendants were kept in jail pending trial.[6]

There were no significant differences revealed in the data between defendants having counsel and defendants lacking counsel on whether or not they received a jury trial. This, however, seems contrary to the expectation that defendants without counsel would be substantially less likely to have a jury trial than defendants with counsel. At least part of the explanation for the rough equality observed is due to the smallness and therefore the relative unreliability of the denominator of those tried on which the "no counsel" percentage is based on the jury treatment line. Jury trials are also a relatively rare phenomenon for defendants regardless of whether they have counsel and regardless of the type of counsel even though jury trials correlate substantially in table 4-2 with being found not guilty.

Likewise, having one's case dismissed or obtaining an acquittal is

Table 4-2
The Correlations Between the Characteristics of Defendants, Their Type of Counsel, and the Criminal Procedure Treatment They Receive

	Non-indigent	*Relatively urban*	*Counsel vs. no counsel*	*Hired counsel vs. provided counsel*	*Public defender vs. assigned counsel*
Non-indigent	—	−05	−21	97	05
Relatively urban	—	—	23	04	24
Counsel vs. no counsel	—	—	—	X	X
Hired counsel vs. free counsel	—	—	—	—	X
Public defender vs. assigned counsel	—	—	—	—	—
Early counsel vs. late counsel	—	—	—	—	—
Received preliminary hearing	—	—	—	—	—
Released on bail	—	—	—	—	—
Short delay	—	—	—	—	—
Jury trial	—	—	—	—	—
Not found guilty	—	—	—	—	—
Probation vs. prison	—	—	—	—	—
Short vs. long prison	—	—	—	—	—

relatively rare after becoming a recorded case in the trial court dockets from which the sample of 1,101 state grand larceny cases was taken. This rarity is at approximately the 10 percent level as contrasted to the greater probability of receiving favorable treatment at the other six stages of criminal procedure. This rarity is shared by both defendants with counsel and without counsel, although defendants without counsel were slightly more likely to plead guilty or be found guilty at trial. Breaking the data down further, however, shows that 27 percent of the defendants who go to trial with counsel are acquitted, but zero percent of the few defendants who go to trial without counsel are acquitted. This is so in view of the many trial matters which require or benefit from having a lawyer such as evidence admissibility, opening and closing argument, direct and cross-examination, jury selection and instruction, deposition presenting, psychological support to the defendant, and knowledge of the law in general.

Although having an attorney may not help much in obtaining a rare dismissal or acquittal because of its rarity, the last two rows of table 4-1 do tend to show that if one is found guilty, having an attorney is helpful in obtaining a suspended sentence or probation, or in obtaining a relatively

Early counsel vs. late counsel	*Received prelim. hearing*	*Released on bail*	*Short delay*	*Jury trial*	*Not found guilty*	*Probation vs. prison*	*Short vs. long prison*
-05	08	42	09	08	07	20	-13
-15	07	07	05	-12	-05	0	07
X	08	11	-23	01	04	07	17
-03	08	51	-13	05	08	24	-14
21	07	-07	13	-03	-07	-14	31
—	-24	-11	29	-03	-11	-03	31
—	—	19	-14	-02	07	06	03
—	—	—	X	10	13	36	05
—	—	—	—	-40	-09	07	03
—	—	—	—	—	37	-11	01
—	—	—	—	—	—	X	X
—	—	—	—	—	—	—	X
—	—	—	—	—	—	—	—

Correlations greater than 10 are underlined.
X = Related by definition.
Decimal points are eliminated.

short prison sentence if there is a prison sentence. This may not be a reflection of the attorney's powers of persuasion over the judge or the jury, especially since relatively few cases are tried and relatively few of the trial cases are jury trials. Instead, it may be a reflection of the attorney's greater ability to engage in plea bargaining with the prosecutor than the defendant can by himself. His attorney knows what the law is and roughly what the empirical likelihood of a conviction is, and is therefore less bluffed into accepting a substantial jail sentence. His attorney, much more so than himself alone, can also more meaningfully threaten to take the case to trial and even to a jury trial with all the time and expense that would mean for the prosecutor.[7]

In the Urban Cases

The second set of percentages in table 4-1 separate out the more urban cases from the less urban cases in order to control for the effects of urbanism on the relation between having counsel and receiving favorable criminal procedure treatment. A county was defined as relatively urban if it had 100,000 or more population and relatively rural if it had less than 100,000 population.

It may be important to control for urbanism because defendants in urban areas are more likely to have attorneys and because criminal procedure treatment may be more favorable at some stages (and more unfavorable at other stages) in urban areas than in rural areas. Thus, what may appear to be a relation between having an attorney and criminal procedure treatment may really be due to the fact that having an attorney and certain kinds of criminal procedure treatment are both co-effects of being a defendant in an urban county.[8]

Table 4-2 shows that there is a +.23 correlation between having an attorney and being tried in a relatively urban county. This is roughly the equivalent of saying that there are about 23 percentage points separating the percentage of urban cases that have counsel from the percentage of rural cases that have counsel. To be more exact, 92 percent of the 640 useable urban cases had counsel, but only 75 percent of the 238 rural cases did so.

Only a set of urban cases are presented in the middle of table 4-1 rather than also a separate set of rural bases because (1) there are more urban cases than rural ones, (2) the rural counsel cases versus the rural no-counsel cases produce findings largely redundant to the urban counsel cases versus the urban no-counsel cases although the differences are somewhat more pronounced in the rural cases, and (3) table 4-1 is thereby more consistent with subsequent tables, particularly where public defenders are compared with assigned counsel, since there were virtually no rural public defenders.

The urban-only cases in the middle of table 4-1 tend to reveal basically the same differences between having counsel and not having counsel as the total set of cases on the left side of table 4-1. Thus, when just looking at urban cases, defendants with counsel are substantially more likely to receive a preliminary hearing, to be released on bail, and to receive relatively long delay while awaiting trial in jail. As in the total sample, the urban counsel cases are like the urban no-counsel cases with regard to receiving a jury trial and not being found guilty although there is more spread on the jury trial variable because it does have a − .12 correlation with urbanism in table 4-2. The urban defendant with a lawyer is also more likely to receive a suspended sentence or probation or a short prison sentence than the urban defendant without a lawyer, but not quite so likely as the rural defendant with a lawyer.

The explanation for the similarity between the counsel versus no-counsel pattern in the urban cases and the total sample (in spite of the + .23 correlation between urbanism and having counsel) lies in the fact that table 4-2 shows there are only very low correlations between being an urban case and receiving favorable (or unfavorable) criminal procedure treatment. Urban areas do tend to give slightly shorter prison terms to convicted defendants in grand larceny cases than rural areas do, especially in comparison to the sentences given in assault cases where rural areas tend to be harsher possibly because larceny in rural areas is more likely to be from individuals rather than business firms. The correlation between urbanism and larceny sentences is not, however, great enough to substantially affect the counsel versus no-counsel comparisons.

In the Non-Indigent Cases

The third set of percentages in table 4-1 separate out the non-indigent or middle-class, cases from the indigent ones in order to control for the effects of indigency on the relation between having counsel and receiving favorable criminal procedure treatment. An indigent defendant in the criminal case data is generally defined as one who was found to be not financially competent to hire his own lawyer. Indigent defendants were thus by definition eligible for free court-provided counsel, at least in those states providing counsel in the early 1960s. Of the 1,101 larceny cases, there were 336 defendants who were categorized as indigents, and 98 percent of them were represented by some kind of counsel. There were 421 defendants who were categorized as non-indigents, and 86 percent of them were represented by counsel. This is consistent with table 4-2, which shows a −.21 correlation between being non-indigent and having counsel, which is semantically the equivalent to a +.21 correlation between being indigent and having counsel.

Unfortunately, the criminal case data did not provide a breakdown of non-indigents into those who were lower middle-class and thus possibly not rich enough to hire their own lawyers although not poor enough to be eligible for a free lawyer, as contrasted to those who were upper middle-class who could more easily hire their own lawyers. Likewise, it is unfortunate that the data did not define indigency in terms of family income so that one could see better what percentage of the poor defendants were going unrepresented.

It may be important to control for indigency or economic class because indigent defendants may be more or less likely to have attorneys and because criminal procedure treatment may be more or less favorable to poor defendants because they are poor. Thus, what may appear to be a relation between having an attorney and criminal procedure treatment may really be due to the fact that having an attorney and certain kinds of criminal procedure treatment are both co-effects of being an impoverished rather than a middle-class defendant.[9]

Only a set of non-indigent cases are presented on the right side of table 4-1 rather than also a separate set of indigent cases because: (1) there are more non-indigent cases than indigent ones, (2) there are virtually no indigent defendants lacking counsel given the way indigency was defined, and (3) if the comparison could be made, indigent counsel cases versus indigent no-counsel cases would probably produce findings largely redundant to the non-indigent counsel cases versus the non-indigent no-counsel cases.

Unlike the urban cases, controlling for indigency does produce some important differences in the counsel versus no-counsel pattern, as shown by comparing the non-indigent cases on the right side of table 4-1 with the total cases on the left side. The direction of the counsel versus no-counsel pattern is generally the same, but the size of the differences is usually greater. Thus, when the counsel cases are compared with the no-counsel cases in the total sample with regard to being released on bail, there is only a difference of 17 percentage points; whereas when the counsel cases are compared with the no-counsel cases in the non-indigent sample with regard to being released on bail there is a difference of 37 percentage points. This shows that when all the defendants are non-indigent and thus approximately equal in their ability to pay the same bail, those who have lawyers are much more likely to be able to arrange for bail terms they can meet even though those among the non-indigent who have lawyers may have committed more severe larcenies.

Likewise, the effect of having a lawyer on producing prolonged delay shows more clearly when all the defendants being compared are non-indigent rather than have the greater mixture of defendants which is present in the total sample. Having counsel also makes a more substantial difference on receiving a suspended sentence or probation when all the defendants are non-indigent.

The explanation for the strengthened impact of counsel on treatment when indigency is held constant simply seems to be that not only does indigency correlate with having counsel (as urbanism does), but it also correlates even more with some types of criminal procedure treatment (which urbanism does not). Thus, table 4-2 shows a +.42 correlation between being non-indigent and being released on bail, and a +.20 correlation between being non-indigent and receiving a suspended sentence or probation of those convicted.

The last row shows a small but unusual negative difference between having counsel and receiving a short prison term of those imprisoned. Thus, 46 percent of the *no*-counsel defendants received short prison terms, but only 37 percent of the defendants with counsel received short terms. This may reflect the fact that counsel is more likely to be hired in the more severe grand larceny cases. It may also reflect the fact that financially better off non-indigents possibly steal larger sums of money, and are also more capable of hiring counsel. When one compares non-indigents with indigents, table 4-2 shows a +.13 correlation between being relatively non-indigent and receiving a longer prison term.

If crudely controlling for economic class, as was done here, brings out the importance of counsel in avoiding unfavorable and possibly illegal criminal procedure treatment, then more accurate controls for economic class and other intervening variables would probably even further bring out the importance of counsel. Given this importance, the question is logically raised as to how to arrange for counsel for those who cannot afford an attorney and who might thereby suffer disproportionately unfavorable treatment in spite of their innocence or low degree of guilt.

Hired Counsel Versus Provided Counsel

One way to provide counsel for those who cannot afford an attorney is the judicare system whereby an indigent defendant can go to the attorney of his choice as non-indigents do, and the government will pay all or a percentage of the reasonable fee charged. This system is contrasted with the system whereby the indigent defendant does not hire his own counsel, but rather is provided with a free counsel who is either a salaried public defender or an ad hoc appointed counsel. Comparing the judicare system with the court-provided attorney is in effect comparing hired counsel with free or provided counsel.

Table 4-3 shows how defendants who have their own hired attorneys differ in their criminal procedure treatment from those who have been provided free attorneys. Unfortunately, there is no way of controlling for indigency in table 4-3 such that one could compare hired counsel of non-indigents with provided counsel of non-indigents or compare hired counsel of indigents with provided counsel of indigents. This is so because non-indigents by definition are ineligible for court-provided counsel and because indigents by definition (and by the absence of judicare systems for criminal cases) are unable to hire their own attorneys.

Table 4-2 shows a +.97 correlation between being a non-indigent and having hired counsel. This is based partly on the fact that in the total sample of cases, there were 323 defendants who were known to be non-indigent, and 99 percent of those non-indigents who had counsel had hired counsel rather than provided counsel. The +.97 correlation also reflects the fact that in the total sample of cases, there were 313 indigent defendants, and

Table 4-3
How Defendants Who Have Their Own *Hired* Attorneys Differ In Their Criminal Procedure Treatment From Those Who Have Been *Provided* Attorneys

Fraction in Sample	*Criminal Procedure Treatment*	*All Cases*			*Urban Cases*		
		Hired Counsel		*Provided Counsel*	*Hired Counsel*		*Provided Counsel*
103 252 514 940	% who wanted only two weeks or *less* for counsel to appear or be appointed	38	–	42	32	–	39
376 476	% who received preliminary hearing	62	+	54	63	+	57
458 873	% who were released on bail	76	⊕	25	78	⊕	25
165 245	% who had short delay of two month's or *less* from arrest to disposition or trial while in jail	50	⊖	64	58	–	64
76 242	% who had jury trial of those tried	31	+	26	31	+	24
138 957	% who were *not* found guilty	13	+	9	12	+	7
320 734	% who received a suspended sentence or probation rather than a prison sentence	61	⊕	37	60	⊕	35
118 266	% who received short prison terms of one year or *less* of those imprisoned	38	⊖	52	34	⊖	55
1101	Number in Sample	347		315	278		242

+ means defendants with *hired* lawyers received better treatment.
– means defendants with *provided* lawyers received better treatment.
The sign is circled where the difference is greater than ten.

only 3 percent of those indigents who had counsel had hired counsel rather than provided counsel.

Table 4-3 shows that one receives more favorable treatment with hired counsel than with provided counsel at all stages of criminal procedure treatment except on the matter of delay and shortness of prison sentence. For example, 76 percent of the defendants who had hired counsel were released on bail, but only 25 percent of the defendants who had provided counsel were. One might argue though that this difference is due to the fact that defendants with hired counsel are more likely to have the money to meet the bail requirements than defendants with provided counsel.

Partially counteracting that economic status argument, however, are three points. First, the left side of table 4-1 shows that indigent defendants with counsel were more likely to be released on bail than non-indigent defendants without counsel, which indicates the influence of the attorney as an important supplement to one's economic status. Second, the size of the 51 percentage points difference (76 minus 25) is substantially larger than any other difference in any of the tables, and such a large difference possibly seems more reasonable to attribute to both economic status and type of counsel than economic status alone. Third, the bail bonds of non-indigent defendants are possibly set higher than the bonds of indigents, thereby partially offsetting the economic status variable. The bonds are possibly set higher because non-indigents have a greater ability to pay and to forfeit, and because non-indigents may be committing more severe grand larcenies as indicated (on the last row of table 4-3) by the longer sentences they are receiving when imprisoned.

Hired counsel was also much more likely to obtain a suspended sentence or probation rather than a prison sentence for his clients than provided counsel was. That difference may, however, be attributed to the fact that provided counsel is representing indigent defendants who may have worse prior records and therefore be worse risks for probation or suspended sentence. Supporting that notion is the fact that there was a +.13 correlation between being indigent and having a prior record in some related federal data.[10]

On the other hand, the left side of table 4-1 on row 6 tends to show that indigent defendants with counsel were more likely to receive a suspended sentence or probation than non-indigent defendants without counsel. Like the bail finding in table 4-1, a higher percentage of the counsel-present cases received a suspended sentence or probation than the no-counsel cases even though the counsel-present cases were more likely to involve indigents than the no-counsel cases.

Like counsel versus no counsel in table 4-1, hired counsel versus provided counsel makes little difference (1) with regard to receiving a jury trial of those tried or (2) with regard to not being found guilty.[11] Hired counsel versus provided counsel also makes little difference with regard to receiving a preliminary hearing. On all three of these treatment variables, however, defendants with hired counsel did receive more favorable treatment than did defendants with provided counsel.

Also like counsel versus no counsel in table 4-1, the hired lawyer takes more time with his case than provided counsel, even when his client is in jail awaiting trial and especially when his client is not in jail awaiting trial. Hired counsel also takes longer to appear in the case than provided counsel does, probably because obtaining hired counsel means shopping around, inquiring among friends, and possibly being turned down by some attorneys more so than obtaining provided counsel does.

There are at least a couple of reasons why hired counsel might obtain more favorable treatment for their clients than provided counsel does. First, if provided counsel is a public defender, he is likely to be overworked and understaffed such that he is unable to give each case as much individual investigation and research as hired counsel may be able to. Second, if provided counsel is an ad hoc assigned attorney, he may be a young inexperienced volunteer; or he may be an older experienced lawyer, but not experienced in criminal law, or only reluctantly representing the defendant.

It may be useful to separate out the urban cases from the total sample of cases on the possibility that the urban cases are disproportionately hired counsel cases (or provided counsel cases) and that urban cases tend to receive more favorable (or more unfavorable) treatment. The right side of table 4-3 does this, but the pattern of hired counsel clients receiving generally more favorable treatment is still preserved. The reason the pattern is still preserved is partly because table 4-2 shows only a +.04 correlation between being relatively urban and having hired counsel rather than provided counsel. This almost zero correlation may reflect such facts as: (1) urban defendants who can afford an attorney are more likely to hire one given the greater formality of the urban legal system; (2) urban defendants who cannot afford an attorney are also more likely to be provided with one; and (3) these two facts balance each other, producing a zero correlation between the variable of urbanism and the variable of hired counsel versus provided counsel. The urban pattern on the right side of table 4-3 also resembles the general pattern on the left side because, as was mentioned in discussing table 4-1, there is little correlation in table 4-2 between urbanism and favorable or unfavorable treatment.

In spite of the fact that hired counsel might be more effective than provided counsel, it is unrealistic to expect the federal, state, or local governments in the near future to adopt a judicare system to enable the poor to obtain hired counsel. This is so largely because the judicare system is more expensive to the government than a public defender, who is paid one salary to handle all the indigent criminal cases during a given year; and it is more expensive than the traditional ad hoc assigned counsel system, where assigned counsel is paid less than the prevailing fee which hired attorneys would receive under judicare.

Public Defender Versus Assigned Counsel

In light of the expense of judicare, the only politically realistic alternatives for providing counsel to the poor are the salaried public defender or the ad hoc assigned counsel. There are variations of the public defender depending on such things as whether he is part time or full time, and whether he covers a single county or rides a circuit of counties. Likewise, there are variations on assigned counsel depending on such things as whether he is paid a fee commensurate with the work done or just a nominal fee or no fee, and whether he is assigned from a volunteer list or assigned in a rotation order regardless of his desires.

Table 4-4 shows how in general the salaried public defender differs from the ad hoc assigned counsel in the criminal procedure treatment of their respective clients. The left side of the table uses the total sample of cases, but this in effect means just using the cases involving indigent defendants, since only indigents are eligible for the services of the public defender or assigned counsel. Thus, there is no set of non-indigent public defender cases to compare with non-indigent assigned counsel cases analogous to the right side of table 4-1.

The table 4-4 comparisons yield mixed findings. On some matters the public defender clients seem to obtain more favorable treatment, and on other matters the assigned counsel clients seem to do so. The public defender client spends less time waiting for a lawyer to be provided than the assigned counsel client does. This is logically so because the public defender is an on-going institution and can be made more readily available; whereas to appoint assigned counsel requires at least one or more hearings or visits to find a willing and able attorney. If waiting time is measured in terms of transpired stages in the criminal justice process rather than transpired days, then assigned counsel does not appear to come on so late compared to the public defender. This lessened difference is due to the fact that the public defender is largely an urban phenomenon, and in urban cases it takes longer for the stages to pass than for the days to pass compared to rural cases.

If one compares having a public defender with having assigned counsel, then both sides of the comparison are represented by counsel. If, however, one compares defendants in counties where the public defender system is the system for representing indigents with defendants in counties where assigned counsel is the system, then all the defendants may not have counsel. Ninety-four percent of the defendants in counties with defender systems had counsel, but only 87 percent of the defendants did in counties with assignment systems. This probably shows that public defenders are slightly less likely to be waived than assigned counsel or are more likely to be appointed before the case is otherwise resolved.

Table 4-4
How Indigent Defendants Who Have *Public Defenders* Differ in Their Criminal Procedure Treatment from Those Who Have *Assigned Counsel*

Fraction in Sample	*Criminal Procedure Treatment*	*All Cases* *Public Defender*		*All Cases* *Assigned Counsel*	*Urban Cases* *Public Defender*		*Urban Cases* *Assigned Counsel*
103 252 514 940	% who waited two weeks or *less* for counsel to appear or be appointed	71	⊕	38	71	⊕	31
376 676	% who received preliminary hearing	62	+	53	62	+	55
458 873	% who were released on bail	18	−	27	18	−	27
165 245	% who had short delay of two months or *less* from arrest to disposition or trial while in jail	75	⊕	60	75	⊕	58
76 242	% who had jury trial of those tried	22	−	26	22	−	24
138 957	% who were *not* found guilty	4	−	9	4	−	7
320 734	% who received a suspended sentence or probation rather than a prison sentence	23	⊖	40	23	⊖	38
118 266	% who received short prison terms of one year of *less* of those imprisoned	81	⊕	44	81	⊕	45
1101	Number in sample	49		266	49		193

+ means defendants who had public defenders received better treatment.
− means defendants who had assigned counsel received better treatment.
The sign is circled where the difference is greater than ten.

According to row 4 of table 4-4, the public defender seems to consume less time preparing his case while the defendant waits in jail pending trial. This may be due to the more specialized experience of the public defender in handling criminal cases and to greater pressures on him to move his cases along faster.[12] He may also have a greater tendency to plead his clients guilty, which might account for their shorter stay in jail pending disposition of their cases. This is partly supported by the slightly higher percentage of public defender clients who plead guilty or who are found guilty (96 percent) than assigned counsel defendants who do likewise (91 percent).

The public defender's possibly greater tendency and ability to plead his clients guilty to a lesser charge may explain why the public defender's clients receive shorter prison sentences of those imprisoned. On the other hand, assigned counsel does seem to try harder for his clients as indicated by the fact that (1) he enables a greater percentage of them to be released on bail even though both sets of clients are indigent,[13] (2) he uses a jury trial for a greater percentage of them, and (3) he, like hired counsel, is more likely to obtain a suspended sentence or probation on their behalf.

Most of these differences between the public defender and assigned counsel do not reflect differences inherent in being a salaried defense lawyer rather than being on an ad hoc assignment. Instead, they seem to reflect the fact that public defenders in the sample are always from urban counties which are often congested, and assigned counsel are at least sometimes from less pressured rural counties. Because of the congestion of heavy urban caseloads, the understaffed public defender is possibly not able to do as thorough or individualized a job as one might expect from his specialized expertise in comparison to less specialized assigned counsel.[14]

Because all the public defenders were in the relatively urban counties, it is impossible to compare rural public defenders with rural assigned counsel in the sample of cases. We can, however, compare urban public defenders with urban assigned counsel. In doing so on the right side of table 4-4, however, we get a pattern of differences quite similar to the pattern on the left side with the total cases. This is due to the fact that the urban public defender cases are the same as the public defender cases for the total sample, and the urban assigned counsel cases are similar to the assigned counsel cases in the total sample since there are more urban than rural cases in the total sample.

Nevertheless, most of the differences on the right side of table 4-4 are smaller than the differences on the left side, showing that holding constant urbanism does decrease the differences between assigned counsel and public defender. The one exception is with regard to earliness of appointment, which does seem to be a real difference inherent on the greater on-going availability of the public defender. The differences between public defender and assigned counsel (just working with urban cases) would probably be even less if population data were readily available for further equalizing the urbanism of the public defender and assigned counsel cases. Unfortunately, the assigned counsel cases on the "urban" side of table 4-4 are probably less urban than the public defender cases. It would also be helpful if we could get data on the financing and caseloads of public defenders' offices so that we could compare well-financed public defenders with less well-financed to see how much of a difference is made by financing and thus staffing per caseload.[15]

Early-Obtained Counsel Versus Late-Obtained Counsel

In discussing table 4-3, it was mentioned that provided counsel appears on behalf of defendants quicker than hired counsel. Likewise, in discussing table 4-4, it was mentioned that the public defender appears on behalf of his clients quicker than assigned counsel does. What is the relationship between early-obtained counsel versus late-obtained counsel and favorableness of criminal procedure treatment?

There are two ways to measure whether counsel is early-obtained or late-obtained. One way involves counting the number of days from arrest to the time counsel appears or is appointed. This is the method that was used in the first row of tables 4-3 and 4-4. The median on this measure was two weeks since in about half the grand larceny cases in the sample, counsel appeared in less than two weeks; and in half the cases, he appeared in more than two weeks. The alternative method is to determine at what stage in the process counsel appeared or was appointed. The median on this measure was "after filing indictment or equivalent but before arraignment" in that about half the cases for which information was available involved counsel at or before that stage, and half afterwards.

The stages-passed measure may make more sense than the days-passed measure because it is worse not to get an attorney until the day of trial (even if that is only five days from arrest) than it is not to get an attorney until thirty days from arrest but before any court hearing. Supreme Court decisions on when counsel should be appointed also specify stages rather than days. On the other hand, it is harmful to wait many days for counsel regardless of what stages transpire because (1) the defendant may be needlessly languishing in jail, (2) witnesses may be forgetting what happened while their statements are not being preserved in depositions, and (3) the defendant may become psychologically depressed thereby hurting his ability to help with the case and to make a good impression on the court.

The days-passed approach rather than the stages-passed approach was used in tables 4-3 and 4-4, also partly for methodological considerations. In the IBM data, the actual stage of counsel's appearance or appointment was not recorded. Instead, what was recorded was "the stage at which counsel is usually appointed in non-capital felonies in the county." The days-passed measure by contrast is based on the individual case rather than the average case from that county although it therefore has more missing information. There is some relationship between the two measures in that if the trial is early, the number of days passed will be early since there are no appointments after trial. The relationship, however, is not high because urbanism correlates negatively with obtaining counsel within a few days, but positively with obtaining counsel before the passage of the median stage.

We shall now discuss how defendants who have early-appointed attorneys differ in their criminal procedure treatment from those who have late-appointed attorneys. There is, however, no table summarizing those relationships for four reasons. First, such a table would probably have to be a double table, one part using the days-passed measure and one part using the stages-passed measure. It is, however, easier to discuss the few situations in which those measures produce different results (as was done with the first row of table 4-4) than to double the data presented. Second, instead of showing all cases, urban cases, and non-indigent cases, it would be necessary to present all cases, urban cases, rural cases, non-indigent cases, and indigent cases in order to adequately show the patterns involved. This is so because (as will be described) the urban pattern is the reverse of the rural pattern, and the non-indigent pattern differs substantially from the indigent one.

Third, early and late counsel (as will be seen) turn out to be just different ways of saying provided and hired counsel (or vice versa) for the urban and rural cases, and just different ways of talking about types of hired counsel or types of provided counsel for the non-indigent and indigent cases. In other words, early and late counsel do not independently reflect the time of appearance or appointment, but rather the type of counsel which has already been discussed with regard to tables 4-3 and 4-4. Fourth, even if early and late counsel could be measured independently from type of counsel, it probably would not produce patterns as substantial as comparing types of counsel does. In other words, time of appearance is probably substantially less important to criminal procedure treatment than is counsel versus no counsel, hired counsel versus provided counsel, and public defender versus assigned counsel. Presenting what would amount to ten sub-tables (two measures times five categories relating to the totality, urbanism, and indigency) would thereby distract from these more important relations.

When all the cases are lumped together, the clients with late counsel tend to receive more favorable treatment than the clients with early counsel. This is so as was brought out in discussing table 4-3 because late counsel tends to be hired counsel, and early counsel tends to be provided counsel. The only exceptions with regard to the more favorable treatment of late counsel clients is with regard to (1) delay in preparing the case and (2) length of prison term for those imprisoned, given the possibly greater severity of grand larcenies committed by non-indigents who hire counsel.

If one just looks to the rural cases, then clients of early counsel receive more favorable treatment. This is so because (unlike the more general urban pattern) early counsel in rural areas tends to be hired counsel since it takes longer to arrange for court-assigned counsel in a rural area than it takes to hire an attorney, and there were no on-going public defenders in the rural cases as of the early 1960s. On the other hand, if one just looks to the urban cases, early counsel tends to correspond to public defender and late counsel to hired counsel.

If one just looks to the indigent cases, then clients of early and late counsel tend to have the same mixed treatment as the patterns present in table 4-4 because early counsel for indigents tends to correspond to having a public defender, and late counsel for indigents tends to correspond to having assigned counsel. If one looks just to the non-indigent cases, the differences are smaller because early and late counsel do not correspond to distinct types like public defender and assigned counsel. Instead, early counsel may mean an attorney that the defendant quickly grabs, possibly in the vicinity of the criminal courthouse, whereas late counsel may mean an attorney for whom the defendant more carefully shops. Thus, although the differences are small, late counsel in the non-indigent cases does obtain more favorable treatment for his client, with the usual exceptions of delay related to preparation and length of prison term related to crime severity.[16]

Some Conclusions

Having an *attorney* is especially important with regard to receiving a preliminary hearing, being released on bail, and receiving a short sentence of those imprisoned. It is also beneficial, although less so, with regard to obtaining a jury trial, a dismissal or acquittal, and a suspended sentence or probation if found guilty. Having an attorney does, however, correlate to the defendant's detriment with increased delay in jail of those defendants who are not released on bail. Detailed analyses and explanations for these summary findings and others below are given in the body of this chapter.

These findings hold up when one analyzes just urban cases or just rural cases because urbanism does not substantially correlate with how one is treated although urban defendants are more likely to have attorneys. These counsel versus no counsel findings are substantially strengthened when one analyzes just non-indigent cases or just indigent cases because indigency does substantially correlate with how one is treated and indigent defendants were more likely to have counsel since by definition indigency is closely related to receiving court-appointed counsel.

Having a *hired attorney* rather than a court-provided one seems especially important with regard to being released on bail and receiving a suspended sentence or probation if found guilty, although these relations are confounded by the relation between economic class and having a hired attorney rather than a court-provided one. It also seems beneficial to have a hired attorney with regard to receiving a preliminary hearing, a jury trial, and a dismissal or acquittal. A hired attorney, however, possibly to the defendant's detriment, is more likely to appear later in the case than a court-provided attorney, is more likely to consume more time while the defendant is in jail pending trial, and is more likely to have clients who commit crimes which possibly merit or at least receive longer prison terms if the defendant is imprisoned.

Having a *public defender* rather than assigned counsel if one is indigent may mean getting an attorney more quickly, having one's case processed faster, and being better represented in (or pushed into) plea bargaining for a lesser sentence to a reduced charge. On the other hand, having assigned counsel may mean more vigorous representation with regard to bail reduction, requesting a jury trial, obtaining a dismissal or acquittal , and obtaining a suspended sentence or probation if convicted.

Having an *early-obtained counsel* may theoretically been an advantage because he can begin his investigation and preparation earlier. As an empirical matter, however, early-obtained counsel tends to mean court-provided counsel rather than hired counsel, especially in the more urban counties where the public defender system is used. Among indigents in the data analyzed, early counsel means having a public defender rather than assigned counsel.

The *policy recommendations* which come from these findings logically lead one to advocate increased provisions for providing attorneys to those who otherwise would not have them if one seeks to protect the innocent from adverse criminal procedure treatment. The hired counsel versus provided counsel findings might lead one to advocate the judicare system for allowing indigents and near indigents to hire their own attorneys who would be paid in whole or in part fron a governmental fund if that were economically and thus politically feasible. In the absence of such a system, an adequately financed public defender system seems most capable of protecting the innocent from maltreatment and conviction. If the appropriate governmental agencies refuse to finance public defender systems proportionate to their heavy caseload, assigned counsel seems most effective especially in less urban areas where caseloads are smaller and can be handled on an ad hoc assignment basis.

In view of the importance of adequate financing for either a hired counsel judicare system or a salaried public defender system, it is important for governmental bodies and society to recognize the importance of providing adequate counsel to those who otherwise cannot afford counsel. Counsel for the poor protects the innocent from conviction and harassment and thereby decreases bitterness toward the system. Without counsel, constitutional rights are less likely to be enforced and more likely to be rendered meaningless. Attorneys also help to bring about orderly reform of the legal system as opposed to resorting to violence and other non-legal tactics to bring legal reform. They can provide an educational function to their clients, thereby preventing some wrong-doing in the future before it occurs. With defense counsel, the American adversary system, which presupposed that truth lies between the opposing attorneys, has at least some chance of obtaining its truth-seeking goal.

Notes

1. The total sample of data can be obtained on computer tape from the Inter-University Consortium for Political Research at the University of Michigan.

2. Grand larceny cases were also one of the most frequently occurring felony cases in the state data. They constituted about 15 percent of the 11,258 cases. Variations on burglary, bad check-passing, and felonious assault also frequently occurred. There seens to be no reason, however, why the effects of alternative types of counsel on criminal procedure treatment should be different between grand larceny cases and these other crimes.

3. Prior relevant studies include: Summers, *Defending the Poor: The Assigned Counsel System in Milwaukee County*, WIS. L. REV. (1969); Skolnick, *Social Control in the Adversary System*, 11 J. OF CONFLICT RESOLUTION 52 (1967). Taylor, A COMPARISON OF COUNSEL FOR FELONY DEFENDANTS (1972); Silverstein, DEFENSE OF THE POOR: THE NATIONAL REPORT (1965); Oaks and Lehman, CRIMINAL JUSTICE SYSTEM AND THE INDIGENT (1968); *The Public Defender and Other Suggested Systems for the Defense of Indigents*, 53 JUDICATURE 242 (1970); Benjamin and Pedeliski, *The Minnesota Public Defender System and the Criminal Law Process: A Comparative Study of Behavior at the Judicial District Level*, 4 LAW & SOC. REV. 79 (1969).

4. These are the points emphasized by the Supreme Court in declaring that the preliminary hearing is a critical stage of prosecution in *Coleman v. Alabama*, 399 U.S. 1 (1970). Table 4-2 does show a +.19 correlation between receiving a preliminary hearing and being released on bond.

5. Not very many of the defendants had their bonds reduced, but 14 percent of the 539 grand larceny defendants in the sample (for whom information was avaialble) who had attorneys had their bond reduced, whereas only 6 percent of the 62 defendants who lacked attorneys had their bond reduced. The average bond for non-indigents for whom bond was set was $2,213; and for indigents, it was $2,054.

6. The relatively greater time consumed in cases where defendants are represented by counsel is even more pronounced where the defendant is not in jail awaiting trial. Thus, 68 percent of the defendants represented by counsel came to trial over ninety days from their arrest, whereas only 29 percent of the defendants who lacked counsel came to trial over ninety days from their arrest.

7. Twenty percent of the 613 grand larceny defendants in the sample for which information was available who had attorneys had their charge reduced, whereas only 2 percent of the eighty-seven defendants who lacked attorneys had their charge reduced.

8. On differences between urban and rural areas with regard to the availability of attorneys and criminal procedure treatment, see Nagel, "*Disparities in Criminal Procedure*," 14 U.C.L.A. LAW REVIEW 1272, 1289-1292 (1967), reproduced in S. Nagel, THE LEGAL PROCESS FROM A BEHAVIORAL PERSPECTIVE (Dorsey, 1969).

9. On differences between indigent and non-indigent defendants with regard to the availability of attorneys and criminal procedure treatment, see *Ibid*., at 1278-1283.

10. *Ibid*., at 1282 and 1303-1304.

11. Of the thirty-nine cases in the sample that went to trial with a hired lawyer, 31 percent resulted in an acquittal; whereas of the 63 cases that went to trial with provided counsel, only 17 percent resulted in an acquittal. This indicates, in combination with Row 6 of table 4-3, that hired counsel makes little difference compared to provided counsel with regard to obtaining a dismissal, but more of a difference with regard to obtaining an acquittal where a lawyer's time and trial skills are more involved.

12. It may appear that the public defender consumes less time than assigned counsel because of the relative shortness of the time consumed from *arrest to trial* when the public defender is involved regardless whether the defendant is released on bond. The time from the public defender's *appointment to trial*, however, may actually be longer than the time from assigned counsel's appointment to trial since the public defender does tend to be appointed earlier.

13. Of the 167 grand larceny defendants who were represented by assigned counsel, 18 percent had their bonds reduced; whereas zero percent of the 45 defendants who were represented by a public defender had their bonds reduced. The lack of subsequent bond reduction by the public defender may be at least partly due to the fact that he is more likely to be present when the original bond is set in view of his earlier appointment.

14. Much of the literature dealing with the problems of public defenders emphasizes their increasingly heavy caseloads and resulting pressures to

plead their clients guilty, even though the quality of attorneys doing public defender work may have improved somewhat in recent years due to stiffer law school admissions, better law school training, and possibly a greater public service orientation. See, e.g., J. CASPER, AMERICAN CRIMINAL JUSTICE: THE DEFENDANT'S PERSPECTIVE (1972), at 106-114; Oaks and Lehman, *supra* note 3; Blumberg, *The Practice of Law as a Confidence Game: Organizational Cooptation of a Profession,* 1 L. & SOC'Y REV. 15 (1967). The Casper book finds that a large amount of the negative reactions of Connecticut prison inmates against the legal system relate to what they perceive as unwarranted disparities between the treatment of defendants represented by public defenders and equally guilty, but better treated defendants having hired attorneys. Casper, *Ibid.* at 100-25. In Illinois the public defender may also lack some trial and appellate vigor because his appointment and retention depends on the chief judge of the circuit.

15. Other comparisons of assigned counsel and public defenders have been made. See Anderson, Warner & Foster, *The Public Defender and Other Suggested Systems for the Defense of Indigents,* 53 JUDICATURE 242 (1970); Benjamin & Pedeliski, *supra* note 3; and Summers, *supra* note 3.

16. For a discussion of the problem of at what point in time counsel should be provided see Silverstein, *supra* note 6, at 75-88. See also A SPECIAL COMMITTEE OF THE ASSOCIATION OF THE BAR OF THE CITY OF NEW YORK & THE NATIONAL LEGAL AID AND DEFENDER ASSOCIATION, EQUAL JUSTICE FOR THE ACCUSED (1959); Hunvald, *The Right to Counsel at the Preliminary Hearing,* 31 MO. L. REV. 109 (1966).

5 Attorney Attitudes Toward the Unpopular and the Poor

The purpose of this chapter is to analyze some data on the nature and correlates of the attitudes and behaviors of attorneys toward unpopular and indigent clients. In this context, "unpopular clients" means clients whose characteristics are perceived by the respondent attorney to arouse such community hostility that acceptance of the case could damage the lawyer's career.[1] "Poor" or "indigent" clients are those who are unable to pay an attorney's regular fee with their own money or through family or friends (where this indigency is known to the attorney at the time the case is accepted).[2]

In the spring of 1970 a questionnaire (included in the Appendix of this chapter) was mailed to a random sample of 474 attorneys across the country. The attorneys consisted of the last practicing lawyer found at every tenth page of the alphabetic sections of the 1970 *Martindale-Hubbell Legal Directory*.[3] Two hundred thirty-nine responses (51 percent of the sample) were received in time to be analyzed.[4] Nearly all the attorneys responded to all the items, but some felt that the categories given did not enable them to indicate the specific nature of their practices. The background characteristics of the responding attorneys seem to correspond roughly to those of American attorneys in general.[5] Given the sample size and questions about its representativeness, this study should be considered an exploratory or pilot study generating tentative conclusions or plausible hypotheses for further testing.

A Profile of the Responding Attorneys

These responses probably fall short of the ideal of those who would like to see lawyers more willing to represent the "unpopular" and the indigent. The percentages of favorable responses, however, probably exceed the expectations of those who are cynical about the legal profession's concern for the "unpopular" and the indigent.[6]

Eighty-two percent of the respondents agreed that "Lawyers should be encouraged to represent the unpopular client" (Item 4). Sixty-three percent would accept as a client an admitted Communist who had been

This chapter was coauthored with Anthony Champagne of Rutgers University and Marian Neef of Harvard University.

charged with forcible overthrow of the government if he was able to pay a normal fee (item 37a). If he were able to pay, 61 percent would accept an admitted Ku Klux Klan member charged with attempting to deprive blacks of their civil rights (item 40a).

Other items are particularly relevant to attitudes toward representing the indigent. These deal with the desirability of different ways of representing the poor in criminal and civil cases. The method least favored is unpaid volunteer or unpaid assigned counsel. For example, only 22 percent of the respondents thought "a desirable system of legal representation for the indigent in criminal cases . . . is unpaid volunteer counsel" (item 48). The method most favored is a salaried government lawyer, either public defender in criminal cases (82 percent thought desirable, item 46) or "Legal Services Agency" in civil cases (81 percent thought desirable, item 50).[7]

Other systems for the provision of legal services include judicare and paid assigned counsel. Judicare was defined in the questionnaire as "a system by which the government would pay 80% of the minimum fee to the attorney accepting the indigent case." Sixty percent thought it desirable for criminal cases (item 43), while 53 percent thought it desirable for civil cases (item 49). Paid assigned counsel is common in criminal cases but thus far is non-existent in civil cases. No state has yet established a statutory or constitutional right to counsel for the indigent in civil cases. Nevertheless, 55 percent of the respondents agreed that "in eviction cases, the court should provide counsel to the indigent defendant" (item 17).

Because an attorney indicates it is desirable that attorneys represent the "unpopular" and "indigent" does not necessarily mean he does so himself. However, 45 percent did indicate they had "defended an unpopular client where an acceptance of the case could have damaged [one's] career" (item 57). In fact, 30 percent stated they lost other clients "because of the case" (item 59). Eighty-one percent indicated they had represented an indigent person accused of a crime (item 53), and 34 percent said they had done so quite often (item 54). Seventy-two percent indicated they had represented indigents in civil cases (item 55), and 40 percent said quite often (item 56).[8]

Variations in Attitudes, Opportunities, and Behavior Toward Defending the Unpopular

Possibly of more interest to others concerned with the legal profession than the mere percentage of positive responses to a given item are the correlations between different items in the questionnaire. These correlations should also have greater validity to reality than do the percentages especially when dealing with a small sample.[9] In other words, one can probably more meaningfully attempt to generalize from the sample of questionnaire respondents to lawyers in general when one is talking about (1) the tendency of certain kinds of responses to vary together or inversely, rather than when one is talking about (2) what percentage of lawyers are likely to respond favorably to a given item.

Table 5-1 shows the correlations between the questionnaire items most related to defense of the "unpopular."[10] The order of the twelve items across and down in the table is from the one behavior item on the left (item 57) to the three specific attitudes (4, 37, and 40) and two types of law practice (74 and 77) that might explain the behavior, to the one general attitude (11) and five background characteristics (84, 83, 92, 90, 93) that might explain the specific attitudes and the opportunities created by the types of law practice. All correlations greater than +.20 or −.20 are underlined.[11]

Some items were left out of table 5-1 for various reasons. Some were redundant, such as different ways of ascertaining "liberalism." Others were omitted because they involved too few attorneys on one side of a dichotomized item, e.g. race (only four were non-white) or sex (only eight were females). In still others, the meaning of the response was too ambiguous. For example, responses about the motivations of other lawyers in rejecting unpopular clients might reflect (1) a projection of the respondent's own un-idealistic values or (2) pessimism about his fellow attorneys' values.

Figure 5-1 takes the data from table 5-1 and attempts to show the possible causal relations among the questionnaire items most related to defending the unpopular. The direction of each arrow indicates the hypothesized causal direction between the related items. An arrow pointing in both directions indicates a hypothesized reciprocal causation between the items.[12]

This causal model of behavior being determined by specific attitudes and opportunities, which in turn are determined by general attitudes and backgrounds or environmental characteristics, is sometimes referred to as the "funnel-shaped theory of behavioral causality." It has received wide support in the voting behavior literature and the judicial behavior literature although in both places discussion of the opportunity variables are relatively neglected (Campbell 1960, pp. 18-37; Murphy and Tanenhaus 1972, pp. 103-11). The tentative findings of this chapter are consistent with this theoretical model, as will be shown below in discussing figures 5-1 and 5-2.[13]

"Constituency-linkage theory" is a related conceptual scheme which might also have predictive and explanatory power. It relates (1) the behavior of lawyers back to (2) their attitudes and (3) their perceptions of their clients' attitudes. These three variables are then related to (4) the actual

Table 5-1
Correlations Between the Questionnaire Items Most Related to Defending the Unpopular

	Have defended unpopular (Item 57)	*Encourage lawyers to defend unpopular* (4)	*Would defend Communist* (37)	*Would defend Klansman* (40)	*Practice primarily personal injury* (74)
Have defended unpopular	—	09	05	09	09
Encourage lawyers to defend unpopular	—	—	39	21	10
Would defend Communist	—	—	—	73	22
Would defend Klansman	—	—	—	—	27
Practice primarily personal injury	—	—	—	—	—
Business and corporate practice	—	—	—	—	—
Economic class liberalism	—	—	—	—	—
Being Jewish	—	—	—	—	—
Democrat	—	—	—	—	—
Relatively young	—	—	—	—	—
Wealthy clients	—	—	—	—	—
Non-metro community	—	—	—	—	—

attitudes of their clients. However, no data were compiled in this study about (3) or (4), so that the constituency-linkage scheme is not available. This "diamond-shaped" alternative model has been used in the legislative behavior literature (Miller and Stokes 1963), and would seem appropriate for future research.

The key question for our purposes here is why some attorneys defend the unpopular more often than other attorneys do. Defending the unpopular seems to depend on two things: (1) having a favorable attitude toward defending the unpopular, and (2) having opportunities to do so.[14] A generally favorable attitude is presumably a reflection of (and possibly a reciprocal cause of) a favorable attitude toward defending both the left-wing and the right-wing unpopular. There is, however, a higher correlation between

Business and corporate practice (77)	*Economic class liberalism (11)*	*Being Jewish (84)*	*Democrat (83)*	*Relatively young (92)*	*Wealthy clients (90)*	*Non-metro community (93)*
−28	−03	−17	11	−12	−15	19
14	28	09	19	20	04	05
–	36	23	19	25	−17	−01
−12	18	−03	03	18	−26	10
−20	09	−17	09	14	−30	−05
—	−11	05	−21	15	40	−14
—	—	26	31	18	−06	−13
—	—	—	18	03	09	−22
—	—	—	—	07	02	−08
—	—	—	—	—	07	01
—	—	—	—	—	—	−35
—	—	—	—	—	—	—

Correlations greater than 20 are underlined.
Decimal points are eliminated.

left-wing defense and unpopular defense in general (+.39) than there is between right-wing defense and unpopular defense in general (+.21). Possibly, when lawyers think of "unpopular clients," they think more readily of left-wing clients.[15] Nevertheless, the highest correlation in figure 5-1 is between being favorable to defending the left-wing unpopular and being favorable to defending the right-wing unpopular (+.73).[16] Possibly these seemingly conflicting attitudes are related to a "liberal" sympathy for the underdog and to a generally favorable attitude toward defending the unpopular.[17]

To supplement the attitudinal relations in the upper half of figure 5-1, it

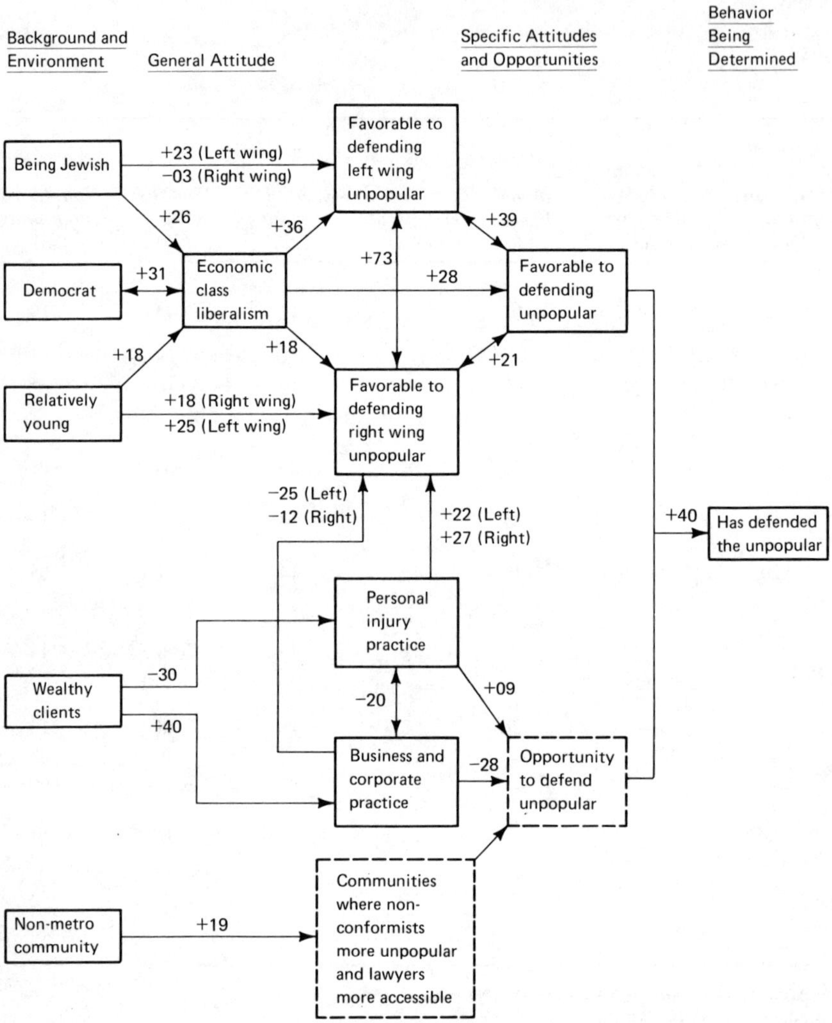

Figure 5-1. Possible Causal Relations Among the Questionnaire Items Most Related to Defending the Unpopular

is helpful to discuss the lower half of the figure, which deals with opportunities to defend the unpopular. No direct information was available regarding such opportunities. That is why this variable is shown as a broken-line rectangle. The correlations on the arrows pointing to this item refer to those between (1) the items from which they come and (2) the item beyond the broken-line rectangle. Such an intervening variable is needed in order to better organize the relationships in the figure.

Personal injury lawyers are more likely to have defended the "unpopular" than business-corporate lawyers, but *not* because the personal injury lawyers have a high degree of sympathy for the underdog. Indeed, the correlation was only +.09 between being a personal injury lawyer and responding favorably to the item used as an indicator of economic class liberalism. A better explanation for the difference in behavior between personal injury lawyers and business-corporate lawyers may be the difference in their clientele. The business-corporate lawyer is much less likely to have an "unpopular person" among his generally wealthier class of clients than a personal injury lawyer among his less affluent ones. The business-corporate lawyer may also fear antagonizing his clientele more than does the personal injury lawyer.[18] Thus the business-corporate lawyer indicates a strong aversion to defending either a Communist or a Klansman (although more so the Communist) even if the client is able to pay the lawyer's normal fee. The personal injury lawyer, on the other hand, indicates a strong willingness to defend either type of "unpopular" client provided they are able to pay his normal fee.

The responses of non-metropolitan or rural lawyers (even more so than the personal injury or business-corporate lawyers) especially support the hypothesis that opportunities as well as attitudes are important in determining whether a lawyer is likely to defend the unpopular. The rural lawyer has a +.19 correlation with defending the unpopular, but a −.13 correlation with "liberalism" and an almost total unwillingness to defend political extremists. Perhaps the explanation is that non-conformists are more readily perceived as unpopular in rural communities, and thus rural communities generate more unpopular cases per lawyer than metropolitan communities do.[19] Thus an "unpopular client" in a rural community might be considered quite "normal" or, at least, less unpopular in a metropolitan community. The rural lawyer has a −.13 correlation with "liberalism," and thus his defense of the unpopular is more likely to be caused by the peculiar nature of his opportunities than by his attitudes.[20]

In general, neither the attitudinal nor the opportunity items shown in figure 5-1 correlate very highly by themselves with having actually defended the unpopular (item 57).[21] However, if one calculates a multiple correlation coefficient combining (1) the three items dealing with attitudes toward the unpopular with (2) the three items dealing with type of law practice, one obtains a somewhat higher correlation of +.40. This indicates that these particular items do tend in combination to account for a substantial amount (but not all) of the variation among attorneys with regard to their having defended the unpopular.[22] The multiple correlation was not higher largely because many of the items in figure 5-1 are not cumulative; they intercorrelate highly, and thus partly duplicate each other.[23]

One way to interpret the multiple correlation is to ask: if we were trying to predict whether a given attorney would say "yes" or "no" to item 57 ("Have you ever defended an unpopular client where an acceptance of the case would have damaged your career"), how much more accurate would our prediction be if we knew the attorney's attitudes and law practice characteristics? Since 55 percent of the respondents answer "no," we would predict accurately 55 percent of the time by always predicting no. Knowing the additional characteristics of the lawyer, our predictive power increases roughly to 70 percent accuracy.[24]

Variations in Attitudes, Opportunities, and Behavior Toward Representing the Indigent

Table 5-2 shows the correlations among the questionnaire items most related to representing the indigent. Figure 5-2, using the data from table 5-2, attempts to portray the possible causal relations among the factors represented by these items.[25] The relevant attitudinal items (at the top of figure 5-2) seem to relate to (1) a willingness to represent the indigent (especially for a fee) and (2) an unwillingness to have others represent the indigent (especially if doing so conflicts with one's own practice). Variable 1 above particularly manifests itself in a desire to see private volunteer counsel paid and a desire to see government reimbursement to private practitioners for representing the indigent, whereas variable 2 above particularly manifests itself in opposition to court-appointed counsel from rotation lists or from government lawyers and an opposition to the OEO legal services program which may be viewed as competing for scarce clients. These two central attitudinal variables (on which information was only indirectly available) seem to correlate highly with each other.

We asked about four basic methods by which the poor can be represented. An indigent may have (A) an attorney who has voluntarily joined a legal aid committee or placed his name on a list of attorneys available to represent the poor with or without pay (volunteer counsel), (B) an attorney who has been sought out by the indigent and who fee is paid by the government the way doctors are paid under medicare (judicare), (C) an attorney who has been appointed by a court to serve with or without pay (court appointed counsel), or (D) an attorney who works on a salaried basis for an OEO legal services program, a legal aid office, or for a public defender's office (salaried attorney). Attitudes toward each of these four methods of representation are measured by questionnaire items 17, and 43 through 52.

The key correlations of responses to alternative methods of providing legal services are shown in the upper half of figure 5-2. Attorneys who are *more* likely to have represented the indigent (at least in criminal cases) are

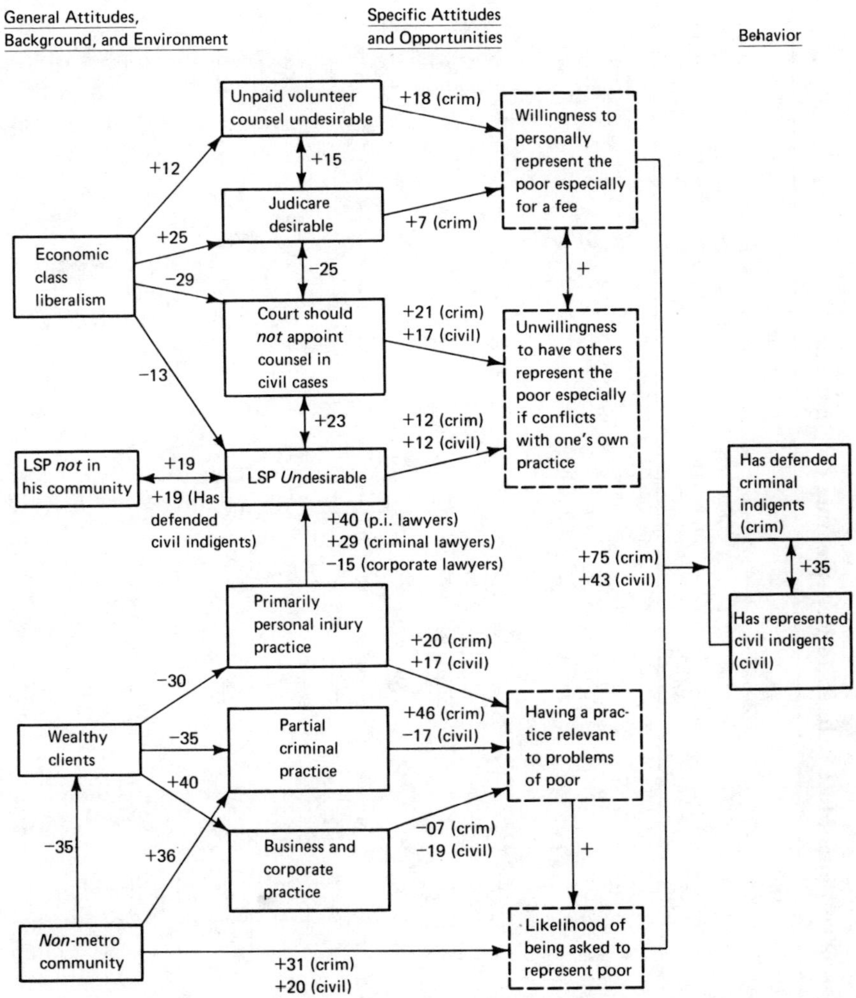

Figure 5-2. Possible Causal Relations Among the Questionnaire Items Most Related to Representing the Indigent

those who consider unpaid volunteer counsel undesirable, and who favor judicare. On the other hand, attorneys who are *less* likely to have represented the indigent in both criminal and civil cases are those who favor court appointed counsel in civil cases (which does not presently exist) and who favor the OEO legal services program (OEO-LSP). This is to say that attorneys are more likely to have represented the indigent if they disapprove expanding the right to court-appointed counsel to include civil cases and if they disfavor the LSP.

Table 5-2
Correlations Between the Questionnaire Items Most Related to Representing the Indigent

	Have defended criminal indigents (Item 53)	*Have represented civil indigents (55)*	*Unpaid volunteer counsel undesirable (48)*	*Judicare desirable (49)*	*Court should not appoint counsel in civil cases (17)*	*LSP undesirable (50)*
Have defended criminal indigents	—	35	18	07	21	12
Have represented civil indigents	—	—	04	−04	17	12
Unpaid volunteer counsel undesirable	—	—	—	15	−07	−08
Judicare desirable	—	—	—	—	−25	−13
Court should not appoint counsel in civil cases	—	—	—	—	—	15
LSP undesirable	—	—	—	—	—	—
Primarily personal injury practice	—	—	—	—	—	—
Partial criminal practice	—	—	—	—	—	—
Business and corporate practice	—	—	—	—	—	—
Economic class liberalism	—	—	—	—	—	—
LSP not in their community	—	—	—	—	—	—
Wealthy clients	—	—	—	—	—	—
Non-metropolitan political community	—	—	—	—	—	—

	Primarily personal injury practice (74)	*Partial criminal practice (82)*	*Business and corporate practice (77)*	*Economic class liberalism (11)*	*LSP not in their community (69)*	*Wealthy clients (90)*	*Non-metro-politan community (93)*
Have defended criminal indigents	20	46	−07	−13	−10	−17	31
Have represented civil indigents	17	−17	−19	−02	17	−14	20
Unpaid volunteer counsel undesirable	10	11	07	12	03	−11	11
Judicare desirable	29	−13	−23	25	04	−08	−04
Court should not appoint counsel in civil cases	07	36	−05	−29	0	−11	20
LSP undesirable	40	29	−15	−13	19	−13	19
Primarily personal injury practice	—	19	−20	09	−02	−30	07
Partial criminal practice	—	—	−12	−18	−10	−35	36
Business and corporate practice	—	—	—	−11	−26	40	−14
Economic class liberalism	—	—	—	—	03	−08	−13
LSP not in their community	—	—	—	—	—	−14	34
Wealthy clients	—	—	—	—	—	—	−35
Non-metropolitan political community	—	—	—	—	—	—	—

Correlations greater than 20 are underlined.

Decimal points are eliminated.

It is interesting to note the types of attorneys who hold these attitudes. The attorney who scores positively on "economic class liberalism" tends to approve of a rather wide range of methods for representing the indigent. He simultaneously favors judicare, court appointed counsel, and OEO-LSP, but disapproves unpaid volunteer counsel. Attorneys who live in communities with OEO-LSPs are more likely to favor the OEO-LSP method than attorneys in communities without them. Pre-existing favorable attitudes probably encourage the establishment of an OEO-LSP, but the operation of the program may also create and reinforce favorable attitudes. If an OEO-LSP exists in their community, they are also less likely to have represented indigents in civil cases—probably because the program lessens the opportunity to do so.

Attorneys in different types of practice also differ substantially in their attitudes toward methods of representing the poor. Both personal injury and criminal lawyers disapprove of OEO-LSP compared to the substantially more favorable corporate lawyers. This may seem contrary to the image of corporate lawyers as conservatives. It is consistent, however, with the notion that personal injury and criminal lawyers are more likely than corporate attorneys to view the legal services program as competing with their practices. Corporate lawyers may view the LSP as a means of relieving them of the unwelcome responsibility of personally representing the indigent. Through this endorsement of the OEO-LSP, the corporate practitioner can participate vicariously in "representing the poor." Some business-corporate lawyers may resent poor persons suing their clients although large corporate businesses tend to have more legal dealings with other large corporate businesses than with poor persons. Lawyers representing certain kinds of businesses may even welcome the additional legal work encouraged by the increased access of indigents to OEO-LSP lawyers.[26]

That personal injury and criminal lawyers have represented the indigent more often than corporate lawyers is explained only in part by attitudes. The content of personal injury and criminal practice is more relevant to the problems of the indigent. The likelihood, therefore, of attorneys in these types of practice having represented the indigent is higher, *regardless* of their personal attitudes. Related information is shown in the lower half of figure 5-2: the correlations are positive between "being a personal injury lawyer" and "having represented the poor" in both criminal and civil cases; the correlations are negative between being a business-corporate lawyer and having represented the poor in these two types of cases. Lawyers who have at least a partial criminal practice, however, had a +.46 correlation with having defended criminal indigents, but a −.17 correlation with having represented civil indigents. A criminal law practice seems to increase the likelihood of being asked to represent the poor, but only in one's specialty. The difference in experience with representing the poor between personal injury and criminal lawyers on the one hand and corporate lawyers on the other is also related to the difference in the relative wealth (item 90) of their fee-paying clientele.

Lawyers operating in non-metropolitan communities are also more likely to be asked to represent the indigent in criminal (+.31) and civil cases (+.20) than are lawyers operating in metropolitan areas. This is probably so in part because the "rural lawyer" is less likely to specialize than the "urban lawyer." This increased "opportunity" makes it more likely he will handle some criminal cases (as is shown by his +.36 correlation with "partial criminal practice"). The clients of the non-metropolitan lawyer are also not as likely to have incomes as high as the clients of the metropolitan lawyer. The combination of more general practice, diverse clientele, and accessibility help explain the rural lawyers' greater representation of the poor. In attitude, however, the rural lawyer is more negative toward court appointed counsel in civil cases (−.20) and the legal services program (−.19) which is less likely to exist in his community.

If we combine the four attitudinal variables from the middle of the top of figure 5-2 with the four law practice variables from the middle and left of the bottom of figure 5-2, we get a +.43 correlation with "having represented civil indigents."[27] We also get an even higher +.75 correlation with "having defended criminal indigents," largely because of the variable of "having a partial criminal practice."[28] In general, "representing civil indigents" does not correlate so highly with the attitudinal or law practice items. That is, if we know a lawyer has represented civil indigents, this does not tell us much about him since there seems to be a great diversity among lawyers who represent civil indigents, but not so much among those who represent criminal indigents.

We know that 72 percent of the sample answers "yes" to item 55, "representing indigents in civil cases," and 81 percent answers "yes" to item 53, "representing indigents in criminal cases." Assuming the sample is representative, we can obtain a prediction accuracy of 72 percent or 81 percent by just predicting a "yes" answer for any attorney. However, also knowing additional attitude and opportunity characteristics, we should now be able to better understand what causes some lawyers to say "yes" and others "no", even if we cannot add to the predictive power of just predicting the most common response.[29]

Some Conclusions and Recommendations

The Interaction of Attitudes and Opportunities

This research indicates that decisions to represent the "unpopular" and the "indigent" are dependent on having certain relevant attitudes and opportunities. Favorable attitudes alone, without any opportunities will, of course, not result in actual representation. However, having opportunities even if negative attitudes are present, may result in actual representation. For instance, rural attorneys are more likely to represent the unpopular and the indigent even though they have relatively conservative attitudes. Having both favorable attitudes and favorable opportunities results in increased representation of the unpopular and the indigent possibly more so than one would expect by simply adding the cumulative effect of each of those two variables.

What we may have here is an excellent example of the phenomenon of joint interaction between two causal variables. If perfect interaction is present, then neither causal variable is capable by itself of producing the effect, but both together will do so. In less than perfect interaction, one variable may produce some of the effect while the other variable produces almost none, but both together produce the effect almost always. In the language of logic rather than statistical social science, each variable in a perfect interaction is a necessary condition and both together are a sufficient condition. Being necessary conditions means the effect cannot occur unless both are present. Being a joint sufficient condition means the effect will always occur when both are present.[30]

In statistical social science, there are many variables external to the two interaction causal variables and the one effect variable which influence their relations. This plus imperfect measurement makes it virtually impossible to ever have two variables which are absolutely necessary conditions and which jointly constitute an absolutely sufficient condition. In the statistical language of percentages and variance explained, a perfect interaction pattern would look like that shown in row 1 of table 5-3. That row indicates that where the questionnaire respondents are unfavorable on both attitudes and opportunities, zero percent of them will represent the clientele group of unpopular or indigent clients. Likewise, zero percent of the respondents will represent the clientele group if the respondents are favorable on attitudes or opportunities, but unfavorable on the other variable. One hundred percent of those respondents who are favorable on both attitudes and opportunities will, however, represent the clientele group if perfect joint interaction between attitudes and opportunities is present.

Columns 5 and 6 indicate ways in which the degree of interaction can be measured. Column 5 shows the average increment in producing the effect from adding the second variable regardless of which is the first variable. In the context of representing the unpopular and the poor, this measure involves determining the difference between the percentage of doubly-favorable attorneys who represent the clientele group and the percentage of singly-favorable attorneys who represent the clientele group. In other

Table 5-3
Interaction Patterns Between Attitudes and Opportunities

	Percentage of Respondents Pepresenting the Clientele Group Who are in the Following Categories:				*Measures of Interaction*	
Clientele Group	*(1) Unfavorable on Both*	*(2) Unfavorable Opportunities Favorable Attitudes*	*(3) Favorable Opportunities Unfavorable Attitudes*	*(4) Favorable on Both*	*(5) Avg. Increment from 2nd Variable*	*(6) Additional Variance Explained from Interaction*
Perfect Interaction Pattern	0%	0%	0%	100%	½ (100 + 100) = 100 pct. points	100% − 0% = 100 pct. points
Unpopular Clients	— (0)	21% (14)	20% (5)	50% (42)	½ (30 + 29) = 29.5 pct. points	>25% − 11% = >14 pct. points
Poor in Criminal Cases	44% (9)	50% (4)	94% (17)	88% (26)	½ (38 − 6) = 16 pct. points	50% − 21% = 29 pct. points
Poor in Civil Cases	29% (14)	80% (5)	69% (29)	75% (20)	½ (−5 + 6) = .5 pct. points	22% − 7% = 15 pct. points

words, this measure involves (1) subtracting the percentage in column 2 from the percentage in column 4, (2) subtracting the percentage in column 3 from the percentage in column 4, and (3) averaging those two differences.

The maximum size that average difference or average increment can be is 100 percentage points as in the perfect interaction pattern. Theoretically one could also obtain a negative 100 percentage points if the percentages in the four columns were 100 percent, 100 percent, 100 percent, and 0 percent. One, however, could then reverse the negative 100 percentage points into a positive 100 by simply reversing the categories on the effect variable or reversing what is considered favorable and unfavorable on the causal variables. Thus the most meaningful minimum increment is zero percentage points, which occurs when all four percentages are equal.

The trouble with the measure in column 5 is that it does not adequately distinguish between (1) the extra causal force gained by adding a second variable that merely adds its own causation to the first variable and (2) the extra causal force gained by the interaction between the two variables. If there is no increment from adding the second variable then there is no additive increment (the first causal force) or joint interaction increment (the second causal force). If there is an increment from adding a second variable, the problem then becomes how much of that increment is additive and how much is interactive or multiplicative.

Column 6 attempts to answer that question by having the computer determine how much of the variation can be accounted for on the effect variable (symbolized Y) by an attitude variable (X_1) and an opportunity variable (X_2) in an additive equation of the form $Y = a + b_1(X_1) + b_2(X_2)$ and then in a multiplicative equation of the form $Y = a + b_1(X_1) + b_2(X_2) + b_3(X_1X_2)$. The little b's indicate the statistical weights assigned to each variable in the parentheses, and the little a indicates the score on the effect variable when both X_1 and X_2 are scored zero or relatively unfavorable. All the variables are scored either 0 for the relatively negative category or 1 for the relatively positive category. Column 6 shows (1) the percentage of variance on the effect variable accounted for by the interactive equation, (2) the percentage of variance accounted for by the additive equation, and (3) the difference between the two.[31]

An analysis of columns 5 and 6 tends to indicate that there is substantial interaction between attitudes and opportunities in the representation of unpopular clients, less substantial in the representation of indigent clients in criminal cases, and possibly no interaction in the representation of indigent clients in civil cases.[32] The explanation for that rank order may lie in the fact that more of a convergence of attitudes and opportunities is required to represent unpopular clients than to represent indigent clients, especially indigent civil clients where little risk is involved. The additional variance explained by interaction on the unpopular client row would be even greater if there were some cases in the category labeled unfavorable on both. For technical reasons, the absence of cases in that category made it impossible for the computer to indicate the full amount of variance accounted for by the interaction term. The exclusion of many attorneys from this analysis because they did not indicate an exclusive specialty in a favorable or unfavorable field of law practice also lowered the sample sizes and decreased the consistency between columns 5 and 6 although those columns do involve different kinds of measures.

In spite of those technical difficulties in carrying out the interaction part of the research design, one can say that there does seem to be an important joint interaction effect from favorable attitudes and favorable opportunities, at least in representing unpopular clients. Interaction effects are not often found in social science, or often looked for, as contrasted to (1) cross-tabulating or correlating one independent variable with one dependent variable, or (2) determining the cumulative although non-interactive effect of two or more independent variables on a dependent variable. In spite of the methodological and substantive value of this analysis, the analysis would not be complete without discussing its policy implications.

Some Policy and Research Implications

By policy implications in this context is meant what do the data tell us regarding how more favorable attitudes and opportunities might be stimulated, assuming the legal profession does want the unpopular and the indigent to be represented. To provide attorneys with better opportunities to defend the unpopular, one would not recommend that more attorneys should move to rural communities where more stigma may be cast on deviant personalities. Likewise, one might not recommend that the way to have more lawyers defend the poor is to have more of them have a more general practice which includes criminal and personal injury work since such a recommendation would run contrary to current efficiency trends towards specialization, especially if there are alternative ways of providing representation of the poor without sacrificing efficiency of attorney operations.[33]

To increase the number of attorneys who participate directly or indirectly in the representation of the unpopular and the poor, it might be more effective to increase the emphasis in law school and among the practicing bar on having a more favorable attitude toward representing the unpopular and the indigent.[34] The increased use of legal clinics in legal education is a step in that direction, as are bar programs to encourage legal aid work (Tucker 1971, 1972). Likewise, Supreme Court decisions endorsing representation of the poor have probably had an important impact on increasing the favorable attitude of the bar toward their representation.

Means should also be developed further by the OEO and the ABA for easing the concerns of personal injury and criminal lawyers with regard to the role of legal services programs. Such lawyers can be put on the referral lists of the LSP agencies to receive fee-paying clients who wander into LSP agencies. They can also be better informed of the fact that only a small percentage of the indigent had ever been to a private attorney for a civil matter before the advent of the legal services program (Carlin and Howard 1965; Levine and Preston 1970; and Denver Law Journal Staff 1971, pp. 115-125).[35]

For the business-corporate lawyer who does not want to get personally involved with the legal problems of indigent clients, there are a number of ways of harnessing his favorable attitude toward seeing the indigent represented. He can participate in the lobbying activities for better legal services programs which the American Bar Association and some state bar associations have promoted. He can contribute financially to supporting charitable legal aid programs and toward providing the local contribution which is needed in OEO legal services programs. He can allow or encourage the younger or more willing members of his firm to participate in the legal aid programs for the poor which have been established by some corporate law firms parallel to the community legal services programs.[36]

In light of the strongly negative response to unpaid assigned and volunteer counsel even among liberal attorneys (items 47, 48, and 52), supplementary payment systems should be devised to bring out those who are willing and able to represent the poor and unpopular as in the federal criminal system.[37] Perhaps judicare can be developed as a supplement to OEO legal services and even to the public defender if the financing can be made available and if the legislative reform, ombudsmen, and test case work of legal services can still be preserved. Those two ''ifs'' represent the leading objections generally given to an expansion of the judicare system.[38]

Since court-appointed counsel is now available in misdemeanor cases in which there is a chance of a jail sentence (*Argersinger v. Hamlin,* 1972), paid court-appointed counsel in civil cases or at least local-government financed legal aid may also become a possibility.[39] Any system which expands the representation of the indigent is also likely to expand the representation of the unpopular since the unpopular so often tend to be indigent, and since the same types of attorneys tend to have the willingness and the relevant abilities to represent both.

Additional research will be needed to supplement this pilot study with regard to the above causal modeling and policy analysis of the effects of various attitudes and opportunities on the representation of the unpopular and the poor. Such research can include more intensive interviewing and case study analysis regarding attorney representation. A larger sample is particularly needed in order to generalize about attorneys having various specialties, environmental backgrounds, attitudes, and other characteristics. The causal modeling might also benefit from the application of more sophisticated statistical techniques such as path analysis rather than rely almost solely on an analysis of the correlation coefficients in the correlation matrices shown in tables 5-1 and 5-2. Further work is also needed with regard to the multiple effects and the interaction effects of various attitude and opportunity variables on the representation of the unpopular and the poor.

Perhaps some future studies might especially focus on such policy issues as the impact on law student and lawyer attitudes of legal clinics, legal services programs, public interest law work, and Supreme Court decisions requiring increased representation of the poor. These developments are too recent to presently determine their long-run effects, but now is the time to begin gathering data for before and after studies while knowledgeable people can still recall the situation before these developments occurred. The accumulation of knowledge concerning motivations and behaviors of lawyers will enable both researchers and policy makers to have a better understanding of the American legal profession.

Appendix
The Questionnaire and the Average Response to Each Item

Some Attitudes and Characteristics of American Lawyers

Lawyers in the items below should be considered as referring to lawyers in your community rather than to American lawyers in general unless the item states otherwise.

I. *Attitude Statements*

Please indicate your attitude toward the statements in the sections below by using the following symbols on the lines provided:

++ agree strongly
+ agree mildly
0 neutral
− disagree mildly
−− disagree strongly
U unknown

Item Number			% Positive Response	
	A.	THE LEGAL PROFESSION		
1	1.	In relation to the hours they put in, lawyers don't make very much money.	64%	Agree
2	2.	Being a lawyer lacks the financial security of salaried executives.	66%	
3	3.	Social science research has little value to the legal profession.	74%	
4	4.	Lawyers should be encouraged to represent the unpopular client.	82%	
5	5.	Courses in legal ethics have the goal of encouraging lawyers to represent unpopular clients.	47%	
	6.	A great advantage of being within the legal profession is the opportunity:		
6		a. to work with people rather than things.	99%	
7		b. for financial gain.	76%	
8		c. for moderate but steady progress rather than the chance of extreme success or failure.	74%	
9		d. to be helpful to others or useful to society	98%	
10		e. to be in a respected position in the community.	97%	
	B.	POLITICAL ATTITUDES		
11	1.	Present laws favor the rich as against the poor.	45%	Agree
12	2.	More government regulation of the economy should be introduced into our society.	15%	
13	3.	Government ownership of industry is likely to lead to inefficiency.	88%	
14	4.	Only people with a definite minumum of intelligence and education should be allowed to vote.	35%	
15	5.	If a person works hard enough he can overcome most handicaps.	17%	
	C.	INDIGENT CLIENTS (An indigent client for this study is a client unable to pay an attorney's regular fee with his own money or through family or friends and this indigency is known to the attorney at the time the case is accepted.)		
16	1.	The poor have failed to secure the fullest measure of legal rights in civil and criminal cases because they have not been able to afford attorneys.	72%	Agree
17	2.	In eviction cases, the court should provide counsel to the indigent defendant.	55%	
18	3.	The losing party should generally be required to pay all the attorney's fees of the other side.	29%	
19	4.	Legal Services Agencies should not attempt law reform.	46%	
20	5.	Legal Services Agencies should not attempt community education programs for the poor as this stirs up litigation.	22%	

21 6. A substantial part of legal education should involve a focus on the legal problems of the poor. 59%

22 7. Law students should be allowed to provide legal assistance to indigent persons. 76%

8. The system of representation of indigents in criminal cases in my community is desirable from the point of view of:

23 a. the poor 84%

24 b. the bar 76%

25 c. the community in general 82%

9. The system of representation of indigents in civil cases in my community is desirable from the point of view of:

26 a. the poor 59%

27 b. the bar 59%

28 c. the community in general 57%

D. UNPOPULAR CAUSES

29 1. If a person involved in an unpopular cause can afford a lawyer but is unable to find a lawyer who is willing to represent him then the judges in my community will appoint counsel. 65% Agree

30 2. The contempt convictions of the lawyers in the recent Chicago conspiracy trial have made me less willing to defend unpopular causes. 12%

31 3. After I got out of law school I was more willing to accept unpopular cases than I am now. 42%

II. *The Relative Desirability of Various Factors*

A. REASONS FOR REJECTING AN UNPOPULAR CLIENT

Please indicate your attitude toward the statements in this section by using the following symbols on the lines provided:

++ highly acceptable
\+ slightly acceptable
0 neutral
– slightly unacceptable
–– highly unacceptable
U unknown

1. The following are possible reasons a lawyer might give in declining the case of an unpopular client:

32 a. the lawyer is too busy. 73% said acceptable

33 b. he has had little trial experience 85%

34 c. the lawyer does not wish to promote or aid the defendant's cause. 51%

35 d. community feeling about the client could damage the lawyer's career. 29%

36 e. the lawyer's own emotional feelings against the client are so strong that he fears that this would preclude him from performing an adequate professional job. 87%

2. Assume that you are a practicing lawyer with considerable experience in criminal law. An admitted Communist, who has been charged with advocating forcible overthrow of the government, asks you to represent him. Would he be acceptable as a client if:

37 a. he was able to pay my normal fee. 63%

38 b. he was able to pay less than my normal fee. 35%

39 c. he was able to pay more than my normal fee. 57%

3. Assume that you are a practicing lawyer with considerable experience in criminal law. An admitted member of the Ku Klux Klan, who has been charged with attempting to deprive Negroes of their civil rights, asks you to represent him. Would he be acceptable as a client if:

40 a. he was able to pay my normal fee. 61%

41 b. he was able to pay less than my normal fee. 34%

42 c. he was able to pay more than my normal fee. 56%

B. SYSTEMS OF LEGAL REPRESENTATION

Please indicate your attitude toward the statements in this section by using the following symbols on the lines provided:

++ strongly desirable
+ mildly desirable
0 neutral
– mildly undesirable
– –strongly undesirable
U unknown

1. A desirable system of legal representation for the indigent in criminal cases in my community is:

43 a. judicare (a system by which the government would pay 80% of the minimum fee to the attorney accepting the indigent case) 60% said desirable

44 b. paid assigned counsel 85%

45 c. paid volunteer counsel 73%

46 d. public defender 82%

47 e. unpaid assigned counsel 9%

48 f. unpaid volunteer counsel 22%

2. A desirable system of legal representation for the indigent in civil cases in my community is:

49 a. judicare 53%

50 b. Legal Services Agency 81%

51 c. paid volunteer counsel 70%

52 d. unpaid volunteer counsel 28%

III. *Experiences in Representing Indigent or Unpopular Clients*

Please place a check mark on the appropriate line. In some cases you have been asked a short answer.

			Yes	*No*
53	1.	Have you ever represented an indigent person accused of crime?	81%	said yes
54		If yes, approximately how many?		
		Few 52%; Many 14%; Very many 34%		
55	2.	Have you ever represented an indigent person in a civil case?	72%	
56		If yes, approximately how many?		
		Few 36%; Many 24%; Very many 40%		
57	3.	Have you ever defended an unpopular client where an acceptance of the case could have damaged your career?	45%	
58		a. Were you associated with the client's cause?	6%	
59		b. Did you lose other clients because of the case?	30%	
60		c. Was your reputation in the community damaged?	10%	
61		d. If yes, was your career damaged in some other way?	10%	

IV. *Background Information*

For the items below, please check the appropriate response.

A. CHARACTERISTICS OF THE COMMUNITY

	1.	The present system of legal representation for the indigent in criminal cases in the community is:		
62		a. judicare	0%	said yes
63		b. paid assigned counsel	47%	
64		c. paid volunteer counsel	3%	
65		d. public defender	2%	
66		e. unpaid assigned counsel	8%	
67		f. unpaid volunteer counsel	0%	
	2.	The present system of legal representation for the indigent in civil cases in the community is:		
68		a. judicare	1%	
69		b. Legal Services Agency	63%	
70		c. paid volunteer counsel	3%	
71		d. unpaid volunteer counsel	26%	

B. CHARACTERISTICS OF LAWYERS

72 1. In which city and state were you born?

2. Is your legal practice primarily:

73,74	6% said yes criminal	16% personal injury
75,76	9% probate	16% governmental
77,78	29% business & corporate	3% matrimonial
79,80	7% real estate	16% other (please specify:
81,82	0% collections	72% partial criminal)

83 3. What is your political party? 45% Democratic 44% Republican 11% Neither

4. What is your religious preference?

84 61% Protestant 16% Catholic 14% Jewish 4% Other 5% None

85 5. What is your race? 98% White 1% Negro 1% Other

86 6. What is your sex? 96% male 4% female

87 7. What was your father's primary occupation?

88 8. Were any of your grandparents born in a country other than the United States? 48% Yes 52% No

89 9. Approximately what percent of your clients are from ethnic and racial minorities?

42% less than 5%	24% 10% to 20%
18% 5% to 10%	16% more than 20%

90 10. What is the approximate dollar income of your average legal client?

9% Under 5,000 a year	10% 15,000 to 20,000 a year
36% 5,000 to 10,000 a year	7% 20,000 to 30,000 a year
26% 10,000 to 15,000 a year	13% 30,000 or more a year

91 11. Have you ever held a political office? 33% Yes 67% No

Thank you for your co-operation.

C. Information from the *Martindale-Hubbell Directory*

92 1. Age. Below the age of 54. 68% Above 54. 32%

93 2. City of practice. More than 100,000 pop. 45% Less. 55%

Notes

1. See note 15 below, the text accompanying it, and the section on "Variations in Attitude toward the Unpopular" in this chapter for further details on the questionnaire items relevant to clarifying the concept of

"unpopular clients" in terms of the survey. See also footnote 19. Footnote 15 and the section "Variations in Attitude toward the Indigent" in this chapter perform a similar function for "indigent clients." Footnote 25 below relates unpopular clients to indigent clients, as does the concluding paragraph of the chapter.

2. The prior quantitative, non-anecdotal literature dealing with the attitudes and behavior of attorneys toward the "unpopular" and the "poor" is slight. Casper (1969) has surveyed radical and ACLU lawyers, but without attempting to systematically compare them with other lawyers. Maddi and Merrill (1971) and Silverstein (1966) surveyed a general sample of lawyers to determine their attitudes toward representation of the poor, but they did not attempt to account for the variation found among the lawyers. Wood (1967, pp. 184-203) does compare criminal and non-criminal lawyers with regard to some aspects of representing indigents in criminal cases.

3. Entrants in the *Martindale-Hubbell Directory* who have lengthy sketches in the biographical section rather than the alphabetic section, however, represent the most complete listing of licensed attorneys in the United States. According to the introductory material on the inside front cover of the *Directory,* all licensed attorneys are included whom the publisher is able to contact and who are willing to be listed. Lawyers who were listed as not currently practicing were excluded from the questionnaire sample which meant excluding lawyers listed as retired lawyers, judges, professors, or in non-legal work. Non-practicing lawyers probably tend to exclude themselves by not being in the listings or by not responding to the questionnaire.

4. A set of the IBM cards containing the responses (and the coding key for interpreting the cards) is available on request from the author to test other hypotheses or to replicate the findings of this chapter.

5. On some of the background characteristics of American attorneys in general, see Blaustein (1954), Handler (1967), Mayer (1967), and Sikes (1971). The responses to questionnaire items 72 through 93 dealing with the background characteristics of the lawyers (as reproduced in the Appendix) show a distribution of characteristics which does not seem out of line with what one would expect from a random sample of American lawyers. Randomly sampling lawyers from the *Martindale-Hubbell Directory* produces approximately the same distribution on sex, age, and city size as the questionnaire respondents. Also see accompanying note 9 below and the text.

6. The percentage of lawyers who responded but gave neither a positive nor negative response to a questionnaire item cannot be calculated from the data given in the Appendix questionnaire. Those respondents,

however, do not contribute to the variation being accounted for on the questionnaire items. Neutral responses on the attitudinal items 1 through 52 average about 15 to 20 percent.

The questionnaire at the end of the article indicates for each item the percentage of attorneys who agreed or indicated a positive response of those attorneys who agreed or disagreed. Thus, on the first item, 64 percent of the attorneys who stated a position agreed that "in relation to the hours they put in, lawyers don't make very much money." By subtracting these percentages from 100, one can obtain the percentage of attorneys who indicated a negative response among those attorneys taking either a positive or negative position.

7. Some lawyers, however, may have been thinking of "legal services agency" as referring to a legal aid agency financed largely out of private funds rather than one financed largely by the Office of Economic Opportunity although the combination of private and governmental financing is becoming increasingly common.

8. There are other interesting items in the questionnaire in the Appendix of this chapter with regard to the legal profession, political attitudes, indigent clients, unpopular causes, reasons for rejecting an unpopular client, systems of legal representation, and experiences in representing indigent or unpopular clients. An interesting item might be (1) one on which one would expect a low positive percentage but yet there is a high percentage, or (2) one on which a high positive percentage is expected but the percentage is low, or (3) one dealing with a controversial issue on which the percentage of lawyers giving a positive response would be inherently interesting regardless whether the percentage is high or low.

9. Blalock (1963, p. 402) says, "A concern with indicating the specific population to which one can generalize may be a blinder which prevents one from attempting to spell out theoretical conditions more exactly" including causal hypotheses.

For example, if one were correlating (1) being young rather than old with (2) being "liberal" rather than "conservative," one might expect a positive correlation (i.e., young lawyers are more "liberal" than old lawyers). This positive association remains valid even if there were a disproportionately large number of young lawyers in the sample in comparison to the total number of lawyers in the nation. One would not, however, expect a biased sample of lawyers accurately to reflect the "liberalism" or "conservatism" of the total population of American lawyers. In other words, a sample of respondents need not be nearly so representative of the total class if one is more interested in determining intrapersonal correlations of characteristics than in sample-to-universe extrapolations. Indeed it is common to over-sample certain groups within a sample so as to have enough of them to make comparisons, even if doing so will distort the general representativeness of the sample.

10. Catch phrases are used to refer to the questionnaire items in table 5-1 in order to save space, but the reader can refer back to the questionnaire in the Appendix to see the exact wording for any given questionnaire item number. Sometimes a questionnaire item is reworded in a negative direction so as to convert what would otherwise be negative correlations into positive ones. For example, community of law practice is referred to as non-metropolitan community rather than metropolitan, and thus the correlation between non-metropolitan community and having defended the unpopular is +.19 rather than −.19.

11. To see all the correlations between one item and all other items, look down the item's column and also across the item's row. For example, in the first row and first column of table 5-1, there is a −.28 correlation between having a legal practice that is primarily "business and corporate" and responding positively to the question, "Have you ever defended an unpopular client where an acceptance of the case could have damaged your career?" A minus correlation means that when one item goes from positive to negative, the other item in the correlation goes inversely from negative to positive. A plus correlation means when one item goes from positive to negative, the other item in the correlation also goes from positive to negative. The number indicates the strength of the correlation and is calculated by a standard formula available in elementary statistics textbooks. What is known as a phi correlation formula is used to calculate the coefficients in tables 5-1 and 5-2 (Guilford 1956, pp. 311-16).

12. Other studies which attempt to determine causal correlations between the characteristics of attorneys include Ladinsky (1963), Carlin (1966), and Nagel and Gagliano (1965). These three studies use attorneys' backgrounds to attempt to account for variations in (1) the hierarchical status within the legal profession, (2) attitudes toward legal ethics, and (3) victory in appellate court cases respectively, rather than for variations in attitudes or behavior toward the unpopular and the indigent.

13. The findings are also consistent with the Blalock-Simon correlation approach to causal analysis. See Blalock (1964) and (1971).

14. A third factor which might be mentioned is that past behavior of defending the unpopular might cause future behavior of defending the unpopular if the experience produces favorable attitudes and reduces unfavorable stereotypes. The same is true of representing the poor. This third factor (in addition to attitudes and opportunities) is, however, partly redundant to the other two and also partly a tautology.

15. Unlike the concept of indigent client (which is defined in the in-

structions to section I-C of the questionnaire), the concept of "unpopular" client is not clearly defined in any one place in the questionnaire. If, however, one puts together the items which most clearly deal with "unpopular" clients (items 4, 37, 40, and 57), a definition of the "unpopular" client emerges like the one given at the beginning of this chapter. Nevertheless, before the questionnaire recipients responded to items 37 and 40, which indicated that "unpopular" clients might include "Communists" or "Klansmen," they responded to item 4 on defense of unpopular clients in general. At that time, the respondents may have been thinking of unpopular clients as being disproportionately left wing (as perhaps they are).

16. Applying the Blalock-Simon causal analysis techniques referred to in footnote 13 above, the +.73 becomes more understandable or at least more consistent with the related correlation coefficients. From economic liberalism alone, one would expect the correlation between variables (1) being favorable to defending the left-wing unpopular and (2) being favorable to defending the right-wing unpopular to be about +.06 (or +.36 times +.18). From being favorable toward defending the unpopular in general, one would expect the correlation between (1) and (2) to be about +.08 (or +.39 times +.21). Likewise, from being relatively young, one would expect the correlation between (1) and (2) to be about +.05 (or +.25 times +.18). One could continue on like this with other background and attitude variables, each of which adds on an additional portion of the explanation of the correlation between defending the left-wing unpopular and defending the right-wing unpopular. Note also the consistency in the direction of the signs.

Also note as a further check on the consistency of that portion of figure 5-1, that through being favorable toward defending the left-wing unpopular, one would expect the correlation between variables (3) economic class liberalism and (4) being favorable toward defending the unpopular in general to be about +.14 (or +.36 times +.39. Likewise through being favorable toward defending the right-wing unpopular, one would expect the correlation between (3) and (4) to be about +.04 (or +.18 times +.21). The sum of these two products (+.14 and +.04) comes fairly close to the actual correlation of +.28 between (3) and (4). The +.18 sum which is predicted does not exactly equal the +.28 actual because of the influence of the other variables in the causal model (and outside the causal model) which are not being controlled for such as the type of law practice which relate to variables (1) and (2) as well as (3) and (4).

17. Liberal sympathy for the underdog or economic class liberalism was originally determined by deriving a composite score from items 11 through 15. However, the respondents' reaction to item 11, (which states, "Present laws favor the rich as against the poor") had a very high correla-

tion with the composite score, and the other items had relatively low correlations. It therefore seemed sufficient and simpler to use item 11 alone as a measure of liberalism. The type of lawyers who had the highest correlation with this liberalism variable were those who identified themselves as Democrats, Jewish, and below the average age of the sample.

Although there is a high correlation between having a favorable attitude toward defending the left-wing unpopular and having a favorable attitude toward defending the right-wing unpopular, Jewish lawyers (unlike young lawyers) were not equally tolerant toward both types of political clients.

18. In addition, the clients of the business-corporate lawyers are "regulars" and may thus exert more influence on him than the clients of the personal injury lawyers who tend to be "one-shot" clients.

19. Rural communities do not generate more "unpopular" cases even on a per laywer basis than metropolitan communities if "unpopular" cases exclusively deal with the prosecution of people as politically extreme on a national scale as Communists and Klansmen. If, however, "unpopular" cases mean unpopular relative to those local community values which might damage a lawyer's career, then in that sense rural communities may generate more unpopular cases per lawyer, or at least they may be perceived as generating more unpopular cases by rural lawyers who may be more sensitive to community values than urban lawyers are. In other words, we are not measuring the extent to which lawyers represent unpopular clients in an absolute sense of unpopularity, but rather in a sense that takes into consideration the fact that (1) unpopularity and damage to one's legal career is relative to one's community, and (2) the amount of psychological risk one takes reflects one's perception of one's community.

20. An additional explanation for why rural lawyers reported more defending of the unpopular might be that rural lawyers are possibly more accessible to clients in general; and rural people, including unpopular ones, are more informed about where and how to obtain a lawyer than urban people. There are, however, fewer lawyers per capita in rural areas than in urban areas; and rural people are generally less informed on most educational measures than urban people, or at least metropolitan people.

The rural lawyer who is almost the only lawyer in town may also feel an obligation to represent all people who come to him, including unpopular cases. In this survey, however, non-metropolitan lawyers are those in cities less than 100,000, not necessarily those in small one-lawyer towns.

21. These bivariate correlations are given in table 5-1.

22. On calculating and interpreting a multiple correlation coefficient, see Guilford (1956, pp. 390-405). Table 5-1 (which is a correlation matrix with missing data on some of the variables) was used as input into the multiple correlation routine on the assumption that the correlations shown

there were roughly representative of the population from which the sample was drawn. All the variables used in this multiple correlation analysis are "either-or" dichotomies.

23. Of the variation in having defended the unpopular which can be predicted by using the six questionnaire items to predict from, about three-fourths is attributable to the predictive power of knowing whether or not a lawyer is a business-corporate lawyer. The remaining one-fourth is about evenly divided among the other five predictive items. None of these six relations, however, is necessarily a causal relation, and the potency of a variable in a multiple correlation relation is as much due (1) to what other overlapping variables are included as it is (2) to the relation between the predictive variable and the variable being predicted.

24. Thus if 100 percent of 100 attorneys who scored positively on the characteristics answered "no" to item 57, and 60 percent of 100 attorneys who scored negatively on the characteristics answered "no" to item 57, then we would have a multiple correlation of roughly .40, and 140 out of 200 (or 70 percent) accuracy prediction from the characteristics. For further detail, see Nagel (1974).

25. Some of figure 5-2 looks like figure 5-1. This is so because there is a +.33 correlation between having defended criminal indigents and having defended the unpopular, and a +.32 between having represented civil indigents and having defended the unpopular. This correlation may be attributed to the fact that the unpopular often tend to be indigent or to identify with the problems of the indigent, and to the fact that both the unpopular and the indigent tend to be social outsiders with whom liberal attorneys sympathize. Nevertheless, there are some important differences between the two figures with regard to the relevant attitudinal and opportunity items and their relations. For one thing, most of the correlations are higher in figure 5-1 than in figure 5-2, possibly because representing the unpopular is more divisive than representing the indigent.

26. The comparison of the attitudes toward the OEO-LSP of personal injury and criminal lawyers on the one hand and business-corporate lawyers on the other is reinforced by the other correlations shown in table 5-2, but not shown in figure 5-2. For example, personal injury lawyers considered judicare *more* desirable than non-personal injury lawyers (+.29 correlation). Corporate lawyers, however, considered judicare *less* desirable than non-corporate lawyers (−.23 correlation). Lawyers handling some criminal work strongly resented the notion of court appointed counsel in civil cases (+.36 correlation with the statement that court should *not* appoint counsel in civil cases), whereas corporate lawyers were more favorable than non-corporate lawyers (−.05 correlation).

For related findings, see Stumpf (1973).

27. Of the variation in having represented civil indigents which can be predicted by the eight variables, most of the predictive power is attributable to knowing whether or not a lawyer is in criminal, personal injury, or business-corporate practice. Some incremental predictive power is also obtainable from knowing his attitude toward court-appointed counsel, but virtually none from the other variables when all eight are taken collectively.

28. Of the variation in having defended criminal indigents which can be predicted by the eight variables, most of the predictive power is attributable to knowing whether or not a lawyer has a criminal practice and secondly whether or not he has a personal injury practice. The other six variables have a trivial incremental predictive power when all eight are taken collectively.

29. On the distinction between prediction accuracy and causal understanding, see Nagel (1966) and (1969, Ch. 13).

30. Perhaps only the opportunity variable is a necessary condition. It may even be both necessary and sufficient at least in the indigent criminal cases as indicated by the 94 percent in column 3 of table 5-3 which shows that 94 percent of the attorneys in the sample with favorable opportunities and unfavorable attitudes were likely to have represented the poor in criminal cases. That 94 percent in itself, however, is not enough to establish favorable opportunities as a necessary condition since approximately 50 percent of the attorneys who were in the relatively unfavorable category on opportunities reported representing the poor in criminal cases. If the opportunity variable were a necessary condition, then the attitude variable would at least be a facilitator since the percentage of attorneys representing unpopular or poor clients does generally go up when moving from column 3 to 4 in table 5-3. The percentage, however, goes up more when moving from column 2 to 4 showing that the opportunity variable is the more important predictor.

31. For further discussion of the statistical interaction phenomena, see Blalock (1972, pp. 463-464, 498-502, 308-309) and Blalock (1960, pp. 178-186). For further discussion of the logic of necessary conditions, see Ruby (1950, pp. 379-385) and Francis (1961, pp. 16-35, 135-154).

32. One attitude item and one opportunity item were used on each row in table 5-2. The attitude item used with unpopular clients was questionnaire item 4, and the opportunities item was questionnaire item 77. The attitude item used with indigent criminal cases was item 17, and the opportunities item was item 82. For indigent civil cases, item 17 provided the attitude variable, and item 77 provided the opportunity variable. These items were chosen because they had the highest correlations with the relevant dependent variable of representing unpopular or indigent clients.

33. As mentioned in note 20, the problem may relate not only to the

above environmental and clientele factors of rural and general practitioners, but also to the supposed increased accessibility and the information of potential clients where rural and general practitioners tend to be prevalent. Regardless of rural-urban differenences, poor people in general (and others too) probably do need more information on how to use legal aid facilities, lawyer referral services, and hired counsel.

34. For literature on getting law students and lawyers to be more favorable toward representing the unpopular and the poor, see Sacks (1961 and 1965), Thurman (1970), and Simon (1966).

35. The *Denver Law Journal* article (1971) also involved a questionnaire designed to determine attorney opinions regarding legal services and the poor. One would think that if the Supreme Court is willing to require the societal payment of court costs for indigents in some civil cases (*Boddie v. Conn.,* 1971) the court might be willing to require the societal payment of lawyers' fees for indigents in some civil cases, since it is harder for an indigent to pay essential lawyers fees than court costs. Legal fees for the poor on public aid may someday be included in public aid payments for certain civil cases like welfare appeals as was planned in the Johnson administration but repealed in the Nixon administration (Dodyk 1969, p. 251).

36. On the involvement of the private bar in legal aid activities, see Pious (1972), Stumpf (1973), Rosenthal and Kagan (1971), Hannon (1969), and Marks (1972).

37. By using the *Martindale-Hubbell Directory,* someone might claim that disproportionately conservative lawyers with favorable attitudes toward judicare were included. The directory, however, is quite comprehensive and disproportionately liberal attorneys may have responded to the questionnaire reflecting their relatively favorable attitudes toward social science research. The high degree of negativism expressed toward unpaid assigned and volunteer counsel, even among and especially among responding attorneys with liberal attitudes, indicates that the favorable attitude toward judicare cannot be attributed to a disproportionate conservative set of respondents.

38. The judicare debate literature includes Brakel (1972), Cole and Greenberger (1973), Goodman and Feuilan (1972), Masotti and Corsi (1967), Pelletier (1967), and Preloznik (1971).

39. The National Legal Aid and Defender Association filed an amicus curiae brief before the U.S. Supreme Court in support of a constitutional right in civil matters in *Slade v. Valley National Bank* as mentioned in 30 NLADA BRIEFCASE 195 (1972). The Supreme Court, however, denied certiorari at 93 Sup. Ct. 445 (1973) with only Justice Douglas voting to grant certiorari. A related test case is being pursued in California by the Western

center on Law and Poverty in *Hunt v. Hackett* as mentioned in 2 NLADA WASHINGTON MEMO 1 (June 1973).

Cases

Argersinger v. *Hamlin,* 407 U.S. 25 (1972).
Hunt v. *Hackett,* 36 Cal. App. 3d 134 (1974).
Slade v. *Valley National Bank,* 409 U.S. 1013 (1972).

References

Blalock, Hubert, *Causal Models in the Social Sciences*. (Chicago: Aldine-Atherton, 1971.

———. *Causal Inferences in Nonexperimental Research*. Chapel Hill: U. of North Carolina Press, 1964.

———. "Some Important Metholological Problems for Sociology." *Sociology and Social Research* 47 (1963): 398.

———. *Social Statistics*. New York: McGraw-Hill, 1972.

Blalock, Hubert and Ann Blalock. *Methodology in Social Research*. New York: McGraw-Hill, 1968.

Blaustein, Albert and Charles Porter. *The American Lawyer*. Chicago: U. of Chicago Press, 1954.

Brakel, Samuel. *Wisconsin Judicare: A Preliminary Appraisal*. Chicago: American Bar Foundation, 1972.

Campbell, Angus, et al. *The American Voter*. New York: John Wiley, 1960.

Carlin, Jerome. *Lawyers' Ethics–A Survey of the New York City Bar*. New York: Russell Sage, 1966.

Carlin, Jerome and Jan Howard. "Legal Representation and Class Justice." *UCLA Law Review* 12 (1965): 381.

Casper, Jonathan. "Lawyers and Loyalty—Security Litigation." *Law and Society Review* 3 (1969): 575.

Cole, George and Howard Greenberger. "Staff Attorneys vs. Judicare: A Cost Analysis." *Journal of Urban Law* 50 (1973): 705.

Dodyk, Paul, et al. *Poverty Law: Cases and Materials*. St. Paul: West Publishing Co., 1969.

Denver Law Journal Staff. *Rural Poverty and the Law in Southern Colorado*. Chicago: American Bar Foundation, 1971.

Francis, Roy. *The Rhetoric of Science: A Methodological Discussion of the Two-by-Two Table*. Minneapolis: U. of Minnesota Press, 1961.

Goodman, Leonard and Jacques Feulian. "The Trouble with Judicare." *American Bar Association Journal* 58 (1972): 476.

Guilford, J.P. *Fundamental Statistics in Psychology and Education*. New York: McGraw-Hill, 1956.

Handler, Joel. *The Lawyer and His Community: The Practicing Bar in a Middle-Sized City*. Madison: U. of Wis. Press, 1967.

Hannon, Philip. "Legal Services and the Local Bars: How Strong Is the Bond?" *California Western Law Review* 6 (1969): 46.

Ladinsky, Jack. "Careers of Lawyers, Law Practice, and Legal Institutions." *American Sociological Review* 28 (1963): 47.

Levine, Felice and Elizabeth Preston. "Community Resource Orientation among Low Income Groups." *1970 Wisconsin Law Review,* p. 80.

Maddi, Dorothy and Frederic Merrill. *The Private Practicing Bar and Legal Services for Low Income People*. Chicago: American Bar Foundation, 1971.

Marks, Raymond. *The Lawyer, the Public, and Professional Responsibility*. Chicago: American Bar Foundation, 1972.

Masotti, Louis and Jerome Corsi. "Legal Assistance for the Poor." *Urban Law Journal* 44 (1967): 483.

Mayer, Martin. *The Lawyers*. New York: Harper and Row, 1967.

Miller, Warren and Donald Stokes. "Constituency Influence in Congress." *American Political Science Review* 57 (1963): 45.

Murphy, Walter and Joseph Tanenhaus. *The Study of Public Law*. New York: Random House, 1972.

Nagel, Stuart. "Multiple Correlation of Judicial Backgrounds and Decisions." *Florida State University Law Review* (1974).

______. *The Legal Process from a Behavioral Perspective*. Homewood, Ill.: Dorsey Press, 1969.

______. "Judicial Prediction and Analysis from Empirical Probability Tables." *Indiana Law Journal* 41 (1966): 403.

Nagel, Stuart and Felix Gagliano. "Attorney Characteristics and Courtroom Results." *Nebraska Law Review* 44 (1965): 599.

NLADA Briefcase [Note] "News." *NLADA Briefcase* 30 (1972): 195.

NLADA Washington Memo [Note] "Cases Pending." *NLADA Washington Memo 1,* (May-June 1973).

Pelletier, George. "English Legal Aid: The Successful Experiment in Judicare." *University of Colorado Law Review* 40 (1967): 10.

Pious, Richard. "Congress, the Organized Bar, and the Legal Services Program." *Wisconsin Law Review* (1972): 418.

Preloznik, Joseph. "Wisconsin Judicare: An Experiment in Legal Services." *American Bar Association Journal* 57 (1971): 1179.

Rosenthal, Douglas and Robert Kagan. *Volunteer Attorneys and Legal Services for the Poor: New York's CLO Program*. New York: Russell Sage, 1971.

Ruby, Lionel. *Logic: An Introduction*. New York: Lippincott, 1950.

Sacks, Howard (ed.). *Proceedings of the Asheville Conference of Law School Deans on Education for Professional Responsibility*. Chicago: American Bar Center, 1965.

Sikes, Bette, et al. *Lawyer Statistical Report*. Chicago: American Bar Foundation, 1971.

Silverstein, Lee. *Defense of the Poor*. Chicago: American Bar Foundation, 1966.

Simon, Rita James. "An Evaluation of the Effectiveness of Some Curriculum Innovations in Law Schools." *Journal of Applied Behavioral Science* 2 (1966): 219.

Stumpf, Harry. *Lawyers and the Poor: An Exploratory Study in Local Bar Politics*. Beverly Hills, Calif.: Sage Publications, 1975.

Thurman, Samuel, et al. *The Legal Profession*. Mineola, N.Y.: Foundation Press, 1970.

Tucker, Marna. *The Lawyer as a Volunteer: Pro Bono Publico Programs for Bar Associations and Professional Organizations*. Chicago: American Bar Association, 1972.

_______. *The Private Law Firm and Pro Bono Publico Programs: A Responsive Merger*. Chicago: American Bar Association, 1971.

Wood, Arthur. *Criminal Lawyer*. New Haven: College and University Press, 1967.

6 Law and Order for the Poor

The Poor, Too, Want Law and Order

It is unfortunate that cries for law and order have acquired a connotation of suppression of black militancy and lessened concern for poverty and discrimination as causes of crime in the streets. It is particularly unfortunate to imply that law and order is a goal of the middle class and an anti-goal of the poor. The truth of the matter seems to be that the poor, too, want law and order; but the law and orderliness they especially want to see enforced is not necessarily the same law and order on which the middle class places such a high priority.

In his capacity as the director of an OEO Legal Services Program in a middle-sized city, this writer has heard numerous complaints from the poor with regard to how the law is administered. The poor are primarily concerned with the law as it relates to their legal rights and obligations as tenants and arrested persons and to a lesser extent as welfare recipients, consumers, employees, and general citizens.

As tenants they frequently complain bitterly of the lack of enforcement of housing codes and the lack of objectivity in public housing operations. Numerous studies have revealed the callousness of housing inspectors, city attorneys, and judges toward a meaningful enforcement of minimum housing standards (e.g., Gribetz and Grad, "Housing Code Enforcement," 66 *Columbia L. Rev*. 1254, 1966). Both the city of Champaign and the city of Urbana, for example, provide for fines of up to $200 a day for each day that each violation continues. In spite of this power, however, it seems that almost never has any fine of any amount been levied for housing code violations in Champaign County. This cannot be interpreted to mean that there are no violations in view of the fact that approximately 60 percent of the houses in the Champaign urban renewal area were found to have serious housing code violations, and 30 percent were so bad they were beyond feasible rehabilitation.

What needs to be done within the law to get these laws enforced are such things as encouraging tenants to call the police and file criminal complaints with regard to serious housing code violations. The police should be as willing to make arrests in these cases as they are in other ordinance violations. A second powerful but seldom-used tool in the state of Illinois is the legal right of Illinois Public Aid to withhold rent from landlords who violate the housing codes. Unfortunately in Champaign County, for example, the Illinois Public Aid people are overly cautious in recognizing their obligation to help improve the housing conditions of their welfare recipients, and there has thus far been only one such rent withholding case in the almost three years that the statute has existed. A recent case in the District of Columbia (*Brown v. Southall Realty Co.*, D.C. App. 238 A.2d—,1968) has now declared that housing code violations make voidable the contractual relationship between any tenant and his landlord.

As for public housing, this area of governmental activity has been far more a matter of government by subjective men than government by objective laws. It would not be hard to develop a rational published point system based on things like income, family size, and current housing for determining the order of admission of applicants to public housing subject to justifiable exceptions for extenuating circumstances. For 30 years until the last few months, nothing approaching such an objective system existed in Champaign County public housing. There was also a lack of impersonal rule-following in eviction matters to say nothing of the lack of procedural due process. In addition (contrary to the equal protection clause of the Constitution, congressional statutes, and federal regulations), three of the six public housing projects are all black and the other three are virtually all white due to discriminatory site selection and the appeasement of discriminatory attitudes held by tenant applicants.

As tenants the black poor particularly complain about the lack of enforcement or lack of existence of open occupancy ordinances. Being confined in the black ghetto when one is financially able to get out, but is not racially able to do so, is certainly depressing to one's ambitions to advance himself. It also leads to an artificial housing shortage causing many blacks to accept expensive, sub-standard housing.

Next to housing, the poor are greatly concerned with lack of lawfulness and objectivity in the administration of criminal justice. A frequently-heard complaint in Champaign County and undoubtedly elsewhere is that the setting of bail too often bears no rational relationship to the likelihood that arrested persons will fail to show up for trial. The Illinois system of allowing release on payment of 10 percent of the bond has reduced the problem, but what is needed is an objective point system (like that developed by the Vera Foundation in New York City) based on items like employment, family status, length of residence, and criminal record. If the probability is high that the defendant will show up for trial, then he should be released without a cash bond no matter how poor he is. If the probability is low, then he should be detained in jail pending a speedy trial no matter how rich he is.

Right to counsel may be the most inportant criminal procedure right because without it the other rights are not very meaningful. Illinois wisely provides for appointing a public defender or assigning counsel to indigents where a jail sentence is possible. Unfortunately, neither the statutes nor the reported precedents provide any objective financial eligibility guidelines for determining indigency. Numerous complaints have been heard at the Champaign County Legal Services Agency that the public defender has been denied to deserving indigents and granted to undeserving non-indigents. Since Legal Services programs use financial guidelines to determine who is entitled to their free help, there is no reason why arraignment magistrates cannot do likewise with regard to the public defender.

It is particularly disturbing to hear so many complaints relating to the lack of the most elementary courtesy on the part of certain judges and certain assistant state's attorneys. Such behavior clearly brings disrespect for law and order among both the black and white poor. More well-known and more flagrant discourtesies by the police and deputy sheriffs have been documented in Chapter 11 of the Kerner Commission's report although only a minority of the law enforcement personnel may be involved.

In the realm of welfare law, there is a notorious lack of objective published standards to guide the township supervisors in determining who is eligible for emergency relief. In some communities, although not so much in Champaign County, studies have revealed blatant disregard for relevant regulations by caseworkers who are more interested in getting welfare recipients off the relief rolls by finding them guilty of wrongdoing than by rehabilitating them (e.g., Reich, "Individual Rights and Social Welfare," 74 *Yale L. J.* 1245, 1965). In reality, the public aid system encourages sloth or dishonesty in reporting outside income by providing for a dollar-for-dollar reduction in welfare benefits for outside earnings rather than providing for a sliding scale like $1 deducted for every $3 earned.

Consumers also complain of dishonest merchants who are not adequately pursued by the Chamber of Commerce or the state's attorney, although in a middle-sized city like Champaign, merchants operate in more of a goldfish bowl atmosphere and possibly tend to be more law-abiding than in larger cities. Potential black employees complain of racial discrimination by business firms and especially by unions, although better enforcement of the Illinois FEPC statute would decrease these complaints.

As general citizens, the poor, both white and black, are bothered by malapportioned legislative districting. The 50-man Champaign County Board of Supervisors, for instance, only allocates 23 seats to the cities of Champaign, Urbana, and Rantoul in spite of the fact that those cities constitute practically all of the county's population. The city of Champaign provides no districts at all for its city council, thereby depriving the poor white neighborhoods and the black ghetto from any representation on the council. Both the poor whites and blacks also complain of their inferior school environments, but that will be partially remedied next year by a one-way busing program.

In conclusion, there is indeed a need for greater law and order, especially with regard to (1) stricter enforcement of housing ordinances and various anti-discrimination legislation and (2) more objective standards in the operations of public housing, the setting of bail, the appointing of the public defender, and the relief work of the township supervisors. The poor cannot fully respect the law if they feel that it is twisted to favor those who are not poor or who are not black. The poor, too, want law and order.

Ombudsmen among the Poor

In the 1968 Law Day edition of The Chicago Daily Law Bulletin, this writer prepared an article entitled, "The Poor, Too, Want Law and Order." It concluded that "there is indeed a need for greater law and order especially enforcement with regard to stricter enforcement of housing codes and anti-discrimination legislation and more objective standards in the operations of public housing, the setting of bail, the appointing of the public defender, and the relief work of the township supervisors." A purpose of this present chapter is to describe one new approach to promoting some aspects of this kind of law and order, namely having ombudsmen among the poor.

An ombudsman is an individual whose job is to *mediate* complaints received from people against governmental personnel or activities with the exception of complaints against judges, legislators, and chief executives. Unlike an arbitrator or a judge, he has no power to hand down decisions binding on the parties. Unlike an attorney, he is not an advocate for either the complainants or respondents.

The idea first came into formal existence in the Scandinavian countries at the national level. It has since spread to Britain and some of the Commonwealth countries. It is now being considered for adoption in various American states and cities including Illinois where both the Republicans and Democrats have introduced ombudsmen bills in the state legislature. A recent boost to the ombudsman idea came on January 27, 1969, when the House of Delegates of the American Bar Association resolved "that state and local governments of the United States should give consideration to the establishment of an ombudsman."

An ombudsman for the poor would specialize in the complaints of the poor either as a separately authorized ombudsman or a special division within a general ombudsman program. He would arrange for one or more neighborhood offices or some other outreach devices designed to facilitate use of his services by the poor. Such specialization is needed in view of the fact that (1) the complaints of the poor against governmental officials then tend to be different than middle class complaints, (2) the poor are more apathetic and pessimistic about the utility of complaining, and (3) the frustrations of the poor are threatening to boil over into antisocial aggression.

The complaints processed deal with government personnel who administer *federal* social security, *state* public aid, or *city* housing codes, or just one of the levels of government if it is deemed that the program should be more narrowly focused. Complaints can come from people living or working in the area to be served and also from legislators who represent the area and who want the ombudsmen to aid the legislators in processing complaints. Complaint against the police can be excluded from the jurisdiction in order to remove the ombudsman from the emotionality, workload, and overlapping of police review agencies and in order to make his establishment more politically realistic. Complaints against judges are logically excluded because of the availability of appellate courts and judicial fitness commissions. Likewise legislators and chief executives are better subject to political and electoral processes than the more narrowly directed redress provided by the ombudsman.

The processing can involve such things as referring citizens to the correct agencies or to an attorney, clarifying unclear communications between citizens and officials, rectifying mistakes, or making policy recommendations to resolve numerous complaints that have a common cause. The ombudsman can also be given subpoena power to question persons or examine records as the ABA recommends. Complaints and inquiries can be received and relayed by phone, mail, or in person with a heavy emphasis on informal mediation rather than formalized procedures.

Existing legal aid programs do not adequately fulfill the functions of an ombudsman mainly because they are so busy processing complaints against private parties, especially against husbands and wives of clients, that they have little time for processing complaints against government officials. Their role is also that of an advocate not a mediator which handicaps their ability to serve as a neutral go-between. Furthermore, they are generally confined to concrete cases as contrasted to the ombudsman who can, for example, look into the problem of improving relations between the fire department and the poor on the basis of reading newspaper articles which mention the stoning of firemen. The ombudsman can also ethically encourage people to tell him what, if anything, is troubling them (or is deserving of praise) without being accused of stirring up litigation.

Like legal aid offices, existing city hall complaint receiving offices also do not represent a complete substitute for the ombudsman concept. They probably tend, in the eyes of the potential complainants especially poor complainants, to be too much associated with the government personnel against whom the complaints might be directed. City hall complaint offices also tend to lack the neighborhood decentralization associated with ombudsmen among the poor.

The Buffalo Ombudsman Project is an existing program roughly approximating what this chapter has in mind. It was established on an experimental basis in 1967 with a grant from the Office of Economic Opportunity that is scheduled to expire in 1969. The director of the project is a distinguished practicing attorney who was chosen by the University of Buffalo with publicized assurances of cooperation from the mayor of Buffalo. The director might have been even more effective, however, if he were jointly chosen by representatives of the city council and the mayor and also representatives of the poor analogous to the way the steel companies and the steelworkers choose a labor arbitrator. With two neighborhood offices and a small staff, he has been processing over 100 complaints a month.

With the endorsement of the American Bar Association and other organizations, the ombudsman idea seems destined to spread in America. It is arriving at an opportune time in view of (1) increased government activity, (2) increased feelings of ineffectiveness on the part of the individual citizens, and (3) increased sensitivity to real and imagined injustices and inequalities. Within the general ombudsman concept, it is hoped that provisions will be made for ombudsmen among the poor so as to promote greater justice, equality, and tranquility where many feel those things have been especially lacking.

7 C. SEX
Women as Litigants

The purpose of this chapter is to describe how women are treated relative to men in criminal, personal injury, and divorce cases—three fields which constitute most of the trial court litigation in American courts. The findings presented will generally be based on quantitative nationwide data. The chapter will particularly examine the extent to which women are disfavored, favored, or treated neutrally as criminal defendants, personal injury plaintiffs, and divorce litigants. It will also discuss some of the effects of having more women as jurors and judges on the relative treatment of male and female litigants.

Women as Criminal Defendants

In the literature dealing with women's rights, researchers have indicated that "in several states higher penalties are imposed on a woman who commits a crime than on a man who commits the same crime."[1] These statements, however, have been based on those few state statutes and appellate test cases which describe the law on the books rather than the law in action. Empirical data have been needed to show how much time the average woman spends in prison as compared to the time spent by the average man, or at least showing the length of sentences given on conviction for various crimes to the average woman as compared to the average man.

Likewise, the literature dealing with discrimination against women has often drawn analogies between American society's treatment of women and of blacks.[2] These analogies may be valid in some fields like employment discrimination where one can sometimes explain both racial and sexual discrimination in terms of the desire of workers to limit competition and the desire of employers to have cheap labor, but the similarities between racism and sexism do not necessarily apply to all fields. Empirical data has also been needed to test the analogy's applicability to the treatment of blacks and women as criminal defendants by comparing black-white sentencing practices with male-female sentencing practices. Additionally, data on presentencing treatment (e.g., being released on bail or receiving a jury trial) might provide valuable comparative insights.

This chapter was coauthored with Lenore Weitzman of the University of California-Davis.

In 1962 Lee Silverstein of the American Bar Foundation (ABF) arranged for attorneys and court personnel in a scientifically determined sample of 194 counties located in all 50 states to systematically compile data on 11,258 criminal cases.[3] The data were primarily designed to study procedures for providing attorneys to indigent defendants. Silverstein, however, included many other variables in his data such as the race, sex, and age of the defendants and the treatment they received at all stages of the criminal justice process from the preliminary hearing through the sentencing stage.

Two basic patterns of discrimination emerge when one uses the ABF data to correlate the background characteristics of criminal defendants with their criminal procedure treatment while holding constant the crime charged.[4] One pattern, which might be called the disadvantaged or disfavored pattern, applies to indigent, black, or elementary-educated defendants. This pattern involves unfavorable treatment at virtually all stages of the criminal justice process including (1) receiving a preliminary hearing, (2) being released on bail, (3) having a hired attorney rather than assigned counsel or no attorney, (4) being subjected to relatively long delay while in jail if not released on bail, (5) receiving a jury trial, (6) being dismissed or being acquitted, (7) receiving probation or a suspended sentence if convicted, and (8) receiving a relatively short sentence if jailed. One could generalize the disadvantaged or disfavored pattern to include personal injury and divorce cases by defining it as a pattern of court behavior in which there is harshness or relative deprivation in both the decisional outcomes and judicial processing of those groups which a society considers to be socially inferior.

The second discriminatory pattern or syndrome might be called the paternalistic pattern. It particularly applies to juveniles under age 21 as contrasted to adults. In criminal proceedings, it involves unfavorable treatment with regard to such safeguards for the innocent as having an attorney or having a jury trial. It involves favorable treatment, however, with regard to being kept out of jail pending trial, not being convicted, and not being sentenced to jail if convicted. One could generalize the paternalism pattern to include personal injury and divorce cases by defining it as a pattern of court behavior in which there is favoritism for the weak in the reluctance to impose negative sanctions, and disfavoritism in the awarding or enforcing of monetary awards and in the informality of judicial processing.

When female criminal defendants are compared with male criminal defendants, the treatment pattern fits the paternalistic mold much more closely than the disadvantaged mold as is indicated in table 7-1. The table separates the cases into those in which the single charge against the defendant was grand larceny (the most common felony against property) and those in which the charge was felonious assault (the most common felony against persons). This property-persons breakdown was made because it was important in understanding the differential treatment found between urban courts (which tend to be relatively more sensitive to crimes against persons) and rural courts (which tend to be more sensitive to crimes against property).[5] The property-persons breakdown was also important in understanding the differential sentencing of blacks who commit larceny (which tends to be a crime between races) and blacks who commit assault (which tends to be a crime within races).[6]

The paternalistic discrimination against and for women (like juveniles), however, applied almost equally in grand larceny and felonious assault cases. Relative to men though, women were somewhat more likely to be jailed in assault cases than in larceny cases. This may be due to the fact that assault is a more manly crime than larceny (as shown by the ratio of male to female defendants in the top and bottom halves of table 7-1), and women are therefore treated more like men when they commit assault than when they commit larceny.

Within the larceny cases (section I) and the assault cases (section II), the data is broken down between the chronological stages that relate to being jailed before or after conviction (rows 1 through 5) and the stages which emphasize formal safeguards for the innocent (rows 6 through 8).[7] Blacks and indigents are particularly discriminated against when it comes to being released on bail. Just the opposite discrimination is evident for women. Of the 63 female larceny-defendants, 76 percent were released on bail; whereas of the 771 male larceny-defendants, only 50 percent were released on bail, giving a difference of 26 percentage points (section I, row 1). This difference is in conformity with the paternalism pattern which shuns keeping juveniles and women in jail pending trial or after conviction. The same jail avoidance phenomenon pending trial can be observed for assault cases where a 19 percentage points difference is present (section II, row 1).

Likewise, women are given more lenient treatment than men if they are convicted. In grand larceny cases, 64 percent of the women received a suspended sentence or probation, whereas only 43 percent of the men did so (section I, row 4). A related although weaker difference is shown for the felonious assault cases (section II, row 4). Of those defendants who actually spent time in jail, there were too few women (20 or less)[8] in the sample to make meaningful comparisons with men as to the length of post conviction imprisonment (rows 5).[9] Possibly as a means of avoiding the imprisonment of women and avoiding the stigma of a criminal record, a lesser percentage of them are convicted than their male counterparts. Thus, it is indicated that 24 percent of the women were acquitted or had their larceny cases dismissed, whereas only 13 percent of the men did (section I, row 3). A similar difference is present for assault cases (section II, row 3).

When it comes to formal safeguards for the innocent, namely having a

Table 7-1
How the Treatment of Females Differs from Males as Defendants in Criminal Cases*

CASE TYPE AND TREATMENT STAGE	*Number of Defendants with Available Info*		*Percentage Receiving the Treatment*		*Difference in percentage points*	*Does paternalism hypothesis seem to be confirmed?*
	Females	*Males*	*Females*	*Males*		
I. GRAND LARCENY CASES						
A. Being jailed						
1. Released on bail	63	771	76%	50%	26	Yes
2. Had less than 2 months delay of those awaiting trial in jail	10	231	60	67	X	Too few women not released on bail
3. Case dismissed or acquited	71	841	24	13	11	Yes
4. Received suspended sentence or probation of those convicted	47	656	64	43	21	Yes
5. Received less than one year imprisonment of those imprisoned	9	241	33	45	X	Too few women imprisoned
B. Formal Safeguards						
6. Received preliminary hearing	42	606	57	55	2	Difference too small
7. Had or given a lawyer	61	781	90	87	3	Difference too small
8. Received a jury trial of those tried	18	283	47	31	X	Too few women

II. FELONIOUS ASSAULT CASES						
A. Being Jailed						
1. Released on bail	43	615	77%	58%	19	Yes
2. Had less than 2 months delay of those awaiting trial in jail	6	152	17	49	X	Too few women not released on bail
3. Case dismissed or acquitted	45	638	36	23	13	Yes
4. Received suspended sentence or probation of those convicted	25	415	44	36	8	Yes
5. Received less than one year imprisonment of those imprisoned	9	172	89	57	X	Too few women imprisoned
B. Formal Safeguards						
6. Received preliminary hearing	31	451	74	73	1	Difference too small
7. Had or given a lawyer	42	620	88	89	1	Difference too small
8. Received a jury trial of those tried	24	262	19	45	26	Yes

* Based on 1,103 grand larceny cases and 846 felonious assault cases from all 50 states for 1962.

lawyer and having a jury trial, the favorable balance toward juveniles and women tends to tip in the other direction. Indeed until the case of *In re Gault*, juveniles in many states did not have a right to court-provided counsel.[10] They still do not have a constitutional right to a jury trial.[11] Since *In re Gault*, although the law has changed, empirical studies have shown that juveniles are still more easily persuaded against exercising and are more reluctant to exercise their right to counsel than are adults.[12]

Table 7-1, however, does not show a discriminatory pattern with regard to having a lawyer when women defendants are compared with men defendants in either larceny cases or assault cases (rows 7). The percentage differences are 3 and 1, respectively, and are too small to explain.[13] Likewise, no discrimination is observed with regard to receiving preliminary hearings (rows 6) although they are probably not as important a safeguard for the innocent as having counsel or a jury trial.[14]

Women, however, in conformity with the paternalism hypothesis, are less likely to receive the formal treatment of a jury trial than are men, at least in assault cases where the difference was 26 percent (section II, row 8). This disparity is contrary to the interests of women since juries are generally less likely to convict than are judges.[15] Conviction by a jury normally requires the unanimous agreement of twelve persons, which is usually more difficult for a prosecutor to achieve than convincing a single judge. One disadvantage of jury trial is that a time-conscious prosecutor may have greater desire to recommend a longer sentence for a jury-convicted defendant than for one who pleaded guilty or took a relatively quick bench trial. The University of Chicago Jury Project research shows that both juries and judges tend to favor women in criminal verdicts, but juries do so to a greater degree.[16]

If juveniles and females are treated paternally in criminal cases (meaning favoritism on jailing and discrimination on jury trial and counsel), then female juveniles are probably treated the most paternally and male adults the least paternally. That is the finding when one uses the American Bar Foundation data to correlate sex and treatment of persons under 21 (while controlling for felonious larceny or assault) although few female juveniles were included in the data.[17] Between these two outer categories of paternalism, the categories of male juveniles and female adults are treated about equally, although male juveniles are less likely to have an attorney, jury trial, or preliminary hearing; whereas the female adults are more likely to be kept out of jail before and after conviction.

When the American Bar Foundation data are used to correlate race and treatment of women defendants, it appears that white women are less likely to be jailed before or after conviction than black women, but they are also less likely to have a lawyer. White women thereby better fit the paternalistic mold. With respect to having a lawyer, however, the data may reflect the greater likelihood of whites being nonindigent and thereby ineligible for court appointed counsel.[18] Black women (unlike black men) do receive more favorable treatment than white men with regard to being jailed before or after conviction, when controlling for felonious larceny or assault. When sexual paternalism and racial discrimination are mixed, the results as to receiving a jury trial follow no consistent pattern.

Looking at table 7-1 from an overall perspective and integrating all of the data, there seems to be a pattern—women are substantially less likely than men to be subjected to jail before or after trial, but are less likely to have a jury trial. The differences discussed were of enough magnitude and based on sufficiently large samples that they could not readily be attributed to chance. However, some of the differences may have arisen from the fact that grand larcenies and felonious assaults committed by women may be generally less to merit a jury trial and less to merit a severe sentence when women are involved.

To the extent that the male and female larceny cases are comparable, and likewise with the assault cases, differences can possibly be explained by judicial attitudes which assume that women and juveniles are weaker and would therefore be more harmed by pretrial and postconviction jailing than would men.[19] The empirical data do show that women and juveniles are less likely to be hardened criminals in the sense that they are somewhat less likely to have prior records.[20] Likewise, judges may feel that both juveniles and women should be treated in a more informal, more fatherly, less legalistic way, and that jury trials and defense counsel interfere with such paternalistic informality. To supplement the behavioral case data of table 7-1 perhaps future psychological questionnaire studies of judicial attitides will throw more light on how judges subjectively view jailing and jury trials for women defendants.[21]

The few statutes which provide different sentences for women and men generally provide for more indeterminate sentences for women,[22] just as juvenile statutes provide more indeterminate sentences for juveniles.[23] Legislators probably think that both women and juveniles are more susceptible to rehabilitation than are males and adults, and that indeterminate sentences contingent on prison progress facilitate rehabilitation. Testing that hypothesis would require determining legislators' attitudes, although it is probable that the more important attitudes concerning increasing or decreasing sexual discrimination are held by the judges who apply criminal statutes that allow for discretion.[24]

Women as Personal Injury Plaintiffs

In personal injury cases, the real defendant is usually an insurance company and thus has no male or female sex, just as the state as plaintiff in criminal cases cannot meaningfully be labeled male or female. Plaintiffs in personal injury cases, however, are sometimes male and sometimes female. What does the empirical data show with regard to their relative treatment?

First it should be noted that the paternalism hypothesis which made some sense in explaining, or at least integrating, data on the treatment of women as criminal defendants does not make sense if applied in the same way to women as personal injury plaintiffs. Personal injury plaintiffs are not in jeopardy of being placed in jail or of being stigmatized with criminal records. The basic issue is whether they should be given a monetary award in a society that has limited monetary resources thereby necessitating priorities. If women are disfavored in receiving monetary awards in society in general, one would expect a similar pattern of negative discrimination to be present in personal injury cases. However, if the paternalism hypothesis is defined as favoritism of the weak when imposing negative sanctions but disfavoritism when awarding or enforcing monetary awards, then either the paternalism or disadvantaged hypothesis would apply and would predict discrimination against women personal-injury plaintiffs.

Just as there were separate stages at which discrimination could occur in criminal cases, so also there are separate stages in personal injury cases. The first stage, analogous to being arrested in criminal cases, involves filing a personal injury complaint. One study of the economics of personal injury cases compiled data on the background characteristics of auto accident victims in the state of Michigan who subsequently became personal injury claimants.[25] The key sex data (summarized on row 1 of table 7-2) shows that of 166 seriously injured male accident victims, 38 percent filed suit; whereas of 178 seriously injured female accident victims, only 30 percent filed suit. The absolute difference of 8 percentage points represents a 27 percent relative increase from the 30 percent base.[26]

The reason a smaller percentage of female victims than male victims filed suit might be due (1) to a possibly higher rate of precomplaint settlements where females are involved or (2) to a possible tendency of females to suffer slighter injuries than males. Perhaps a more meaningful explanation is that women are encouraged to be less aggressive in asserting their legal rights in personal injury cases, just as they may be less aggressive in asserting their right to trial by jury in criminal cases.

Once a suit is filed, the next stage is establishing the defendant's liability to the plaintiff. In the Department of Transportation study of personal injury claims, nationwide data shows virtually no difference between males and females with regard to the likelihood of their respective claims being paid when bench, jury, and nontrial cases are lumped together (row 2).[27] Also, there is no difference between male and female victory percentages in jury-trial cases, at least when adult and minor plaintiffs are lumped together (row 3). This data comes from the nationwide compilation of the Jury Verdict Research Corporation of Cleveland, Ohio.[28] It further shows that there is a lower victory rate for both sexes in cases that have to go to a jury decision (row 3) as contrasted to cases that are settled with or without a trial (row 2), possibly because the nontrial cases more clearly favor the plaintiff.

A discriminatory pattern begins to appear if one compares adult male plaintiffs with adult female plaintiffs (row 4) since adult male plaintiffs win 76 percent of their jury trials and adult female plaintiffs win 69 percent of theirs.[29] Sexual discrimination is possibly less prevalent in comparing girl minors and boy minors than in comparing women adults and men adults since minors (especially pre-teenage minors) probably tend to be perceived as children, whereas adults tend to be perceived as women and men. One can also readily see that both male and female adults have a better chance of winning than male and female children (comparing row 4 and row 3), probably because child plaintiffs often negligently contribute to their injuries and because juries identify more with the adult defendant than the child plaintiff.

Once liability has been established, the next stage conceptually (although the two may occur concurrently) involves determining the amount of money to be awarded. Little difference appears in the average amount awarded to male and female plaintiffs when adults and minors are lumped together (row 5, like row 3) although a small percentage difference may involve a substantial number of dollars.[30] When adult female plaintiffs are compared to adult male plaintiffs, the pattern of amounts awarded is more favorable to men (row 6, like row 4).[31] Males averaged 6 percent above the expected awards to plaintiffs for similar types of injuries, medical expenses, and lost wages whereas females averaged 2 percent below what would be expected.

The more interesting male-female comparisons relate to specific kinds of personal injuries rather than to personal injuries in general. For example, when husbands sue for their losses caused by their wives' injuries, they collect more than wives collect when wives sue for their losses caused by their husbands' injuries (row 7).[32] This is so in spite of the fact, as previously shown (row 6), that when women sue for their own injuries they tend to collect less than do men. In other words, men collect (1) more for their own injuries and (2) more vicariously for injuries to their women than women collect vicariously for injuries to their men. Note also that there are more than eleven times as many sample suits by husbands for the losses of their wives' services than by wives for the losses of their husbands' services (row 7). The 28 wife-plaintiff suits represent a big increase from the 1964 Jury Verdict Research Report which showed only 3 such cases. Indeed, in some states the law still allows only husbands, not wives, to sue

Table 7-2
How the Treatment of Females Differs from Males as Victims and Plaintiffs in Personal Injury Cases*

	Number of Persons with Available Info.		*Differential Treatment*				
Treatment Stage and Case Type (1)	*Female Plaintiffs (2)*	*Male Plaintiffs (3)*	*Female Plaintiffs (4)*	*Male Plaintiffs (5)*	*Absolute Size of the Difference (Cols. 5-4) (6)*	*Relative Size of the Difference (Cols. 6÷4) (7)*	*Does Discrimination hypothesis seem to be confirmed? (By Col. 7) (8)*
I. SUIT FILED							
1. Suit filed by serious injury victims	178 victims	166	30%	38%	8	27%	Yes
II. LIABILITY ESTABLISHED							
2. Claim was paid in bodily injury cases	11,979 victims	13,059	80%	77%	3	4	Diff. too small
3. Victory in jury trial cases (to plaintiffs of all ages)	5,522 plaintiffs	—	61%	62%	1	2	Diff. too small
4. Victory in jury trial cases (to adult plaintiffs)	2,795	3,976	69%	76%	7	10	Yes

III. AVERAGE AMOUNT AWARDED							
5. Award in jury trial cases (to plaintiffs of all ages)	376	—	−2% below average	+1% above average	3	X	Diff. too small (Col. 6)
6. Award in jury trial cases (to adult plaintiffs)	2,795	3,976	−2% below average	+6% above average	8	X	Yes
7. Award for loss of victims services (to spouse plaintiffs)	28	314	$5,585	$6,524	$939	17	Yes
8. Award for victims death (to spouse plaintiffs where victim employed age 21-29)	—	—	$67,524	$39,820	$27,454	41	Yes (as to victim's worth) No (as to plaintiff)
9. Award for urino-genital injuries	—	—	$11,835	$31,966	$20,131	170	Yes

* Based on data compiled by Alfred Conard, Dep't of Transportation, and the Jury Verdict Research Corporation.

for the loss of a spouse's services, this stemming from a time when wives were almost considered property of their husbands.[33]

The generally larger amounts awarded to male plaintiffs (row 6) may be partially explained by the greater earning power of males, temporarily or permanently reduced by the injury. Personal injury juries have no control over this factor which reflects employment and educational discrimination against women. The most permanently damaging injury is death, and as expected men are valued there more highly than women (row 8).[34] The difference, however, may be less than anticipated because a wife-plaintiff seeking to collect for a killed husband as contrasted to a husband-plaintiff is seeking to collect for a killed wife, thereby mixing discrimination as to the victim's sex with favoritism as to the plaintiff's sex.

There are some injuries that are not generally relevant to one's work capacity, and therefore differences in the amounts awarded to male and female plaintiffs for such injuries cannot be readily explained in terms of differential earning power. Urino-genital injuries are an example since probably few men or women in the Jury Verdict sample make a living from their genitalia, and if they did, they probably would not have so informed the jury. Nevertheless, the inequality pattern here was greater than it was with any other type of bodily injury. The average male plaintiff who won a urino-genital injury case in the sample studied collected $31,966, whereas the average female plaintiff in similar cases collected only $11,835 (row 9).[35] This represents an absolute difference of $20,131 or a relative difference of 170 percent. In other words, male genitalia seem to have been valued almost three times as much as female genitalia. This may be an indication of a sexist view in the American court system. Much of the difference, however, may be due to the fact that urino-genital damage to the male rather than the female plaintiffs is usually more severe and more likely to be permanent.[36]

Looking at table 7-2 from an overall perspective integrating all the data, there seems to be a pattern in which adult women are less likely than men to file suits, to establish liability, or to receive a relatively high award, especially for certain types of injury. In that regard, the possible discrimination pattern of women plaintiffs is more like that of black plaintiffs than juvenile plaintiffs. In personal injury cases, children,[37] blacks,[38] and women, in that order, have greater difficulty establishing liability than adults, whites, and men. Thus, given this order of discrimination against children, blacks, and women on a victory rate continuum, women plaintiffs are closer in treatment to blacks than to children. Women, however, are closer to children than to blacks on a damages-awarded continuum with blacks furthest behind.

The extent to which women are less likely than men to establish liability and also to collect higher damages for similar injuries can probably be traced back to employment and educational discrimination, to the traditional subordination of women in the family, to a rationing of limited monetary resources, and in some cases to Freudian castration and other sexual anxieties (possibly indicated in the genitalia award comparisons). As these possible causal factors diminish through societal and legal change, the differential victory rates and damages awarded should become more equal.

Women as Divorce Litigants

Prevailing public opinion may conceive of divorce cases as a manifestation of female domination or even exploitation of men since only women litigants normally seek and obtain alimony or child support.[39] In spite of this, empirical data on women as divorce litigants may show actual male domination and exploitation.

Although women tend to be the formal plaintiffs in divorce cases,[40] existing data indicates that this is a nominal status, and that the husband in reality takes the de facto rather than the de jure initiative in dissolving the marriage.[41] Among the poor, desertion by the husband is a frequent substitute for divorce and is a major cause of eligibility for welfare aid.[42] The fact that wives seem to have better formal grounds for divorce and thus become the plaintiff-complainants possibly shows greater provocation on the part of husbands.[43] Although women have become more independent as a result of increased employment opportunities, they are still more economically dependent on their husbands than vice versa, and they would therefore tend to resist divorce if it were not for their husbands' cruelty, nonsupport, desertion, or other provocation.[44]

In descriptions of the divorce trial process, there are references to the often degrading paternalistic procedures to which women litigants are subjected.[45] Begging for alimony may be particularly degrading even if alimony is considered (1) income accrued as a result of inadequately compensated wifehood and motherhood and (2) payment for obtaining educational rehabilitation and training.[46] Seeking child support may also be a frustrating ordeal even if judges recognize the concept as covering (1) some of the considerable work mothers must do in caring for children and (2) some of the considerable out-of-pocket expenses involved in raising children which husbands have fathered. In custody disputes, a double standard of morality may prevail which condemns extramarital activities by wives, but tolerates them by husbands.[47] In some states this double standard allows husbands to obtain divorces on sexual grounds which are not available to wives.[48]

The real test of possible discrimination in the judicial process, however, is not at the initiation or suit-filing stages or even at the judgment stage, but rather at the judgment-enforcement stage. To a lesser extent, this reasoning also applies to personal injury and criminal cases, but a much higher percentage of the results of those cases are determined at the presentencing and predamages stages. In addition, data do not seem to be available on the collection of personal injury damages by sex as contrasted to the awarding of damages, or on the paroling of convicts by sex. Data are available, however, showing what happens to monetary judgments awarded to women divorce litigants.

Table 7-3 shows the probability of a divorced woman collecting any child support money. It is based on data gathered by Kenneth Eckhardt from a 1955 sample of fathers who were ordered in divorce decrees to pay child support in a Metropolitan Wisconsin county.[49] Within one year after the divorce decrees, only 38 percent of the fathers were in full compliance with support orders (row 1). Twenty percent had only partially complied, and in some cases partial compliance only constituted a single payment. Forty-two percent of the fathers made no payment at all. By the tenth year, the number of open cases had dropped from 163 to 149 as a result of the death of fathers, the termination of parental rights, or the maturity of children. By that year, only 13 percent of the fathers were fully complying, and 79 percent of the fathers were in total noncompliance.

If noncompliance is so great with child support orders, it is probably even greater with alimony orders although alimony orders are relatively infrequent.[50] It should be noted that the original child support orders probably did not meet the full support needs of the children.[51] Some of the orders may also have been further reduced judicially when the father re-married, or when his financial status otherwise worsened. Thus, if only a minority of husbands pay anything and even those pay a substantially less-than-full support order, most child support is actually carried by the mother or by the state.

In spite of available sanctions like contempt of court, civil action, and criminal prosecution, and in spite of the state's incentive to avoid unnecessary welfare payments, legal action is seldom initiated against nonpaying fathers (last column of table 7-3). This is so especially as children grow older and probably require even more support money. Only 19 percent of the 101 nonpaying fathers at the end of the first year had legal action taken against them, and only one percent of the 128 nonpaying fathers in the tenth year. Indeed, of all criminal and civil court orders, monetary divorce awards (and small claims judgments)[52] are probably the least complied with and the least enforced.

The explanation for the nonenforcement is not that fathers are unable to comply since: (1) support orders consider the ability of the father to pay;

Table 7-3
The Probability of a Divorced Woman Collecting Any Child Support Money
(by years since the court order)

Years Since court order	*Number of open cases*	*Full Compliance*	*Partial Compliance*	*No Compliance*	*Non-Paying Fathers against whom whom legal action was taken*
One	163	38%	20%	42%	19%
Two	163	28	20	52	32
Three	161	26	14	60	21
Four	161	22	11	67	18
Five	160	19	14	67	9
Six	158	17	12	71	6
Seven	157	17	12	71	4
Eight	155	17	8	75	2
Nine	155	17	8	75	0
Ten	149	13	8	79	1

Based on data from Kenneth Eckhardt, "Deviance, Visibility, and Legal Action: The Duty to Support," 15 *Social Problems* 470, 473-474 (1968).

and (2) Eckhardt's data shows that less able working-class fathers are more likely to be prosecuted than more able middle-class fathers because (a) their ex-wives are more likely to be on welfare and (b) they are more likely to already have criminal records.[53] A possible explanation for nonenforcement lies in the promale bias of the prosecutors, judges, and legislators who could more meaningfully enforce the law. An additional explanation may be the greater complexity of nonsupport cases (especially where interstate enforcement is involved) and the greater age of such claims compared to other, more current cases.

More vigorous prosecution may not be a realistic remedy for the nonenforcement of child support orders, although it may be merited in flagrant cases. Instead, a dignity-preserving system of social insurance might more effectively cover the situation. The concept of survivorship under social security could be expanded to include children of a deserted or divorced father as well as a deceased father.[54] Other social alternatives include child allowances, negative income tax, or an expanded family assistance plan.[55] A national program of wholesome daycare centers[56] and government stimulation of employment opportunities[57] would also enable women to work who wish to do so, rather than to rely on child support or welfare.

The Effect of the Sex of the Jury

The unequal treatment of male and female litigants may be affected by whether the judge is a man or a woman and by whether the jury is predominantly male or female.[58] Because there are few female judges, and no data found comparing them with male judges vis-à-vis male and female litigants, this section of the chapter will deal solely with male and female jurors, but one can possibly extrapolate the findings to male and female judges.[59] Likewise, because of the rare occurrence of jury trials in divorce cases, there seems to be no data available on how male-dominated juries differ from female-dominated juries vis-à-vis male and female divorce litigants.[60]

There are five meaningful hypotheses which one can formulate concerning the effect of the sex of jurors on male-female treatment in criminal and personal injury cases. One hypothesis, which may be called opposites-attract hypothesis, predicts that men will favor women and women will favor men.[61] A second, the chivalry hypothesis, predicts that men will favor women and women will also favor women because supposedly women need special treatment. Third is the brainwashing hypothesis which says that men will be favored by both men and women because they have been indoctrinated to believe that men are more valuable. Fourth is the equality hypothesis which says men favor neither sex, and women favor neither sex. This is the implicit or explicit hypothesis of cases which have found no denial of equal protection in state actions which systematically decrease the chances of women serving on juries.[62] Fifth is the likes-attract hypothesis which predicts that men favor men, and women favor women.

With regard to criminal cases, the most relevant data seems to be contained in a quantitative empirical study by Arnold Rose and Arthur Prell.[63] A sample of students taking courses in introductory sociology and social psychology at the University of Minnesota in 1953 were asked what sentences they would hand down if they were serving as judges or jurors in a variety of hypothetical fact situations. One situation involved a male convicted of a certain crime. Elsewhere on the list, another situation involved a female convicted of the same crime. The male respondents tended to give the male defendant a lower sentence than the female defendant, whereas the female respondents tended to give the female defendant a lower sentence than the male defendant.[64] In other words, men tended to favor males and women tended to favor females. To the extent this finding can be extrapolated to real juries or real judges, it confirms the likes-attract hypothesis.

With regard to personal injury cases, there are data available on real, not just simulated, juries. Table 7-4 presents data from the Jury Verdict Research Corporation on how the treatment of females and males differs in personal injury cases when considering the sex of the jury. The upper half of the table answers the question: "If I know the sex of the plaintiff, what can I predict with regard to victory and damages before male-dominated and female-dominated juries?" The lower half of the table answers the question: "If I know the dominant sex of the jury, what can I predict with regard to victory and damages for male and female plaintiffs?"

Both parts of the table show that holding constant the sex of the jury makes no significant difference with regard to establishing liability. Both parts, however, show that holding constant the sex of the jury makes a substantial difference with regard to the average amount awarded. For instance, male-dominated juries gave awards to male plaintiffs that averaged 12 percent above the expected average for the type of injury, medical expenses, and lost wages (row 3); whereas male-dominated juries gave female plaintiffs awards that averaged 17 percent below the expected average. With female-dominated juries, the direction of favoritism between female and male plaintiffs was reversed (row 4). The validity of the likes-attract hypothesis is further reinforced by other data on the average amounts awarded (rows 7 and 8). Note, however, that although women favor women, they do so to a lesser extent than men favor men.

In table 7-4 and to a lesser extent in table 7-2 discrimination, or at least inequality, between men and women seems to be greater in the amount of damages awarded than in the establishment of liability. Some of the difference between these two stages may be attributed to the fact that extremely large awards (those over $100,000) tend to be rendered for work accidents resulting in crippling injuries. Relatively few women are injured in such circumstances.[65] In table 7-4, however, the type of injury (*e.g.*, whiplash) and the out-of-pocket expenses are statistically controlled in calculating percentage above or below the expected average. Some of the difference in liability versus damages may be due to the fact that the differential earning power rationale only applies to assessing damages, not to establishing liability, and male jurors may place more emphasis on that rationale than do female jurors. Much of the difference may also be attributed to the greater subjectivity involved in determining damages. Thus, prejudice is more easily exercised there than in the more objective legalistic decision of establishing liability. Likewise, the greater inequality present at bail and sentencing stages in criminal cases as compared to procedural safeguards may be partly attributable to the relatively greater subjectivity and lesser legalistic restraint involved in bail-setting and sentencing.

Since table 7-4 shows that disparities in the treatment of male and female litigants can be affected by the sex of the decisionmakers, this should be further reason for society to seek an increase in the number of women judges and jurors in addition to more democratic representation. In order to obtain more women judges, it is necessary to encourage more

Table 7-4
How the Treatment of Females Differs from Males as Plaintiffs in Personal Injury Cases When Considering the Sex of the Jury*

Treatment Stage and Jury Sex	*Number of Cases with Available Information*		*Differential Treatment*		*Difference*	*Does hypothesis seem to be confirmed that men and women favor own sex?*
	Female Plaintiffs	*Male Plaintiffs*	*Female Plaintiffs*	*Male Plaintiffs*		
I. LIABILITY ESTABLISHED						
1. Victory with a predominantly *male* jury	117	149	63%	65%	2	Diff. too small
2. Victory with a predominantly *female* jury	35	63	60%	68%	8	Diff. too small
II. AVERAGE AMOUNT AWARDED						
3. Award with a predominantly *male* jury	117	149	−17% below average	+12% above average	29	Yes
4. Award with a predominantly *female* jury	35	63	+17% above average	+3% above average	14	Yes

Treatment Stage and Plaintiff Sex	*Female Juries*	*Male Juries*	*Female Juries*	*Male Juries*	*Difference*	*Does hypothesis seem to be confirmed that plaintiffs are better off with jurors of their own sex?*
III. LIABILITY ESTABLISHED						
5. Adult *male* Plaintiffs	63	149	68%	65%	3	Diff. too small
6. Adult *female* Plaintiffs	35	117	60%	63%	3	Diff. too small
IV. AVERAGE AMOUNT AWARDED						
7. Adult *male* Plaintiffs	63	149	+3% above average	+12% above average	9	Yes
8. Adult *female* Plaintiffs	35	117	+17% above average	−17% below average	34	Yes

* Based on data contained in Jury Verdict Research Corp., *Personal Injury Valuation Handbooks*, 3676-87 Report 71) (1966).

women to become law students and eligible lawyers.[66] As for jurors, a majority of states by law still allow women to be more easily excused or exempted from jury service than men, probably resulting in an underrepresentation of women on the juries of those states.[67] In some states, however, women may already approximate 50 percent of the jurors. A Pennsylvania study showed an unbalance toward male jurors in Lancaster County, an unbalance toward female jurors in Philadelphia County, and approximate equality in Allegheny County.[68] These wide variations under the same state law seem to illustrate the empirical importance of local administrators and judges with regard to jury selection laws.

Conclusions

Looking at tables 7-1, 7-2, 7-3, and 7-4 from a general overall perspective, one can conclude that women as litigants do not receive the same treatment that men receive as litigants. In criminal cases, women are much less likely to be jailed before or after conviction and are also less likely to have a jury trial than are men charged with the same crime. In personal injury cases, adult women are less likely to win than adult men, and they collect substantially smaller awards, especially for certain types of injuries and especially before male-dominated juries. In divorce cases, where there is always a woman on one side and a man on the other, the woman seems to win if one analyzes only divorce decrees; but she generally loses if one analyzes collection records.

These findings seem consistent with how women are generally treated in American society. There exists a paternalistic protectiveness, at least toward white women, that assumes they need sheltering from manly experiences such as jail and from subjection to the unfriendliness of overly formal proceedings in criminal or family law cases. At the same time, however, when it comes to allocating limited valuable resources like personal injury monetary awards or child support money, women are more likely to be slighted than their male counterparts.

Perhaps more equal treatment will be achieved by increasing the awareness of disparities in the treatment of male and female litigants and by increasing the representation of women as jury and judicial decision-makers. More specifically focused changes in the legal system are needed to improve the legal process for both men and women.

For example, the remedy for disparities in the jailing of women does not lie in reducing their release on bond or increasing their post-conviction imprisonment. Instead, a more socially useful remedy probably lies in providing pretrial release for all persons, regardless of sex, mainly on the basis of their likelihood of appearing for trial, possibly using the quantitative methods devised by the Vera Institute.[69] Likewise, society needs to provide posttrial sentencing for all persons, regardless of sex, on the basis of the likely rehabilitation and deterrent effects of imprisonment, possibly using a more scientific approach than has heretofore been used in sentencing.[70]

Along related lines, the remedy for disparities in personal injury awards and child support collections probably does not lie in lowering the damages awarded to males or in more vigorously prosecuting wayward fathers. Instead, society may need to try collective action like no-fault insurance[71] and expanded social security.[72] These measures, however, will probably still not eliminate whatever discrimination exists against women litigants until discrimination against women in general is further decreased in accordance with current trends.[73]

Notes

1. Seidenberg, *The Submissive Majority: Modern Trends in the Law Concerning Women's Rights*, 55 CORNELL L. REV. 262 (1970). *See also* L. KANOWITZ, WOMEN AND THE LAW 167-72 (1969) [hereinafter cited as KANOWITZ]; Schulder, *Does the Law Oppress Women?* in SISTERHOOD IS POWERFUL, 139, 153 (R. Morgan ed. 1970).

2. *E.g.*, C. BIRD, BORN FEMALE 110-25 (Pocket Book rev. ed., 1971); K. MILLETT, SEXUAL POLITICS 23-58 (1970).

3. Some of the data were the basis for L. SILVERSTEIN, DEFENSE OF THE POOR IN CRIMINAL CASES IN AMERICAN STATE COURTS (1965) in which the data compilation methods are described at pages 175-79, 183-86, and 207-12. The data can now be obtained on magnetic tape or punched cards from the Inter-University Consortium for Political Research at Ann Arbor, Michigan.

4. For further details on these and other disparities in criminal procedure see S. NAGEL, THE LEGAL PROCESS FROM A BEHAVIORAL PERSPECTIVE 81-112 (1969) [hereinafter cited as NAGEL]. Those pages also provide some reinforcing data from the federal courts, but the sample of women in the federal criminal cases used is too small to be meaningful.

5. *Id.* at 98-101.

6. *Id.* at 94. *See also* M. WOLFGANG, CRIME AND RACE: CONCEPTIONS AND MISCONCEPTIONS (1964).

7. No data were compiled on the arrest stage prior to the preliminary hearing. Women, however, may be arrested for some crimes that equally guilty men are not arrested for (*e.g.*, prostitution), and men may be arrested for some crimes that equally guilty women are not (*e.g.*, statutory rape).

KANOWITZ, *supra* note 1, 15-25. Likewise no data were compiled on the parole stage subsequent to sentencing. Women, however, may be more readily paroled than men for similar crimes (as indicated by their more readily receiving pretrial release and postconviction probation), although imprisoned women may represent a subsample of women who are particularly high recidivisits. While in prison, women may also be treated differently than men. *See* D. WARD & G. KASSENBAUM, WOMEN'S PRISON (1965); Tittle, *Inmate Organization: Sex Differentiation and the Influence of Criminal Subcultures*, 34 AM. SOC. REV. 492 (1969).

8. Twenty was used as a cut-off partly to make theoretical sense out of the data presented and partly because Guilford says: "If one asks, How small is N before we have a small sample? . . . Some place it is as low as 20." J. GUILFORD, FUNDAMENTAL STATISTICS IN PSYCHOLOGY AND EDUCATION 217 (4th ed. 1956). Guilford also says that special statistics should be used when any frequency is expected by chance to be less than 10. *Id.* at 234-35. If the number of females on a row is 20 or less, then by chance 10 or less should receive favorable treatment, and 10 or less unfavorable.

9. There would have been more imprisoned men and women on row 5 if convicted defendants ordered to serve indeterminate sentences had been included. Indeterminate sentences were excluded because they lack preciseness for making comparisons, unless one obtains data on time actually served, or unless one somewhat arbitrarily translates indeterminate sentences into determinate ones by averaging the minimum and maximum when those two figures are available. Of the 363 women in the total sample of 11,258 cases who received sentences, 27 percent received indeterminate sentences; while 35 percent of the 5,898 men who received sentences received indeterminate ones. Such sentences are associated with more serious crimes (*e.g.,* murder and arson) which men are more likely to commit relative to women than the less serious crimes (*e.g.,* bad checks). Even when the crime is held constant, however, the above data show men usually receive a slightly higher percentage of indeterminate sentences. Such sentences generally have higher maximums and sometimes even higher minimums than the fixed sentences for the same crimes and probably result in longer prison stays. These indeterminate-sentence findings are thus consistent with the fixed-sentence findings in that under both types of sentences, women tend to receive shorter sentences than men.

10. *In re* Gault, 387 U.S. 1 (1967).

11. McKeiver v. Pennsylvania, 403 U.S. 528 (1971).

12. Lefstein, Stapleton & Teitelbaum, *In Search of Juvenile Justice: Gault and Its Implementation*, 3 L. & SOC. REV. 491 (1969).

13. The cut-off level in this chapter is between differences that are too small to explain (7 percent and under) and differences that merit an expla-

nation (9 percent and over). A percentage difference of 8 is the gray area in terms of making theoretical sense out of the empirical data presented.

A difference of approximately 8 percent is attributable to chance less than 5 times out of 100 if the total sample size on which it is based (males plus females) is about 150. GUILFORD, *supra* note 8, at 178-82, 190-92, and 538-39. The smallest total samples in tables 7-1, 7-2, and 7-4 tend to be as large as or larger than 150. Such a probability calculation assumes one has hypothesized the direction of the difference between males and females as has been done in the tables in light of the paternalism hypothesis. *Id.* at 207-08.

14. Of these three safeguards, only preliminary hearings have not been made a due process right for adults by the Supreme Court. *See* Duncan v. Louisiana, 391 U.S. 145 (1968) (jury trial), and Gideon v. Wainwright, 372 U.S. 335 (1963) (right to counsel). For a discussion of the functions of preliminary hearings, defense counsel and jury trials see D. FELLMAN, THE DEFENDANT'S RIGHTS (1958); L. ORFIELD, CRIMINAL PROCEDURE FROM ARREST TO APPEAL (1947).

15. H. KALVEN & H. ZEISEL, THE AMERICAN JURY 55-65 (1966).

16. *Id.* at 191-218. Juries relative to judges may be especially sympathetic to women relative to men in more serious crimes and also in less manly crimes. This might explain why the lawyers of women defendants asked for jury trials more in grand larceny cases than in felonious assault cases. Larceny is generally a more serious crime bringing a more severe sentence, as indicated by comparing the percentages on row 5 (length of sentence) of the larceny section with row 5 of the assault section. Larceny is also a less manly crime, as indicated by the female to male ratio in the larceny and assault sections of table 7-1.

17. Where the sample sizes are large enough to compare length of postconviction incarcerations of female and male juveniles, female juveniles on the average are confined about two months longer when the nature of the crime is not held constant between females and males. CHILDRENS BUREAU, U.S. DEP'T OF HEALTH, EDUCATION AND WELFARE, STATISTICS ON PUBLIC INSTITUTIONS FOR DELINQUENTS (1970). The longer confinement is generally justified on the grounds that young girls are more in need of protection, especially sexually, from the outside world than young boys are. See K. Olson, For Her Own Protection: A Case Study of the Conditions of Incarceration for Female Juvenile Offenders in the State of Connecticut, 1971 (unpublished paper, Yale Law School). In the Connecticut juvenile data, the main commitment reasons for boys were breaking and entering (33 percent), theft (22 percent), and car theft (20 percent); whereas for girls the main reasons were runaway (30 percent), pregnancy (16 percent), and sexual misconduct (15 percent). There were too few boys

and girls committed for the same reason to be able to hold the "crime" constant.

18. The correlation coefficient is +.16 being white and being nonindigent in the 1,949 state criminal cases on which table 7-1 is based, and the correlation is +.20 between being nonindigent and lacking an attorney. The correlation is +1.00 between being classified as nonindigent and not having a court-appointed attorney in the federal data. These correlation coefficients are numbers similar in meaning to those in the "Difference" column of table 7-1 although the differences in table 7-1 are not stated as decimals, and the plus and minus signs are eliminated.

19. Judges may also give shorter sentences to women than to men convicted of the same crimes because judges think the weaker nature of women also makes them (1) less dangerous to society, (2) more deterred from repeating their crime, and (3) more easily rehabilitated. These points are in conformity with the custodial, deterrence, and rehabilitation goals of imprisonment.

20. NAGEL, *supra* note 4, at 111. The correlation between being a man and having a prior record, however, was only +.08 in the federal data, and prior record was unavailable for the defendants in the state data.

21. A questionnaire answered by 118 state and federal supreme court judges who were serving in 1955, contained the statement that "women are not the equals of men in intelligence and organizing ability." Seventeen percent of the judges agreed, and 73 percent disagreed. Nagel, *Off-the-Bench Judicial Attitudes*, in JUDICIAL DECISION-MAKING 29, 32, 53 (G. Schubert ed. 1963). No questions were asked, however, which specifically dealt with judicial attitudes toward the jailing of women and jury trials for women defendants. Only 12 percent of a nationwide sample of state legislators agreed with the same questionnaire item. NAGEL, *supra* note 4, at 199, 205.

22. See note 1 *supra* and statutes discussed in Commonwealth v. Daniels, 430 Pa. 642, 243 A.2d 400 (1968); United States *ex rel.* Robinson v. York, 281 F. Supp. 8 (D. Conn. 1968). Even if both women and men are subject to indeterminate sentences, the average sentences given and especially served may differ. See notes 7, 9 & 17 *supra*.

23. D. TAFT, CRIMINOLOGY 618 (1950).

24. After this chapter was written, a *New York Times* study headlined: "Crime Rate of Women up Sharply Over Men's." N.Y. Times, June 13, 1971, at 1, col. 1. The article quotes Phil Levin, a social work consultant to the Dallas police, as saying, "We in the criminal justice system are becoming less tolerant of women. They are becoming apprehended more frequently and not sheltered as in the past." *Id.* at 72, col. 5. This may portend decreased paternalism toward women criminal defendants in the future.

25. A. Conrad, J. Morgan, R. Pratt, C. Voltz, R. Bombaugh, Automobile Accident Costs and Payments 259 (1964).

26. Relative percentages are shown in table 7-2 so as to provide a common measure for comparing: (1) differences between percentages like those on row 1; and (2) differences between dollar amounts like those on row 7. An increase of 10 percentage points also means more if one starts at 5 percent than if one starts at 80 percent. Where a relative percentage can be calculated, its size is referred to in determining whether the discrimination hypothesis seems to be confirmed.

27. 1 U.S. Dep't of Transportation, Automobile Personal Injury Claims 15 (1970).

28. 4 Jury Verdict Research Corp., Personal Injury Valuation Handbooks, Rep. No. 41, at 2025-26 (1964) [hereinafter cited JVR]. Sometimes the JVR Handbooks do not give the exact sample size of female or male plaintiffs on which their percentages or dollar amounts are based as indicated by the dashes in columns 2 and 3 of table 7-2, but the sample sizes are generally quite substantial in view of the extensive data collected unless the JVR Handbooks indicate otherwise. For an analysis of the concepts and methods of the Jury Verdict Research Corporation see Nagel, *Statistical Prediction of Verdicts and Awards*, 1963 Modern Uses of Logic in Law 135.

29. 6 JVR, Rep. No. 62, at 3451-56 (1966).

30. 4 JVR, Rep. No. 41, at 2027-29 (1964).

31. 6 JVR, Rep. No. 62, at 3451-56 (1966).

32. 2 JVR, Rep. No. 113, at 555, 567-68 (1969).

33. Kanowitz, *supra* note 1, at 80-85, 160, 167.

34. *Compare* 2 JVR; Rep. No. 102, at 425-26b (1969) *with id.*, Rep. No. 100, at 407-08b (1968).

35. *Compare* 2 JVR, Rep. No. 116, at 850-52 (1970) *with id.*, Rep. No. 117, at 865-65b (1970).

36. *Id*. If females who lose their child-bearing ability in an accident could be compared with males who lose their propagating ability, the damages awarded would probably be more equal since severity and permanence would be held constant and since women have been especially valued in society for their child-bearing ability.

Although one might think women would receive higher awards for facial scarring injuries than men, given society's emphasis on feminine beauty, the average awards for both sexes are about equal although the especially high awards tend to go to women. 6 JVR, Rep. No. 70 at 127-29F (1966).

37. The victory rate for children under 12 is 46 percent versus 61.3 percent for plaintiffs in general. If children collect anything, they tend to

either get very little or very much as compared to the general population. Their very small and large damage awards, however, give them an average award close to the general population if they collect. 5 JVR, REP. NO. 45, at 3025-32 (1964).

38. The victory rate for blacks is 57 percent as compared to 61.3 percent for plaintiffs in general. Damage awards to black plaintiffs average 15 percent lower than to plaintiffs in general. 5 JVR, REP. NO. 43, at 2076-79 (1964).

39. Hofstadter & Herzog, *Common Sense About Alimony*, HARPERS, May 1958, at 68; Lobseng, *Are Divorce and Alimony Unfair to Men?* READER'S DIGEST, Oct. 1959, at 193.

40. In a 1963 sample of divorce cases in 22 states, wives were plaintiffs in 72 percent of the cases, and husbands were plaintiffs in 28 percent. DIVISION OF VITAL STATISTICS, U.S. DEP'T OF HEALTH, EDUCATION & WELFARE, DIVORCE STATISTICS ANALYSIS 39 (1967) [hereinafter cited as HEW, DIVORCE STATISTICS].

41. On the basis of extensive interviewing of a sample of 425 divorced women, Goode concludes that "the husband more frequently than the wife is the first to desire a divorce; and . . . it is the husband more often than the wife who adopts (whether consciously or not) a line of behavior, a 'strategy', which forces the other spouse to suggest a divorce as the appropriate solution." W. GOODE, AFTER DIVORCE 133 (1956).

42. Seventy-six percent of the 1,300,000 families receiving benefits under the aid to families with dependent children program in 1967 involved families where the father was absent from the home. NAT'L CENTER FOR SOCIAL STATISTICS, U.S. DEP'T OF HEALTH, EDUCATION & WELFARE, FINDINGS OF THE 1967 AFDC STUDY: DATA BY STATE AND CENSUS DIVISION, pt. 1, table 22 (1970). Categories of absence include desertion (18 percent), nonmarriage to the mother (28 percent), divorce (13 percent), separation (12 percent), and imprisonment (3 percent). *Id.* In 35 percent of the families, the father's whereabouts were unknown. *Id.*, table 24. On middle class desertion see L. Weitzman, Social Suicide: A Study of Missing Persons, June 1970 (unpublished Ph.D. dissertation in Columbia University Library).

43. An alternative explanation for why wives are often made the plaintiff in divorce cases is because both husband and wife realize the wife has a better chance of winning. In divorce cases where decrees were granted, the wife as plaintiff lost only about 2 percent of the time (*i.e.*, the husband was granted the decree); whereas the husband as plaintiff lost about 10 percent of the time (*i.e.*, the wife was granted the decree). HEW, DIVORCE STATISTICS, *supra* note 40, at 39.

44. The formal legal grounds given in a 1963 nationwide sample of

divorce decrees are cruelty (54 percent), non-support (19 percent), desertion (18 percent), and indignities (16 percent). Other grounds are less than 3 percent. Grounds may be multiple, HEW, DIVORCE STATISTICS, *supra* note 40, at 49.

45. Tomasson, *Women as Property*, NEW REPUBLIC, Sept. 19, 1970, at 15.

46. On the goals to be served by alimony and child support, see H. CLARK, THE LAW OF DOMESTIC RELATIONS IN THE UNITED STATES § § 14.1, .5, at 441-42 (alimony), § 15.1 (child support) (1968).

47. At first glance, it may appear to be a victory for the wife to obtain custody of (and responsibility for) the children which she does about 95 percent of the time. W. GOODE, *supra* note 41, at 311. Husbands, however, admitted that they agreed with the custody decrees 85 percent of the time. *Id.* at 313.

48. KANOWITZ, *supra* note 1, at 96-98. For example, a common provision allows husbands to divorce wives who were pregnant at the time of the marriage, but wives cannot divorce husbands who have made other women pregnant at the time of the marriage. *Id.* at 96.

49. Eckhardt, *Deviance, Visibility, and Legal Action: The Duty to Support*, 15 SOCIAL PROBLEMS 470 (1968).

50. In an analysis of 12,000 Chicago divorce cases, the wife requested postdivorce alimony in only 7 percent of the cases and waived it in 93 percent. M. VIRTUE, FAMILY CASES IN COURT 92 (1956). In 1922, which is the last year the Census Bureau kept alimony data, their data showed alimony was decreed in 15 percent of a nationwide sample of decrees although women were less independent at that time than in the 1950s. P. JACOBSON, AMERICAN MARRIAGE AND DIVORCE 126 (1959). For an in-depth analysis of alimony and other matters in a sample of 40 Kansas divorce cases, see Hopson, *The Economics of a Divorce: A Pilot Empirical Study at the Trial Court Level*, 11 KAN. L. REV. 107 (1962).

51. The smallness of child support and property settlements in divorce decrees is discussed with empirical data in W. GOODE, *supra* note 41, at 218-23. Of 172,000 minor children involved in divorces in Chicago in 1949-50, one third were awarded no child support at all. Robson, *The Law and Practice of Divorce–The Judge's Point of View*, in UNIVERSITY OF CHICAGO LAW SCHOOL CONFERENCE ON DIVORCE 4 (Conference Ser. No. 9, 1952).

52. L. Weitzman, Non-Compliance with Small Claims Court Orders (forthcoming). The legal actions referred to in table 7-3 are contempt proceedings for noncompliance with the divorce decree, rather than prosecution for nonsupport.

53. Eckhardt, *supra* note 49, at 475.

54. A. SCHORR, EXPLORATIONS IN SOCIAL POLICY 21-68 (1968).

55. *See* Family Assistance Act of 1971, H. R. 6020, 92d Cong., 1st Sess. (1971). CASES AND MATERIALS ON LAW AND POVERTY 281-317 (P. Dodyk, gen. ed. 1969).

56. *See* F. RUDERMAN, CHILD CARE AND WORKING MOTHERS (1968); *Special Issue on Day Care*, 44 CHILD WELFARE 124 (1965).

57. *See* C. WILCOX, TOWARD SOCIAL WELFARE: AN ANALYSIS OF PROGRAMS AND PROPOSALS ATTACKING POVERTY, INSECURITY, AND INEQUALITY OF OPPORTUNITY 103-17, 179-92, 211-27, 291-329 (1969).

58. The concern here is only with the effect on sexual discrimination (not on sentences or awards in general) of changing the sexual representation of judicial decision-makers. Studies that deal with the effect on sentences or awards in general are not directly relevant. Such studies include R. SIMON, THE JURY AND THE DEFENSE OF INSANITY 109 (1967) which shows that housewives are less punitive than men in burglary and possibly other theft cases, but more punitive in father-daughter incest and possibly other male-female sex crimes.

59. For a comparison of the effects of various background characteristics (other than sex) on the decisional propensities of judges (rather than jurors), see NAGEL, *supra* note 4, at 227-44.

60. "Of several thousand divorce cases [in Chicago], juries were used in only three." M. VIRTUE, *supra* note 50, at 58.

61. A. White, *Selecting the Jury*, in SUCCESSFUL JURY TRIALS: A SYMPOSIUM 119, 123 (J. Appleman ed. 1952) says: "If you are representing a personable young man, try to seat kindly old ladies in the jury box. If you are representing an attractive young woman, have as many male jurors, old or young, as possible."

62. KANOWITZ, *supra* note 1, at 28-31.

63. Rose & Prell, *Does the Punishment Fit the Crime? A Study in Social Valuation*, 61, AM. J. SOC. 247 (1955).

64. *Id.* at 257.

65. 4 JVR REP. NO. 41, at 2027 (1964).

66. Sassower, *Women in the Law: The Second Hundred Years*, 57 A.B.A.J. 329 (1971); White, *Women in the Law*, 65 MICH. L. REV. 1112 (1967).

67. For a compilation of state laws with respect to jury service by women as of January 15, 1965, see AMERICAN WOMEN: THE REPORT OF THE PRESIDENT'S COMMISSION ON THE STATUS OF WOMEN AND OTHER PUBLICATIONS

OF THE COMMISSION 242 (M. Mead & F. Kaplan ed. 1965). *See also* KANOWITZ, *supra* note 1, at 28-31.

68. Vanderzell, *The Jury: A Community Cross-Section*, 19 WEST. POL. Q. 136 (1966). In the jury *panel* list for the Los Angeles courts, women constituted about 63 percent of the names. Holbrook, *Composition of Juries as a Group* in CIVIL JUSTICE AND THE JURY 195, 198 (C. Joiner ed. 1962). A majority of Los Angeles attorneys and judges who were interviewed also indicated they thought women were over-represented on actual juries. *Id.* Both Pennsylvania and California are among the minority of states that do not by law make it easier for women to be excused from jury service. See note 67 *supra*.

69. *See* D. FREED & P. WALD, BAIL IN THE UNITED STATES (1965); R. GOLDFARB, RANSOM: A CRITIQUE OF THE AMERICAN BAIL SYSTEM (1965); Ares, Rankin & Sturz, *The Manhattan Bail Project: An Interim Report on the Use of Pre-Trial Parole*, 38 N.Y.U.L. REV. 67 (1963).

70. N. WALKER, SENTENCING IN A RATIONAL SOCIETY (1971); PRESIDENT'S COMMISSION ON LAW ENFORCEMENT AND ADMINISTRATION OF JUSTICE, TASK FORCE REPORT: THE COURTS 14-36 (1967); S. RUBIN, THE LAW OF CRIMINAL CORRECTION 109-150 (1963).

71. W. BLUM & H. KALVEN, PUBLIC LAW PERSPECTIVES ON A PRIVATE LAW PROBLEM: AUTO COMPENSATION PLANS (1965); G. CALABRESI, THE COSTS OF ACCIDENTS: A LEGAL AND ECONOMIC ANALYSIS (1970); R. KEETON & J. O'CONNELL, BASIC PROTECTION FOR THE TRAFFIC VICTIM (1965).

72. See notes 51-52 & the accompanying text *supra*.

73. For a discussion of current trends concerning general discrimination against women and the forces responsible for the trends see AMERICAN WOMEN: THE REPORT OF THE PRESIDENT'S COMMISSION ON THE STATUS OF WOMEN (1963); C. EPSTEIN & W. GOODE, THE OTHER HALF: ROADS TO WOMEN'S EQUALITY (1971); W. GOODE, WORLD REVOLUTION AND FAMILY PATTERNS (1963).

8

D. GEOGRAPHICAL AND PARTISAN DISCRIMINATION

The Effects of Legislative Reapportionment on the Passage of Non-Expenditure Legislation

The Problem and the Literature

The *Baker vs. Carr* decision of March 26, 1962 was the beginning of the Supreme Court's role in the reapportionment of state election districts. On June 15 and 22, 1964, the Court handed down decisions concerning apportionment in fifteen states. In one of these decisions, *Reynolds vs. Sims,* the Court went so far as to reject the "federal analogy" by holding that both houses of state legislatures should be based on population and that the state must "make an honest and good faith effort to construct districts, in both houses of its legislature, as nearly of equal population as is practicable."[1] By November, 1966, at least thirty-six states had completed successful reapportionments. Only five of the states had reapportioned without litigation having been brought against them. The remaining states were still in the process of reapportioning. A number of states have had successive reapportionment plans turned down by the courts, and in a few cases court-drawn plans have been placed in effect.[2] The court decisions stimulated, in one way or another, reapportionment in all fifty states by the end of the decade.

Despite the success of Court policy in inducing the reapportionment of state legislatures, it was still unclear whether this massive reapportionment would have the beneficial effects that political reformers had predicted. In regard to subsequent changes in party strength, the *National Civic Review* of February 1967 reported that "nationwide, the side effects of redistricting have balanced each other out, although substantial upheaval has taken place within specific states."[3] In an analysis of the 1966 and 1968 sessions of the Virginia General Assembly, Thomas Wells states the following:

> Quantitatively, reapportionment permitted the urban character of the state to be reflected accurately in the legislature. The number of seats changed was minimal but the effect was much greater in terms of turnover of legislative members. Many of the freshman members, including some who represented rural districts, were disappointed with the lack of opportunity for effective legislative action and impatient with the older leadership which appeared to reject new policy outlooks. The

---

This chapter was coauthored with William Cantrall of Coe College.

most significant internal change in 1966 and 1968 was a switch in philosophy from providing minimal services to a more realistic and progressive attitude of providing for needs.[4]

In the case of Georgia, Hawkins and Welchel report that "gains in total urban membership in Georgia's General Assembly have not been matched by proportionate gains in influence positions."[5] The report indicates that any change in policy due to reapportionment may be held up for some time due to the internal structure of the legislative bodies, and especially because of committee systems where seniority arrangements result in a lack of turnover in key positions.

These early reports do not come close to answering all of the reformers' claims for the beneficial effects of reapportionment. In attacking the reformers' claims, Brady and Edmonds cite Charles Shulls' list of eight major policy areas, which supposedly have been adversely affected by malapportionment, and use them as a basis for testing the reformers' case: "(1) Labor and management; (2) Support of public education; (3) Highway fund distribution; (4) Local government subsidies and support; (5) Social welfare programs; (6) Taxation and public finance; (7) Legislative organization; (8) Imbalance of party strength."[6] In investigating six of these eight areas using several types of analysis, Brady and Edmonds come to the conclusion that apportionment has little, if any, independent effect on public policy output.[7]

In a correlation analysis of the independent effect of malapportionment on policy outcomes in the fields of education, welfare, highways, public regulation, and taxation, Thomas Dye concludes that "for the most part, variations in public policy among the states are *not* associated with malapportionment."[8] It should be noted that most of Dye's dependent variables are dollar figures, some others being the number of laws introduced, school dropout rate, pupil-teacher ratio, and size of school districts. Dye cites the generally low level of the correlations and the fact that controlling for apportionment does not seriously affect the relationships between economic development and policy outcomes to indicate the lack of effect of apportionment.[9]

In an analysis of the above-mentioned studies of apportionment and others, William Bicker points out several deficiencies.[10] One problem has been the widespread use of state expenditure outputs as dependent variables. As Bicker indicates, if the control of state expenditure is largely out of the hands of the state legislatures then state expenditure variables would be the worst possible place to observe the effect of apportionment. Anton's description of the narrow limits of action which state officials have in the determination of expenditures gives some support to this hypothesis.[11] Another problem in earlier studies has been the lack of an adequate test of the dynamic impact of reapportionment over time.[12]

The Research Design

In an attempt to alleviate these deficiencies, the present study investigates the relationship between apportionment and non-expenditure outputs manifested in state statutes. Secondly, in addition to static analysis, this study attempts to measure the impact of a *change* in apportionment on *changes* in policy as contrasted to those previous studies which utilized only a one-point-in-time approach.

Since our general hypothesis is that well apportioned states will tend to have "liberal" or urban-oriented state laws, our dependent variables are usually dichotomous scores—whether or not a state has a certain law or regulation at a specific point in time. For the same reasons as the reformers, we expect the laws in well apportioned states to be more liberal. The fact that urban areas were those which tended to be underrepresented, and the fact that urban residents tended to support liberal laws (which were more relevant to urban problems and the urban way of life) led the reformers to believe that an increase of urban representation because of reapportionment would lead to more liberal legislation. We expect that the change in apportionment patterns brought about by the courts in the last decade will be found to be associated with changes in state policy in a liberal or urban-oriented direction.

An increase in a voting group in a legislative environment should tend to produce more legislation which is in that group's interest due to the group's increased voting power in the legislature. Vote trading and logrolling make it possible for groups who do not constitute a majority in a state to pass legislation favorable to their interests. As Buchanan and Tullock have shown, a vote trading and logrolling situation can lead to more nearly optimal solutions in terms of preferences and intensity of preferences than can the simple majority rule situation.[13] Therefore, we suppose only that the better represented a group is, the more likely it is that the group will find legislation passed that is to its liking. Apportionment is important in influencing state policy to the extent that it correlates with the representation of groups interested in a certain policy. The apportionment of the urban versus rural interests in the states is important both in terms of the historical development of malapportionment and in terms of the frequency of urban-rural splits on state policy issues.

Four different measures of apportionment were chosen as the independent variables. The first is the Schubert-Press apportionment score which is a mathematically sophisticated measure of apportionment. The second measure is the David-Eisenberg index of urban representation, which computes the value of a vote in the largest urban counties of each state. The third measure is the population variance ratio, which is the ratio of the population of the largest legislative district to that of the smallest. If a measure is determined for both houses of a state legislature, one can divide by two to get an average measure.[14]

Each of these three measures has some failings. The population variance ratio only takes into account two districts for each house, the largest and the smallest, and ignores any variation in the other districts. The population variance ratio does have the advantage of being a primary criterion used by the courts.[15] The Schubert-Press apportionment score does not take into account discrimination against important political groups in the state. The David-Eisenberg index does take into account discrimination against one important political group, but there may be some question about its legitimacy when used for interstate comparisons.[16]

Our fourth measure of apportionment is partisan malapportionment, which indicates the extent to which party voting strength in the state is reflected in the makeup of the state legislature. Partisan malapportionment was measured by comparing the party split of state legislative seats to the party split of the statewide votes for congressional candidates.

The dependent variables (state policies) were gathered through sources such as the *Book of the States* and the *Statistical Abstract of the United States* and from the Munger-Shaffer-Webber legal data set and from the Cho-Frederickson apportionment data set.[17] The variables are dichotomous or ordinal measures of state policy in the areas of: (1) racial equality; (2) violence reduction; (3) labor legislation; (4) women's liberation; (5) highway safety and beauty; (6) public employees; (7) parochial school aid; (8) welfare regulation; and (9) divorce reform.

Each of the selected state laws was subjected to a correlation analysis with the measures of apportionment. The correlations controlled for the (1) economic development of the state as measured by median family income, (2) regionalism dichotomized as north and south, and (3) the degree of party competition in the legislature as measured by closeness to a 50 percent split, and (4) partisanship in the legislatures as measured by the percentage of Democrats present. Because of the inherent relationship between partisan malapportionment and the party competition and partisanship variables, only economic development and regionalism were controlled in the partial correlations involving partisan malapportionment. The control variables were selected because of their theoretical relationship to the "liberalness" of a state and because of their widespread use and significance in explaining state legislative policy in previous studies.

The level of significance that is used is the .05 level for a one-tailed test since the direction of the relationship has been predicted. This means that correlations greater than .23 in the direction hypothesized could not have occurred purely by chance-error in more than about 5 samples out of 100, and will therefore be assumed to be real, not chance relations.

The Effects

Malapportionment in the Early 1960s

The results of the analysis for the first time period, 1960-62, are presented in Table 8-1. In the area of racial equality, a definite correlation with apportionment is found, with the apportionment of rural interests as measured by the David-Eisenberg index exhibiting the greatest correlation. David-Eisenberg correlates significantly with public accommodations 1962, open housing, fair employment, and a general measure, even when other influences are controlled. Partisan malapportionment correlates generally in the predicted direction, but is significant only in the case of public accommodations 1960. The Schubert-Press score is significant only in the case of public accommodations 1962. Overall, apportionment seems to have a substantial influence on the racial equality area.

In the case of the violence reduction area, the partial correlation coefficients are not significant, but tend to be in the predicted direction.

The occurrence of minimum wage laws is not quite significantly associated with apportionment, but is in the predicted direction.

Under the area of women's liberation, both the Schubert-Press and the David-Eisenberg indexes are fairly highly correlated with the occurrence of equal pay for women's laws in the states. The correlations for equal employment are in the predicted directions, but are not significant.

In the area of highway safety, David-Eisenberg correlates significantly with more stringent seat belt requirements, compulsory insurance, billboard regulation, and stricter vehicle inspection. Schubert-Press also correlates significantly with compulsory insurance and strict vehicle inspection.

None of the relationships under public employee rights is significant.

In sum, for the first time period, apportionment, and especially the David-Eisenberg index, is significantly related to laws and regulations in the areas of racial equality, women's liberation, and highway safety.[18]

Reapportionment in the Late 1960s

The 1962 measure of the Schubert-Press scores and the David-Eisenberg index were used again in the 1968 analysis in addition to the later period apportionment scores. The earlier scores were used because: (1) it was thought they might show an indication of a time-lag effect of apportionment, and (2) it was expected that the later period apportionment scores would show much less variance than in the early period and hence would be

Table 8-1
Relations Between Apportionment and Legislative Policy (Early 1960s)

Measures of Apportionment, Economics, and Politics / *1960 to 1962 Laws*	Schubert-Press Measure (1962)	David-Eisenberg Measure (1962)	Population Variance Ratio (1962)	Partisan Malapportionment (1962)	*Controlling for Political and Economic Variables* S-P (1962)	D-E (1962)	P.V.R. (1962)	P.M.A. (1962)
A. Racial Equality								
1. Public Accommodations (62)	35*	46*	03	33*	33*	40*	08	17
2. Open Housing	16	31*	02	29*	10	24*	−01	15
3. Fair Employment	06	34*	01	33*	−03	24*	05	15
4. General Racial Equality	21	44*	02	36*	15	35*	05	18
5. Public Accommodation (60)	20	35*	−10	55*	−06	11	01	29*
B. Violence Reduction								
6. Restricted Capital Punishment (62)	−03	27*	15	17	−12	06	22	02
7. Death Penalty Sentencing (60 to 62)	−08	−23*	15	−14	05	−15	02	04
8. Death Penalty Executions (60 to 62)	−24*	−24*	06	−25*	−15	−18	01	−11

C. Labor Legislation								
9. Minimum Wage	26*	29*	−27	−11	21	21	−21	−10
D. Women's Liberation								
10. Equal Pay	42*	56*	−17	34*	39*	48*	−09	10
11. Equal Employment	11	15	10	14	08	10	17	07
E. Highway Safety and Beauty								
12. Stricter Seat Belt Requirements	04	29*	05	−17	−05	25*	06	−17
13. More Extensive Physical Examination	−08	−03	09	19	−11	−02	−07	21
14. Compulsory Insurance	26*	18	10	04	30*	25*	03	01
15. Stricter Billboard Regulation	15	32*	08	−08	11	23*	02	07
16. Higher Minimum Driving Age	−25	02	−25	02	−33	−12	−25	−16
17. Incentives for Drivers' Education	−10	02	−25	−07	−12	−16	−21	−01
18. Stricter Vehicle Inspection	23	28*	−23	−06	24*	27*	−15	−13
F. Public Employee Rights								
19. Allowed to Join Teachers' Union	−01	04	−04	−03	−05	−13	05	−10
20. Allowed to Join Police Union	−08	−10	−10	05	−11	−28	−03	−04
21. Allowed to Join Firemen's Union	−05	−01	−03	10	−06	−16	02	05

* Significant at .05 level for a one-tailed test.

Decimal points are eliminated from the correlations.

less useful measures. Indeed, our 1968 measure of population variance ratio showed much less variance and was even negatively correlated with the 1962 score, meaning those states which scored relatively low in the 1962 scored relatively high in 1968.

The results of the analysis for the second time period, 1966-69, are presented in Table 8-2. In the area of racial equality, the David-Eisenberg (1962) score correlates significantly with public accommodations 1968, open housing, fair employment, the general measure, and the Munger-Shaffer-Weber measure of fair housing. The correlations with anti-miscegenation laws are in the predicted direction but are not significant. David-Eisenberg (1967) correlates significantly with fair employment and in the predicted direction with the rest.

The significant correlations found under violence reduction are those with execution sentencing, executions, and weighted gun control measure. The weighting scheme weights the gun laws in terms of their effectiveness in reducing gun deaths.[19]

Under labor legislation, the David-Eisenberg index correlates negatively (in the predicted direction in this case) with the existence of right to work laws.[20]

In the case of women's liberation, both the Schubert-Press and the David-Eisenberg measures are associated with equal pay laws.

Under highway safety, Schubert-Press is related to stricter vehicle inspection, and David-Eisenberg (1962) is related to compulsory insurance, billboard regulation, and stricter vehicle inspection. David-Eisenberg (1967) is related to higher minimum driving age and incentives for drivers' education.

David-Eisenberg (1962) is also related to aid to parochial schools in the form of transportation. In the area of public aid, apportionment is significantly associated with lenient residence requirements and against a practice of giving clothing or food in lieu of general assistance funds, as is David-Eisenberg (1967). Population variance ratio is associated with eligibility for people able to work. The direction of the relationships with some of the other policies in this area indicates that the influence of apportionment may not be cohesive in the area of welfare regulation.

Apportionment has been found to relate significantly and in the direction predicted with 1968 state policies in the areas of racial equality, violence reduction, labor legislation, women's liberation, highway safety, parochial school aid, and welfare regulation even when other influences are controlled.

Changes in Apportionment Over the 1960s

To investigate the effect of change in apportionment on change in state

Table 8-2
Relations Between Apportionment and Legislative Policy (Late 1960s)

Measures of Apportionment, Economics, and Politics						*Controlling for Political and Economic Variables*				
1966 to 1969 Laws	Schubert-Press measure (1962)	David-Eisenberg measure (1962)	David-Eisenberg (1967)	Population Variance ratio (1965)	Partisan malapportionment (1966)	S-P (1962)	D-E (1962)	D-E (1967)	P.V.R. (1965)	P.M.A. (1966)
A. Racial Equality										
1. Public Accommodations (68)	14	39*	10	−11	04	11	29*	20	−10	07
2. Open Housing	27*	46*	17	−04	03	21	36*	08	03	05
3. Fair Employment	15	38*	25*	−10	−02	−07	23*	25*	−14	00
4. General Racial Equality	21	47	24*	−07	02	16	37*	21	−09	05
5. Public Accommodation (66)	21	35*	28*	−06	00	−02	14	22	−33	−02
6. Fair Housing (66)	31	45*	17	−06	07	24*	38*	08	−05	09
7. Anti-Miscegenation	15	37*	30*	−08	04	13	22	18	02	06
B. Violence Reduction										
8. Restricted Capital Punishment (68)	14	27*	08	04	15	04	19	−01	−02	15
9. Death Penalty (66)	−08	−16	09	06	−15	−02	−12	14	09	−15
10. Death Penalty Sentencing (63 to 66)	−14	−26*	−13	−06	−25*	−04	−21	−05	03	−25*
11. Death Penalty Executions (63 to 66)	−27*	−42*	−12	−03	−01	−21	−41*	−09	−02	−01
12. Purchase Permit Required for Hand Guns	18	21	06	−41	00	17	18	05	−41	01
13. License Required for Concealed Weapon	13	14	−07	−22	10	−09	06	−14	−24	10
14. Gun Control (# of Gun Regulations)	20	26*	02	−10	05	19	22	06	−09	06

* Significant at .05 level for a one-tailed test.

Table 8-2 (continued)

Measures of Apportionment, Economics, and Politics / *1966 to 1969 Laws*	Schubert-Press measure (1962)	David-Eisenberg measure (1962)	David-Eisenberg (1967)	Population Variance ratio (1965)	Partisan malapportionment (1966)	*Controlling for Political and Economic Variables* S-P (1962)	D-E (1962)	D-E (1967)	P.V.R. (1965)	P.M.A. (1966)
15. Gun Control (# of Gun Regulations weighted in Terms of Effectiveness in Reducing Gun Deaths)	24*	33*	12	−17	10	24*	28*	10	−17	11
C. Labor Legislation										
16. Right to Work	−07	−43*	−21	−10	07	−01	−36*	−19	09	06
17. Minimum Wage	28*	27*	20	02	−06	22	15	−15	01	−06
D. Women's Liberation										
18. Equal Pay	36*	41*	22	−08	00	36*	28*	14	−15	00
19. Equal Employment	14	16	16	−30	08	14	04	12	−32	−09
20. Birth Control Dissemination Allowed	13	−07	−05	00	09	15	−01	02	01	10
21. Abortions Allowed to Protect Health	01	−11	−06	−14	−09	01	−09	−08	−17	−10
E. Highway Safety and Beauty										
22. Stricter Seat Belt Requirements	03	19	10	03	15	00	18	10	04	−15
23. More Extensive Physical Examination	01	13	00	−11	−21	04	11	−01	−09	−21
24. Compulsory Insurance	21	26*	−10	−12	05	23	30*	11	−12	05
25. Strict Billboard Regulation	12	42*	07	−12	00	−07	34*	−02	12	−02

26. Higher Minimum Driving Age	−11	15	31*	−01	00	−21	04	26*	−03	00
27. Incentives for Drivers' Education	−18	−10	28*	08	03	−21	−11	30*	08	04
28. Stricter Vehicle Inspection	23	19	00	−24	−05	37	34*	09	−24	−05
F. Public Employee Rights										
29. Allowed to Join Teachers' Union	−04	17	−15	−07	13	−04	09	−27	−09	15
30. Allowed to Join Police Union	−09	−01	−25	03	07	−17	−13	−35	04	08
31. Allowed to Join Firemen's Union	06	15	−20	−38	06	−01	04	−30	−42	07
G. Parochial School Aid										
32. Transportation	24*	48*	29*	06	01	20	41*	24*	05	02
33. Textbooks	−07	06	06	01	03	−07	18	06	−04	01
H. Welfare Regulation (General Assistance)										
34. Allow Assistance to those Physically Able to Work	−23	−42	−24	19	10	−13	−20	−12	23*	14
35. Do Not Require Recipient to Take Public Works Job	07	19	−19	−07	03	−03	02	10	−03	−03
36. Do Not Require Recipient to Take Job Offer in State	22	37*	19	−16	−06	11	17	07	−14	−07
37. Require Recipient to Name the Father of Illegitimate Child	−12	−18	−14	−11	−07	−15	−21	−18	−07	−08
38. Do Not Provide Food, Clothing In Lieu of General Assistance	12	31*	31*	12	−23	10	26*	29*	13	−22
39. Shorter Residence Requirements in General	16	31*	03	16	16	15	29*	02	16	17
40. Shorter Residence Requirements for General Assistance	32*	43*	27*	16	−08	28*	29*	20	22	−08

* Significant at .05 level for a one-tailed test.

policy, it was decided to forego the use of difference scores (i.e., apportionment 1966 minus apportionment 1962 equals change or difference in apportionment), and instead to utilize residualized gain scores as suggested by George W. Bohrnstedt.[21] Following Bohrnstedt's recommendation, a measure of apportionment as of 1966 was correlated with state policy 1968 while partialling out or statistically controlling for the influence of apportionment 1962 and state policy 1962. As Bohrnstedt points out, the use of a difference score often results in the change score being negatively related to the score on the same variable as of time one because the entities who started out low tend to undergo the highest change over time.[22] Since the best predictor of a variable in time two is generally that same variable in time one, it is necessary to partial out the influence of the time one variable when checking for the influence of another variable over time. In the case of the present analysis, since what was to be determined was the influence of change in apportionment on change in state policy, both apportionment and the specific state policy as of time one were partialled out.

The David-Eisenberg measure was used for the change analysis because of its theoretical appropriateness regarding urbanism malapportionment, in addition to its strong showing in the static analysis.

The results of the change analysis are presented in Table 8-3. Change in apportionment is significantly related to change in public accommodations, incentives for driver education, and drug addiction as a ground for divorce. By far the larger number of the non-significant correlations are in the predicted direction. These results appear even more positive when one considers the frequently low number of states which underwent state policy change during this short time period.

Some Conclusions

In regard to the results shown by the various measures of apportionment, it is apparent that the David-Eisenberg measure of urban representation accounts by far the largest number of significant relationships. It is felt that the importance of the David-Eisenberg index is due to the fact that it measures the apportionment of an important political group, namely the residents of urban areas. It will be noted that most, if not all, of the state policies with which David-Eisenberg is correlated are policies which are likely to be of interest to the urban population. The better represented a state's urban population is, the more likely it is that the state will have liberal and urban-oriented state policies. This study suggests that the increased representation of urban areas brought about in many states through reapportionment should lead to more liberal, urban-oriented policies in the states.

Table 8-3
Relations Between Change in Apportionment and Change in Legislative Policy (Over the 1960s)

Change in Policy	*David-Eisenberg Measure*	*Controlling for Political and Economic Variables*
A. Racial Equality		
1. Public Accommodations (62 to 68)	18	25*
2. Open Housing	13	07
3. Fair Employment	17	21
4. General Racial Equality	22	23
5. Public Accommodation (60 to 66)	26*	24*
B. Violence Reduction		
6. Restricted Capital Punishment	08	06
7. Death Penalty	14	16
8. Death Penalty Sentencing	−03	−05
9. Death Penalty Executions	11	10
10. Gun Control (# of Gun Regulations)	−04	−05
C. Labor Legislation		
11. Right to Work	−08	−10
12. Minimum Wage	06	09
D. Women's Liberation		
13. Equal Pay	11	10
14. Equal Employment	12	13
E. Highway Safety and Beauty		
15. Stricter Seat Belt Requirements	−02	−02
16. More Extensive Physical Examination	02	01
17. Compulsory Insurance	−01	−01
18. Strict Billboard Regulation	00	−02
19. Incentives for Drivers' Education	35*	36*
20. Stricter Vehicle Inspection	−10	−05
21. Higher Minimum Driving Age	10	06
F. Public Employee Rights		
22. Allowed to Join Teachers' Union	−04	−11
23. Allowed to Join Police Union	−06	−11
24. Allowed to Join Firemen's Union	−14	−19
G. Grounds for Divorce		
25. Adultery	00	00
26. Cruel and Inhuman Treatment	−03	02
27. Non-Support	00	01
28. Habitual Drunkeness	−02	03
29. Drug Addiction	55*	57*

* Significant at .05 level for a one-tailed test.

The Schubert-Press measure of apportionment has less of an impact on state policies, although it does correlate significantly in a few areas.

The population variance ratio between the largest and the smallest districts in each state seems to be the least useful measure. Because of court-ordered reapportionment, and the use of the population variance ratio by the courts as a criterion for reapportionment, this measure exhibits little variance between the states as of 1966 and, hence, can show little influence on state policy.

Partisan malapportionment, the extent to which the legislature matches the partisan make-up of the state, appears to correlate rather strongly with state policy in the early 1960s until one controls for region and economic development, when the correlations tend to become insignificant. This pattern is due to the fact that southern states tend to have a so much larger percentage of Democratic legislators compared to the Democratic vote for congressional representative that they score as very malapportioned, and they do tend to have few liberal laws.

Significant and independent associations between apportionment and state policy have been shown to exist in the areas of racial equality, labor legislation, women's liberation, highway safety, parochial school aid, violence reduction, and welfare regulations. For these policy areas, the arguments of the reformers can be accepted as having a factual basis. Apportionment, contrary to the implications of earlier studies, does indeed seem to play a significant and independent role in the determination of state policy, at least in non-expenditure state policies as studied here. The findings of this study suggest that one should expect, as a result of reapportionment, a greater orientation of state policy to the interests of those areas previously underrepresented.

Notes

1. *Reynolds v. Sims,* 377 U.S. 533 at 571-84.

2. "Little effect felt in party control: national picture same but states shift," 56 National Civic Review 95 (February 1967).

3. *Ibid.*

4. Thomas Wells, "A Pattern Emerges," 57 National Civic Review 457 (October 1968).

5. Brett W. Hawkins and Cheryl Welchel, "Reapportionment and Urban Representation in Legislative Influence Positions: The Case of Georgia," in Policy Analysis in Political Science 419-422, Sharkansky, ed. (Chicago: Markham, 1970).

6. D. Brady and D. Edmonds, "*The Effects of Malapportionment on Policy Output in the American States,*" The Laboratory for Political Research, Report No. 3, Department of Political Science, University of

IOWA, a paper prepared for the annual meeting of the Midwest Conference of Political Scientists held in April 1966.

7. Brady and Edmonds, p. 3.

8. T. R. Dye, POLITICS, ECONOMICS, AND THE PUBLIC: POLICY OUTCOMES IN THE AMERICAN STATES (Chicago, Rand McNally (1966) 3.273.

9. Dye, pp. 273-277.

10. Bicker, "*The Effects of Malapportionment in the States–A Mistrial,*" in REAPPORTIONMENT IN THE 1970'S 151-201 Polsby, ed. (Berkeley: University of California Press, 1971).

11. Anton, "*Roles and Symbols in the Determination of State Expenditures,*" 209-223 in *Ibid.,* Sharkansky, ed.

12. Although it is useful to know how reapportionment affects legislative responsiveness to public opinion, as in the Cho-Frederickson research (Cho and Frederickson, "*Apportionment and Legislative Responsiveness to Policy Preferences in the American States,*" paper presented at the New York Academy of Sciences Conference on Democratic Representation and Apportionment, November 1972), there are some defects in their approach that are avoided by dealing with how reapportionment affects the passage of controversial state legislation. First, if legislative opinion and public opinion seem to have moved closer together subsequent to reapportionment, they may be due more to a change in public opinion than to a change in reapportionment-produced legislative opinion. Second, public responses to for-or-against survey questions may not be reflected in legislative output because there is no meaningful intensity measure included in the responses. On the other hand, legislative output does reflect intensity feelings through the horse-trading which is part of the legislative process. Third, the positioning of the fifty states on the public opinion variables did not involve a survey made in all fifty states, but rather a projection of what the public opinion positions would be in each state based on the state's demographic characteristics and what is known about people with similar characteristics. Such projections may make public opinion seem to be more similar to legislative opinion than it really is since legislators may also be acting on stereotyped projections.

13. J. Buchanan and G. Tullock, THE CALCULUS OF CONSENT: LOGICAL FOUNDATIONS OF CONSTITUTIONAL DEMOCRACY 119-145 (Ann Arbor, Mich.: U. of Michigan Press, 1962).

14. After this chapter was in press, it was realized that it probably would have been more meaningful to have just measured the degree of the most malapportioned house of a two-house legislature. This is so because the most malapportioned house can (and is probably more likely to) veto the liberal legislation that constitute the dependent variables of this re-

search. Thus, with that more politically meaningful measure, perhaps even stronger correlations between reapportionment and the passage of controversial state legislation would have been found.

15. Baker, "*Implementing One Man, One Vote: Population Equality and Other Evolving Standards in Lower Courts,*" in National Municipal League, CONFLICTS AMONG POSSIBLE CRITERIA FOR RATIONAL DISTRICTING (New York: National Municipal League, 1969).

16. Schubert and Press, "*Measuring Malapportionment,*" 58 AMERICAN POLITICAL SCIENCE REVIEW 302-327 (1964).

17. For further detail on the Munger-Shaffer-Webber data set, see W. Shaffer and R. Webber, "*Political Responsiveness in the American States,*" (paper presented at the 1972 American Political Science Association meeting). The authors gratefully thank Ronald Webber of Indiana University for supplying them with his data and Yong Cho of Akron University and George Frederickson of Indiana University for supplying them with their data.

18. One might object that for every 100 correlations, one would expect at least five to be automatically statistically significant at the .05 level regardless of empirical reality. There are at least three defects in such a view. First, many more than five percent of the correlations in Tables 8-1 and 8-2 are statistically significant at the .05 level. Second, the entities that were used in this study (namely the fifty states) do not represent a sample from some larger universe, but rather the total universe of American states in existence. Thus, all the correlations can be considered representative of the universe, and the problem becomes not which ones are attributable to chance, but rather which ones are strong enough to merit further causal discussion. Third, each correlation has no greater chance of going below the .05 level of chance probability because of the other correlations than a balanced coin has of going heads because prior flips went tails. Neither the coin nor the desk calculator has any memory of the prior flips or correlations; nor has it any goal to achieve evenness in the results.

19. Geisel, Roll, and Wettick, "*The Effectiveness of State and Local Regulation of Handguns: A Statistical Analysis,*" DUKE LAW JOURNAL 650-659 (1969).

20. Other correlations that were hypothesized to be negative because they involved conservative policies consisted of death penalty sentences, death penalty executions, and requiring welfare recipients to name the father of an illegitimate child.

21. Bohrnstedt, "*Observations on the Measurement of Change,*" in SOCIOLOGICAL METHODOLOGY 1969 113-133 Borgatta, ed. (San Francisco: Jossey-Bass, 1969).

22. *Ibid.*, 117. As an example, the correlation between our 1962 measure of population variance ratio and a difference score measure of change in population variance ration was –.99. This almost perfect inverse relationship is due to the movement of all states regardless how low they were on apportionment in the early 1960s to nearly perfect reapportionment in the late 1960s as measured by the somewhat crude population variance ratio.

9 Computers and the Law and Politics of Redistricting

The purpose of this chapter is to describe the theory and practice associated with bipartisan constitutional computer-aided redistricting.

The Theory

The theory behind bipartisan constitutional computer-aided redistricting essentially consists of three normative criteria which any systematic legislative redistricting scheme probably ought to seek to achieve. First, the redistricting system ought to be feasible so that it keeps computer time and other costs down to a minimum. Second, the system ought to provide legislative districts that will be approximately equal in population per representative so as to satisfy the Supreme Court's equality criterion, and the districts should be so shaped as to satisfy other legal requirements that relate to contiguity. Third, the system should consider the impact of the resulting districting on incumbents and on party balance so as to minimize the unhappiness which redistricting might otherwise produce for political leaders and for diverse political viewpoints.

These three criteria are summarized in the phrase "bipartisan constitutional computer-aided redistricting." The adjective "computer-aided" refers to computer feasibility. It also emphasizes that the computer aids in redistricting like an elaborate desk calculator and does not do the redistricting itself. The adjective "constitutional" refers to the federal and state legal requirements with regard to equality and contiguity. The adjective "bipartisan" refers to promoting mutual party interests rather than ignoring the partisan impact that all redistricting inevitably has.[1]

Computers can usefully supplement traditional hand methods of redistricting. This is so because the computer when adequately instructed has great accuracy, speed, versatility to satisfy many criteria simultaneously including legal and political criteria, ability to break deadlocks by facilitat-

Thanks are owed to Joseph Vitale of the Yale Computer Center for his help in developing the recent changes in the computer program on which this chapter is based. This chapter represents a substantially revised version of a paper presented at the 1971 Spring Joint Computer Conference sponsored by the American Federation of Information Societies. This research is one of a series of policy science studies on measuring and achieving effects of alternative legal policies partly financed by the National Science Foundation grant GS-2875, but NSF is not responsible for results.

ing political compromises, ability to minimize disruption to incumbents, inexpensiveness relative to the quality of the results, and flexibility to allow for local variations and special considerations. The key questions in this chapter relate to what criteria the computer instructions should seek to satisfy and to what extent various redistricting programs have addressed themselves to those criteria.

Satisfying Computer Feasibility

There are two general aspects of computer feasibility to be met. One relates to the internal logic of the computer program so that it will be capable of satisfying the legal and political goals without using unrealistic or excessive amounts of time or money. The other aspect relates to making the computer input and output as economical and as convenient to handle as possible.

Internal Logic. A logical approach to computer-aided redistricting if one had unlimited computer time and funds available might be to establish an overall criterion of goodness; have the computer generate every possible combination of precincts or census tracts into a given number of districts in the area to be redistricted; and then apply the optimizing criterion to each of the districting patterns in order to determine which districting pattern maximizes the criterion.

Assuming agreement could be obtained among lawyers and politicians on a composite optimizing criterion, such an approach would lack computer feasibility. With any realistic number of precincts or census tracts larger than forty, the number of different districting patterns into which they could be made quickly becomes astronomical and unwieldy.[2]

A simple alternative to trying all possible combinations is to start with the prevailing districting pattern; move each precinct or census tract from the district that it is in into every other district; each time a move is made, check to see if the districting has been improved in light of the optimizing criterion; and each time an improvement is made, use that districting pattern as the one to be improved upon until no further improvements can be made.[3]

This method can avoid making a high percentage of the moves that would be made in the all-combinations method by inserting into the computer program certain prerequisites that must be met before a move can even be checked against the optimizing criterion. For example, no move of a precinct from its present district to another district will be made if the move will cause either the district *to* which the precinct is moved or the district *from* which the precinct is moved to become noncontiguous—such that one could not go from any point in the district to any other point in the district without leaving the district. Likewise, no precinct will be moved from its present district if it is the only precinct or unit within the present district thereby destroying the district and decreasing the number of districts. In addition, the district from which a precinct is moved must be different from the district to which the precinct is moved.

The above system of moving each precinct from its present district to every other district in order to obtain successive improvements can also be supplemented by simultaneously trading a precinct from one district for a precinct from another district. Every pair of precincts gets an opportunity to be involved in such a trade provided the above mentioned prerequisites with regard to contiguity, multiple-precinct districts, and diverse districts are met. When a trade is attempted, the resulting redistricting combination is checked against the legal and political optimizing criterion to see if an improvement has been made, just as in the single precinct moving approach.[4]

Alternatives to the moving-and-trading approach other than the all-combinational approach include such techniques as the pie-slices approach of Myron Hale,[5] the diminishing-halves approach of Edward Forrest,[6] and the transportation-warehousing algorithm of Weaver and Hess.[7] A comparative analysis by Michael Strumwasser emphasizing the computer feasibility aspects of these alternative approaches concluded: "The generalized swapping alogorithms (moving-and-trading), following closely the human approach to such a problem, offer a better solution than either geometric allocation (the pie-slices and diminishing-halves approach) or mathematical programming (the transportation algorithm). While the latter two approaches are aesthetically satisfying, the simplifying assumptions are violated in practice."[8]

Input and Output. Computer input for meaningful redistricting requires population data in order to provide equality, data on which units touch each other in order to provide contiguity, and data on political party and possibly racial information in order to facilitate political compromises. The population data can be obtained via Census Bureau tapes, microfilms, or published reports or via inexpensive census processing firms like DUALabs of Arlington, Virginia.[9] Economic feasibility is greatly increased if larger and fewer units can be used for redistricting. To achieve this, an auxiliary program can determine whether a larger unit needs to be broken into smaller units if: in itself it is excessively larger than an ideal district; or it is smaller than an ideal district, but when combined with any adjacent unit, the combination will be excessively larger.

The list showing which units touch each other can be prepared by hand and then checked for accuracy by determining: whether every touching relation is reciprocal such that when unit A is listed as touching unit B, then unit B is also listed as touching unit A; and whether all unit identification numbers that are said to be touched are actually numbers of units in the area to be redistricted. Instead of hand preparation of these touchlists, one can use a digitizer like the ones manufactured by the Calma Company of Sunnyvale, California, which can be rented by the hour at various service bureaus. The user moves an electronic pointer over the lines on the prevailing districting map after keypunching the identification number of the unit being traced. This process causes the X and Y coordinates (or latitudes and longitudes) of points along the lines to be fed into a mini-computer. The computer can then list or punch out which units touch each other by determining which units share a common line.

To obtain the political party data for each unit may involve going to records in the secretary of state's office, county courthouses, or political party files. The party vote for candidates for relatively unknown offices (such as the Board of Trustees of the University of Illinois) can also be used as a measure of party affiliation for each unit. This work may require aggregating or translating party data from precinct units into census tracts or other census units. A digitizer combined with a keypunch and mini-computer as described above can also aid in this aggregating and translating process.

Because the Hess-Weaver and other approaches generally begin from many starting points (rather than from the existing districting pattern), these approaches can produce many equally valid plans which adds a further feasibility complication (as well as possibly unnecessary deviation from the existing pattern). With the moving-and-trading approach, however, one can in effect randomize the starting data without changing the starting map by simply shuffling the input cards, since this will create a new order of moves and trades. Computer running time and the quality of the results are further improved if the initial districting pattern has high population equality among the districts.

Computer *output* can be verbal so as to indicate a district number for each precinct number and population equality and political information for each district. As a supplement, the computer output can also be in the graphic form of a plotted map using equipment like that manufactured by the Tektronix Corporation of Beaverton, Oregon or unit numbers displayed on a cathode ray tube on which there is a map overlay.[10] Verbal output can be supplemented with a map when the new output represents an improvement in equality or political representation over the old output. If the computer just gives verbal output, one can draw districts by hand on a map, which is made easier if the computer lists the perimeter units for each district.

Both the verbal and map output can be presented to the user as part of a man-machine interaction system whereby the user can make changes in the output or input and get almost instant feedback as to the population or party effects of his changes. For example, after the computer has arrived at one or more optimal redistricting patterns in light of the quantitative criteria in the computer program, the user can sit at a console terminal and try to improve upon the optimum by telling the computer to move one or more units from the districts they are in to certain other districts.[11] If the user is not able to make an improvement, he will be especially pleased with the computer's output. If he is able to do so, this will reflect personalized criteria that were not included in the quantitative program. Postoptimizing improvements may also be based on trading a few units from one district for a few units from another district since the computer program may only allow for one-for-zero moves or one-for-one-trades.

In addition to using the man-machine interaction system for making moves and trades and obtaining quick feedback, the user can use the system to make changes in the input data or criteria such as changing the number of districts, the maximum deviation from equality allowable, the percentage which is considered a safe margin of victory for a political party or black civil rights group to seek to achieve, or changing which input districts will be considered not subject to change. These kinds of changes can be experimented with until a redistricting plan is generated that has the characteristics which most satisfy what the user wants to achieve.[12]

Satisfying the Legal Requirements

The legal requirements which any computer-aided redistricting scheme should satisfy consist of equal population per district and generally contiguity within each of the districts.

Equal Population. Equality of population can be measured in a variety of ways. The crudest way, although sometimes quite dramatic, is to present the ratio between the most populous single-member district and the least populous single-member district in the area being redistricted. This simple approach obviously ignores all the information available about the population of the non-extreme districts. At the most complex end of a continuum of equality, measures would be such esoteric figures as the geometric mean[13] or the inverse coefficient of variation.[14] These complex measures have no legal standing in that they have never been cited as appropriate for measuring equality in a published court decision or a statute.[15]

The measure of equality most favorably cited by the Supreme Court is division of the total population of the state or area to be districted by the number of districts or seats in the legislature in order to determine the ideal population per district or per representative; and then determination of the percentage by which the population of each actual district deviates from this ideal population.[16]

If the percentage deviation from ideal is more than a few percentage points, then the districting probably represents a violation of the equal protection clause of the Constitution and the democratic notion of one man, one vote. Thus in the recent Supreme Court case dealing with the equality standard, Missouri's congressional districting was declared unconstitutional even though no district deviated from the ideal by more than 3.13 percent. Justice Brennan delivering the opinion of the Court stated that the "standard requires that the State make a good-faith effort to achieve precise mathematical equality."[17]

It should be noted that no matter how low the average deviation is; if there is even one district that has a substantial percentage deviation from the ideal, the whole districting will probably be held unconstitutional. This must be recognized in writing the optimizing criterion even though mathematicians find it more aesthetic to minimize or maximize averages.[18]

In states where there are multi-member districts each involving different numbers of representatives, the courts talk in terms of population per representative rather than population per district. Someday the courts may recognize that one voter who is a member of the majority interest group in a district with two representatives and 2,000 people has more political power than one voter in a district with one representative and 1,000 people, since the first voter can determine who two representatives will be.[19] Where multi-member districts are allowed, the computer moving system requires that each unit carry a fractional seat with it as it moves from district to district, although the number of seats per district is always rounded to whole numbers.

Contiguity. Contiguity of districts is the second legal requirement. It is usually stated as a requirement in state constitutions or state statutes, or prevails as a matter of custom with minor exceptions, although it is not a United States Supreme Court requirement. A district is contiguous if one can go from any point in the district to any other point without leaving the district. For two intra-district units to touch or be contiguous they must share part of a common line no matter how small, not merely a common point. Legal boundaries of land areas adjacent to bodies of water normally extend over a portion of the water at least for the purpose of court and police jurisdiction if not for the purpose of ownership, and these extended boundaries should generally be used in determining contiguity, not the shoreline.

Contiguity is sought for many purposes including the purpose of simplifying redistricting by eliminating many alternative combinations of precincts, enabling legislators to have easier access to their constituents, decreasing partisan gerrymandering, encouraging people of similar interests to be together in the same district, and making districting patterns more understandable and more aesthetically appealing.

A district can be contiguous and not compact, and likewise it can be compact and not contiguous. Compactness can either mean being geographically like a circle or a square,[20] or it can mean having its people clustered close together regardless of the shape of the perimeter of the district.[21] Compactness is not a legal requirement. In fact the Supreme Court recently said, "A State's preference for pleasingly shaped districts can hardly justify population variances."[22] Likewise the Court seemed to disparage the value of population compactness as well as geographical compactness by saying, "to accept population variances, large or small, in order to create districts with specific interest orientations is antithetical to the basic premise of the constitutional command to provide equal representation for equal numbers of people."[23]

In spite of the importance the Supreme Court has given to equality and the non-importance it has given to compactness, and in spite of the importance the states have given to contiguity, a number of redistricting programs heavily emphasize compactness at the expense of equality and do not guarantee contiguity.[24]

Satisfying the Political Requirements

It can be demonstrated that if the precincts, census tracts, or other building blocks out of which districts are made are small enough, then virtually perfect equality can be provided while still allowing room for taking political interests into consideration. Given this leeway, it seems reasonable to expect the politicians to want computer-aided redistricting to minimize disruption to incumbents, and to facilitate political compromises.

The Options. Disruption to incumbents can be legally minimized by the following techniques: the prevailing districting plan can be used as a starting point rather than starting from an undistricted map of the state; districts that already come sufficiently close to the ideal population can be removed from the redistricting; one can select building blocks from which districts are built with the knowledge that these units will not be broken into smaller pieces; no move will be consummated if the new districting is merely equal in value to the previous one, rather than an improvement as measured by the optimizing criterion; and redistricting can be done to satisfy the equality requirement and then district lines can be drawn so as to make the number of districts dominated by the Democrats or Republicans as equal as possible to the number before the redistricting.[25]

Political compromises can be facilitated in various ways if the computer redistricting scheme inputs information on the number of Democrats and Republicans in each precinct or building block. For example, the computer can quickly show the Democrats and Republicans what is the maximum number of districts which they could each dominate given the Court's equality requirements and the partisan information. From these outermost positions, both sides can work in toward a compromise. Once the equality requirement has been met, the computer simply shifts from an equality optimizing criterion to a Democratic or a Republican optimizing criterion in order to reveal those outermost positions.[26]

Some compromises might require that districts in certain sections of the state be drawn to favor the Republicans up to a specified point and that districts in other sections be drawn to favor the Democrats up to a point while providing court-required equality. The computer can aid in this kind of politically-oriented redistricting, but only if it has been programmed to provide for such a political option.

An option can also be exercised within the computer program to make the percentage of districts dominated by the Democrats (or Republicans) as close as possible to the percentage of Democrats (or Republicans) in the state. Doing so provides a kind of proportional representation without the complicated voting procedures which are usually associated with proportional representation.[27] This is probably the fairest of the political options. Proportional representation can be similarly provided for minority ethnic groups like blacks or Spanish-speaking Americans.

An additional option can easily be added to the program whereby the computer seeks to maximize the number of districts in which neither the Democrats nor the Republicans have more than about 51 percent of the two-party vote. This would please political scientists who feel competitive districts make for more responsible representatives, but might displease politicians who prefer greater margins of safety.

Finally, the computer also facilitates political compromises by quickly providing information on the partisan composition of the districts in various tentative redistricting plans. The man-machine interaction described above is especially helpful in providing quick feedback on the effects of using different options, criteria, and input data.

Legality and Programming Aspects. In the most recent relevant Supreme Court decision relating to political considerations, the Court said, "Problems created by partisan politics cannot justify an apportionment which does not otherwise pass constitutional muster."[28] The implication is that if the reapportionment otherwise passes constitutional muster, then problems created by partisan politics and legislative interplay can be legitimately considered.

In spite of the Supreme Court's refusal to declare political line drawing unconstitutional where population equality is provided,[29] the Court may someday say that the equal protection clause is prima facie violated if the districting plan gives the minority party a substantially lower percentage of the districts than the percentage of minority party members in the state. This would be the case, for example, if the minority party constitutes 40 percent of the people in the state, but the lines are drawn so that the minority party dominates only 15 percent of the districts.

William Below and Michael Strumwasser have prepared computer programs that do seek to minimize disruption to incumbents and facilitate political compromises.[30] Other programs, however, have lacked any attempt to consider their partisan effects although some have been labeled nonpartisan. Labeling a redistricting program nonpartisan does not make it nonpartisan if the results change the partisan balance of power as they are likely to do. The nonpartisan label has merely meant that the computer program so labeled ignores the partisan effects of its work, and thus cannot facilitate political compromises or minimize political disruption.[31] Robert Dixon in his comparative analysis of alternative computer approaches particularly emphasizes the importance of political sophistication and understanding the political impact of computer-aided redistricting.[32]

The Practice

A computer program that was written in 1964 to satisfy the requirements of computer feasibility, constitutionality, and bipartisanship has thus far had some limited applications which might be worth reporting. Further applications are anticipated after the 1971 state legislatures decide on the procedures they intend to follow in redistricting the fifty states for congressional and state legislative purposes.

1960s Bipartisan Computer Redistricting

The first application of the bipartisan constitutional program consisted of experimental debugging runs made to convert ninety downstate Illinois counties from twenty-one districts down to eighteen districts.[33] Using counties, rather than precincts or census tracts, as the building blocks out of which to make districts greatly limited the flexibility to maneuver. Under current constitutional standards, units smaller than counties would be a court-ordered requirement.[34] Nevertheless, the redistricting was able to convert the original twenty-one districts, in which eight violated the Illinois constitutional requirement of no more than twenty percent deviation, into eighteen contiguous districts in which none violated the Illinois constitutional requirement. This conversion took only eighty-one seconds of computer running time.

After meeting the Illinois constitutional requirement, the program generated various politically-oriented districting patterns. They ranged from a pattern in which the Democrats obtained a majority in only twenty-two percent of the eighteen districts, up to a pattern in which the Democrats obtained a majority in thirty-nine percent of the districts. This ability to provide alternative political patterns could have facilitated the Republicans making some concessions in the downstate area in return for related concessions by the Democrats in the Chicago area. Instead both parties moved so slowly trying to develop political compromises that the constitutional deadline passed and an at-large election had to be held to choose the state legislature.

The next application of the bipartisan constitutional program was by William Below working for the California Assembly Committee on Elections and Apportionment in 1965.[35] According to his report, "The program was applied to Assembly districts in Los Angeles, Orange, San Francisco, and Santa Clara counties. In San Francisco, the use of the program served only to verify that a particular set of goals was not obtainable. In each of the other counties, plans were produced which the committee staff considered good enough to submit to committee members and the affected incumbents. Three out of the thirty-one districts in Los Angeles (those which underwent the greatest change), were included in the assembly bill almost exactly as the program produced them. The plans for Orange and Santa Clara Counties were slightly changed on the advice of the incumbents."[36]

Below also reports that "members of the committee staff with no data processing experience became proficient at specifying the initial plans, weights, and desired proportions necessary to use the program."[37] Below's version of the program added increased flexibility by allowing different political goals for each district rather than just having an overall political goal for the area to be redistricted, interspersing moving and trading rather than doing all the trading after completing all the moving, developing techniques for translating census areas into political areas, simplifying the information inputed to preserve contiguity, and translating the program into the Fortran programming language.

The third application of the bipartisan constitutional program was by C-E-I-R, Inc., for the Illinois Republican Party in 1965. Norman Larsen, who handled the application for C-E-I-R, reported that the politicians were more interested in being quickly and accurately provided with useful information on the characteristics of the districts in a variety of tentative redistricting plans than they were in having the computer produce an optimum output.[38] The Republican Party was the minority party in the

Illinois legislature at that time, and its districting patterns were less influential on the final result than the Democratic districting patterns. Nevertheless, the Republican Party leaders did buy $31,000 of computer redistricting consulting services, and they appeared to be satisfied with what they obtained.

Like Below in California, Larsen in Illinois made various changes in the program to take into consideration the fact that thousands of townships and other units were used to create the districts rather than a mere 90 counties as in the original example. The contiguity checks in particular were streamlined. Continuous intermediate output was generated to allow a monitoring of convergence toward an optimum. Time-saving conditions were also introduced to eliminate various kinds of moves that were not likely to lead to an improvement.

1970s Redistricting Thus Far

Although the 1970s redistricting has just begun, there are already a number of applications of the bipartisan constitutional computer-aided redistricting approach described above. One interesting application is the use of the approach by the Lawyer's Committee on Civil Rights under Law in order to prepare districting plans for various states (such as Mississippi and Virginia) so as to provide proportional representation for blacks which they might otherwise not receive.[39]

The Mississippi Senate, for example, prepared a plan which tended to group black-dominated counties with white-dominated counties so as to provide a disproportionate number of districts which would be white-dominated. The districts so created were assigned a number of representatives equal to the nearest whole number that corresponds to the ratio between the district's population and the ideal population of 40,000 (which was determined by dividing the state's population by fifty-five Senate seats). Although this multi-member system provided good population equality across districts, the computer approach was able to provide even better equality and more black representation. This was so even when counties were used as units, but especially when units smaller than counties were used within the larger counties.[40]

Safe black districts having close to the ideal population were in effect removed from the redistricting by indicating that their units only touched a nonexisting unit with identification number 0. Safe black districts were created by finding units that have a black majority and adding them to adjacent units until the ideal district population was reached with a safe black majority. The more such unchangeable districts are created, however, the less flexibility there is in providing equal population among the remaining districts across the state. A safe black district may sometimes require a black population percentage over sixty percent in view of the fact that blacks are less likely than whites to be over 18 and eligible to register, to register if eligible, to vote if registered, and to vote their interests out of fear that the ballot may not be secret or that a black representative will be ineffective.[41]

Armed with computer-generated plans, the Lawyers Committee has for the time being successfully challenged the Mississippi redistricting, in the federal district courts under the equal protection clause of the Constitution,[42] and the Virginia redistricting in the Department of Justice's approval procedures under the 1965 Voting Rights Act.[43]

Another recent interesting application of bipartisan redistricting relates to redrawing the federal judicial circuits. The Federal Judicial Center has been using the computer approach described above mainly to equalize the workloads and the number of trial judges among the circuits. The Center has been experimenting with different numbers of circuits, with or without splitting states, and with or without seeking compactness. The circuit court lines could also be drawn so as to better equalize the political ideology among the circuits. This can be done by having the computer try to group the states so the percentage of Johnson or Humphrey voters relative to Goldwater or Nixon voters is approximately equal in all circuits. Such inter-circuit political homogeneity would aid in promoting uniformity in circuit court decisions, thereby decreasing inter-circuit conflict and the burden on the Supreme Court of resolving such conflict.[44]

As an alternative way of equalizing the political ideology among the federal circuit courts, one could try to draw the lines so as to give each circuit the same percentage or average of conservative or liberal appellate judges residing in the circuit. The conservatism of each appellate judge could be meaningfully approximated by determining the percentage of times he voted for the prosecution in criminal cases and the percentage of times he voted for the insurance company or other defendant in personal injury cases for a given recent year. Changing which judges sit on which circuit courts will clearly influence the political orientation of those circuits. Conservatives would probably like to see more conservative circuits, and liberals would like to see more liberal ones. The logical compromise is to try to make all the circuits like the average circuit on conservatism. Thus far, however, the Federal Judicial Center has refused to consider the political- or decisional-direction implications of circuit court redistricting in the computer runs that have been made.

Other applications of the bipartisan computer redistricting approach include the redistricting of the Nottingham area of England where Sherwood Forest is located.[45] The program is being used by George Leyland Associates of Boston on behalf of the Republican Party in such states as

Illinois and New Mexico. It is also being used by William Below (now of American Computer Resources of Los Angeles) on behalf of members of the Democratic Party in California. Moshman Associates of Washington, D.C., and the National Corporation for Policy Research and Operation of New York City are making the approach available on a nationwide bipartisan basis.

The experience received in applying the program for Republicans, Democrats, legislatures, courts, blacks, Englishmen, and others has shown that the bipartisan constitutional computer-aided redistricting approach is feasible from the three viewpoints of computer technology, constitutional law, and political realism. The approach would clearly be less meaningful if it failed to satisfy fully these three essential criteria. It is anticipated that other versions of this basic program and approach will be developed and applied to the 1970s redistricting which is now getting underway across the country.

Notes

1. A computer program that seeks to achieve all three of these criteria and their sub-criteria simultaneously is described in Nagel, "*Simplified Bipartisan Computer Redistricting,*" STANFORD LAW REVIEW, pp. 863-899, 7 (1965); and S. Nagel, THE LEGAL PROCESS FROM A BEHAVIORAL PERSPECTIVE (Homewood, Ill.: Dorsey, 1959, 321-359.

2. R. S. Garfinkel and G. L. Nemhauser, "*Optimal Political Districting by Implicit Enumeration Techniques*." 16 MANAGEMENT SCIENCE, pp. 495-508 (1970).

3. The essence of this precinct moving system was first developed by Kaiser, "*An Objective Method for Establishing Legislative Districts*," 10, MIDWEST JOURNAL OF POLITICAL SCIENCE, pp. 200-213 (1966).

4. For a system that adds multiple-unit trades to the basic moving and trading system, see C. R. Cope, REGIONALIZATION PROJECT: FINAL REPORT TO CAMBRIDGE PROJECT ON COMPUTER REDISTRICTING WORK (Cambridge, Mass.: M.I.T. Dept. of Urban Studies and Planning, 1971).

5. M. Hale, REPRESENTATION AND REAPPORTIONMENT (Columbus, Ohio: Political Science Dept., Ohio State University, 1965). See also M. Hale, "*Computer Methods of Districting*" in REAPPORTIONING LEGISLATURES, Howard Hamilton (ed.), (Columbus, Ohio: Chas. Merrill, 1966).

6. Edward Forrest, "*Apportionment by Computer*," 4, AMERICAN BEHAVIORAL SCIENTIST, (1964) pp. 23, 35.

7. Weaver and Hess, "*A Procedure for Nonpartisan Districting: Development of Computer Techniques*," 72, YALE LAW JOURNAL, (1963). A

revised version of their approach is described in CROND, Inc., REDIST: PROGRAM DESCRIPTION AND USER MANUAL (New York: National Municipal League, 1967). Hess and Weaver have recently added a moving and trading option to their program.

8. Strumwasser, "*A Quantitative Analysis of Political Redistricting*" (master's thesis) (UCLA School of Business Administration, 1970). See also RISE, Inc., PROPOSAL FOR THE REAPPORTIONMENT OF THE CALIFORNIA ASSEMBLY (March, 1970) available from 417 South Hill Street, Los Angeles. Other studies have endorsed the goal of a "computer approach that more closely approximates the political reality of districting," Castellan, "*Political Apportionment by Computer*," 1 BROWN UNIVERSITY COMPUTING REVIEW, pp. 5, 7, (1967); or the goal to "simulate closely the actual decision making process," C. M. Cope, "Municipal Boundaries in Nottingham 1937-1967" (Bachelors dissertation, Cambridge University, 1968), p. 61.

9. Instead of inputing total population figures, one can use narrower measures such as voting age population or registered voters provided doing so "produces a distribution of legislators not substantially different from that which would have resulted from the use of a [total] population basis." *Ely v. Klahr*, 91 S.Ct. 1803 (1971). See also R. Dixon, DEMOCRATIC REPRESENTATION: REAPPORTIONMENT IN LAW AND POLITICS (New York: Oxford U. Press, 1968), pp. 501-503.

10. Forrest, "Electorate Reapportionment Mapping," 7, DATA PROCESSING MAGAZINE, (July, 1967), pp. 52-54, and Davis *et al*. "*Legislative Districting by Computer*," JURIMETRICS JOURNAL (1968), pp. 77-98.

11. See Stevens, "*On the Screen: Computer Aided Districting*," in CONFLICTS AMONG POSSIBLE CRITERIA FOR RATIONAL DISTRICTING (New York: National Municipal League, 1969), pp. 40-49; and Stevens, "*A Report on the Feasibility of GEODATA: A Man-Machine System for Political Districting*" (Cambridge, Mass.: M.I.T. Center for International Studies, 1968).

12. An interaction system available for this kind of parameter and data editing is IBM, CONTROL PROGRAM-67/CAMBRIDGE MONITOR SYSTEM USER'S GUIDE (1970).

13. Kaiser, "*A Measure of the Population Quality of Legislative Apportionment*," 62, AMERICAN POLITICAL SCIENCE REVIEW (1968), pp. 208-215.

14. Schubert and Press, "*Measuring Malapportionment*," 57 AMERICAN POLITICAL SCIENCE REVIEW (1964), pp. 302-327.

15. Baker, "*Implementing One Man, One Vote: Population Equality and Other Evolving Standards in Lower Courts*," in CONFLICTS AMONG POSSIBLE CRITERIA FOR RATIONAL DISTRICTING (New York: National Munici-

pal League, 1969), pp. 24-29, 32. Baker content-analyzed 232 redistricting case opinions.

16. For example, *Kirkpatrick v. Preisler*, 394 U.S. 526, 529 (1969).

17. *Kirkpatrick v. Preisler*, 394 U.S. 526, 530 (1969). Although *Kirkpatrick* dealt with congressional districting, its standards would probably equally apply to *state* legislative districting. In fact the equal protection clause which applies to state districts, more explicitly requires equality than Article I of the Constitution which applies to congressional districts. In *county* board redistricting, the Supreme Court, however, has indicated it will allow deviations at least as high as twelve percent if necessary to preserve town lines, *Abate v. Mundt*, 91 S.Ct. 1904 (1971).

18. The programs developed by Below and Kaiser only optimize averages rather than force outliers under a maximum cutoff. Below, "*The Computer as an Aid to Legislative Reapportionment*" in AN ALI-ABA COURSE OF STUDY ON COMPUTERS IN REDISTRICTING (Philadelphia: American Law Institute, 1965); and Kaiser, op. cit.

19. Banzhaf III, "*Weighted Voting Doesn't Work: A Mathematical Analysis*," RUTGERS LAW REVIEW, 19 (1965), pp. 317-343; and Banzhaf III, "*Multi-member Electoral Districts–Do They Violate the 'One Man, One Vote' Principle,*" 75 YALE LAW JOURNAL, (1966), 1309-1338. Multi-member districts also facilitate denying representation to minority ethnic groups in such districts. The recent case of *Whitcomb v. Chavis*, 91 S.Ct. 1858 (1971), however, continued to hold that merely having multi-member districts is not unconstitutional unless the challenger can show a pattern indicating purposeful discrimination against minority groups.

20. Reock, "*Measuring Compactness as a Requirement of Legislative Apportionment*," 5 MIDWEST JOURNAL OF POLITICAL SCIENCE, (1961), pp. 70-74.

21. Weaver and Hess, op. cit.

22. *Kirkpatrick v. Preisler*, 394 U.S. 526, 536 (1969).

23. *Ibid.*, at page 533.

24. Weaver and Hess, *Op. Cit.* Forrest, *op. cit.* The Kaiser program also lacks a guarantee of contiguity, Kaiser, "*An Objective Method*," pp. 200-213. By emphasizing compactness, the Hess-Weaver program usually achieves contiguity, but not always. The most recent version of their program has an option to signal noncontiguity, but not to force or guarantee contiguity.

25. A redistricting option can also be added to insure that all districts or a maximum number of districts will contain the residence of only one incumbent legislator as was done in the Arizona computer redistricting described in *Ely v. Klahr*, 91 S.Ct. 1803 (1971).

26. For a discussion of the computer programming that is involved in both the equally optimizing criterion and the various political optimizing criteria, see S. Nagel, *op. cit.*

27. James Weaver impliedly defines "nonpartisan" as providing proportional representation by stating, "A procedure blind to politics should provide a random opportunity for changes in the party in power, hopefully approximating the partisan ratio in the area." Weaver, FAIR AND EQUAL DISTRICTS: A HOW-TO-DO-IT MANUAL ON COMPUTER USE, (New York: National Municipal League, 1970), 3. The Weaver-Hess program, however, makes no attempt to provide proportional representation (that is, to approximate the partisan ratio) other than by blind hope. It is a nonpartisan process to flip a coin to determine which party will get all the seats in a state legislature, but the results will clearly disproportionately favor the winning party and thus be partisan. The latest version of the Hess-Weaver program will indicate how many estimated Democrats and Republicans are in each district, but will not seek to provide proportional party representation.

28. *Kirkpatrick v. Preisler*, 394 U.S. 526, 533 (1969).

29. *WMCA v. Lomenzo*, 382 U.S. 4 (1965); and Dixon, *op. cit.* pp. 475-99.

30. Below, *op. cit.* Strumwasser, *op. cit.* Both of these programs are based on the Nagel program, *op. cit.*

31. This is true of the programs of Weaver-Hess, *op. cit.*; Forrest, *op. cit.*; Hale, *op. cit.*; and Kaiser, "*An Objective Method.*" It is also true of the more obscure programs of Harris, "*A Scientific Method of Districting,*" BEHAVIORAL SCIENCE, 9 (1964), pp. 219-225; and Thoreson and Liittschwager, "*Computers in Behavioral Science: Legislative Districting by Computer Simulation,*" BEHAVIORAL SCIENCE, 12 (1967), pp. 237-247.

32. Dixon, *op. cit.*, pp. 526-35.

33. See Nagel, *op. cit.*

34. In *Kirkpatrick v. Preisler*, the Court said "we do not find legally acceptable the argument that variances are justified if they necessarily result from a State's attempt to avoid fragmenting poljtical subdivisions by drawing congressional district lines along existing county, municipal, or other political subdivision boundaries." 394 U.S. 526, 533 (1969). But see the *Abate* case mentioned in note 17.

35. Below, *op. cit.* Information on the California application also comes from 1965 correspondence between William Below and this writer.

36. *Ibid.*, p. 7.

37. *Ibid.*

38. In a report from Norman Larsen to Jack Moshman of C-E-I-R, Inc. dated November 1, 1965.

39. Providing proportional representation to blacks might affect proportional representation of Democrats. The criterion being maximized can, however, incorporate both kinds of proportional representation by seeking to minimize the product of the deviation from the desired percentage of blacks and the deviation from the desired percentage of Democrats. An exponent of N can be attached to the deviation that is considered N times as important to consider as the other deviation.

40. For further detail on the Mississippi computer redistricting, see C. Ross Cope, *op. cit.*, note 4.

41. To protect the interest of minorities in safe districts, legislation could provide special minority representation devices such as cumulative voting (see Dixon, *op. cit.*, pp. 520-27) or legislation could make it easier to have contested elections and primaries where minorities could represent an important swing bloc.

42. *Connor v. Johnson*, Civil Action 3830 (decided by United States District Court for the Southern District of Mississippi, May 18, 1971). A stay was granted by the United States Supreme Court to the Lawyers Committee in order to develop single-member districts for Hinds County where Jackson is located. *Connor v. Johnson*, 91 S.Ct. 1760 (1971). As of January, 1972, the Mississippi redistricting is still in litigation. *Connor v. Williams*, 92 S.Ct. 656 (1972).

43. *Howell v. Mahan*, Civil Action 105-71-N (decided by United States District Court for the Eastern Division of Virginia, May 24, 1971). On other aspects of black redistricting, see Dixon, *op. cit.*, pp. 463-75, 116-17; and *Whitcomb v. Chavis*, 91 S.Ct. 1858 (1971) where the Court held that states have no affirmative constitutional obligation to provide black proportional representation, but they do have an obligation to provide equality of population per representative among districts, and they can provide black proportional representational if they want to do so.

44. On the need for greater inter-circuit homogeneity, see Carrington, "*Crowded Dockets and the Courts of Appeals: The Threat to the Function of Review and the National Law*," HARVARD LAW REVIEW, 82 (1969), pp. 542, 585-604. On redistricting of courts in general, see Dixon, *op. cit.*, pp. 559-64.

45. C. Cope, "*Municipal Boundaries in Nottingham 1937-1967*" (Bachelors dissertation, Cambridge University, 1968). See also C. R. Cope, "*Regionalization and the Electoral Redistricting Problem*," AREA, 3 (1971), pp. 190-195.

Part III Improving Judicial Personnel

The previous section (Chapters 3 through 9) emphasized the importance of decreasing discrimination against weak litigants by providing for such things as (1) legal principles like those embodied in the Bill of Rights and the Fourteenth Amendment to the Constitution, (2) institutions and attitudes designed to facilitate having legal counsel for the poor and the unpopular, and (3) more equitable representation of minority groups on juries and in legislative bodies. Those legal principles, however, are more likely to be complied with if there are more competent judges serving in the courts. More competent judges also help achieve other accepted goals like decreasing procedural delay and increasing the responsiveness of the courts to socially needed legal changes.

Chapter 10 attempts to measure judicial competency on the United States Supreme Court by looking at some of the evaluations of the individual justices who have served since 1789. The positioning of the justices by Felix Frankfurter and John Frank into those who were considered great and those who were considered not so great was particularly relied upon. With this measure, the chapter attempts to determine what background and other characteristics are associated with Supreme Court greatness. Such findings are relevant to evaluating policy recommendations requiring prior judicial experience, restricting dissenting opinions, and providing ethnic and geographical balance on the Court.

Chapter 10 starts with a measure of competence and attempts to determine what causes variation among judges on that measure. Chapter 11, on the other hand, starts with a proposed cause of competence-variation, namely method of selection, and attempts to determine what effects that proposed cause will have. In comparing elected and appointed judicial systems, the chapter concentrates on (1) backgrounds and decisional propensities of elected judges and interim-appointed judges sitting on the same state supreme courts hearing the same cases, (2) the relative nonpartisanship and technical competence of various elected and appointed state supreme courts, (3) voting behavior of the electorate in judicial elections, and (4) appointing behavior of presidents and governors in judicial appointments.

One judicial personnel problem that has been frequently discussed in the judicial behavior literature is the problem of measuring and possibly decreasing the influence of judges' backgrounds on their decisions. The previous literature has tended to relate backgrounds to decisions, one background characteristic at a time. Chapter 12 attempts to deal with the problem of the combined influence of judicial backgrounds on judicial decisions within state supreme courts. It emphasizes the relevance of fourteen different background and attitude characteristics taken in combination for explaining variation among judges serving on the same state supreme courts with regard to their criminal case and economic case decisions. The methodology used can also include institutional differences as independent variables for explaining and decreasing the variations found. Before determining how to reduce background-decisional correlations, we need to know to what extent such relations exist, especially in light of the fact that any given judge is a combination of many background characteristics working together rather than one at a time. Data on background-decisional relations can also be helpful in determining on what background characteristics judges may need more balance.

10 Characteristics Associated With Supreme Court Greatness

From George Washington's appointees in 1789 up to but not including John Kennedy's appointees in 1960 there were ninety-two Justices who served on the United States Supreme Court. Virtually all of them were highly qualified individuals. Some of them, however, have been acclaimed by legal scholars as having been outstanding. Felix Frankfurter named nineteen who were likely to be considered pre-eminent.[1] John Frank, another scholar of the Court, has named a longer, possibly less selective group of twenty-three.[2] All but three of the nineteen named by Frankfurter also were named by Frank, which indicates a substantial degree of consensus.[3] Both the Frankfurter and Frank lists exclude Justices who were appointed subsequent to 1932. If one were applying criteria like those Frankfurter and Frank seemed to use, one might choose five post-1932 Justices.[4] The sixteen on whom both Frankfurter and Frank agreed plus these five Justices will constitute the "great" Justices for the purpose of this article.

Birth and Youth

Of the ninety-two Supreme Court Justices, thirty-nine were born in the Northeast, nineteen in the Midwest, twenty-nine in the South, and only five in the West.[5] Of the thirty-nine born in the Northeast, 31 per cent were considered great judges in contrast to 11 per cent from the Midwest, 17 per cent from the South, and two out of five from the West. (See table 10-1, line 1.) With the exception of the small group from the West, the northeastern group contributes the highest proportion of great judges. This difference might be attributable to the presence of better schools in the Northeast and possibly to the progressivism that is associated with urbanism of that area.

As for better schools, John Schmidhauser classified the law schools of all the judges as either being law schools of high standing when attended or law schools of average standing. Line 2 of the table shows that sixty-seven of the ninety-two judges went to high standing law schools.[6] Of these judges, one-fourth were considered great as contrasted to only one-sixth of the judges who went to average standing law schools. These data, however,

AUTHOR'S NOTE: My thanks to John Schmidhauser of the University of Iowa for the use of his data on Supreme Court Justices and also to Joan Kerns and Judith Williams, who are former graduate students at the University of Illinois, for their aid in processing some of the data.

Table 10-1
How Different Groups of Supreme Court Justices Differ in Being Considered Great

GROUP 1 JUSTICES (Found to be more associated with greatness)	*GROUP 2 JUSTICES (Found to be less associated with greatness)*	*Number Group 1*	*Number Group 2*	*% of Group 1 Who Were Considered Great*	*% of Group 2 Who Were Considered Great*	*Differences*
1. Northeast	Other regions	39	53	31%	17%	+14
2. High standing law school	Other	67	25	25	16	+ 9
3. Non-Protestant	Protestant	9	81	44	21	+23
4. Judges in family	No judges in family	25	67	28	21	+ 7
5. Humble economic status	Nonhumble economic status	11	81	27	22	+ 5
6. Not former judge	Former judge	34	58	41	12	+29
7. Below average age at appointment	Above average age at appointment	40	52	33	15	+18
8. Democrat	Republican	43	46	23	22	+ 1
9. Appointed within party lines	Appointed across party lines	83	9	23	22	+ 1
10. Frequent dissenter	Not frequent dissenter	28	64	50	11	+39
11. High on overruling	Low on overruling	31	40	32	23	+ 9
12. Chief Justice	Not Chief Justice	14	78	29	22	+ 7

are incapable of indicating the extent to which attending a high standing law school promotes greatness as contrasted to indicating that having the abilities of a potentially great judge causes one to be more likely to attend and be accepted at a high standing law school.

Religion seems to be a correlate of greatness that is noncausal in nature. The findings indicate that more than two-fifths of the nine non-Protestants on the Court were considered great in contrast to one-fifth of the eighty-one Protestants. (Line 3) In view of the handicaps of being non-Protestant in the legal world until recently, one would not expect that being Jewish or Catholic would make it easier to become a great judge. The explanations may be that (1) when the President appoints a Jew or Catholic to the Supreme Court, he is more careful to appoint an especially well-qualified one in order to avoid criticism, and (2) those Jews and Catholics who managed to be considered for such an appointment were unusually capable of overcoming social barriers.

There are some background characteristics of Supreme Court Justices that did not substantially correlate with judicial greatness, although one might have expected them to do so. Coming from a family containing a judge made a difference of only seven percentage points, although it is interesting to note that twenty-five of the ninety-two judges did come from these families. (Line 4) Likewise, being able to rise up from a family that had humble economic status only made a difference of five percentage points, and only eleven of the judges came from these families.[7] (Line 5)

Pre-Court Activity

The most controversial precourt activity with regard to its degree of relevance to greatness is prior judicial experience. A majority of fifty-eight out of the ninety-two judges did have this experience, but only 12 per cent of these judges were considered great. (Line 6) On the other hand, 41 per cent of the judges lacking this experience were considered great, thereby producing a substantial difference of twenty-nine percentage points in a direction opposite to what one might have hypothesized. It seems unlikely that prior judicial experience could be so harmful to being a great judge, although lower court work could make a Supreme Court Justice more provincial or more legalistic than a judge without this experience. John Frank explains the negative correlation between prior judicial experience and greatness by noting that lower judicial "positions have traditionally paid very little, and able men who did not have independent means have frequently been unable to accept them".[8]

A better or further explanation, however, is that there is a strong correlation between having no prior judicial experience and being appointed to the Court at a relatively young age. This correlation logically follows from the fact that one grows older while obtaining prior judicial experience. Line 7 further indicates that those judges who are appointed to the Court below the average age of appointment (*i.e.*, below 53 years of age) are more likely to be considered great. Youthful appointees tend to be considered great for two reasons: First, they must have accomplished more than older appointees in a shorter period of time to merit such an appointment; second, and perhaps more important, they tend to serve on the Court for a longer period of time, thus having greater opportunity to write more opinions and become better known.

An indication of the nonpartisan nature of the greatness categorizing is the fact that there is no correlation between political party affiliation and whether a judge is considered great. Of the 43 Democrats 23 per cent were considered great, and so were 22 per cent of the 46 Republicans. (Line 8) Related to party affiliation is the phenomenon of a President making appointments across party lines. On the one hand, when making an appointment from the opposite party, the President might tend to appoint a person who is not so likely to bring prestige to the other party. On the other hand, it might require a very good person to attract the President to go across party lines. These two factors tend to balance each other. As a result, line 9 shows virtually no relation between appointing across party lines and obtaining great Justices. According to Glendon Schubert, nine of the ninety-two Justices were initially appointed to the Court across party lines.[9]

Court Activity

The one variable in the table that has the highest correlation with greatness is the frequent dissenter.[10] Line 10 shows that half of the frequent dissenters were among the great judges, as contrasted to only about 10 per cent of those not considered to be frequent dissenters. The reason for the strength of the relation partly lies in the fact that those judges who are most remembered as dissenters are those who had the foresight or fortune to have their dissenting positions eventually become majority positions. The concept of dissenter as used here may thus partly include the quality of one's dissents as well as the quantity. One would therefore expect such pioneering judges to be disproportionately among the great judges.

On the other hand, being high on overruling[11] correlates to a much lower extent with being considered great (a nine percentage point difference (Line 11)). Unlike the concept of dissenter, the concept of overruler has no qualitative element in that it is based on giving each judge a score equal to the percentage of time he was on the majority side in the eighty-one overruling cases from 1789 onward that have been isolated by Sidney Ulmer.[12]

Finally, line 12 indicates that having been chosen to be a Chief Justice is not much of an indication of past or future greatness since 29 per cent of the fourteen Chief Justices were considered great as compared to 22 per cent of the seventy-eight non-Chief Justices.

Related Findings Among Federal District Judges

To determine further the characteristics that are associated with judicial quality, I drew a random sample of 100 judges from the 239 federal district judges listed in the *Directory of American Judges*, which was published in 1955. The *Federal Supplement* court reports of 1955 were checked to find the cases that these 100 judges heard, and each case was checked in *Shepard's Citations* to determine whether it was reversed on appeal, affirmed or not appealed. Each judge was then given an ability score by examining the percentage of his cases that were appealed, the percentage of his appeals that resulted in reversals and the percentage of his cases that were reversed. Finally, the ability scores for the judges were correlated with their characteristics as provided by the *Directory of American Judges*.

It is interesting to note that when characteristics were used like those in the Supreme Court study, similar findings were generally revealed. Thus, for example, 65 per cent of the fifty-seven scorable judges on the lower federal courts who had no prior judicial experience had above average ability scores, whereas only 43 per cent of the twenty-one judges who had some prior judicial experience has above average ability scores. Likewise, differences in the same direction as occurred with Supreme Court judges were found with regard to region and religion. Being a Democrat, however, led to less frequent reversals than being a Republican, probably because of the dominance of Democratic viewpoints on the federal appellate bench in 1955.

Conclusions and Implications

From the Supreme Court analysis one can conclude that certain types of judges on the Supreme Court are more likely to be considered greater than others. These types of judges who (1) were born in the Northeast, (2) went to high standing law schools, (3) were non-Protestants, (4) had no judicial experience prior to their appointment, (5) were appointed before reaching age 53 and (6) were considered to be frequent dissenters.

From these findings one can further conclude that from the point of view of encouraging the appointment of great judges, it would be unwise to require that appointees have prior judicial experience or that they be older than they have been, unless one has a different goal in mind, such as the appointment of more conservative judges. Likewise, restrictions on dissenting opinions for the sake of unity might suppress potentially great judges as well as foresightful opinions. It also may be unwise to tamper unduly with the custom of (1) having at least one Jewish and one Catholic seat on the court, and (2) disproportionately appointing judges from the Northeast and from high standing law schools unless one is seeking to promote some kind of proportional representation.

On the other hand, these findings, dealing as they do with the collective characteristics of the judges, have little value in choosing specific future judges. In making this choice, the important characteristics to look for are those that are more directly related to Supreme Court greatness. These characteristics generally include a brilliant intellect, an ability to write well, a deep knowledge of law and society, a willingness to work hard, a strong personality, an ability to get along with one's colleagues and a high level of success in one's prior activities. In addition to these facets of greatness, it would also be appropriate or at least realistic for a President to look for appointees who have value systems compatible with his and whose appointments may help to improve his image with important interest groups.

Notes

1. Frankfurter, *The Supreme Court in the Mirror of Justices*, 105 U. PA. L. REV. 781 (1957). The nineteen judges in chronological order of appointment are: Marshall, W. Johnson, Storey, Taney, Curtis, Campbell, Miller, Field, Bradley, Harlan (1st), Matthews, Brewer, Brown, E. White, Moody, Hughs, Holmes, Brandeis and Cardozo.

2. FRANK, MARBLE PALACE: THE SUPREME COURT IN AMERICAN LIFE 43-44 (1961). The seven Justices named by Frank who were not named by Frankfurter are: McLean, Davis, Waite, Taft, Sutherland, Butler and Stone.

3. The three Justices names by Frankfurter but not by Frank are: Mattheys, Brown and White. Although Frankfurter mentioned these three Justices, he indicated doubts about them.

4. Black, Frankfurter, Douglas, Jackson and Warren were the post-1932 pre-1960 Justices.

5. The Northeastern states consist of Connecticut, Maine, Massachusetts, New Hampshire, New Jersey, New York, Pennsylvania, Rhode Island and Vermont.

6. Schmidhauser, *The Justices of the Supreme Court: A Collective Portrait*, 3 MIDWEST J. POL. SCI. 1, 25, 29-31 (1959).

7. *Id.* at 6-16.

8. *Supra* note 2, at 47.

9. SCHUBERT, CONSTITUTIONAL POLITICS: THE POLITICAL BEHAVIOR OF SUPREME COURT JUSTICES AND THE CONSTITUTIONAL POLICIES THAT THEY MAKE 37 (1960). Brandeis is not included in the nine because of the unclearness of his party affiliation at the time of his appointment. Crossover appointments of Associate Justices to Chief Justice also are not counted.

10. Evans, *The Dissenting Opinion: Its Use and Abuse*, 3 MO. L. REV. 129 (1938); ZoBell, *Division of Opinion in the Supreme Court: A History of Judicial Disintegration*, 44 CORNELL L. Q. 186 (1959); and Schmidhauser, *Stare Decisis, Dissent, and the Background of the Justices of the Supreme Court of the United States*, 14 TORONTO L. J. 194 (1962).

11. Schmidhauser, *supra* note 10, at 200-201.

12. Ulmer, *An Empirical Analysis of Selected Aspects of Lawmaking of the United States Supreme Court*, 8 J. PUB. L. 414 (1959).

11 Comparing Elected and Appointed Judicial Systems

There is a great deal of literature on the hotly debated topic of how American judges ought to be selected.[1] Indeed, it was part of the national high school debate topic in 1971.[2] There has, however, been a lack of empirical data systematically comparing elected and appointed judges and the criteria by which they are chosen, with some exceptions.[3]

It is the purpose of this chapter to discuss some data that have been compiled and appropriate ways of compiling additional data in order to compare elected and appointed judicial systems. Comparisons might appropriately deal with (1) backgrounds and decisional propensities of elected judges and interim appointed judges sitting on the same state supreme courts hearing the same cases, (2) the relative non-partisanship and technical competence of various elected and appointed state supreme courts, (3) voting behavior of the electorate in judicial elections, and (4) appointing behavior of presidents and governors in judicial appointments.

Elected judicial systems are those in which the judges are supposed to be initially voted into office by the general public in a special or general election, partisan or non-partisan, with or without primaries. Appointed judicial systems are those in which all the judges are initially appointed by the governor, legislature, or combination of both with or without provision for subsequent recall or approval-rejection elections.[4] Mention is made in the chapter of where variations within the elected systems seem to produce differences in results, and likewise with variations within the appointed systems.

The Judicial Behavior of Comparing Elected and Appointed Judges

Decisional Propensities and Backgrounds

General Liberalism. A big difficulty with trying to compare elected judges with appointed judges is that they are usually thought of as serving on different courts hearing different cases. If that were always so, then any differences found between them might be readily attributed to differences found between (1) the cases they hear, (2) the laws of the states in which they operate, or (3) the social, economic, and political climate of their respective states.[5] There are, however, many interim appointed judges serving on state supreme courts along with elected judges hearing exactly the same cases under the same legal rules within the same state social climate.[6] These interim appointed judges fill out the unexpired terms of judges who die, resign, or retire.

Interim appointed judges may not be the same as judges who never stand for election (since interim judges generally are voted upon in the next election subsequent to their interim appointments), but they do represent a form of judicial selection closer to appointment than the purely elected judge does. Whatever substantial differences are found between *interim* appointed judges and elected judges can probably be extrapolated to be even greater between *fully* appointed judges and elected judges.

Table 11-1 shows how the decisional propensities of appointed judges differ from those of elected judges, using the nonunanimous decisions of the state supreme courts of 1955 on which both appointed and elected judges were present. Appointed judges here refer to judges on elected courts who were initially selected through an interim appointment although they may have subsequently run for election. Nineteen hundred fifty-five is the most recent year for which these data and related data are conveniently available, but there is no reason to believe that appointed judges differ from elected judges any more or less in later years. Originally fifteen (rather than nine) types of cases were used, but six types of cases were eliminated because the number of appointed judges or elected judges for which nonunanimous cases were available was less than twenty.[7]

Hearing the same cases as their interim appointed counterparts, table 11-1 shows that elected judges tend to be on what might be considered the liberal side in nonunanimous cases in seven of the nine types of cases although by only a small margin in the seven types of cases. Union versus management cases provide an illustrative example of the table 11-1 findings. In these cases, 50 percent of the 24 elected judges (serving with interim appointed judges) decided above the average of their respective courts for the union, whereas a lesser 40 percent of the 25 appointed judges decided above the average of their respective courts for the union.

One explanation that might be offered for why elected judges in general tend to be on the liberal side is that Democratic judges are more likely to be elected judges (given that Democrats tend to dominate the electorate especially with relatively unknown judicial candidates), and Democratic judges are more likely to decide liberal (given the relatively liberal nature of the Democratic party). Thus, being elected and voting liberal might correlate with each other because they are co-effects of being a Democrat. This explanation is faulty, however, as indicated by the last two columns, which show that if one only compares elected Republicans with appointed Republicans or if one only compares elected Democrats with appointed Democrats on the same courts, then the elected-appointed differences generally become stronger, not weaker. The elected-appointed differences show up much more when all the judges are Republicans than when all the judges are Democrats. This may be so because being a Republican, at least in the 1950s when these data were gathered, was a less unifying variable (among diversely selected judges on the same state supreme court) than was being a Democrat.

The explanation for the greater liberalism of elected judges possibly lies in the fact that elected judges may be more likely to be lawyers who have risen up from the political ranks and who have characteristics more like those of the general population or at least the more liberal elements in the general population. Appointed judges, on the other hand, may be more likely to be lawyers who formerly worked for the top conservative law firms from which they were appointed. This kind of explanation is partly confirmed in table 11-2 which does show that elected judges are more likely to be Democrats, members of a minority religion, and more likely to have high liberalism attitude scores. Their background and attitude characteristics were determined by checking various who's who directories and by sending the supreme court judges a mailed attitude questionnaire.

The reason political party is held constant in the last two columns of table 11-2 is to show that if one correlates a liberal background or attitude characteristic with being an elected rather than appointed judge, then the relation is not due to the intervening variable of party affiliation. For example, having a liberal attitude (L) may correlate with being a Democrat (D) rather than a Republican, and being a Democrat (D) may correlate with being an elected (E) rather than an appointed judge. Even so, having a liberal attitude (L) correlates with being an elected judge (E) even if one makes this analysis just with Republican judges or just with Democratic judges. Likewise most of the other findings in table 11-2 are consistent regardless whether one uses all the judges, just the Republican judges, or just the Democratic judges.

One interesting finding in table 11-2 is shown in row 3. It indicates (on courts which had some appointed and some elected judges and also some Protestants and some Catholics) that 39 percent of the elected judges were Catholics, and only 19 percent of the appointed judges were Catholics. This finding conflicts with the notion that "minorities have a better chance of placing their man by appointment than by election [because] governors are anxious to curry the favor of minority blocs and appointments are a very popular way to do it."[8] That notion does not adequately recognize that the

Table 11-1
Differences in the Decisions of Appointed and Elected Judges (Using the Nonunanimous Decisions of the State Supreme Courts of 1955 on which both Appointed and Elected Judges Were Present)

Type of Issue	*% of Appointed Judges Above Their Court Average*	*Base of this % (apptd. judges)*	*% of Elected Judges Above Their Court Average*	*Base of this % (elected judges)*	*Difference between the Percents (in % pts.)*	*Difference just for Republican judges*	*Difference just for Democratic judges*
PUBLIC LAW							
Criminal Law							
1. For the defense in criminal cases	41%	88	43%	79	+ 2	+16	− 6
Administrative Law							
2. For the administrative agency in business regulation cases	49	59	58	52	+ 1	+14	−10
Civil Liberties Law							
3. For finding a constitutional violation in criminal cases	41	32	47	34	+ 6	+22	+ 6
Tax Law							
4. For the government in tax cases	60	53	34	62	−26	−40	−15

PRIVATE LAW							
Family Law							
5. For the wife in divorce settlement cases	43	35	46	26	+ 3	+47	+ 6
Business Regulations Law							
6. For the labor union in union-management cases	40	25	50	24	+10	+28	+13
7. For the consumer in sales-of-goods cases	38	32	56	41	+18	+14	+16
Personal Injury Law							
8. For the injured in motor vehicle accident cases	62	89	41	71	−21	−21	−20
9. For the employee in employee injury cases	41	71	49	65	+ 8	+ 8	+ 4

Table 11-2

How the Backgrounds and Attitudes of Appointed Judges Differ from Those of Elected Judges (Based on the State Supreme Courts of 1955 on which there was diversity on selection method and on the background differences)

Group 1 (Hypothesized to be more likely to be appointed)	*Group 2 (Hypothesized to be more likely to be elected)*	*% of Appointed Judges in Group 2*	*Base of this Percentage (apptd. judges)*	*% of Elected Judges in Group 2*	*Base of this Percentage (elected judges)*	*Difference between the percents*	*Difference Just for Republican Judges*	*Difference Just for Democratic Judges*
I. GOOD DECISIONAL PREDICTORS								
1. *Party*								
Republicans	Democrats	27	37	50	40	+23	0	0
2. *Religion*								
Protestants	Catholics	19	37	39	23	+20	+51	− 9
3. *Liberal Attitudes*								
Low general liberalism score	High general liberalism score	37	24	60	25	+23	+24	+17
II. GOOD VOTE-GETTING IMAGE								
4. *Education*								
Attended high tuition law school	Attended low tuition law school	74	35	54	39	−20	−38	−16
5. *Years of Judicial Experience*								
More than 17 years	17 years or less	52	21	36	11	−16	−27	−24
6. *Scholarly Honors*								
Honored as scholars	Did not so indicate	75	20	45	11	−30	−75	+29

judicial slatemakers of political parties where there are substantial minorities may be even more anxious to curry the favor of minority blocs.

Some Specific Types of Cases. Tax cases and motor vehicle accident cases did not follow the general pattern of elected judges being more liberal in table 11-1. The explanation in tax cases might be that there is no clearly liberal position in tax cases unless one knows the type of tax (e.g., income or sales) or the type of taxpayer (e.g., corporate or consumer). Liberals do tend to favor the government in business regulation cases, but they disfavor the government in criminal cases, particularly where constitutional rights are involved. Some otherwise liberal judges have been known for their anti-government decisions in tax cases such as Judge Musmanno of the elected Pennsylvania Supreme Court.[9]

The explanation for motor vehicle accident cases may be more complicated. Like the tax cases, they may involve a mixture of issues as to both liability (on which liberals tend to find for the plaintiff) and damages (on which liberals sometimes do not think in dollar amounts as large as more wealthy types do, provided liability has been established). The personal injury cases may also be less ideological than the other types of cases and thus they may not split liberal elected judges from conservative appointed ones as well as more divisive types of cases. The degree of divisiveness of the type of case can be determined by calculating the average percentage of dissents for each type of case or the average margin of victory for each type of case. Tax and personal injury decisions did not correlate as highly with party,[10] ethnic background,[11] or liberalism attitudes[12] as did business regulation, employee injury criminal, or many other types of cases.

Perhaps another explanation for why elected judges were not so liberal in motor vehicle accident cases is indicated by the portion of table 11-2 which shows judges who are put up for election rather than receive an interim appointment from the governor generally have good vote-getting images by way of having (1) attended a prestige law school (and thus come from wealthier backgrounds), (2) served many years in a prior judgeship (and thus are older judges), and (3) received scholarly recognition by way of publication[13] or membership in scholarly honorary organizations (and thus are more established). These are not good general decisional predictors like party, religion, and liberalism; but they do happen to have a relatively high correlation with voting against the monetary claims of the injured party in motor vehicle accident cases.

Maybe elected judges given their education, judicial experience, and scholarly honors tend to be more legalistic in diciding cases than appointed judges. This might cause them to have a greater propensity to reverse trial court decisions favoring the injured plaintiff in spite of the plaintiff's contributory negligence which legally bars him from recovering. This kind of trial court illegality is probably more likely to occur in motor vehicle accident cases than in the other types of cases.

Although the above explanations make some empirical sense, the deviant nature of the motor vehicle accident cases may be partly due to the chance presence of some untypical elected or appointed judges. The judges on the motor vehicle accident row are not the same set of judges as those on the other rows of table 11-1 since the judges on a row depend on which judges or courts heard nonunanimous motor vehicle accident cases in the sample year among the total judges used. Although chance might explain one type of case, it is not so likely to explain seven or eight out of the nine, especially when one considers the size of the differences between the elected decisional propensities and the appointed decisional propensities (at least with Republican judges), and when one considers the size of the samples of the elected and appointed judges on which the percentages are based.

One finding in table 11-1 possibly worth separate mention is the finding with regard to how elected judges differ from appointed judges in criminal cases. On the one hand, it might be argued that elected judges are *more* likely to favor the defense because elected judges tend to be more liberal in their decisional propensities, attitudes, and backgrounds. On the other hand, it might also be argued that elected judges are *less* likely to favor the defense because elected judges tend to be more sensitive to public opinion, and public opinion demands more convictions and severer sentences. Perhaps both these explanations balance each other, and as a result table 11-1 shows virtually no difference between elected and appointed judges in criminal cases.

Related to the above finding in criminal cases is the notion that although elected judges may be more liberal on economic matters than appointed judges (especially when one controls for political party), elected judges may be less liberal on civil liberties matters than appointed judges. This lack of civil liberties liberalism may be due to majoritarian public pressures to play down the rights of radical speakers and minority racial groups. In the sample of state supreme court judges, however, there were too few free speech cases or race relations cases to test this hypothesis although elected judges were slightly more liberal in table 11-1 on the constitutional rights of criminal suspects.

A related untested hypothesis is that judges with long terms of office (especially lifetime tenure) are more likely to decide in favor of broadening free speech and minority rights than are judges with short terms of office who are more subject to the majoritarian pressures of periodic elections. In data not shown in table 11-1, judges with above average terms of office (over eight years) were slightly more liberal in handling the constitutional rights of criminal suspects even though there is a strong negative relation between being elected and having a long term of office.

Nonpartisanship and Technical Competence

Just as the interim appointed judges were compared with elected judges with regard to their decisional propensities and backgrounds, so also comparisons could be made with regard to their nonpartisanship and technical competence. These two characteristics, however, tend to be more associated with courts rather than with judges. Thus, it makes more sense to talk of a court being nonpartisan by virtue of its balanced party representation than an individual judge being nonpartisan. Likewise, if the technical competence of a state supreme court is measured by the percentage of times it is upheld by the United States Supreme Court or favorably cited by other state supreme courts, then such a measure of competence accrues to the judges on that state supreme court collectively rather than to its individual judges.

Nonpartisanship. For that reason, the methodology of within-court comparisons was not used in a related article by this writer dealing with the relative partisanship of elected and appointed judges.[14] The key data in that article, which are reproduced here on row one of table 11-3, show that judges on appointed courts tend to be more nonpartisan than judges on elected courts in the sense that they were less likely to vote like typical Democrats or typical Republicans. A typical Democratic judge or an atypical Republican judge tended to vote in favor of the administrative agency in business regulation cases, the claimant in unemployment compensation cases, and the employee in employee injury cases. A typical Republican or an atypical Democrat tended to vote in the opposite direction in nonunanimous cases of these three types on courts having both Democratic and Republican judges present.[15]

Long term of office correlates positively with being appointed and positively with nonpartisanship. Long term, however, does not explain the positive correlation between being appointed and nonpartisanship because the correlation remains when long tenured *appointed* judges are compared with long tenured *elected* judges on row two. Likewise, appointed judges are not more objective in suppressing their values than elected judges, as is indicated on row three by the fact that *appointed* judges with liberal questionnaire attitudes tended to vote just as liberally as *elected* judges with liberal questionnaire attitudes.

Another possible explanation for the positive correlation between being appointed and nonpartisanship is the hypothesis that appointed judges are more atypical of their political party with regard to their attitudes than are elected judges because appointed judges must usually be nominated or approved by some bipartisan body and are sometimes appointed by governors across party lines. This explanation was tentatively discarded when it was found that appointed judges are just as likely to be conservative

Table 11-3

Some Aspects of How Elected Judges Differ from Appointed Judges on Nonpartisanship and Technical Competence

Group 1 (A Quality Often Thought to be Less Desirable	*Group 2 (A Quality Often Thought to be More Desirable)*	*Number of Judges or Courts*				
		Elected	*Appointed*	*% Elected in Group 2*	*% Appointed in Group 2*	*Difference between Percentages*
I. NONPARTISANSHIP		(Judges on Elected Courts	(Judges on Appointed Courts)			
1. Judges who voted in *accordance* with their party pattern	Judges who voted *contrary* to their party pattern	47	18	15%	39%	+24
2. Judges who voted in *accordance* with their party pattern	Judges who voted *contrary* to their party pattern	20 (all with over 8-year terms)	17	15	41	+26
3. Judges who voted in *accordance* with their value position	Judges who voted *contrary* to their value position in criminal cases	59	6	64	67	+3

4. Being a liberal Democrat or conservative Republican	Being a conservative Democrat or liberal Republican	17	8	50	53	+3
5. Having a *less* nonpartisan role perception	Having a *more* nonpartisan role perception	—	—	>50?	<50?	+?
II. TECHNICAL COMPETENCE		(Elected Courts)	(Apptd. Courts)			
6. Courts having *below* average prestige	Courts having *above* average prestige	38	10	37%	40%	+3
7. Courts deciding *below* average number of cases per judge per year	Courts decinding *above* average number of cases per judge per year	31	11	42	18	−24
8. Courts *not* clearing their full annual docket	Courts clearing their full annual docket	30	9	57	89	+32

Democrats or Liberal Republicans as elected judges are (as is shown on row 4).

Possibly the best explanation for the positive correlation (other than attributing it to chance in spite of the size of the correlation and the size of the sample) is that judges on appointed courts consciously or subconsciously view their roles as being more nonpartisan than do judges on elected courts. Unfortunately, none of the questionnaire or interviewing surveys of state judiciaries have specifically dealt with how they perceive their relations with Democratic or Republican party positions (as is indicated by the blanks and question mark on row 5). Appointed judges may have a more positive attitude toward judicial lawmaking rather than mere law-finding, but such a role perception does not necessarily relate to partisanship or nonpartisanship.[16]

Technical Competence. One could measure the relative technical competence of elected and appointed state supreme courts by determining for each state supreme court (1) the esteem in which they are held by law professors through a mailed questionnaire, (2) the frequency with which their opinions are included in law school casebooks, and (3) the extent to which they are favorably cited by other courts. All three prestige-competence measures were used by Rodney Mott to rank the forty-eight state supreme courts during the 1930s.[17] No more recent ranking has been prepared.

Row 6 in table 11-3 shows that there is virtually no difference in the relative prestige of the elected and appointed state supreme courts using the Mott combined prestige ratings. The top five state supreme courts were New York, Massachusetts, Illinois, New Jersey, and California. At that time only Massachusetts and New Jersey were appointed courts although California subsequently adopted an appointive system. There is likewise virtually no difference between elected and appointed courts if the components of the combined prestige index are used since the components correlate so highly with the combined index and with each other.

Determining the prestige or competence of state supreme courts by looking to favorable mentions by law professors, casebooks, or other courts may, however, be more a reflection of the quantity of cases generated by the economy and society of the state than a reflection of the technical competence of the court. Likewise, the percentage of times a state supreme court is upheld by the United States Supreme Court (or favorably cited by law professors) may be more a measure of the ideological similarity between the two levels of courts rather than a measure of technical competence.

A measure of technical competence that at least at first seems less subjective than using the ratings of law professors or other courts is to determine the relative ability of elected courts (1) to handle many cases per judge per year or (2) to clear their full annual docket of appeals. The Institute of Judicial Administration in 1954 prepared a report entitled "Statistics on Work of Highest State Appellate Courts," which contains the latest available raw data in one place for making such a comparison.[18]

Row 7 shows that a higher percentage of elected courts (42 percent) were below the national average with regard to the number of cases decided per judge for 1953 as contrasted to the appointed courts (18 percent). Row 8, however, shows that a lower percentage of elected courts (57 percent) failed to decide as many appeals in 1953 as had been argued or submitted as contrasted to the appointed courts (89 percent).

These two rows of comparisons, however, are not very meaningful in view of the fact that the different state supreme courts seem to have highly different notions of what constitutes a case. For instance, some include and some exclude certiorari denials in counting cases submitted and cases decided. Inconsistent definitions of what constitutes a case thus seem to explain why the elected supreme court of the state of Florida, for example, claims to have decided 991 cases in 1953 and the appointed court of New Jersey claims to have decided only 163.

There may be some value in using the ratings of law professors and other courts to determine the technical competence of state supreme courts provided that some statistical adjustments are made to control for the quantity of cases each court generates and the liberalism ideological factor. There also may be some value in using case output and backlog statistics provided there is a common definition of what constitutes a case. A more sophisticated measure of whether the decisions were objectively correct may, however, be impossible by virtue of the inability to measure "objectively correct" especially when one is dealing with the kind of policy-oriented problems which exist at the state supreme court level. What is objectively correct may ultimately depend on one's liberal or conservative value position, which takes us back to comparing elected and appointed judges on their decisional propensities.

Comparing the Selection Behavior of Judicial Voters and Appointers

Voting Behavior in Judicial Elections

In order to compare elected and appointed judicial systems, it makes sense not only to compare the judicial behavior of elected and appointed judges, but also to compare the selection behavior of judicial voters and appointers.[19]

Voting Turnout. A charge that is frequently made in attacking the elected system is to point out how few voters participate in judicial elections.[20] This may be true when judicial elections are held separately from general elections. When judicial elections are held at the same time as general elections, however, the percentage of general election voters who also participate in the judicial elections tends to run about 80 or 90 percent. For example, in a poll conducted by Elmo Roper and Associates of voters in the combined New York state general and judicial election of November, 1954, 82 percent of the general election voters also participated in the judicial election.[21] In a nationwide sample of 47 combined congressional and judicial elections from 1950 to 1962 on which data were available, all of them involved over 90 percent of the congressional voters participating in the simultaneous judicial elections.[22] The New York figure may have been less than 90 percent because the simultaneous judicial election involved an especially long separate ballot.

When those who attack judicial elections mention low voter participation, they are implying that those who do participate are not representative of the general population of those eligible to vote. If the actual participants (regardless of how small the percentage) is representative of the general population, then no harm is done by the low participation with regard to obtaining a representative cross-section sample. Table 11-4 provides some information with regard to the extent to which judicial election participants differ from those who do not participate. The data in the table come from the same Roper poll previously mentioned. Line 1 indicates there is no difference between the percentage of Democrats who participated in the general and judicial election and the percentage of Republicans who participated in the general and judicial election. The top half of table 11-4 shows that the general-plus-judicial voters do not differ substantially from the just-general votes with regard to sex, age, urbanism, or even economic class.

On the other hand, those who participate in the general election do differ substantially from those who do not. Seventy-five percent of all those polled who identified themselves as Republicans indicated they voted in the election for governor which was held the same day as the judicial election, whereas only 61 percent of those who identified themselves as Democrats did so. Seventy percent of the males polled voted in the gubernatorial election, but only 61 percent of the females did. There were even sharper differences between those whom the Roper pollsters defined as poor people and those defined as not poor. There was also an 18 percentage-point difference between people living in smaller communities (who vote more) and people living in larger cities (who vote less).[23] There is a less sharp difference along age lines over forty-five and under forty-five, although age differences might be more apparent if the data were broken down into ten-year age categories.

Table 11-4
How Voters Who Participate in Judicial or General Elections Differ from Those Who Do Not (Using Data from the 1954 New York State Elections)

Group 1 *(Hypothesized to be lower participants)*	*Group 2* *(Hypothesized to be higher participants)*	*Number in Each Group* *(1)*	*(2)*	*% of Group 1 Voters Who Participate*	*% of Group 2 Voters Who Participate*	*Difference Between Percentages*
I. JUDICIAL ELECTION VOTERS (Of Those Voting in the General Election)						
1. Democrats	Republicans	336	327	83%	83%	0
2. Female	Male	372	439	78	85	+ 7
3. Under 45	Over 45	406	405	79	84	+ 5
4. Over 250,000 population	Under 250,000 population	500	311	83	80	− 3
5. Poor people	Not poor	176	609	76	84	+ 8
II. GENERAL ELECTION VOTERS (Among Citizens Age 21 or Older)						
1. Democrats	Republicans	554	436	61%	75%	+14
2. Female	Male	644	629	58	70	+12
3. Under 45	Over 45	651	622	63	66	+ 3
4. Over 250,000 population	Under 250,000 population	872	401	59	77	+18
5. Poor people	Not poor	364	855	50	72	+22

Thus, it appears that those who participate in judicial elections are more representative of general voters than those who participate in general elections are representative of the general public. It also appears that judicial voters are no less representative of the general public than general voters are. In spite of the lack of representativeness which general voters have as to important background characteristics, it has not been seriously proposed that voting for governor should somehow be replaced with an appointive process. Instead, the emphasis has been on trying to increase voting turnout in general elections rather than abolishing them.

Voting turnout can be increased in judicial elections (at least close to the level of voting turnout in general elections) if judicial and general elections are held simultaneously as previously indicated. It is sometimes argued, however, that judicial elections should be held at a separate time from general elections even though that might greatly reduce the judicial voting turnout. The argument is made that holding judicial elections at the same time as general elections causes voters to be more likely to vote irrationally on the basis of the political party affiliation of the judicial candidates. It is therefore appropriate to discuss data relating to the factors which judicial voters consider in judicial elections.

Factors Considered in Voting. First, it should be pointed out that it may not be so irrational in terms of maximizing the voter's interests for him to consider party labels and even ethnic surname connotations in judicial voting. This may be so in view of previous data which this writer has compiled which show Democratic judges do differ substantially from Republican judges in their decisional propensities in many important types of cases.[24] For instance, in a sample of sixty state supreme court judges serving on bipartisan state supreme courts in 1955 and hearing nonunanimous business regulation cases, 68 percent of the twenty-five Democratic judges were above the average of their court in deciding for the administrative agency, whereas only 23 percent of the thirty-five Republican judges were above their court average. Similar, although smaller, differences divided the Democratic judges from the Republican judges with regard to voting for the defense in criminal cases, the tenant in landlord-tenant cases, the labor union in union-management cases, the consumer in sales of goods cases, the employee in employee injury cases, and what might be considered the liberal direction in various other cases.

Previous data also shows Catholic and other minority-ethnic judges do differ from Protestant and other majority-ethnic judges in their decisional propensities in important types of cases.[25] The differences are generally not so great or so consistent as with party affiliation, but ethnic affiliation does bear some predictive relation to the decisional behavior of the judges being voted upon. For instance, in a sample of fifty-seven state supreme court judges serving on state supreme courts in 1955 having both Catholic and Protestant judges present and hearing nonunanimous criminal cases, 56 percent of the eighteen Catholic judges were above the average of their court in deciding for the defense, whereas only 31 percent of the thirty-nine Protestant judges were above their court average. Similar differences divided Catholic judges from Protestant judges with regard to voting for the administrative agency in business regulation cases, the employee in employee injury cases, and voting for the liberal direction in various other cases. Related differences were also found between judges whose family names indicated exclusively British ancestry as contrasted to judges whose family names indicated at least partial non-British ancestry.

Even if it were not generally in conformity with the voter's interests to consider party label or ethnic connotations, it should be pointed out that party and ethnic voting may be as prevalent in general elections as in judicial elections. A high percentage of voters in general elections do vote on the basis of party label.[26] Of those voters who indicated their source of information about judicial candidates in the Roper poll of the 1954 New York judicial election, 39 percent said they just supported the party ticket, 21 percent said newspaper recommendation, 15 percent said they consulted family and friends who are not lawyers, 7 percent said they consulted family and friends who are lawyers or bar association recommendations, and 17 percent mentioned other sources.

A meaningful way to compare party voting in judicial and general elections would involve determining the percentage Democratic vote of the two-party vote in a state supreme court judicial election held at the same time or as close in time as possible to a congressional election.[27] This was done in a nationwide sample of 112 congressional districts for bipartisan congressional elections held in 1960. In those congressional districts dominated by the Democratic party,[28] one would expect the percentage of Democratic vote in judicial elections to be greater than the percentage of Democratic vote in the accompanying congressional election if party label is indeed more important in judicial elections. Table 11-5, however, shows that of thirty-four congressional districts dominated by the Democrats for which information was available, in only one of the districts was the percentage of Democratic vote in the judicial election greater than the percentage of Democratic vote in the congressional election. Among the seventy-four usable congressional districts dominated by the Republicans, in forty of them the percentage of Republican votes in the judicial election was greater than the percentage of Republican votes in the congressional election, and in thirty-four of the districts, those two percentages were reversed.

This means that of the 102 usable congressional districts, only 40 percent confirm the hypothesis that the dominant political party will re-

Table 11-5
How Voters in Judicial Elections Differ from Voters in General Elections With Regard to Party and Ethnic Voting
(General Hypothesis: The dominant party or ethnic group will receive a higher percentage of votes in judicial than in general elections)

I. Testing the Hypothesis that the Dominant Political Party Will Receive a Higher Percentage of Votes in Judicial than in Congressional Elections (where both elections are bipartisan)

	Dominant Party in the Congressional District: Republican	Dominant Party in the Congressional District: Democrat
% Dem. Vote in Judicial Election Greater than % Dem. Vote in Cong. Election	Hypo. Refuted 34 districts	Hypo. Confirmed 1 district
% Rep. Vote in Judicial Election Greater than % Rep. Vote in Cong. Election	Hypo. Confirmed 40 districts	Hypo. Refuted 27 districts

% Confirmed = 41/102 or 40%;
% Refuted = 61/102 or 60%

II. Testing the Hypothesis that Anglo-Saxon Ethnic Surnames Will Receive a Higher Percentage of Votes in Judicial than in Congressional Elections (where both elections are bi-ethnic)

	Anglo-Saxon Candidate is with Dominant Party in Which Election: Both Elections or Neither Election	Anglo-Saxon Candidate is with Dominant Party in Which Election: Only in One of the Two Elections
% Anglo-Saxon Vote in Judicial Election Greater than % Anglo-Saxon Vote in Congressional Election	Hypo. Confirmed 9 districts	Hypo. Untestable 3 districts
% Anglo Saxon Vote in Judicial Election Less than % Anglo-Saxon Vote in Congressional Election	Hypo. Refuted 6 districts	Hypo. Untestable 7 districts

% Confirmed = 9/15 or 60%;
% Refuted = 6/15 or 40%

ceive a higher percentage of the votes in judicial elections than in congressional elections, and 60 percent of the districts refuted the hypothesis. It may be that voters believe that it is less proper or meaningful to vote party label in judicial elections and therefore may be more likely to look to other criteria in making judicial choices. It may also be that the criteria voters use in choosing judges has less of a correlation with political party than the more ideological criteria they use in choosing congressmen.

On the other hand, ethnic voting may be more important in judicial than in congressional elections, even if party voting is not. To determine this, one needs a sample of paired judicial and congressional elections in which both elections involve a candidate with an Anglo-Saxon name running against one with a non-Anglo-Saxon name. To control for the advantage which a candidate has who is with the dominant party, the only districts in which the ethnic hypothesis is testable are those in which the Anglo-Saxon candidate is with the dominant party in both of the two elections or in neither. The bottom half of table 11-2 indicates there were fifteen such districts on which data was compiled. Sixty percent of those fifteen districts confirm the hypothesis that the percentage of Anglo-Saxon votes in the judicial election is greater than the percentage of Anglo-Saxon votes in the congressional election. This means that the ethnic split was generally greater in judicial elections. It may be due to the need of judicial voters to resort to ethnic surname connotations where the voters lacked more personalized knowledge of the candidates, especially where there are nonpartisan ballots. It may also be due to the reluctance of voters to emphasize ethnic considerations in congressional elections where ethnic balance on the ticket is not considered as important as it is on a multiple-judge court.

Appointing Behavior in Judicial Appointments

In discussing factors considered in judicial election voting, it was pointed out (1) that party and ethnic voting may not be so irrational and (2) that party and ethnic voting may not be so much more prevalent in judicial than in congressional or general elections. It should also be pointed out that emphasis on party and ethnic considerations by voters may not be so strong as it is among governors and presidents in making judicial appointments, to which we should now turn.[29]

Appointing in One's Own Image. Presidents and governors do strongly consider party affiliation in making judicial appointments, as indicated by the high percentage of appointments within party lines. For example, of 102 appointments to the United States Supreme Court from John Jay through William Rehnquist, there have been only nine appointments across party lines.[30] Eight of the nine involved Republican presidents appointing a Democrat to the court, possibly in light of the fact that Democrats have generally constituted a numerical majority in America even when Republicans have occupied the White House. Justice Burton, a card-playing friend of Harry Truman, was the only Republican appointed by a Democratic president. During the period from 1860 to 1960, over 95 percent of the appointments to lower federal courts by Democratic presidents were Democrats, and almost 95 percent of the appointments by Republican presidents were Republicans.[31]

State governors in making appointments to state supreme courts are somewhat more likely to appoint across party lines. Thus, only eight of thirty-six presidents appointed across party lines, but in a sample of nineteen state governors, eleven made at least one appointment across party lines. State governors make more such appointments because in some appointive states (like Missouri) they are required by law to do so;[32] and in some elective states they possibly feel an obligation to occasionally replace a retired, deceased, or resigned judge by a member of the same party. Although presidents and governors may choose within party lines more so than voters do, presidents and governors supplement party information with personalized data which voters often lack.

Appointments across ethnic lines have been slightly more rare than appointments across party lines. Thus, thirty-five of the thirty-six presidents through Richard Nixon have been Protestants. Only seven of the Protestant presidents have appointed either a Catholic or a Jew to the Supreme Court, as contrasted to eight who made appointments across party lines. The one non-Protestant president (John Kennedy) made only one appointment to the Supreme Court, and that appointment was also a non-Protestant (Arthur Goldberg).

In the sample of nineteen state governors, sixteen were Protestants, two Catholic, and one unknown. Nine of the sixteen never appointed a Catholic or Jew, although seven of the sixteen appointed at least one Catholic or Jew. The two Catholic governors both appointed at least one Catholic or Jew. The reason for fewer appointments along religious lines than along party lines may relate to the greater visibility, feeling of need, and the presence of legal requirements for bipartisan supreme courts but not for bi-ethnic supreme courts. Using a national sample of state supreme courts, political parties are much better represented in comparison to the general population than are the diverse American ethnic groups.[33]

By appointing judges like themselves, the presidents and governors not only promote their ideological causes and satisfy party patronage rewards, but they also possibly receive direct feedback decisions favorable to the appointer when the appointer's powers are involved in litigation before the court. For example, in the case testing the constitutionality of President Truman's seizure of the steel mills during the Korean War, 50 percent of his appointees voted in favor of Truman, whereas only 20 percent of the Roosevelt holdovers voted in favor of Truman.[34] This case tends to confirm the hypothesis that a greater proportion of judges appointed by the president are likely to vote for him than are the judges not appointed by the president.[35]

In a sample of one hundred famous Supreme Court cases involving presidential power (as shown in table 11-6, twenty-three confirmed the above hypothesis, eleven refuted it, and forty neither refuted nor confirmed it because the percentage of the president's appointees favoring him equalled the percentage of the president's non-appointees favoring him (which happens when the cases are unanimous or there is a zero correlation between being the president's appointee and voting in favor of him).[36] Twenty-six of the cases were unusable because they did not contain some judges who where the president's appointees and some who were not. Since 23 cases confirmed and only 11 refuted, this amounts to 68 percent confirmation.

Likewise, there is substantial confirmation of the hypothesis on row 2 of table 11-6 for the hypothesis that a greater proportion of the judges from the president's party are likely to vote for him than are the judges from the opposite party. Sixty-four percent of the usable, non-zero correlation cases confirmed the hypothesis.

For a president to appoint a former governor or president to the Supreme Court is also a form of appointing someone like one's self. Although there were only nineteen non-zero correlation cases in which some former governors or presidents were present, twelve of these nineteen involved a greater proportion of those former chief-executive judges voting for the president. However, merely having been a former governmental administrator does not seem to be enough to enable a judge to strongly empathize with the president, as is indicated on row 4 where there were more refutations than confirmations of the hypothesis that a greater proportion of the judges who had been governmental administrators are likely to vote for the president.

Other Factors Considered in Appointing. Although appointing in one's own image may be a very important factor in judicial appointments, other factors may also be important as well as interesting to discuss. These other factors include a desire to appoint judges who (1) will later be acclaimed for their judicial greatness, (2) will be approved by the legislature, (3) are young and will thus carry the appointer's ideology on the court for many years, and (4) possibly have had prior judicial experience. It may be interesting to try to determine what types of governors or presidents are most likely to appoint great, approved, young, or experienced judges, as well as judges across party or religious lines.

Table 11-7 shows the correlation between various appointer characteristics and various characteristics of judicial appointees where the ap-

Table 11-6
How Victory for the Appointer Relates to What Judges He Appoints (Using 100 famous Supreme Court cases involving presidential power)

Hypothesis	*# Cases Not Having Both Groups Being Compared (Thus Unusuable)*	*# Cases Refuting Hypothesis*	*# Cases neither Refuting Nor Confirming (Unanimous or Zero Correlation Cases)*	*# Cases Confirming Hypothesis*	*Percentage of Cases Confirming Rather than Refuting*
1. A greater proportion of the judges *appointed by the president* are likely to vote for him (than are the judges not appointed by the President).	26	11	40	23	68%
2. A greater proportion of the judges *from the president's party* are likely to vote for him (than are the judges from the opposite party).	7	13	57	23	64%
3. A greater proportion of the judges who *had been governors or presidents* are likely to vote for the President (than are judges without such experience).	56	7	25	12	68%
4. A greater proportion of the judges who *had been governmental administrators* are likely to vote for the president.	0	23	62	15	39%

Table 11-7
How Appointers Who Make Generally Praiseworthy Appointments Differ from Those Who Do Not

	APPOINTER CHARACTERISTICS						
Appointer / *Appointee* (APPOINTEE CHARACTERISTICS)	*Governor Not President*	*Former Lawyer*	*Former Legislator*	*College Educated*	*Republican Not Democrat*	*Opposition Controlled Legislature*	*Member Minority Religion*
Some Great Judges	X	11	–04	01	–08	<u>48</u>	X
All Accepted by Legislature	X	<u>21</u>	<u>21</u>	–01	06	–10	12
Most Had Prior Judicial Experience	14	<u>22</u>	<u>22</u>	–07	<u>24</u>	19	–11
Some Across Party Lines	<u>30</u>	10	–11	<u>28</u>	29	<u>23</u>	07
Some Minority Religion	18	–05	–16	13	–05	11	35

X = Information on this variable was available only for presidents or was otherwise limited.
Underline indicates correlation greater than 20.
Decimal points preceding each correlation are not shown.

pointee characteristics are often considered praiseworthy. The data for table 11-7 come from analyzing the characteristics of thirty-four presidents through President Kennedy and the characteristics of the Supreme Court judges they appointed.[37] Table 11-7 also includes data on sixteen governors and their appointed judges serving in 1955 in states where all the supreme court judges are appointed by the governor.[38] Information on the greatness of the judges who were appointed is available only for presidents and Supreme Court justices, using the lists of Felix Frankfurter and John Frank.[39] Information on whether some of the appointments were rejected by the legislature is also only readily available for presidents and Supreme Court justices.

The relationships that are particularly interesting to discuss are those involving a positive or inverse correlation between two of the variables that is greater than +20 or −20. For example, reading down each column or appointer characteristic the first such substantial correlation is the +33 one between being a governor rather than a president and making some appointments across party lines. This correlation may be due to the fact that some state laws which provide for appointive systems require the governor to provide some party balance on the supreme court, but nothing in the federal Constitution or statutes requires the president to do so. Governors are also more likely than presidents to appoint some Supreme Court judges who are Catholics or Jews rather than Protestants. This may be due to the lower visibility of appointments at the governor level than at the presidential level and to the fact that in some states Catholics and Jews have a much higher percentage of the population than they do in the nation as a whole.

Appointers who are former lawyers seem more capable of obtaining the consent of their legislatures to their appointments (+21) possibly because of their greater negotiating ability and experience, but also because there is a substantial correlation between being a former lawyer and a former legislator since so many legislators are lawyers. Appointers who are former lawyers also tend to appoint mord supreme court judges who have had prior judicial experience than non-lawyer appointers do (+26) possibly because lawyers tend to think of supreme court judging as being more legalistic than non-lawyer appointers do. Like former lawyers, the former legislator tends to have his appointments more readily accepted by the legislature and tends to appoint prior judges. This may partially reflect the former legislator's greater awareness of how to win over the legislature.

College-educated in the fourth column refers to having at least a bachelors degree prior to 1900 or a graduate or professional degree after 1900. College-educated appointers tend to appoint more across party lines and more judges of minority religions. This might reflect the possible fact that better educated appointers might be more concerned with ability than with party loyalty or ethnic acceptability. Better educated presidents, however, were no more likely to appoint great judges than less educated presidents.

The more political characteristics represented in the next two columns reveal some of the higher and more interesting correlations. Republican appointers, for instance, are more likely to appoint supreme court judges with prior judicial experience than are Democratic appointers. This may reflect the relative conservatism due to the increased age of appointees who have had prior judicial experience and the relative conservatism of Republican appointers. Republican appointers are also more likely to make appointments across party lines than are Democratic appointers. This conforms to the finding not shown that there is a +20 correlation between being a Republican appointer and having an opposition-controlled legislature, which may cause a Republican appointer to feel a greater need to make more Democratic appointments than for Democratic appointers to feel the need to make Republican appointments. Republican appointers are more likely to have opposition-controlled legislatures because for most of the time periods involves in the data, Democrats constituted a majority of the legislature's electorate although the electorate may have chosen a Republican as chief executive.

Having an opposition-controlled legislature produces the high correlation of +48 with appointing some great judges. Apparently appointers have a greater tendency or need to pick better qualified or at least more acceptable appointees if the appointer's party does not control the consent process in the legislature. This would also help to explain why appointers who have opposition-controlled legislatures tend to make more appointments across party lines and tend to appoint judges more likely to have prior judicial experience.

In the last row of the last column, once again we see the tendency of appointers like voters to appoint in their own image. Thus, there is a +35 correlation between an appointer being a member of a minority religion and his appointing some supreme court judges who are also members of a minority religion. As mentioned before, there has been only one president who was a non-Protestant (namely John Kennedy) and his only appointment to the Supreme Court was also a non-Protestant (namely Arthur Goldberg). This same phenomena of like begets like also appears in the governor appointment data.

Bar Association Preferences. In order to more fully consider appointer behavior in judicial appointments, it might be helpful to determine what kinds of judges tend to receive high bar association endorsements. This is so because bar associations and lawyers seek to play important roles in the selection of judges in appointive systems by way of their membership on nominating commissions as in Missouri, or by way of their membership on legislative approval committees like the U.S. Senate Judiciary Committee. Even in judicial elections, bar associations seek to have an informal influence on determining the judges by way of their electoral endorsements.[40]

Table 11-8 shows how proposed federal judges who are rated relatively high by the ABA differ from those who are rated relatively low, using 270 appointees to the federal district and circuit courts from 1953 to 1962.[41] "Rated high" means they were declared to be exceptionally well qualified or well qualified. "Rated relatively low" means they were declared to be just qualified or unqualified before their appointment. The general hypothesis is that proposed judges having background characteristics more associated with liberalism will be rated higher than proposed judges having background characteristics more associated with conservatism. It is further hypothesized that higher ratings will go to judges having characteristics associated with technical competence and nonpartisanship. The general findings do not strongly support the liberalism hypothesis, but they provide more support for the technical competence and nonpartisanship hypothesis.

The top or liberalism half of table 11-8 shows how political party, ethnic background, and bar association affiliations relate to how high the judicial ratings are. Sixty-four percent of the 104 Democratic judges received high ratings, which is virtually equal to the 63 percent of the 153 Republican judges who received high ratings. It was thought that this equality might be due to high ratings being given to conservative sourthern Democratic judges offsetting the possible low ratings being given to liberal northern Democratic judges. However, there is still virtually a zero difference between the percentages when northern Democrats are compared with northern Republicans and when sourthern Democrats are compared with sourthern Republicans.

American Bar Association preferences as manifested in their ratings do not significantly relate to whether the proposed judges are Catholic or Protestant. The ratings correlate more highly with whether the appointees have southern or eastern European ancestral nationality as contrasted to western or northern European ancestral nationality. There was also a 15 percentage points difference between the percentage of foreign-born judges receiving high ratings and the percentage of native-born, but this difference could be attributable to the fact that there was only a small sample of eight foreign-born judges.

The most relevant pressure groups to which potential judges can be members are probably bar associations since they take a stand (often conservative) on many issues that are involved in litigation.[42] Judges who indicated membership in the American Bar Association in *Who's Who in America* did not receive higher ratings than judges who did not indicate ABA membership. Judges who were ABA leaders, however, did tend to

Table 11-8

How Proposed Judges Who Are Rated Relatively High by the ABA Differ from Those Who Are Rated Relatively Low (Using 270 appointees to the Federal Judiciary from 1953 to 1962)

Group 1	*Group 2*	*Number of Judges in Each Group (1)*	*(2)*	*% Group 1 Receiving High Rating*	*% Group 2 Receiving High Rating*	*Difference Between the Percentages*
I. CONSERVATISM CHARACTERISTICS						
(Less Associated with Conservatism)	(More Associated with Conservatism)					
A. POLITICAL PARTY						
1. Democrats	Republicans	107	153	64%	63%	− 1
2. Northern Democrats	Northern Republicans	62	120	66	67	+ 1
3. Southern Democrats	Southern Republicans	45	33	61	63	+ 2
B. ETHNIC BACKGROUND						
4. Catholic	Protestant	40	126	60	62	+ 2
5. South or East Europe	West or North Europe	27	233	52	65	+13
6. Foreign born	Native born	8	245	50	65	+15

Table 11-8 (continued)

Group 1	*Group 2*	*Number of Judges in Each Group (1)*	*(2)*	*% Group 1 Receiving High Rating*	*% Group 2 Receiving High Rating*	*Difference Between the Percentages*
C. BAR ASSOCIATION AFFILIATIONS						
7. No ABA indicated	Indicated ABA membership	43	222	63	64	+ 1
8. No state bar indicated	Indicated state bar assoc. membership	50	209	52	66	+14
9. No local bar indicated	Indicated local bar assoc. membership	63	202	57	66	+ 9
II. NONPARTISANSHIP AND TECHNICAL COMPETENCE						
(Less Associated with Non-P. & Tech. Comp.)	(More Associated with Non-P. & Tech. Comp.)					
A. NONPARTISANSHIP						
10. More active in party	Less active in party	97	163	55%	68%	+13
11. Some legislative exp.	No legislative exp.	52	203	54	68	+14
12. Some govt. executive experience	No govt. executive experience	185	69	60	77	+17

B. TECHNICAL COMPETENCE						
13. No books or articles indicated	Books or articles published	186	84	59	74	+15
14. No academic experience indicated	Academic experience	198	45	66	60	− 6
15. Little trial experience	Much trial experience	64	99	63	71	+ 8
16. No judicial experience	Some judicial experience	159	107	59	69	+10
III. MIXED CHARACTERISTICS						
(Less Associated with Conservatism and Maybe Competence)	(More Associated with Conservatism and Maybe Competence)					
A. AGE						
17. Under 45	45 and over	70	135	56	64	+ 8
B. TYPE OF LAW PRACTICE						
18. Criminal, Domestic, or Administrative	Corporate or Financial	14	103	43	66	+23
19. Under five-man firm	Firm with five or more	150	103	56	73	+17

receive higher ratings than judges who were mere members. Membership in state and local bar associations did correlate more highly with the ratings, possibly because membership in these bar associations was more likely to be accompanied by leadership roles than membership in the far larger, more diluted ABA.

There are substantial correlations between the characteristics relating to nonpartisanship and receiving high ratings. For instance, those judges who had been less politically active received higher ratings than those who had been more politically active. To be classified as politically active meant holding elective political office, being a committeeman for either political party, or being a national convention delegate. Likewise, those proposed judges who had no prior legislative experience or no prior government executive experience also tended to receive higher ratings.

The characteristic related to technical competence that correlated most highly with ABA ratings was whether the proposed judge in his *Who's Who* biography listed any books or articles published. It does follow that one who published about law should be more technically competent to write judicial opinions and decide legal matters. Row 5, however, shows the ABA preferred judges with no academic experience by six percentage points over those with academic experience. This may reflect the fact that academic experience correlates with a lack of practicing lawyer experience which the ABA considers more important, although academic experience might correlate with technical competence if all other things were held constant.

The most relevant practicing lawyer experience is trial work which does correlate with higher ratings. It makes sense that lawyers who have had extensive courtroom experience would make better judges. An even more relevant form of experience from the point of view of technical competence might be prior judicial experience. This characteristic also correlates with higher ratings. A more detailed breakdown of the prior judicial experience characteristic indicates that with additional years of judicial experience goes higher ratings if the lower judge is proposed for a higher federal judicial appointment. The preference of the ABA for judges with prior judicial experience in table 11-8 is consistent with the preference of appointers who are former lawyers for judges with prior judicial experience in table 11-7.

Prior judicial experience correlates with age as well as ABA preference. Age possibly correlates with both increased technical competence and increased conservatism. Row 17 shows that older proposed judges are somewhat more likely to receive higher ratings than younger judges. This is especially so if one divides the judges by age into more than two intervals. Thus, 44 percent of those under thirty-four received high ratings, 57 percent of those between thirty-five and forty-four, 65 percent of those between forty-five and fifty-four, and 67 percent of those fifty-five and older. These figures just include district court judges because the circuit court judges tend to be appointed at older ages and there are fewer of them.

Type of clients is another mixed characteristic that may correlate with conservatism and possibly technical competence such that it is hard to explain which of these two correlations accounts for the higher ratings which lawyers with a more prestigeful type of clientele have over lawyers with a less prestigeful type of clientele. Thus, row 19 contains the largest difference between the percentages in that it shows that 66 percent of the 103 lawyers who primarily had corporate and financial clients received high ratings, whereas only 43 percent of the fourteen lawyers who specialized in criminal, domestic, or administrative law practice received high ratings. The nature of the law practice of the proposed judges was mainly determined from consulting material in the *Martindale-Hubbell Legal Directory*. Related to type of clientele is size of law firm. Lawyers from larger, more prestigeful law firms did receive higher ratings possibly because of the presumed technical competence which large firm members tend to have, but also possibly because large firm members are likely to be bar association leaders. Degree of urbanism as a separate characteristic is not shown in the table because it correlates highly with size of law firm.

To supplement the above analysis of ABA ratings, one could determine the decisional propensities of the 270 appointees by analyzing their opinions to see if the judges with higher ABA ratings tend to be more conservative in business regulation and other types of cases which tend to separate conservative from liberal judges. In a study which had that as one of its purposes, no substantial decisional differences were found.[43] That study, however, did not compare high rated federal judges with relatively low rated judges hearing the same cases on the same three-judge districts courts or multiple-judge circuit courts the way elected judges were compared with interim appointed judges in the beginning of this chapter. Therefore the findings might be muddied by differences between the cases heard by high rated judges and those heard by low rated judges.

One could try to get at the technical competence of the 270 appointees by doing a follow-up on their opinions to see to what extent they were either upheld or cited favorably in subsequent cases. Appellate decisions were found for 147 of the district court appointees. Of eighty-five appointees who were highly rated, 33 percent were affirmed more than 80 percent of the time; whereas of sixty-two appointees who were not so highly rated, only 23 percent were affirmed more than 80 percent of the time. Using Shepard's Citations to determine how favorably or unfavorably the judge's opinions were treated by a subsequent court for 202 usable judges revealed that 20 percent of the highly rated appointees were *favorably* cited more than 40 percent of the time, whereas only 15 percent of the less highly rated appointees were favorably cited more than 40 percent of the time. Thirty-five percent of the less highly rated appointees were also *unfavorably* cited, but only 23 percent of the highly rated appointees were unfavorably cited.

Thus, it seems that bar association ratings, at least at the federal level, seem to correlate rather weakly with conservative background and decisional characteristics. They do correlate a little more strongly with background and decisional characteristics that relate to nonpartisanship and technical competence, but even there, their predictive power seems quite limited.

Some Conclusions

Pulling together all the findings presented leads one to conclude that maybe elected and appointed judicial systems do not differ as much in their results or in the behavior of voters and appointers as the debate literature would have us believe.[44] It may, however, be more interesting to find little or no difference where a big difference was generally thought to exist or argued over than to have simply confirmed the conventional wisdom.[45] Nevertheless, there are some important differences between the two systems of judicial selection.

Comparing Judicial Behavior

Elected judges serving on the same courts as interim appointed judges do seem to be slightly more liberal in their decisions as, for example, in business relations cases involving consumers or unions. The liberalism differences show up especially when one only makes comparisons between elected Republican judges serving with appointed Republican judges. Offsetting these liberalism differences, however, is the fact that the appointed judges were more likely to decide in favor of the injured party in motor vehicle accident cases.

Likewise elected judges serving on the same court as interim appointed judges do seem to have (1) more liberal-predicting backgrounds with regard to party and ethnic affiliation and (2) more liberal off-the-bench attitudes even if political party is held constant. Partially offsetting that liberalism is the possibility that elected judges are partly slated and elected for their greater vote getting image, and they thus tend to have more conservative prestige law school degrees, years of judicial experience, and scholarly honors.

Judges on appointed courts were found to be more likely to vote contrary to the pattern of their political party than judges on elected courts even when length of tenure was held constant. This finding, however, could not be explained in terms of greater attitudinal objectivity or having off-the-bench attitudes atypical of one's party although it might possibly be explained in terms of differential role perceptions of appointed and elected judges.

There was virtually no difference between the elected and appointed courts on such measures of prestige or competence as the esteem in which they are held by law professors, the frequency their opinions are used in casebooks, or the extent they are cited favorably by other courts. Likewise nothing meaningful could be concluded with regard to the ability of elected and appointed courts to process a large number of cases per judge or a large number of cases per cases-submitted mainly because of the inconsistencies among the courts as to what constitutes a "case."

Comparing Selection Behavior

Two frequent charges made against elected judicial systems are that the voters have such a low turnout in judicial elections as to make the elections meaningless and that when the voters do vote they do not do so in a meaningful way. On turnout, the data indicate that over 90 percent of the voters in general elections will vote in judicial elections if (1) the judicial elections are held at the same time as the general elections and if (2) they do not have an especially long ballot. The data also show those who vote in judicial elections are at least as representative of the general public as those who vote in general elections.

Voters in judicial elections may consider the political party and ethnic affiliation of the candidates when casting their votes. Empirical data, however, do tend to indicate that Democratic judges do differ in their decisional propensities from Republican judges, and that Catholic judges do differ from Protestant judges. The empirical data further show that voters in judicial elections consider party affiliations less than voters in general elections although they seem to consider ethnic affiliations more.

On the other side of the total picture, the appointments by presidents and governors highly correlate with political party and ethnic considerations in that a very high percentage of their appointments are within their own political party and ethnic group especially among presidents. By appointing judges like themselves, the presidents and governors not only promote their ideological causes and satisfy party patronage rewards, but the data indicate they are thereby more likely to receive favorable decisions when their powers are involved in litigation before the court, especially if their appointees had been former chief executives themselves.

When one attempts to correlate a variety of characteristics of presidents and governor appointers with the characteristics of their judicial appointees, a number of findings are revealed. For example, former lawyer-legislators are more likely to appoint judges with prior judicial experience and are more likely to have their appointments accepted by the legislature. Presidents are more likely to appoint great justices to the Supreme Court when the opposition party controls Congress. Appointments across party lines are more likely to be made by governors than presidents, by better educated appointers, by Republican appointers, and when the opposition party controls the legislature.

Bar associations often try to play an important part in judicial appointments at the president and governor level as well as in judicial elections. A systematic empirical analysis of what kind of judicial nominees get relatively high American Bar Association ratings tends to show that the ABA does not have a partisan political preference or a religious preference in its ratings. The ABA does have more of a preference for (1) bar association leaders although not mere members; (2) for non-activism in partisan, legislative, or executive politics; (3) for authorship and prior courtroom experience, and (4) for lawyers in large firms engaged in corporate law practice. The ABA ratings correlate weekly with subsequent liberal-conservative decisional behavior of appointers, but a little more strongly with subsequent affirmance and favorable citation of appointers.

Making a Policy Choice

From all these data, one should be in a better position to make an evaluative comparison between elected and appointed judicial systems, or at least to see better what additional data is needed. In addition to empirical data, an evaluative comparison requires an awareness of what goals one considers desirable and possibly how much relative weight to give each goal. Thus if one highly values liberalism and public participation but does not so highly value nonpartisanship and technical competence, he may be more likely to prefer an elected system to an appointed system. Empirical data, however, can help inform one at least roughly on how much or how little of a difference in liberalism, public participation, nonpartisanship, or other variables there is between elected and appointed systems.

If elected judges are more liberal than appointed judges (from the same political party on the same court) on economic matters but less liberal on civil liberties matters as hypothesized, then it looks like a hopeless dilemma if one wishes to equally maximize or minimize both these ideological goals. One may, however, be able to *maximize* both by having elected judges but with lifetime or long tenure like Pennsylvania where the supreme court is elected, but they have twenty-one year terms. Likewise one might be able to *minimize* both kinds of liberalism by having appointed judges who periodically run for reelection against opposition or on their record. That is the situation in Missouri where the supreme court is appointed but stands for reelection every ten years, and at least one judge was defeated for his civil liberties liberalism by a press campaign conducted by a conservative St. Louis newspaper.

Although the method of selection may correlate with a judge's economic background, and although term of office may relate to the amount of anti-civil liberties majoritarian pressure to which he is subjected, neither the method of selection nor the term of office seems to correlate very highly or consistently with technical competence, honesty, wisdom, and other non-ideological virtues. There was, however, some correlation in the data (1) between being *appointed* and deciding cases contrary to one's expected political party pattern and (2) between being *elected* and attending a prestige law school, having years of judicial experience, and having received scholarly honors. What is possibly needed to supplement the provisions for method of selection and term of office on these non-ideological criteria is a non-ideological commission concerned with technical competence, honesty, and wisdom in slating nominees for election or appointment and in removing judges who grossly fail to continue to meet these standards.

Such a commission for nomination and removal proceedings could perhaps consist of five people: one judge, one law professor, one practicing lawyer, and two public representatives, or some other similar combination. The commission could be required to have no more than three persons from the same political party. They could be appointed by the governor with the consent of the legislature and with staggered terms so no one governor could appoint all the members at one time.[46] The judicial members could be appointed by the state supreme court and the lawyer members by the state bar association.

In the election process, two such commissions would be needed. One commission could aid the Democratic slatemakers and would be required to have the same occupational breakdown as the removal commission but consist only of Democrats chosen in a Democratic primary. The other commission could aid the Republican slatemakers and be chosen in a Republican primary. These judicial election commissions (like the Missouri nominating commission) could by law have the power to require the slatemakers to choose judicial candidates from within the commission's recommended list or at least to choose a percentage of the candidates from the lists. This is analogous to the way the Democratic and Republican statewide slatemakers in Illinois rely on the Democratic alumni committee and the Republican alumni committee of the Alumni Association of the University of Illinois in slating candidates of the Illinois Board of Trustees.

Some of the above policy provisions (like those dealing with a possible nominating commission to supplement the elected and appointed processes) go beyond the quantitative data presented, but all the above policy choices can obtain some insights and partial support from the quantitative data. Equipped with a hierarchy of values and access to raw or analyzed data, one should be able to make a policy choice that will better achieve one's goals on this controversial issue of elected versus appointed judicial systems.[47]

Notes

1. Bibliographies include AMERICAN JUDICATURE SOCIETY, SELECTED READINGS ON THE ADMINISTRATION OF JUSTICE AND ITS IMPROVEMENT 1-26 (1967); Smith, *Bibliography: Judges–Appointment and Removal–Selected Writings* (Yale Law Library, 1970); American Judicature Society, *Judicial Selection and Tenure* (1970); F. KLEIN, JUDICIAL ADMINISTRATION AND THE LEGAL PROFESSION—A BIBLIOGRAPHY 173-204 (1963); R. DAHL & C. BOLDEN, THE AMERICAN JUDGE—A BIBLIOGRAPHY 38-69 (1968).

2. Goldman, *American Judges: Their Selection, Tenure, Variety and Quality,* 61 CURRENT HISTORY 1 (1971).

3. Exceptions include R. WATSON & R. DOWNING, THE POLITICS OF THE BENCH AND THE BAR (1969); B. HENDERSON & T. C. SINCLAIR, JUDICIAL SELECTION IN TEXAS—AN EXPLORATORY STUDY (1964); Canon, *The Impact of Formal Selection Processes on the Characteristics of Judges–Reconsidered,* 6 LAW & SOC'Y REV. 579 (1972); Levin, *An Empirical Evaluation of Urban Political Systems: The Criminal Courts* (paper presented at the 1969 Amer. Pol. Sci. Assoc. meeting); Jacob, *The Effect of Institutional Differences in the Recruitment Process: The Case of State Judges,* 13 J. PUB L. 104 (1964). Although these items contain some systematic quantitative data for comparing elected and appointed judges, they generally do not control for other important variables besides method of selection which might cause differences or similarities between their elected and appointed judges. See note 5 below and the accompanying text.

4. See the annual editions of the BOOK OF THE STATES (Council of State Governments, since 1936) for the judicial selection methods that were used in each state since the 1930s.

5. These are the kinds of variables that are generally not controlled for in the quantitative comparative studies cited in note 3.

6. Herndon, *Appointment as a Means of Initial Accession to Elective State Courts of Last Resort,* 38 N. DAK. L. REV. 60 (1962).

7. Twenty was used as a cut-off partly to make theoretical sense out of the data presented and partly because Guilford says: "If one asks, How small is N before we have a small sample? . . . Some place it is as low as 20." J. GUILFORD, FUNDAMENTAL STATISTICS IN PSYCHOLOGY AND EDUCATION 217 (4th ed. 1956). Guilford also says that special statistics should be used when any frequency is expected by chance to be less than 10. *Id*. at 234-35. If the number of elected or appointed judges on a row is 20 or less, then by change 10 or less should be above their court average and 10 or less should be below.

8. Winters & Allard, *Two Dozen Misconceptions about Judicial Selection and Tenure,* 48 J. AM. JUD. SOC'Y 140 (1964).

9. G. SCHUBERT, THE JUDICIAL MIND—THE ATTITUDES AND IDEOLOGIES OF SUPREME COURT JUSTICES 1946-1963, 150-154 (1965).

10. Nagel, *Political Party Affiliation and Judges' Decisions,* 55 AM. POL. SCI. REV. 843 (1961) and reprinted in S. NAGEL, THE LEGAL PROCESS FROM A BEHAVIORAL PERSPECTIVE 193 (1969) [hereinafter cited as LEGAL PROCESS].

11. Nagel, *Ethnic Affiliations and Judicial Propensities,* 24 J. POL. 92 (1962).

12. S. Nagel, *Off-the-Bench Judicial Attitudes* in JUDICIAL DECISION-MAKING 29 (G. Schubert ed. 1963), reprinted in LEGAL PROCESS 199.

13. For further detail on the meaning of high tuition law schools, see Nagel, *Judicial Backgrounds and Criminal Cases,* 53 J. CRIM. L. C. & P. S. 333 (1962), reprinted in LEGAL PROCESS 227. For further detail on the meaning of years of judicial experience and scholarly honors, see Nagel, *Off-the-Bench Judicial Attitudes* in *op. cit.* note 12 at 41-42.

Herbert Jacob also found that elected trial court judges were generally more likely to have attended a prestige law school than appointed trial court judges, but both types of judges were about the same on law school honors and on having little prior judicial experience. See Jacob, *op. cit.* note 3.

14. Nagel, *op, cit*. note 10, at 848-850.

15. As further support for the finding, when elected judges are compared with interim appointed judges with regard to deciding contrary to one's party pattern, a higher percentage of the appointed judges do decide contrary than do the elected judges, especially among Republican judges. Francis Lee, however, finds no significant difference between judges on the appointed courts of California, Massachusetts, New Jersey, and Missouri on nonpartisanship as compared to the judges on the elected courts of New York, Pennsylvania, Ohio, and Wisconsin. F. Lee, *Judicial Selection: An Explanatory Variable of Judicial Behavior on Bipartisan State Supreme Courts* (U. of Pa. Ph.D. dissertation, 1970).

16. Vines, *The Judicial Role in the American States–An Exploration* in FRONTIERS OF JUDICIAL RESEARCH 461 (J Grossman & J. Tanenhaus eds. 1969).

17. Mott, *Judicial Influence,* 30 AM. POL. SCI. R. 295 (1936).

18. Institute of Judicial Administration, STATISTICS ON WORK OF HIGHEST STATE APPELATE COURTS (1954).

19. Studies of voting behavior in judicial elections include Jacob, *Judicial Insulation–Elections, Direct Participation, and Public Attention to the Courts in Wisconsin,* 1966 WIS. L. R. 801 (1966) and Ladinsky and Silver, *Popular Democracy and Judicial Independence: Electorate and Elite Reactions to Two Wisconsin Supreme Court Elections,* 1967 WIS. L. REV. 128 (1967), but they were not designed to compare judicial elections with general elections or judicial elections with executive appointment.

20. Winters & Allard, *op. cit.* note 8, at 140.

21. E. Roper, A STUDY OF VOTER AWARENESS OF JUDICIAL CANDIDATES IN ELECTIONS (mimeographed report, 1954) and Klots, *The Selection of Judges and the Short Ballot,* 1955 RECORD OF N.Y.C.B.A. 103.

22. See the text accompanying table 11-5 for further information on the source of the data.

23. If the area, however, gets small enough to be classified as rural-farm, the voting turnout drops almost to the relatively low percentages of New York City and Buffalo.

24. Nagel, *op. cit.* note 10. Other works which find Democratic judges differ from Republican judges include D. Leavitt, *Political Party and Class Influences on the Attitudes of Justices of the Supreme Court in the Twentieth Century* (paper delivered at the 1972 Midwest Political Science Association meeting); Feeley, *Another Look at the 'Party Variable' in Judicial Decision-Making: An Analysis of the Michigan Supreme Court*, 4 POLITY 91 (1971); M. Feeley, *Comparative Analysis of Decision-Making on State Supreme Courts* (University of Minnesota thesis, 1969); Ulmer, *The Political Party Variable in the Michigan Supreme Court,* 11 J. PUB. L. 352 (1962); Goldman, *Voting Behavior on the United States Courts of Appeals, 1961-1964,* 60 AM. POL. SCI. REV. 374 (1966). No significant differences were found by Adamany, *The Party Variable in Judges' Voting: Conceptual Notes and a Case Study,* 63 AM. POL. SCI. REV 57 (1969) and Walker, *A Note Concerning Partisan Influences on Trial Judge Decision-Making,* 6 L. & SOC'Y REV. 645 (1972).

25. Nagel, *op. cit.* note 11. Other works which find Catholic judges differ from Protestant judges include: Vines, *Federal District Judges and Race Relations Cases in the South,* 26 J. POL. 337, at 353 (1964); Ulmer, *Dissent Behavior and the Social Background of Supreme Court Justices,* 32 J. POL. 580 (1970); *Social Background as an Indicator to the Votes of*

Supreme Court Justices in Criminal Cases: 1947-56 Terms (forthcoming); no significant differences were found by Goldman, *op. cit.* note 24.

26. A. CAMPBELL et al., THE VOTER DECIDES 88-111 (1954).

27. If judicial elections held simultaneously with general elections had a separate straight-party level or box, then one could simply determine the percentage of straight-party judicial voters and compare it with the percentage of straight-party general election voters. There is, however, no separate straight-party indicator for judicial elections, and this writer has found no data on straight-party voting in judicial elections.

28. "Dominated by the Democratic party" here means that in the five congressional elections from 1952 through 1960, the Democratic candidate in the district won at least three times. If the Republican candidate won at least three times, then the district is considered to be Republican-dominated.

29. Studies of the process whereby presidents or governors appoint judges include Watson, *op. cit.* note 3; J. GROSSMAN, LAWYERS AND JUDGES—THE ABA AND THE POLITICS OF JUDICIAL SELECTION (1965); JOHN SCHMIDHAUSER (ed.), CONSTITUTIONAL LAW IN THE POLITICAL PROCESS 183-232 (1963); Chase, *Federal Judges: The Appointing Process* 51 MINN. L. REV. 185 (1966); SCIGLIANO (ed.), THE COURTS—A READER IN THE JUDICIAL PROCESS 65-97 (1962); D. DANELSKI, A SUPREME COURT JUSTICE IS APPOINTED (1964); and Goldman, *Judicial Appointments to the United States Courts of Appeals,* 1967 WIS. L. REV. 186 (1967). With the exception of the Watson book, these studies are not, however, designed to compare the appointing process with the electing process.

30. The nine Supreme Court appointments across party lines were (1) Democrat Nelson who was appointed by Whig Tyler, (2) Democrat Field appointed by Republican Lincoln, (3) Democrat H. Jackson appointed by Republican Harrison, (4) Democrats Lurton and (5) J. Lamar appointed by Republican Taft to the Court, (6) Democrat Butler appointed by Harding, (7) Cardozo appointed by Hoover, (8) Burton appointed by Truman, and (9) Brennan who was an Eisenhower appointee. Brandeis is generally considered to have been a Democrat at the time he was appointed by Wilson, although a Republican prior to 1912. G. SCHUBERT, CONSTITUTIONAL POLITICS—THE POLITICAL BEHAVIOR OF SUPREME COURT JUSTICES AND THE CONSTITUTIONAL POLICIES THAT THEY MAKE 37, 709-712 (1960).

31. Miller, *Politics and the Courts: The Struggle for Good Judges,* 42 A.B.A.J. 939 (1956).

32. COUNCIL OF STATE GOVERNMENTS, COURTS OF LAST RESORT OF THE FORTY-EIGHT STATES, Table 4 (1955).

33. Nagel, *op. cit.* note 11 and Nagel, *Unequal Party Representation on the State Supreme Courts,* 45 J. AM. JUD. SOC'Y 62 (1961).

34. *Youngstown Sheet* & Tube Company v. Sawyer, 343 U.S. 579 (1952). The two Truman appointees who voted against him said they would have voted in his favor if there was danger of invasion (Burton) or if Congress had not passed a statute governing seizures (Clark).

35. On some relations between the president and the Supreme Court, see R. SCIGLIANO, THE SUPREME COURT AND THE PRESIDENCY (1971).

36. The writer gratefully thanks Gary Hoskin of SUNY at Buffalo for the work he did on compiling some of these data as part of a seminar paper.

37. CONGRESSIONAL QUARTERLY SERVICE, CURRENT AMERICAN GOVERNMENT 65-68 (1963).

38. The sixteen governors were Adams of New Hampshire, Boggs of Delaware, Bradford of Massachusetts, Carvel of Delaware, Cross of Maine, Dale of New Hampshire, Donnelly of Missouri, Driscoll of New Jersey, Hildreth of Maine, Knight of California, Meyner of New Jersey, Marby of New Hampshire, Payne of Maine, Saltonstall of Massachusetts, Smith of Missouri, and Warren of California.

39. Frankfurter, *The Supreme Court in the Mirror of Justices,* 105 U. PA, L. REV. 781 (1957); J. FRANK, MARBLE PALACE: THE SUPREME COURT IN AMERICAN LIFE 43-44 (1961); and Nagel, *Characteristics of Supreme Court Greatness,* 56 A. B. A. J. 957 (1970). The sixteen justices that they both agreed had achieved greatness were Marshall, W. Johnson, Story, Taney, Curtis, Campbell, Miller, Field, Bradley, Harlan (1st), Brewer, Moody, Hughes, Holmes, Brandeis, and Cardozo.

40. However, less than one percent of the voters in the Roper poll (*op. cit.* note 21) mentioned bar association recommendations as being helpful in deciding which judge to vote for even though bar association recommendations was one of five answers suggested by the pollsters. Bar association recommendations are more influential in the presidential appointment process. See Grossman, *op. cit.* note 29.

41. The writer gratefully thanks Linda Nielsen Metzler for the work she did in processing some of these data as part of her master's thesis. Metzler, *Characteristics of Federal Judges Preferred by the American Bar Association* (U. of Illinois master's thesis, 1965). Most of the raw data were generously provided by Joel Grossman of the University of Wisconsin.

42. J. SCHMIDHAUSER, THE SUPREME COURT—ITS POLITICS, PERSONALITIES, AND PROCEDURES 65-99 (1960).

43. Goldman, *op. cit.* note 24.

44. For references to the debate literature, see note 1 above.

45. Examples include studies showing that: (1) the definition of criminal insanity may be irrelevant to outcomes in criminal cases; (2) the occurrence of equal apportionment may be irrelevant to legislative policy outcomes; or (3) the abolition of the principle of contributory negligence may be irrelevant to court congestion. *See* R. SIMON, THE JURY AND THE DEFENSE OF INSANITY (1967); R. DIXON, DEMOCRATIC REPRESENTATION: REAPPORTIONMENT IN LAW AND POLITICS 574-581 (1968); and Rosenberg, *Comparative Negligence in Arkansas–A "Before and After" Survey,* 13 ARK. L. REV. 89 (1959).

46. On the Missouri nominating commission, see Watson, *op. cit.* note 3. On removal commissions, see the symposia on *Judicial Misconduct* in 48 J. AM. JUD. SOC'Y 163 (1965).

47. On systematic legal-policy evaluation, see Mayo & Jones, *Legal-Policy Decision Process: Alternative Thinking and the Predictive Function,* 33 GEO. WASH. L. REV 318 (1964); and Nagel, *Optimizing Legal Policy,* U. FLA. L. REV. 577 (1966), reprinted in LEGAL PROCESS 360.

12 Multiple Correlation of Judicial Backgrounds and Decisions

The Basic Research Design

In the early 1960s this writer published a series of articles describing the relation between the backgrounds of judges and judicial decisional propensities.[1] The basic research design used for this project was divided into three components. The first step was to establish a number of hypotheses, for example: if judges possess a particular background characteristic, then it may be possible to predict that they also generally possess a specific decisional propensity.[2] Next, the hypotheses were tested through compilation and analysis of data supplied from carefully selected sources.[3] The data sources for this analysis were the judicial decisions and background characteristics of the judges on every state supreme court that was bi-group with respect to the background characteristic under investigation;[4] compilations were based on all the nonunanimous decisions reached by these courts during their 1955 term.[5] After statistical analysis of the data, conclusions about the presence and strength of the proposed relationship could be drawn.[6]

One relation investigated during this period was that hypothesized to exist between political party affiliation and a propensity to favor the defense in criminal cases. The specific hypothesis used was: "Democratic judges have a greater tendency to decide for the defense in criminal cases than do Republican judges."[7] To test the hypothesis, it was necessary to compare: (1) the percentage of Democratic judges (the +X position) who decided for the defense in criminal cases more often than their supreme court did (the +Y position) with (2) the percentage of Republican judges (the −X position) who decided for the defense more often than their supreme court did (the +Y position).[8] The conclusion drawn from these comparisons was that, compared to other background characteristics, political party affiliation is a relatively accurate predictor of decisional propensities among state supreme court judges hearing criminal cases.

Some reviewers of this early research indicated that determining the relations between two or more background characteristics and two or more decisional propensities simultaneously could lead to additional insights about the relation between a judge's background and the judicial rulings he made.[9] The purpose of this chapter is to provide such a multiple correlation analysis of judges' backgrounds and decisions.[10]

Some Problems in the Original Research Design

The original research design is unsuitable without modification for multiple correlation analysis because a judge's decisional propensity was measured by comparing his behavior with that of his court. This was necessary to guarantee that comparison would be made only among judges hearing the same cases at the same time.[11] Using the original design to compare the decisional propensities of Catholic and Protestant judges who belong to the same political party (*i.e.*, holding party constant) would require finding at least one state supreme court whose members included Catholic Democrats, Catholic Republicans, Protestant Democrats and Protestant Republicans. One would then compare (1) the percentage of Catholic Democratic judges whose decisions for the defense in criminal cases exceeded the average of their state supreme court with (2) the percentage of Protestant Democratic judges who decided for the defense more often than did their court. One would repeat this procedure for Catholic Republican judges and Protestant Republican judges.

To evaluate the combined effect of religion and party affiliation would require a similar comparison of Catholic Democrats, Catholic Republicans, Protestant Democrats and Protestant Republicans. The probability of finding a state supreme court with at least one member in each of these four categories is very small.[12] If one wishes to assess the combined effect of more than two background variables, the opportunity to make the necessary comparisons becomes even less likely.[13]

Modifications to Allow Multiple Correlation Analysis

As an alternative research design, one can first determine the correlation between each background characteristic, X, and the judges' decisional propensities in criminal cases, Y. To do this requires one to introduce the statistical concept of the correlation coefficient, denoted r_{xy}.[14] This coefficient may assume any value between +1.00 and −1.00. The closer r_{xy} is to +1.00, the stronger the positive relationship between X and Y; the closer r_{xy} is to −1.00, the stronger the negative relationship between X and Y.[15] The closer r_{xy} is to 0.00 in value, the weaker the relationship is between X and Y.[16]

The sources used in the original design can again supply the necessary data to compute each correlation coefficient. Only bi-group courts are used because religion, party or any other background characteristic cannot explain differences in the decisions of members of the same court if the members of the court all share or all fail to share the background characteristic under study.[17] Only cases decided nonunanimously are used because these are the only cases in which there are differences to explain. The size of the sample from which each correlation is determined will vary because the number of judges serving in 1955 on bi-group courts depends upon the background characteristic being studied—in other words, upon the number of $+X$ and $-X$ judges who are members of each court that has at least one $+X$ and at least one $-X$ judge.[18]

As the next step, one can place these correlation coefficients in a correlation matrix[19] from which a multiple correlation analysis[20] or a multiple regression analysis[21] can be completed. Forming the matrix requires the assumption that the number of judges upon which each correlation is based (denoted N) is in some sense a representative sample of the set of judges upon which each correlation could have been based. Assuming that the sample[22] used is representative of the population[23] from which it was drawn is less reasonable when, as here, membership in the sample set is not randomly determined.[24] When one interprets the results, however, he can allow for the possibility that a group of judges is not randomly representative of the whole. For example, if Democratic judges are found to be more liberal[25] than Republican judges, one could observe that only northern courts were bipartisan. One would then realize that northern Democrats are being compared with northern Republicans because the bi-group or bipartisan criterion of the sample set prevents any comparison between southern Democrats and northern Republicans hearing the same cases on the same court.[26]

The Non-Multiple Correlation Results

The main results this writer obtained from such a multiple correlation analysis of judicial characteristics and decisions are exhibited in table 12-1. The twelve background variables and two attitudinal variables used in this writer's prior research appear again for two reasons: (1) to establish continuity between the present and earlier research and (2) to take advantage of the predictive power of the previous background variables.[27] The background variables studied include political party affiliation, pressure group affiliation, ethnic affiliation, pre-judicial occupation, education, age, and size of hometown.[28] The only change made in the set of background variables has been the substitution of the variable of economic liberalism[29] for the variable of liberalism, primarily because the latter lacked the clarity and specificity needed to do a more meaningful analysis.[30]

The two dependent variables examined here are both decisional propensities. The first is the tendency of a judge to decide for the defense in criminal cases more often than does his state supreme court. Since all the cases examined were decided by a state supreme court, the issues em-

Table 12-1
The Non-Multiple and Multiple Relations Among Judicial Characteristics and Decisions

Background Characteristics (the category hypothesized to be more liberal is mentioned first)	*Criminal Case Decisions*			*Economic Case Decisions*		
	1. Correlation with Above Average Defense Propensity for One's Court	*2. Usable Judges in Sample*	*3. Additional Variance Accounted For (%)*	*4. Correlation with Above Average Liberalism Propensity for One's Court*	*5. Usable Judges in Sample*	*6. Additional Variance Accounted For (%)*
I. Party						
1. Democrat vs. Republican	+.26	85	11%	+.37	103	44%
II. Pressure Groups						
2. Not a member of business group vs. is	+.01	80	0	−.05	99	—
3. Not a member of ABA vs. is	+.12	190	1	+.02	224	1
4. Not a member of nativist group vs. is	+.11	44	4	+.11	50	3
III. Occupations						
5. Not a former businessman vs. was	+.12	97	—	+.13	112	10
6. Not former prosecutor vs. was	+.12	181	3	−.03	222	2

IV. Education						
7. Attended low tuition law school vs. high	−.12	70	3	+.05	91	3
V. Age						
8. Under 65 vs. over 65	−.02	134	—	+.08	168	—
VI. Geography						
9. Practiced initially in a large city vs. small town	00	68	0	−.10	81	13
VII. Ethnic						
10. Catholic vs. Protestant	+.25	59	13	+.05	77	9
11. Low income Prot. denom. vs. high	+.09	108	2	−.03	140	—
12. Part non-British ancestry vs. only British	+.09	180	2	+.01	213	1
VIII. Attitudes						
13. High economic liberalism score vs. low	−.18	75	3	+.11	86	—
14. High criminal liberalism score vs. low	+.25	75	1	+.07	86	4
TOTALS (regardless of sign)	1.74	1446	43%=R^2	1.21	1752	90%=R^2
AVERAGES (regardless of sign)	.12	103	4%	.09	125	9%

phasized were legal rather than factual; that is, the issues presented were often procedural or constitutional questions of law rather than trial-level determinations of fact.

The second dependent variable reflects the tendency of a judge to find more often than his state supreme court: (1) for the administrative agency in business regulation cases; (2) for the claimant in unemployment compensation cases; (3) for the tenant in landlord-tenant cases; (4) for the debtor in creditor-debtor cases; (5) for the consumer in sale-of-goods cases; (6) for the injured party in motor vehicle accident cases; (7) for the labor union in union-management cases; and (8) for the employee in employee injury cases. Calculating a judge's position with respect to this second dependent variable requires computation of a composite decision score for each judge. To obtain this composite score, the decision scores of each judge for each of these eight categories of cases were added together and then the sum was divided by the number of categories for which he received a score.[31] Thus each judge was assigned a score indicating that his behavior in economic cases was more or less liberal than that of his court.[32]

Table 12-1 is divided into two parts, with data for the criminal cases in the first three columns and the data for the economic cases in the last three columns. In both parts, the first data column lists the one-to-one (or zero-order[33]) correlation coefficients between each background characteristic and a judge's tendency to find for the defense in criminal cases more often than did his state supreme court. The second column shows the size of the sample[34] of judges who supplied data to compute these correlation coefficients. Judges are included in a sample only if (1) they serve on courts that are bi-group[35] with respect to an independent background variable; (2) they have heard cases involving the dependent variable issue; and (3) they reached a nonunanimous decision in at least one of these cases.

All the background characteristics can assume only one of two values; they are described so that the category hypothesized to be more liberal[36] is mentioned first. A positive entry in the first and fourth data columns indicates support for the general hypothesis that there is a correlation between the liberal background characteristics and finding for the defense in criminal cases and for the generally economically weaker party in the civil cases considered. The table shows that political party affiliation is a relatively good predictor of a judge's vote in both criminal cases and civil cases involving economic issues.[37] Religious affiliation is also an indicator of judicial behavior in these situations, although it probably does not directly cause a judge to favor the defendant or the state in a criminal case.[38] There is also a positive correlation between a judge's not having been a former businessman (for example, a director, executive or proprietor) and his support for the economic underdog.[39]

Of course, correlation alone does not indicate causation.[40] One must look beyond these correlation coefficients to prove the accuracy of hypotheses explaining the apparent relations. Party affiliation probably does not cause decisional propensities or liberal attitudes; it may, however, reinforce pre-existing attitudes that are partially responsible for a judge's choice of political party.[41] Additionally, religious affiliation probably causes neither attitudes nor decisional propensities, nor is it usually a result of pre-existing attitudes. Even more than party affiliation, religious affiliation is a consequence of social values transmitted by the individual's family. The explanation for the correlation probably lies in the link between particular religious affiliations and (1) membership in distinct economic classes, (2) urban living and (3) reaction to discrimination. A more detailed analysis of causal relationships necessitates the investigation of correlations among the background variables themselves. Such a study would require statistically controlling for certain variables while allowing others to vary within this same sample of judges.[42]

There are two negative correlation coefficients of substantial magnitude appearing in the first column of table 12-1. These correspond to the independent variables (1) tuition-cost of a judge's law school education and (2) attitude on economic issues. Graduates from law schools with low tuition (especially commuter law schools) might be expected to be more liberal in criminal case dispositions because students at these schools frequently come from lower socioeconomic backgrounds. One might predict that their youthful experiences would give these judges more empathy for the defendant in criminal cases. Each judge in the sample, however, was a member of the state supreme court when this data was gathered. Thus those judges who attended law schools with low tuition experienced a form of the rags-to-riches phenomenon. Persons from modest backgrounds who achieve high economic status are often not particularly tolerant of those of lower economic status.[43] These individuals may feel that others, like themselves, should be able to overcome a disadvantaged background. This attitude could explain partially the negative correlation between attending a low tuition law school and being above one's court average on propensity for the defense.

The civil liberties nature of many of the criminal cases in part may account for the negative correlation between an attitude of economic liberalism and partiality for the defendant. Some studies have found positive correlations of only small magnitude or even negative correlations between economic liberalism and civil-liberties liberalism, especially among ethnic Democrats living in large cities.[44] More influential than the nature of the cases, however, is the nature of the judges in the sample. This becomes clear when the judges are categorized according to party and religious affiliation, because these were the two background characteristics displaying the strongest correlation with decisional propensities in criminal cases (see table 12-1). Examination of the correlation matrix[45] reveals that the variables of political affiliation and of economic attitudes have a positive correlation coefficient, but the correlation coefficient relating a judge's political affiliation and his attitude toward treatment of criminals is negative.[46]

Similarly, the correlation coefficient relating religious affiliation and economic attitudes is positive while the coefficient for religious affiliation and attitude toward treatment of criminals is negative. Thus these correlations suggest that the non-concurring correlations (1) between political affiliation and the two attitudinal variables and (2) between religious affiliation and the two attitudinal variables may explain the negative correlation between liberal economic attitudes and favoring the defense in criminal cases.

For the economic cases the only negative correlation of substantial magnitude involved the variable of geography (see table 12-1). One could hypothesize that judges who practiced law in small towns would assume a more conservative position in economic cases than those who practiced in a large city. This notion is supported by the finding that rural people, possibly because of their greater self-sufficiency, are often less sympathetic to the liberal side in economic cases.[47] State supreme court judges who practiced initially in large cities, however, were more likely to be associated with firms that practiced corporate law on behalf of the business side in economic cases;[48] judges who started their legal careers in small towns were more often either sole practioners or associates of firms in general practice,[49] with professional experience that more likely included criminal defense work.

The Results of Multiple Correlation Analysis

In this section the significance of the entries in the third and sixth columns of table 12-1, the columns labeled "additional variance accounted for," will be explained. To enable the reader to appreciate the importance of these entries, however, it is necessary to introduce a few more statistical concepts.

A background characteristic has "accounted for *x* percent of the variance" in the decisional propensity being studied when the variation among the positions of the judges in the sample with respect to this background characteristic can explain *x* percent of the variation observed among the judges' positions with respect to the decisional variable.[50] The third data column of table 12-1 lists the percentage of variance in judges' tendencies to favor the defense in criminal cases that is accounted for by a specific background characteristic when controlling for all the background characteristics in the table. The sixth data column contains similar information concerning variance in judges' tendencies to favor the economically liberal side in certain classes of civil cases. Columns one and four, by adding to more than 1.00 reveal some information about the overlap[51] among the background characteristics as predictor of judicial behavior in civil and criminal dispositions. The overlap among these independent variables is not great enough that one can obtain a prediction of judicial behavior with maximized accuracy by using only the background characteristic with the highest correlation coefficient.[52] To test the predictive power of all the independent variables interacting with each other, one must resort to multiple correlation analysis.

Multiple Correlation

This term indicates the part of the total variation in the dependent variable that can be explained by all the interacting independent variables.[53] One cannot simply add the correlation coefficients or the squares of the correlation coefficients[54] to determine how much of the total variance the independent variables explain. Given the overlap in the percentage of variance for which these variables account, such a computation could result in a sum greater than 100 percent; this would be statistically meaningless. By using more sophisticated multiple correlation analysis, one can eliminate the overlap in variance explained and thus ensure that the sum of the percentages listed in the third or the sixth column does not exceed 100 percent.

Computation of the Multiple Correlation Coefficient

This coefficient indicates the strength of the relationship between a dependent variable and two or more interacting independent variables.[55] The variance-accounted-for figures, which appear as the last entries of columns three and six of table 12-1, were obtained by the use of a computer. A correlation matrix that showed the correlations among all the background variables[56] supplied the input data for the computer program. The program assumed that each correlation was based on the same sample size. However, since the correlations were based on samples of different sizes (see columns 2 and 5 of table 12-1), some of the correlations are mathematically inconsistent with each other. Consequently, the computer was unable to calculate the value of standardized regression weights[57] for some of the characteristics. These standardized regression weights are used in the computation of both the multiple correlation coefficient and the additional variance for which a background variable accounts. Dashes in the "variance accounted for'' columns indicate that the computer could not calculate the weight for the corresponding variable.

Another consequence of the disparity in sample sizes was the need to modify slightly the basic formula for calculating additional variance. Failure to make the change could have resulted in a set of percentages for which the sum exceeded 100 percent.[58] If $X_1, X_2, \ldots, X_{14}$ denote the 14 background characteristics, let B_i and r_i be the standardized regression weight and the correlation coefficient corresponding to X_i. Then for each independent variable X_i, the basic formula to calculate the additional variance, V_i, for which X_i accounts would be:

$$V_i = r_i B_i .$$

Then, if R^2 denotes the multiple correlation coefficient,

$$R^2 = \Sigma V_i = \Sigma (r_i B_i).$$

That is, R^2 is the sum of the additional variances for which each independent variable X_i accounts.[59]

The Meaning of the Multiple Correlation Results

The third and sixth columns of table 12-1 do not greatly alter the rank order of unsigned correlation coefficients from the first and fourth data columns, respectively.[60] In most cases, those background variables with comparatively large correlation coefficients also accounted for a relatively large part of the total variance explained. One should note, however, that a background variable that has a low correlation with one of the dependent variables may still increase the amount of variance explained by, in effect, filtering out irrelevant portions of other background variables with which it correlates.[61]

By itself each judicial characteristic cannot explain a large part of the variance among judges' decisional propensities. For example, if one were to rely only upon political party affiliation to predict a judge's tendency to find for the defense in criminal cases, one could account for only 7 percent of the variance (or .26 squared); using the twelve variables for which standardized regression weights could be computed, one can account for 43 percent of the variance by just using the variables of political party affiliation, attitude on economic issues and attitude toward treatment of criminals. Column 3 of table 12-1 shows that these three variables had substantial, non-redundant correlations with a tendency to hold for the defense in criminal cases.

The effect of multiple correlation used to interpret data collected from judges hearing civil cases involving economic issues is more dramatic. Without this more sophisticated analysis, political party affiliation accounts for only 14 percent of the variance.[62] When adjustments for the effect of other variables are made, however, political party affiliation can account for 44 percent of the variance. If the sum of the additional variance explained by each of the ten variables for which the computer could find standardized regression weights (see table 12-1, column 6) is computed, approximately 90 percent of the variance of the dependent variable can thus be explained. While correlation analysis focuses upon the strength of relationships among the variables,[63] regression analysis uses the independent variables to define an equation that explains and predicts the value of the dependent variable.[64] If one constructs a regression equation to predict a judge's position in appropriate civil cases from the ten "usable" variables,[65]

$$R^2 = .90 \text{ and } R = .95$$

imply that there will be a 68 percent reduction in the degree of error that would result if one simply predicted that each judge would have the average of all the scores of the total sample.[66]

An Alternative to Multiple Correlation to Measure Prediction Accuracy

In this chapter, the writer has used the total variance explained by a set of independent variables to measure the accuracy of these variables for collectively predicting judicial behavior in a limited context. There is, however, an alternative approach that is possibly more appealing to an individual's common sense. Regression analysis may be used to predict decisional propensity when specific values are assigned to each of the background variables. For example, one can derive the regression equation to predict a judge's propensity to hold for the defense in criminal cases. Then he can apply this equation to each judge to predict whether his decisional score will be above or below his court's average score. A judge is labeled a misprediction if either his actual score or the score predicted on the basis of his background characteristics is above the court average and the other is below. The percentage of all predictions that are mispredictions offers another measure of accuracy of the predictions.[67] Although its meaning is initially more difficult to comprehend, prediction accuracy measured by the "varience-accounted-for" method should correspond reasonably well to that calculated by the mispredictions method.[68]

Sampling Limitations Upon the Statistical Methods

Both the variance-accounted-for method and the mispredictions method described the strength of the multiple correlation. Neither indicates the probability that the multiple correlation coefficient might really be zero and that chance sampling distortion[69] is responsible for the apparent magnitude of the coefficients. Statistical methods indicate that the likelihood of obtaining a multiple correlation as large as those obtained in table 12-1, namely .66 and .95, from an average sample size of 103 and 125 respectively is less than one in one thousand if the multiple correlation coefficient is really zero.[70] (Recall that $R = 0$ would indicate that there was no linear relationship among the dependent and independent variables.)[71] One could also make similar calculations to test the statistical significance of each correlation coefficient and each additional variance explained by the background characteristics.[72] The value of performing such tests upon these statistics, however, is questionable partly because these tests assume that (1) the data have a normal curve distribution; (2) the variances of all the variables are equal; and (3) the variables satisfy a linear equation of the form $Y = \Sigma(b_i X_i) + a$.[73] The data collected from the sample may fail to meet these conditions adequately. Moreover, the sample of judges used was not randomly selected from the population of judges; it represents the usable sample of state supreme court judges serving in 1955 who satisfied the other requirements discussed in the preceding two sections of this chapter.[74] It is also true that statistical significance depends more upon the size of the sample than upon the magnitude of the correlation obtained.[75] Finally, few would argue that the background characteristics of judges have a zero correlation with their judicial decisions, although some do contend that the correlation is low or, in some sense, not high enough.[76]

Some Conclusions

The methodological purpose of this chapter has been to show some of the things that can be done using multiple correlation techniques to supplement non-multiple correlation techniques in analyzing the relations between judicial background and attitudinal characteristics and judicial decisions. In addition to this methodological purpose, the chapter has further indicated the importance of political party as a predictor of judicial propensities in criminal cases and, especially, in cases involving economic conflict.[77] It has also indicated in the multiple correlation context that the religious orientation of judges is an important predictor of their decisional propensities in criminal cases and their pre-judicial association with the business world is an important predictor in economic cases.

Although judicial backgrounds may be useful in predicting those judges or categories of judges who will be above or below the average of their court on various types of decision scores[78] (or at least those scores associated with economic or criminal cases), judicial background variables are not as useful for predicting the outcomes of cases in general. This is so largely because being above or below the average of one's court is determined only by those cases in which the judges on one's court differ, and such cases may only constitute about 12 percent of the cases heard by the average state supreme court.[79] Even in those cases, one may be more interested in knowing whether the plaintiff or the defendant will win and why than in knowing how the judges' votes will be split. To make such predictions requires an analysis of the factual and legal variables present in the cases used for the predictions and in the cases to be predicted; one or more factual variables may relate to the dominant or plurality party, religion, or pre-judicial occupation on the court.[80]

In spite of the limitations on judicial background analysis for predictive purposes, such analysis does help improve the legal process. It is useful for providing a better understanding of the determinative factors in judicial decision-making.[81] It also enables one to demonstrate better the need for making judges more representative of the people over whom they judge, since it enables one to show that certain background characteristics have a substantial relation to certain judicial propensities.[82] Furthermore, if one finds a relatively high correlation between the background characteristics of some judges and their decisional propensities, then one can make statements about methods of decreasing these correlations by analyzing how low-correlation judges, or their courts, differ from high-correlation judges.[83] Finally, an analysis of these relations can provide some data that might be helpful to voters in the selection of judges and to lawyers in the selection of jurors.[84]

Although this writer has tried to extend raw judicial background analysis to these broader purposes, much remains to be done along the lines suggested. It is hoped that the methods described here and in materials cited in the notes will be applied to other courts, judges, cases, countries and time periods to obtain more findings and to build better theories for understanding and improving the legal process.[85]

Notes

1. *See* Nagel, *Off-the-Bench Judicial Attitudes*, in JUDICIAL DECISION-MAKING 29 (G. Schubert ed. 1963); Nagel, *Political Party Affiliation and Judges' Decisions*, 55 AM. POL. SCI. REV. 843 (1961); Nagel, *Judicial Backgrounds and Criminal Cases*, 53 J. CRIM. L.C. & P.S. 333 (1962);

Nagel, *Ethnic Affiliations and Judicial Propensities*, 24 J. POL. 92 (1962); Nagel, *Testing Relations Between Judicial Characteristics and Judicial Decision-Making*, 15 W. POL. Q. 425 (1962).

2. *See* S. Nagel, THE LEGAL PROCESS FROM A BEHAVIORAL PERSPECTIVE 14 (1969).

3. *See id*. 15-20.

4. The background characteristics used were defined so that a judge would belong to one of two categories. For a discussion of the problems encountered in positioning the judges, see Nagel, *Testing Relations Between Judicial Characteristics and Judicial Decision-Making*, 15 W. POL. Q. 425, 428-30 (1962). A court was bi-group with respect to a background characteristic (such as political party) if it had at least one member included in each category (that is, at least one Democrat and one Republican). To understand why it was necessary to restrict the sample to bi-group courts, see note 17 and accompanying text *infra*.

5. Nagel, *Testing Relations Between Judicial Characteristics and Judicial Decision-Making*, 15 W. POL. Q. 425 (1962), gives more detailed information about the methods used to gather and analyze the data for this early research. The year 1955 was the only year for which the valuable Directory of American Judges was published. The time period used is referred to in this article as a possible explanatory variable where it may be relevant, although the general findings do not appear to be time-bound.

6. S. NAGEL, *supra* note 2, at 20-23.

7. Nagel, *Testing Relations Between Judicial Characteristics and Judicial Decision-Making*, 15 W. POL. Q. 425, 427 (1962).

8. Because it is used here to predict the presence of a decisional propensity, political party affiliation is called an independent variable. The letter X is usually used to represent such a variable. Since the propensity to favor the defense is the behavior to be predicted, it is regarded as the dependent variable. The letter Y usually denotes the dependent variable. In this case each usable member of the sample set can assume only one of two possible positions with respect to each variable: either a judge is a Democrat or he is a Republican; either he finds for the defense in criminal cases more often than his supreme court or he does not. Arbitrarily, one position with respect to the independent variable X will be considered positive (denoted $+X$) and the other position negative (denoted $-X$). In the same way, one position with respect to the dependent variable is considered positive and the other negative.

The results of the data collection can be summarized in a four-cell table that can be used later to compute a statistical measure of the strength of the hypothesized relationship. *See* note 14 *infra*.

9. H. GLICK & K. VINES, STATE COURT SYSTEMS 82-84 (1973); W. MURPHY & J. TANENHAUS, THE STUDY OF PUBLIC LAW 103-11 (1972); Grossman, *Social Backgrounds and Judicial Decision-Making*, 79 HARV. L. REV. 1551 (1966); Grossman, *Social Backgrounds and Judicial Decisions: Notes for a Theory*, 29 J. POL. 334 (1967). Some aspects of Grossman's articles were questioned in Goldman, *Backgrounds, Attitudes, and the Voting Behavior of Judges: A Comment on Joel Grossman's "Social Backgrounds and Judicial Decisions*," 31 J. POL. 214 (1969). Grossman responded in *Further Thoughts on Consensus and Conversion: A Reply to Professor Goldman*, 31 J. POL. 223 (1969).

10. The IBM card data and coding key from which all the calculations in this article are made are available on request from this writer or from the Inter-University Consortium for Political Research at Ann Arbor. Tables showing the names of the judges, their backgrounds, their decisional propensities and the citations to the cases used are available in Nagel, Judicial Characteristics and Judicial Decision-Making (unpublished dissertation, Northwestern University Microfilms Order No. 62-865, 1961). These materials can be used for checking the calculations or for secondary analysis.

11. Failure to control for these important case determinants when comparing judges can easily lead to spurious results. For example, Glendon Schubert compares northern trial judges with southern trial judges in union-management cases later heard by the United States Supreme Court, and he finds the southern trial judges decided in favor of the union about the same percentage of times as did the northern judges. G. SCHUBERT, JUDICIAL BEHAVIOR: A READER IN THEORY AND RESEARCH 458 (1964). Southern union-management cases, however, may be much easier to decide in favor of the union, given the possibly more clear-cut violations of the National Labor Relations Act by southern employers. *See* R. Downing, The Federal Courts and Labor Relations Policy, 1936-1954: A Study of Judicial Decision-Making (unpublished dissertation in University of Illinois at Urbana-Champaign Library, 1956).

The meaning of findings in other studies is also weakened because the authors did not account for differences in the cases heard by different groups of judges. *See, e.g.*, D. Bowen, The Explanation of Judicial Voting Behavior from Sociological Characteristics of Judges (unpublished dissertation in Yale University Library, 1965); Goldman, *Voting Behavior on the United States Courts of Appeals, 1961-64*, 60 AM. POL. SCI. REV. 374 (1966); Schmidhauser, *Stare Decisis, Dissent, and the Background of the Justices of the Supreme Court of the United States*, 14 TORONTO L.J. 194 (1962). Richard Schwartz, however, has clearly indicated his awareness of this comparability problem. Schwartz, *Judicial Objectivity and Quantitative Analysis*, in 1963 MODERN USES OF LOGIC IN LAW 141-42. *See also* R.

WATSON & R. DOWNING, THE POLITICS ON THE BENCH AND THE BAR 311 (1969); Sacks, Book Review, 67 AM. POL. SCI. REV. 221 (1973) (reviewing GLICK, SUPREME COURTS IN STATE POLITICS (1971)).

12. The average number of members of a state supreme court is seven; among its seven members, a court is not likely to have at least one judge belonging to each of these four categories.

13. This kind of partitioning or fractionization approach to the problem of partial and multiple correlation was used with regulatory agency commissioners in Nagel & Lubin, *Regulatory Commissioners and Party Politics*, 17 ADMIN. L. REV. 39 (1964). That research, however, did not require that all usable agencies have all the categories of commissioners being compared, although the research did use being above or below the decisional average of one's agency in a liberal direction as the decisional variable.

14. *See* J. GUILFORD, FUNDAMENTAL STATISTICS IN PSYCHOLOGY AND EDUCATION 135 (3d ed. 1956).

For the general formula to compute r, see P. HOEL, INTRODUCTION TO MATHEMATICAL STATISTICS 165 (3d ed. 1962). Because each variable discussed in this article assumes only one of two values, however, the computation of r_{xy} can be greatly simplified. To evaluate r_{xy} in the special case, the following steps suffice. *Step 1*. Construction of a four-cell illustrating the distribution of the data collected:

	−Y	+Y
+X	A	B
−X	C	D

This table indicates that (1) in A cases, the $+X$ and $-Y$ positions were taken, (2) in B cases, the $+X$ and $+Y$ positions were taken, (3) in C cases, the $-X$ and $-Y$ positions were taken, and (4) in D cases, the $-X$ and $+Y$ positions were taken.

Step 2. Then r_{xy} can be computed using the formula:

$$r_{xy} = \frac{BC - AD}{\sqrt{(A + B)(C + D)(A + C)(B + D)}}$$

S. NAGEL, THE LEGAL PROCESS FROM A BEHAVIORAL PERSPECTIVE 128 (1969).

Data collected by this author can now be used to compute the correlation coefficient between political party affiliation and a tendency to favor the defense in criminal cases (the first entry in the first column of table 12-1, pp. 000-000 *infra*).

The four-cell constructed from the data looks like this:

	*At or below the average of one's court on the decision score**	*Above the average of one's court on the decision score*	*Totals*
Democratic Judges	18	22 (55% of 40)	40
Republican Judges	31	14 (51% of 45)	45

*Decision score represents the proportion of times voting for the defense in criminal cases. Unanimous cases were excluded, since they have no bearing on the direction of the position of judges relative to other judges sitting on the same court.

Id. at 190.

In this example,

$$A = 18 \qquad B = 22$$

$$C = 31 \qquad D = 14$$

Substituting these numbers in the formula for r_{xy}, one sees that

$$r_{xy} = \frac{(22 \times 31) - (14 \times 18)}{\sqrt{(18 + 22)(31 + 14)(18 + 31)(22 + 14)}} \cong 24$$

There is a "rule-of-thumb" that can be used to estimate r_{xy} in the cases considered here:

When both the [independent] predictor variable and the [dependent] outcome variable provide for only two categories . . . the correlation coefficient is approximately [see note 33 *infra*] equal to (1) the percentage of cases *positive* on the predictor variable that are also positive on the outcome variable minus (2) the percentage of cases *negative* on the predictor variable that are positive on the outcome variable.

Id. at 147.

15. H. Blalock, Social Statistics 377 (2d. ed. 1972) [hereinafter cited as Social Statistics]. The reader must remember:

The interpretation of a correlation coefficient as a measure of the strength of the . . . relationship between two variables is a purely mathematical interpretation and is completely devoid of any cause or effect implications. The fact that two variables tend to increase or decrease together *does not* imply that one has any direct or indirect effect on the other.

P. Hoel, Introduction to Mathematical Statistics 164 (3d ed. 1962) (emphasis added). *See, e.g.*, the example illustrating this warning, *id.* at 164-65.

16. SOCIAL STATISTICS 377. $r_{xy} = 0$, however, does not imply that there is no relationship between the variables since r_{xy} may only be measuring the linear relation and a non-linear relation may be present. *See* P. HOEL, INTRODUCTION TO MATHEMATICAL STATISTICS 377-78 (3d ed. 1962).

17. When this writer used judges serving on one-party courts in the correlation of political party and decisions, the correlation dropped greatly although the sample sizes increased since more judges could become members of the sample. Similarly lowered correlations were observed when the writer used judges serving on courts that were homogeneous with regard to other background characteristics being correlated.

18. *See* notes 4 & 8 *supra*.

19. The correlation matrix for the 14 background characteristics is a rectangular array of 14 rows and 14 columns. The entry in column j, row i is the correlation coefficient relating the ith independent variable X_i to the jth independent variable X_j. *See* SOCIAL STATISTICS 386-87 (1st ed. 1960).

20. *See* notes 53-63 and accompanying text *infra*, discussing multiple correlation analysis.

21. *See* notes 64-66 and accompanying text *infra*, discussing multiple regression analysis.

22. The statistical term "sample" refers to the subset of the "population" (see note 23 *infra*) contributing the data on which the statistical computations are based and from which statistical inferences are drawn. P. HOEL, INTRODUCTION TO MATHEMATICAL STATISTICS 64 (3d ed. 1962).

23. The statistical term "population" refers to the totality of all possible contributors of data for a statistical investigation; a specific population is always defined by naming its unique properties. *See* J. GUILFORD, FUNDAMENTAL STATISTICS IN PSYCHOLOGY AND EDUCATION 155 (3d ed. 1956).

24. A sample is randomly determined if "*every individual in the population has an equal chance of being chosen* [as a member of the sample]. *The selection of any one individual is also in no way tied to the selection of any other*." *Id*. at 156. The problems caused by using a sample that was not randomly selected are discussed in *id*. at 157-58; SOCIAL STATISTICS 142-45, 523-24.

25. The term "liberal" in this context corresponds to "the viewpoint associated with the interests of the lower or less privileged economic or social groups in one's society and (to a less extent) with acceptance of long-run social change." Nagel, *Political Party Affiliation and Judges' Decisions*, 55 AM. POL. SCI. REV. 843, 846 (1961).

26. In an unpublished review dated May 26, 1973, of this manuscript and the multiple correlation methods which it uses, Robert Ferber (an editor of the *Journal of the American Statistical Association*) wrote: "I do

not have any major comments on how to improve the goodness of fit . . . . All things considered, I think you have done as much as you could do with these data."

27. For more detailed information about these background characteristics, see Nagel, *Judicial Backgrounds and Criminal Cases*, 53 J. CRIM. L.C. & P.S. 333 (1962).

28. The number of variables could be increased by inserting into the regression equation (see notes 68-70 *infra*) variables that represent (1) the squares or exponents of certain of the 14 variables if non-linear relations were suspected and (2) the product of certain pairs of the 14 variables if joint interaction effects on the dependent variable were suspected. *See* SOCIAL STATISTICS 459-64, 502-06. Similarly, the number of variables could be decreased (thereby reducing the multicollinearity or intercorrelations among them) by constructing a single score for a related block of variables within the 14 variables. *See id.* at 457, 503.

29. See note 25 *supra*.

30. The statement in the mailed questionnaire used to measure the economic liberalism attitude read, "Present laws favor the rich as against the poor." Judges were asked whether they strongly agreed, mildly agreed, had no opinion, mildly disagreed or strongly disagreed with this statement. The statement used to measure a liberal attitude towards treatment of criminals was, "Our treatment of criminals is too harsh; we should try to cure, not to punish them." For more information about the questionnaire see S. NAGEL, *Judicial Attitudes and Those of Legislators and Administrators*, in THE LEGAL PROCESS FROM A BEHAVIORAL PERSPECTIVE 199 (1969); Nagel, *Off-the Bench Judicial Attitudes* in JUDICIAL DECISION-MAKING 29 (G. Schubert ed. 1963). The response rate was as follows: 139 judges replied to the questionnaire (with 118 usable replies), 136 failed to reply, and 38 were known to have died before the questionnaires were mailed.

In the correlation and regression analysis used to generate table 12-1, the two attitude variables were each coded with five categories or degrees, and the twelve background variables were coded as dichotomous.

31. Nagel, *Political Party Affiliation and Judges' Decisions*, 55 AM. POL. SCI. REV. 843, 844 (1961), describes how the decision score for each category would be computed.

32. See note 25 *supra*.

33. The zero-order correlation coefficient is defined in note 8 *supra*. This coefficient is computed without recognition of the possible effect of other intervening variables. When these effects are recognized, multiple correlation techniques must be used to measure the correlation between any two variables. If the effect of *n* other variables is statistically con-

trolled, the correlation coefficient relating two variables is called an *n*th order partial correlation coefficient.

The correlations in the first column of table 12-1 do not correspond exactly to the differences between percentages shown in Nagel, *Judicial Backgrounds and Criminal Cases*, 53 J. CRIM. L.C. & P.S. 333, 335 (1962), because r_{xy} is not exactly equal to the difference between the percentage of $+X$ judges who are $+Y$ and the percentage of $-X$ judges who are $+Y$. *See* Nagel, *Applying Correlation Analysis to Case Prediction*, 42 TEXAS L. REV. 1006, 1009-10 (1964); notes 4 & 8 *supra*. The substantial deviation with regard to the education variable is explained by a typographical error in the earlier article.

34. See note 22 *supra*.

35. See note 4 *supra*.

36. See note 25 *supra*.

37. Other research that finds Democratic judges differing from Republican judges includes the following: J. Beatty, An Institutional and Behavioral Analysis of the Iowa Supreme Court—1965-1969 (unpublished dissertation in University of Iowa Library, 1970); M. Feeley, A Comparative Analysis of State Supreme Court Behavior (unpublished thesis in University of Minnesota Library, 1969); G. SCHUBERT, QUANTATIVE ANALYSIS OF JUDICIAL BEHAVIOR 129-42 (1959); J. Herndon, Relationships Between Partisanship and Decisions of State Supreme Courts (unpublished dissertation in University of Michigan Library, 1963); D. Leavitt, Political Party and Class Influences on the Attitudes of Justices of the Supreme Court in the Twentieth Century (unpublished paper delivered at the 1972 meeting of the Midwest Political Science Association); Barber, *Partisan Values in the Lower Courts: Reapportionment in Ohio and Michigan,* 20 CASE W. RES. L. REV. 401 (1969); Feeley, *Another Look at the "Party Variable" in Judicial Decision-Making: An Analysis of the Michigan Supreme Court,* 4 POLITY 91 (1971); Goldman, *Voting Behavior on the United States Courts of Appeals, 1961-64*, 60 AM. POL. SCI. REV. 374 (1966); Ulmer, *Politics and Procedure in the Michigan Supreme Court*, 17 SW. SOC. SCI. Q. 375 (1966); Ulmer, *Leadership in the Michigan Supreme Court*, in JUDICIAL DECISION-MAKING 13 (G. Schubert ed. 1963); Ulmer, *The Political Party Variable in the Michigan Supreme Court*, 11 J. PUB. L. 352 (1962).

Less significant differences between the two groups of judges were found in Adamany, *The Party Variable in Judges' Voting: Conceptual Notes and a Case Study*, 63 AM. POL. SCI. REV. 57 (1969); Beiser & Silberman, *The Political Party Variable: Workmen's Compensation Cases in the New York Court of Appeals*, 3 POLITY 521 (1971); Walker, *A Note Concerning Partisan Influences on Trial-Judge Decision Making*, 6 LAW & SOC. REV. 645 (1972).

Although Ken Dolbeare's presentation seems to contain arithmetic errors and does not involve judges hearing the same cases, his data show (1) that 6/17 or 35 percent of his Democratic judges decided for the administrative action in zoning cases and (2) that 7/23 or 30 percent of his Republican judges decided for the administrative action, contrary to his reported findings. A similar recalculation of his data can be made with regard to religion and zoning cases. K. DOLBEARE, TRIAL COURTS IN URBAN POLITICS 77-78 (1967).

38. Works that find a difference between the decisional propensities of Catholic and Protestant judges include: Ulmer, *Dissent Behavior and the Social Background of Supreme Court Justices*, 32 J. POL. 580 (1970); Ulmer, *Social Background as an Indicator to the Votes of Supreme Court Justices in Criminal Cases: 1947-56 Terms*, 17 MIDWEST J. POL. SCI. 662 (1973); Vines, *Federal District Judges and Race Relations Cases in the South*, 26 J. POL. 353 (1964). No significant differences were found by Chase, Green & Mollan, *Catholics on the Court*, THE NEW REPUBLIC, Sept. 26, 1960, at 13; Goldman, *Voting Behavior on the United States Courts of Appeals, 1961-1964*, 60 AM. POL. SCI. REV. 314 (1966).

39. This writer attempted to determine the relation between political party (and other related background characteristics) and judicial propensities on the national supreme courts of Australia, Canada, India, Ireland, and the United Kingdom simultaneously, using the same within-court bivariate comparisons described here. The general findings involved substantially lower correlations and thus apparently a lower ideological component than with the American court data, possibly because American courts (1) have more discretion to create judge-made law under the American common law system; (2) have more power to nullify legislative and administrative acts under the American judicial review system; (3) have more ideological leeway given the subjectivity of such key constitutional concepts as equal protection and due process; (4) are often elected, thus injecting partisan and ideological side effects; and (5) can at the state supreme court level be less visible and thus less inhibited in their ideological divisions.

40. SOCIAL STATISTICS 442-44; P. HOEL, INTRODUCTION TO MATHEMATICAL STATISTICS 164-65 (3d ed. 1962).

41. Values cause party affiliation more than party affiliation causes values, but party affiliation and its accompanying activities can reinforce prior values. *See* Adamany, *The Party Variable in Judges' Voting: Conceptual Notes and a Case Study*, 63 AM. POL. SCI. REV. 57 (1969); Nagel, *Political Party Affiliation and Judges' Decisions*, 55 AM. POL. SCI. REV. 843 (1961).

42. *See* H. BLALOCK, CAUSAL INFERENCES IN NONEXPERIMENTAL RESEARCH (1964); H. BLALOCK, CAUSAL MODELS IN THE SOCIAL SCIENCES (1971).

43. For a discussion of the relation between wealth and conservatism, see R. CENTERS, THE PSYCHOLOGY OF SOCIAL CLASSES (1949); V. KEY, PUBLIC OPINION AND AMERICAN DEMOCRACY 121-52 (1961); A. CAMPBELL, P. CONVERSE & D. STOKES, *The American Voter* 333-401 (1960) [hereinafter cited as A. CAMPBELL].

44. For a discussion of liberalism and ethnic Democrats, see S. LIPSET, POLITICAL MAN (1960); R. SCAMMON & B. WATTENBURG, THE REAL MAJORITY (1970).

45. See note 19 *supra*.

46. The matrix reveals that Democratic party affiliation and liberal economic attitudes have a correlation coefficient of +.30 while Democratic party affiliation has a negative correlation coefficient of −.03 with a liberal attitude towards rehabilitation of criminals. Being Catholic had a +.06 correlation with liberal economic attitudes and a correlation of −.16 with a liberal attitude towards criminal rehabilitation. The non-concurring correlations among these four variables seem to be the key to explaining the "inconsistency" between a judge's having liberal economic attitudes and failing to favor the defense in criminal cases. Political affiliation and the attitudinal variables predict the outcome in economic cases more reliably than they predict the outcome in either civil liberties or appellate criminal cases. Nagel, *Political Parties and Judicial Review in American History*, 11 J. PUB. L. 328 (1962).

47. For a discussion of the relation between urbanism and liberalism, see A. CAMPBELL 402-440; V. KEY, *supra* note 43, at 99-120.

48. *See* S. Nagel, Judicial Characteristics and Judicial Decision-Making (unpublished dissertation, Northwestern University Microfilms Order No. 62-865, 1961).

49. *See id.*; data described in note 10 *supra*.

50. SOCIAL STATISTICS 454-55.

51. If there is a substantial correlation between two independent variables, the second will explain essentially the same variation in the dependent variable as the first. Therefore, to account for as much variation as possible in the dependent variable requires that the independent variables selected have moderately high correlations with the dependent variable and low correlation with each other. *Id.* at 456.

52. *See* note 14 *supra*.

53. SOCIAL STATISTICS 429.

54. *See* note 51 *supra*.

55. J. GUILFORD, FUNDAMENTAL STATISTICS IN PSYCHOLOGY AND EDUCATION 392 (3d ed. 1956).

56. *See* notes 19 & 33 *supra*.

57. *See* J. GUILFORD, FUNDAMENTAL STATISTICS IN PSYCHOLOGY AND EDUCATION 394 (3d ed. 1956). The standardized multiple regression weights are not shown because they are useful only as intermediate mathematical values generated by canned computer programs either (1) to determine the amount of additional variance in the dependent variable explained by each independent variable or (2) to obtain unstandardized regression weights. This latter class of weights are needed to define a regression equation or formula for predicting the position of judges with respect to the dependent variable being studied. *See* notes 64-67 and accompanying text *infra*. The unstandardized regression weights are not shown because there is no attempt in this article to develop a 14-variable prediction equation.

The goal here is to say something meaningful about the relative and collective importance of the 14 background variables for predicting or explaining variations in the two decisional variables.

58. If the sizes of the samples used to compute the correlation coefficient were equal, then the additional variance explained by each independent variable would be calculated by multiplying the correlation coefficient for each characteristic by the corresponding standardized multiple regression weight. J. GUILFORD, FUNDAMENTAL STATISTICS IN PSYCHOLOGY AND EDUCATION 397 (3d ed. 1956). *See also* Tanenhaus, Schick, Muraskin & Rosen, *The Supreme Court's Certiorari Jurisdiction: Cue Theory*, in JUDICIAL DECISION-MAKING 111 (G. Schubert ed. 1963); Ulmer, *Social Background as an Indicator to the Votes of Supreme Court Justices in Criminal Cases: 1947-56 Terms*, 17 MIDWEST J. POL. SCI. 622 (1973). Instead of multiplying the correlation coefficient by the corresponding standardized regression weight to determine the additional variance explained by each independent variable, Bowen squared the partial correlation coefficient. D. Bowen, The Explanation of Judicial Voting Behavior from Sociological Characteristics of Judges (unpublished dissertation in Yale University Library, 1965). There does not seem to be any statistical support for Bowen's method, however.

59. The basic formula for calculating the additional variance accounted for has to be slightly modified because the basic formula may result in a set of about 14 percentages whose sum exceeds 100 percent. The basic formula as mentioned in the correlation coefficient (symbolized r) times the standardized regression weight (symbolized B) for each independent variable. The sum of these products should equal the multiple correlation squared (symbolized R^2) if the number of judges used in calculating each correlation coefficient were the same. If the values shown in the third data column are symbolized V, then the ratio of $(r \cdot B)$ to the sum of the $(r \cdot B)$'s should be equal to the ratio of V to R^2. Thus, each V in the third data column algebraically equals $(r \cdot B \cdot R^2)$ divided by the sum of the $(r \cdot B)$'s. This means (where "/" is read "is to," and "=" is read "as") that if $(r \cdot B)/\Sigma(r \cdot$

$B) = V/R^2$, or if $(r \cdot B)/V = \Sigma\ (r \cdot B)/R^2$, then V equals $(r \cdot B \cdot R^2)$ divided by $\Sigma\ (r \cdot B)$.

The equation $V = (r \cdot B \cdot R^2)/\Sigma\ (r \cdot B)$ using the absolute unsigned value of $r \cdot B$ is more meaningful than simply saying $V = r \cdot B$ because $r \cdot B$ can be a negative number, and the variance accounted for cannot be negative since adding any variable increases R^2 to some extent. Even without missing data, the above equation provides a meaningful way of allocating the variance accounted for to each individual variable, since all of the V's are positive, they all sum to R^2 and they are proportional to $r \cdot B$'s.

60. This statement can be interpreted to mean that if the magnitude of the correlation of X_i was greater than that of X'_i then X_i also explained more of the variance in the dependent variable than X'_i did.

61. *See* J. GUILFORD, FUNDAMENTAL STATISTICS IN PSYCHOLOGY AND EDUCATION 402-03 (3d ed. 1956). The nationality of a judge's ancestors may be an example of such a filtering or suppressor variable, since it has a low correlation with a judge's decisional propensities in economic cases, but a high correlation with political party affiliation. Its removal from the regression equation, however, resulted in a substantial reduction in the multiple correlation coefficient. It may exert a filtering effect by removing a portion of the non-ideological component from the party variable because some ethnic groups tend to join the Republican or Democratic party more from inertia and group reinforcement than because of the party's ideology.

62. To calculate the variance in judges' decisional propensities in economic cases explained by party affiliation while ignoring the effect of the other variables, one must square the correlation coefficient, .37 (see table 12-1). *Id.* at 378.

63. SOCIAL STATISTICS 454.

64. *Id.* at 429-30.

65. The "usable" variables are those for which a standardized regression weight could be calculated, that is, those variables for which a dash does not appear in column 6 of table 12-1.

66. The reduction in error is the result of subtracting $\sqrt{1 - R^2}$ from 1.00, where $R^2 = .90$. The quantity $\sqrt{1 - R^2}$ is called the coefficient of alienation and indicates the lack of relationship between the dependent and independent variables. J. GUILFORD, FUNDAMENTAL STATISTICS IN PSYCHOLOGY AND EDUCATION 375 (3d ed. 1956).

67. This mispredictions method perhaps should be called the "mispostdictions" method since the events being predicted have already occurred.

68. This mispredictions method is used in Nagel, *Predicting Court Cases Quantitatively*, 63 MICH. L. REV. 1411 (1965); Ulmer, *Dissent Be-*

havior and the Social Background of Supreme Court Justices, 32 J. POL. 580 (1970). The mispredictions method could not be meaningfully applied to enough judges involved in table 12-1 because it requires that each judge be usable on each background characteristic. For more detailed information about the mispredictions method, see Nagel, Prediction Accuracy Percentages as a Supplement to Correlation Coefficients (unpublished paper available from the writer on request).

69. *See* SOCIAL STATISTICS 523-24; note 24 *supra*.

70. To reach this conclusion, the values given in table 12-1 for R^2, the square of the multiple correlation coefficient, N, the average size for the sample, and k, the number of usable independent variables, are substituted in the formula:

$$[R^2/1-R^2] \cdot [(N-k-1)/k] = F$$

SOCIAL STATISTICS 464-65. Turning to an F probability table, letting $n_1 = k$ and $n_2 = N-k-1$, reveals that either R^2 appearing in table 12-1 could have occurred purely by chance less than one time in a thousand if the true value of R is 0. *Id.* at 465, 572. Even if N is allowed to equal the smallest sample size appearing in columns 2 or 5 of Table 1, the F probability table shows that either R^2 could have occurred by chance less than five times in a hundred. *Id.* at 570.

71. *See* note 16 and accompanying text *supra*.

72. SOCIAL STATISTICS 397-407, 466-67.

73. *Id.* at 464-65.

74. *See* notes 17-18 and accompanying text *supra*.

75. SOCIAL STATISTICS 293.

76. Grossman says: "Bowen's findings cast clear doubt on the explanatory power of background variables taken by themselves." Grossman, *Social Backgrounds and Judicial Decision-Making*, 70 HARV. L. REV. 1551, 1561 (1966) (footnote omitted). Murphy and Tanenhaus quote Bowen as saying, "[T]he sociological background characteristics of these judges . . . are generally not very helpful." W. MURPHY & J. TANENHAUS, THE STUDY OF PUBLIC LAW 107 (1972). In a paper summarizing his results, however, Bowen says:

> [T]he predictive power of these variables [party, region, religion, prestige of schools attended, age, and tenure] is generally quite low when they are taken by themselves . . .
>
> . . . .
>
> . . . [W]hen we take all six independent variables and examine their total contribution the picture brightens considerably. The six sociological characteristics together will explain anywhere from 20% to over 40% of the variance in these cases.

And to put the situation bluntly, explaining somewhere around a quarter to better than a third of the variance is not, in current political science, to be sneezed at.

D. Bowen, The Explanation of Judicial Voting Behavior From Sociological Characteristics of Judges 18-19 (undated)(unpublished paper available from Bowen or from this writer). Bowen makes similar observations in his dissertation. D. Bowen, The Explanation of Judicial Voting Behavior From Sociological Characteristics of Judges 19, 57 (unpublished dissertation in Yale University Library, 1965).

77. For a list of other articles reaching this conclusion, see note 37 *supra*.

78. For a definition of decision score see note 14 *supra*.

79. One study found dissenting opinions in an average of 13% of the state supreme court cases investigated. On particular supreme courts dissent was present in between 49% (New York) and 0% (Tennessee) of the cases. *See* Canon & Jaros, *State Supreme Courts–Some Comparative Data*, 42 STATE GOVERNMENT 260, 264 (1969).

80. S. NAGEL, THE LEGAL PROCESS FROM A BEHAVIORAL PERSPECTIVE (1969), attempts to discuss the legal process by focusing upon its legal, factual and personnel aspects rather than by examining only the personnel aspect totally in isolation. *See id.* at 132-72.

81. For a good analysis of the causal role of background and attitudinal characteristics, along with legal and factual elements, in determining one kind of judicial propensity, see J. HOGARTH, SENTENCING AS A HUMAN PROCESS (1971), especially 211-28, 341-82. In comparing judges' sentencing patterns, however, Hogarth does not control for the nature of the crimes or cases that the judges hear; some judges may hear more serious cases and their doing so may correlate with their background characteristics. For example, certain types of judges (*e.g.*, female, older or Catholic judges) may hear or not hear a disproportionate number of certain types of cases (*e.g.*, rape, juvenile or abortion cases respectively) because of their interest or because of the control counsel may exercise in allocating the cases. These imbalances in case allocation may thereby make certain judges appear to be more severe or lenient than their fellow judges.

82. *See* Nagel, *Characteristics of Supreme Court Greatness*, 56 A.B.A.J. 957 (1970); Nagel, *Unequal Party Representation on the State Supreme Courts*, 45 J. AM. JUD. SOC'Y 62 (1961).

83. For example, appointed or long-tenured judges may have a lower correlation between their party affiliation and decisional propensities than elected or short-tenured judges. *See* S. NAGEL, COMPARING ELECTED AND APPOINTED JUDICIAL SYSTEMS (1973).

84. *See id.*; Nagel & Weitzman, *Sex and the Unbiased Jury,* 56 JUDICATURE 108 (1972).

85. A good recent example of the application of multiple correlation analysis to judicial backgrounds and decisions is S. Goldman, Voting Behavior on the U.S. Courts of Appeals Revisited (paper presented at the 1973 APSA annual meeting). Goldman's paper contains a larger sample of judges than does Ulmer's recent *Midwest Journal* study, *supra* note 58, but does not provide equally good control over the uniformity of the cases heard by the judges.

Part IV
Improving Procedural Efficiency

In addition to decreasing discrimination against weak litigants and improving the competence of judicial personnel, the legal process should be structured so as to operate as efficiently as possible. Efficiency means achieving its objectives at minimum cost or maximizing its objectives without exceeding its available budget. Chapter 13 describes how the methodology associated with linear programming can be used to minimize costs or maximize benefits in the operations of the legal system. The operations with which Chapter 13 particularly deals are those involved in providing legal services to the poor. More specifically, it uses as an example to illustrate its methodology the problem of rationally allocating funds between routine case handling and law reform work.

The methodology used in Chapter 13 has been applied to business and economics problems and also to defense strategy. It has, however, received little use in legal policy-making in spite of its power as a tool for generating insights into how to allocate most efficiently scarce funds or other resources. Although it is applied here to the legal services problem, related methodologies could be used for more efficiently handling such problems as how to maximize one's net benefits in plea bargaining or personal injury settlements, how to allocate judicial personnel most efficiently, or how to better sequence the stages of the legal process so as to minimize waste and maximize productivity.

In order to apply either the correlation approach for testing the effects of alternative legal policies (as was done in Chapters 4, 7, 10, 11, and 12) or the linear programming approach for allocating scarce resources to diverse alternatives (as was done in Chapters 9 and 13), one must be able to measure with some degree of meaningfulness the goals one seeks to achieve. A common goal when one talks about improving procedural efficiency in courts or administrative agencies is the goal of reducing delay. Delay in this context, however, does not merely refer to time consumed (which is fairly easy to measure), but rather to unnecessary time consumed (which is not as easy to measure). Chapter 13 discusses three methods for measuring unnecessary delay in terms of the difference between time actually consumed and time expected to be consumed in light of (1) past trends, (2) the average time consumed, and (3) comparisons with other courts or agencies, all while attempting to control for variations in the complexity of the cases.

This measurement methodology from Chapter 14 can be applied to other problem situations where one might be interested in the difference between the real effects of a legal policy and its ideal effects, or the difference between empirical measures and normative measures. As indicated toward the end of the chapter, such a problem is involved in measuring the degree of possibly illegal discrimination in the legal process against weak litigants, as contrasted to mere differences between types of defendants or litigants. Other measurement problems are involved in procedural efficiency studies such as how does one measure aesthetic damage in an environmental policy situation, or how does one devise a checklist to measure satisfaction in the evaluation of legal services agencies.

13 Minimizing Costs and Maximizing Benefits in Providing Legal Services To the Poor

Introduction

Purposes and Literature

This chapter has two purposes, a general and a specific one. The general purpose is to describe how legal policy decisions involving the allocation of scarce resources can be optimized, or at least improved upon, through the application of some simple, easy-to-understand concepts of linear regression analysis combined with linear programming, and also nonlinear regression analysis combined with differential calculus. The specific purpose is to describe the application of the above model to the optimum allocation of budgets of the legal services agencies of the Office of Economic Opportunity between routine case handling versus broader law reform work.

The linear programming methodology emphasized here has been well developed by mathematicians.[1] It has received wide application to business and economic problems.[2] There have also been works calling for its increased use in political policy problems,[3] but there have been few applications in areas other than defense strategy.[4] As yet there seems to have been no published application of linear programming methodology to a problem involving decisions as to what should be the law on a controversial legal issue or how the law might be best implemented.[5]

There has been a substantial literature developed concerning evaluations of the OEO Legal Services Program.[6] The literature includes a running debate over the relative effort that should be allocated to case handling versus law reform.[7] Unfortunately, most of the allocation-debate literature tends to be somewhat emotional and lacking in quantitative data with regard either to how the effort is empirically allocated in various types of agencies or to how the empirical effort ought to be allocated in light of given goals.

Data

From 1969 to 1972 the Urban Institute of Washington and the Auerbach and Kettelle corporations of Philadelphia prepared and applied objective evaluation forms for evaluating the work of over 200 legal services agencies across the country.[8] Teams of expert evaluators representing diverse perspectives were chosen under the supervision of the Office of Legal Services.[9] They spent at least a few days in each agency conducting many interviews and observing procedures to determine on a structured scale how each agency scored on over a hundred different rating criteria (including one overall rating), as well as many cost and background variables. The total cost of this massive data gathering was approximately $1,500,000. In this chapter, this data base provides the raw material for illustrating the linear programming methodology for choosing between case handling and law reform legal services activities.

The Auerbach data provide complete information for 51 unnamed legal services agencies with regard to the following basic variables used in this analysis: (1) the total budget per year for each agency, symbolized B; (2) the total planned participants per year, symbolized P; (3) the percentage of law reform and related activities other than routine case handling,[10] symbolized %L, and (4) the overall project rating or satisfaction score, symbolized S.

From these four variables one can create the four transformed variables needed for the linear programming analysis. First, the number of dollars spent per participant[11] for law reform (symbolized $L) equals %L times B/P. Second, the number of dollars spent per participant for case handling (symbolized $C) equals (100% − %L) times B/P. Third, the number of dollars spent per participant in total equals B/P or $L + $C. Fourth, S (meaning project satisfaction) can range from a low of 1 to a high of 12.[12]

The Kettelle data provide complete information on the four basic variables for only 16 agencies as contrasted to the Auerbach 51 agencies. Because the Kettelle data are based on a smaller sample, they will not be used in this chapter as much as the Auerbach data. They will, however, be occasionally referred to at least in the notes because they do provide an additional sample of agencies, they provide more meaningful measurement on some of the variables, and the raw Kettelle data are more readily available to the general public.[13]

Two of the 51 agencies were eliminated from the analysis of the Auerbach data because they were so deviant from the average agency with regard to dollars spent per participant.[14] Without those two deviant agencies, the average agency spent a total amount of $68.34 per participant, $62.18 (or 91 percent) on case handling and $6.16 (or 9 percent) on law reform.[15] The two deviant cases spent a total amount per participant of $633.94 and $294.20, respectively.[16]

The especially interesting question is not how much money did the average agency actually spend for case handling and for law reform, but rather how much money should the average agency spend for case handling and law reform in order to minimize costs at a given satisfaction level or to maximize satisfaction at a given cost level? That type of question is what the rest of this chapter is designed to answer.

Basic Concepts

The methodology for making an optimum choice between activity variables depends on whether the dollars spent for each activity produce a constant change or increase in satisfaction or benefits (the constant returns situation), or whether dollars spent produce an increase in satisfaction but at a decreasing rate (the diminishing returns situation). Constant returns can be thought of as a straight line relation between dollars spent and satisfaction obtained, whereas diminishing returns represent a curved line or logarithmic relation between expenditures and satisfaction. The constant returns assumption enables one to use linear regression and linear programming to find the optimum allocation, whereas the diminishing returns assumption (which is more empirically realistic) may require the use of nonlinear regression and differential calculus to optimize the allocation. These terms will all be defined and explained without assuming any prior knowledge more sophisticated than high school algebra.

Optimizing programming can be defined as a procedure whereby one finds the optimum allocation of something between two or more alternatives in light of a given minimizing or maximizing goal (called the objective function) and in light of given constraints or conditions. In order to be linear rather than nonlinear programming, both the goal and the constraints must involve only relations between variables that are straight-line or constant return relations, as previously mentioned.

In any policy-making problem involving the allocation of scarce resources to two or more activities,[17] the generalized normative constraints or desired conditions will be as follows:

1. The minimum level for alternative activity number one which the allocation *should* allow.
2. The maximum level for alternative number one which the allocation should allow.
3. The minimum level for alternative number two (and so on for additional alternatives).
4. The maximum level for alternative number two (and so on for additional alternatives).
5. The minimum total cost. (The minimum is generally the sum of the minimums for each alternative activity.)

6. The maximum total cost. (The maximum is generally the total budget available.)
7. An equation showing how each activity relates to the total cost. Total cost = Activity 1 + Activity 2.
8. The minimum benefit level.
9. The maximum benefit level.
10. An equation showing how each activity relates to the total benefits. Total benefits = Benefits with zero cost + (Weight 1 · Activity 1) + (Weight 2 · Activity 2).

In a policy-making problem involving possible costs and possible benefits, one might seek to:

1. Minimize costs at a given benefit level.
2. Maximize benefits at a given cost level.
3. Maximize benefits minus costs.

What follows involves a more detailed explanation of these basic concepts, particularly as applied to the legal services allocation problem.

Choosing Among Legal Services Activities Assuming a Constant Return to Dollars Spent

Constraints or Conditions to Satisfy

Nonbenefit Constraints. Figure 13-1 graphically shows all of the ten constraints involved in the legal services problem for the average legal services agency in the Auerbach data sample. For the first constraint, the minimum desired level for law reform activity for the average agency is $6.83 out of the total budget of $68.34 per participant. This figure was arrived at by taking 10 percent of the total budget in view of the fact that 10 percent seems to be the minimum desired allocation of the evaluators.[18] The maximum level for law reform activity which the allocation should allow is $13.67 or 20 percent of the total budget. This percentage corresponds to the highest category on which the variable was scored that described the percentage of effort devoted to law reform.[19]

For the third constraint, the minimum desired level for case handling activity in the average agency is $54.67 out of the total budget of $68.34 per participant. This figure was arrived at by taking 80 percent of the total budget in view of the fact that if law reform can constitute only a maximum of 20 percent, then case handling must constitute a minimum of 80 percent.

The maximum level for case handling activity which the allocation should allow is $61.50 or 90 percent of the total budget.[20] This percentage corresponds to the fact that if law reform must constitute a minimum of 10 percent, then case handling must not constitute more than 90 percent.

The minimum total cost is $61.50. This is arrived at by summing the minimum $L which is $6.83 and the minimum $C which is $54.67. If the alternative activities had no minimum expenditures other than zero dollars and our only goal was to minimize costs regardless of satisfaction obtained, then spending zero dollars would be the optimal solution. There is no way of spending negative dollars. The graph, however, does not show the point where zero law reform dollars and zero case handling dollars are spent because the graph begins at the $46 level of case handling since none of the constraint lines are drawn in the region below $46 of case handling.

For the sixth constraint, the maximum total cost per average agency is $68.34. This maximum cost constraint is shown by the diagonal line running from northwest to southeast. At its southeast extremity, the line indicates that if zero dollars were spent on law reform, $68.34 from the total budget could be spent on case handling or vice versa. At its northwest extremity, the line indicates that if $46 were spent on case handling, $22.34 from the total budget could be spent on law reform or vice versa. Once those two points are connected by a straight line, any point along the diagonal straight line involves an allocation of law reform dollars and case handling dollars that add up to $68.34. This line is sometimes called an equal cost line because the total costs at any point on the line are equal, or it is sometimes called a consumption possibility line because it indicates the total amount of money available to be consumed.

That maximum line, like the minimum total cost line, also represents one version of the equation involved in constraint seven. The general version of constraint 7 is $L + $C equals total cost. Total cost, however, does not necessarily have to be the total budget since the total cost can range from zero dollars on up to $68.34.

Benefit Constraints. The minimum total benefit level desired by the evaluators seems to be a rating score of 7.00, or 7 units of satisfaction, because a project below that level is referred to as a "project [that] has internal problems [and] requires technical assistance," whereas a project at that level is referred to as a "project operating efficiently."[21] The maximum total benefit level is a rating score of 12.00, or 12 units of satisfaction, because the rating scale did not allow for the possibility of any ratings higher than 12.00. In order to show the minimum benefit level of 7.00 or the maximum benefit level of 12.00 on figure 13-1, it is necessary to understand how to derive a constraint 10 equation showing how each activity relates to the total benefits.

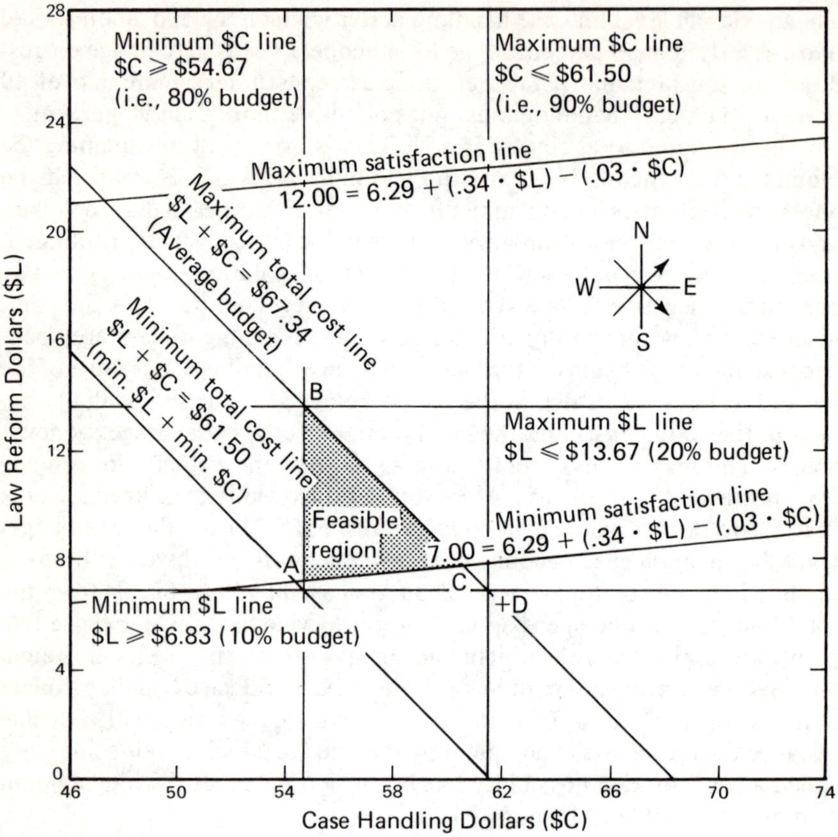

Point A is where total cost is minimized within the constraints.
$L = $7.06 $C = $54.67 %C = $61.74 S = 7.00

Point B is where satisfaction is maximized within the constraints.
$L = $13.67 $C = $54.67 TC = $68.34 S = 9.27

Point C is where total cost is maximized and satisfaction is minimized within the constraints.
$L = $7.46 $C = $60.88 TC = $68.34 S = 7.00

Point D is where the average LSP agency in the survey is.
$L = $6.16 $C = $62.18 TC = $68.34 S = 6.51

All dollar amounts refer to dollars per planned participant.

Figure 13-1. Allocating $L and $C to Minimize Costs or Maximize Benefits (with constant returns)

If we wanted to draw a straight line depicting an equation relating law reform dollars spent and satisfaction obtained, we could plot on a two-dimensional graph 49 dots corresponding to the 49 legal services agencies for which we have complete information in the Auerbach data. Each dot shows for each agency (1) how many dollars it spent for law reform per participant as indicated by the position of the dot relative to the horizontal axis and (2) how many units of satisfaction it provided to the diverse evaluators as indicated by the position of the dot relative to the vertical axis.

Through algebraic means, one can fit a line to those dots that will minimize the square of the distances from the dots to the line. This regression line can then be expressed as an equation with the form $S = a + (b \cdot \$L)$. The "a" geometrically represents the distance from the zero point to the point where the line crosses the vertical axis, and in economic terms it represents the number of units of satisfaction obtained without spending any law reform dollars. The "b" geometrically represents the degree to which the line slopes, and in economic terms it represents the ratio between a change in $L and the corresponding change in S. A similar regression line can be constructed to show the relation between $C and S. Likewise, these two regression lines can be combined into one multiple regression line showing the relation between both $L and $C simultaneously related to S with the overlap between $L and $C statistically removed. Such a multiple regression line[22] can be expressed as a constraint 10 equation having the form $S = a + (b_1 \cdot \$L) + (b_2 \cdot \$C)$.

When the above regression analysis is carried out by hand or with a computer with the 49 legal services agencies, the regression equation relating $L and S is $S = 4.67 + (.29 \cdot \$L)$, and the regression equation relating $C and S is $S = 7.58 - (.02 \cdot \$C)$. These figures indicate that $L has a positive correlation with satisfaction obtained, but $C has a negative correlation with satisfaction obtained.[23] Many of the evaluators were present or former legal services attorneys, law professors, lawyers, social work administrators, and community analysts who favor a more broadly effective legal services program in terms of improving the conditions of the poor. It is therefore understandable that money spent for law reform might tend to satisfy such evaluators more than money spent for case handling. It is, however, not so easy to understand why money spent for case handling would produce a negative or inverse correlation with satisfaction obtained rather than just a lower correlation.

One further explanation for why additional dollars spent on case handling might correlate with decreased satisfaction is that additional case handling activity may empirically mean reduced law reform activity, thereby producing reduced satisfaction (although both $C and $L can theoretically increase or be high).[24] Another explanation is that the cities where the most case handling dollars per participant are being spent are those cities that had especially explosive low satisfaction or high dissatisfaction to begin with in the middle 1960s when OEO legal services began, thereby causing extra money to be spent on them, including $C. In other words, the low satisfaction caused the high spending rather than the reverse. In fact, if data over time could be obtained, one might find that in the high spending areas, the satisfaction has increased although it is still lower than in the low spending areas.[25] As an additional explanation, perhaps increased spending may also produce rising expectations or rising standards such that satisfaction goes down because the standards set by the evaluators have gone up faster than the achievement. It seems unlikely that increased case handling expenditures in themselves would produce lowered satisfaction.[26]

When the above-mentioned multiple regression analysis is carried out, the constraint 10 regression equation relating \$L and \$C simultaneously to S is S = 6.29 + (.34 · \$L − (.03 · \$C). This regression equation yields a multiple correlation coefficient of .78 out of a possible 1.00 correlation. If we set S equal to the minimum S of 7.00, then we can plot constraint 8 showing what combinations of \$L and \$C will achieve a rating of 7.00. Given this multiple regression equation with S = 7.00, then by simple algebra and arithmetic, one can see that \$L = (.09 · \$C) + \$2.09, and \$C = (11.33 · \$L) − \$23.67. We then find any two points on this equation line and connect the two points to determine the equation line. For example, we can find that the value of \$L is \$6.23 when \$C = \$46.00, and that the value of \$C is \$66.97 when \$L = \$8.00. This yields a minimum benefit line with a slight slope from the southwest to the northeast.

Likewise, if we set S equal to the maximum S of 12.00, then we can plot constraint 9, showing what combinations of \$L and \$C will achieve a rating of 12.00. Given the above multiple regression equation with S = 12.00, one can see that \$L = (.09 · \$C) + \$16.80, and \$C = (11.33 · \$L) − \$190.33. This line can be plotted by finding two points on it, such as the point corresponding to an \$L of \$23.00 and a \$C of \$70.26, and the point corresponding to a \$C of \$46.00 and a \$L of \$20.94. This yields a maximum benefit line also with a slight slope from southwest to the northeast which is parallel to, but higher than, the minimum satisfaction line.[27]

Both the minimum and maximum benefit lines are sometimes called equal benefit, equal product, or indifference lines because the benefits obtained by any allocation corresponding to a point on either line are equal to any other point on that line. Like equal cost lines, equal benefit lines normally slope from northwest to southeast (although not with the same slope), meaning that a reduction in expenditure on one activity requires an increase in expenditure on the other activity in order to hold constant the total benefits (or the total costs in the case of an equal cost line). Both the Auerbach and the Kettelle data, however, indicate equal benefit lines which have a positive (rather than an inverse) relation between \$L and \$C, meaning (1) when there is an increase in \$L, there has to be an increase in \$C in order to keep the total benefits from rising, and (2) when there is a decrease in \$L, there has to be a decrease in \$C in order to keep the total benefits from falling. This relation follows from the fact that $L correlates positively with satisfaction, and $C correlates negatively with satisfaction, as previously mentioned. If one could obtain data to statistically control for: (1) the prior satisfaction level before the increase in $C, and (2) the change in standards or rising expectations, then both $L and $C might correlate positively with satisfaction, and the equal benefit line would have an inverse slope from northwest to southeast rather than a positive slope from southwest to northeast.

Regardless of which way any of the lines in figure 13-1 slope, the optimization techniques of linear programming are applicable so long as the lines block off a closed surface of the figure in which the optimum allocation point must lie. It is those optimization techniques to which we now turn.

Goals to Optimize

When the above ten constraints are determined, one can then easily determine the optimum allocation between the activity variables in order to minimize costs or maximize benefits, either graphically or through the use of a computer.

Minimizing Costs. If one wants to minimize total costs while obtaining the minimum satisfaction level of 7.00, then from figure 13-1, one can see that point A will involve the optimum allocation between law reform dollars and case handling dollars. This is the point where the minimum satisfaction line intersects the minimum $C line, slightly above the minimum $L line. At this point, $C equals $54.67, and $L equals $7.07. If one plugs those values of $C and $L into the regression equation given in constraint 10, then those values will produce a satisfaction level of exactly 7.00.[28] Note that the optimum cost line through point A is not the same as the minimum cost line, which is just below point A, because the minimum cost line is below the minimum satisfaction line at point A, meaning no feasible combination of $L and $C adding up to only the minimum cost will give a satisfaction level of 7.00.[29]

The sum of the values for $C and $L is only $61.74, representing a saving of $6.60 from the $68.34 total budget available. This average savings of $6.60 per participant per legal services agency adds up to a large sum of money available for establishing additional legal services agencies if one multiplies the $6.60 by the total number of Legal Services Program participants across the country. The average agency in the Auerbach sample of 201 agencies had 3,369 participants. Given the fact that in 1970 there were about 300 legal services agencies across the country, this would mean more than 1,000,000 participants in the total program. A million participants times a savings of over \$6.00 per participant means a savings of more than \$6,000,000 which was more than 10 percent of the \$58,000,000 total national budget for the OEO Legal Services Program in 1970.[30] This follows from the fact that a \$6.60 saving per participant represents about 10 percent of the \$68.34 available per participant. With the additional \$6,000,000, many communities in need of legal services agencies could be provided with them.

The reason point A represents the optimum cost-minimization point is because it is the point on the minimum satisfaction line that is farthest away from the maximum cost line and yet not below either the minimum \$C line or the minimum \$L line. Any allocation point closer to the maximum cost line would waste money, even though it would be within the feasible region where all the minimum and maximum constraints are satisfied. Likewise, any allocation point farther from the maximum cost line would fail to satisfy the minimum constraints on S and \$C, and ultimately on \$L and total cost.

Instead of saying the cost-minimization point is to spend \$54.67 on case handling per participant and \$7.07 on law reform in order to obtain a satisfaction level of 7.00, it would generally be more meaningful to state the proper allocation in terms of percentages. The optimum percentage of an agency's budget to allocate to \$C should be 80 percent because that is the minimum percentage that can be allocated to \$C. One should not allocate more than 80 percent to \$C because doing so will either reduce satisfaction, as the Auerbach and Kettelle data indicate, or will at least probably not increase it as much as using the extra money for law reform.

The total remaining 20 percent of the budget should not be allocated to law reform, however, if one wants to minimize costs with a minimum satisfaction level since less than a 20 percent allocation will achieve the minimum 7.00 satisfaction. The exact percentage to allocate to \$L will vary for each agency somewhere between 10 percent (the minimum \$L) and 20 percent (the maximum \$L), depending on the agency's total budget. To determine the exact percentage to allocate to \$L, (1) calculate 80 percent of the total budget to determine \$C, (2) plug that figure in place of \$C in the combined constraint 8 and 10 formula $7.00 = 6.29 + (.34 \cdot \$L) - (.03 \cdot \$C)$, (3) solve for \$L, and (4) divide this solution of \$L by the total budget to determine the percentage of the total budget to allocate to \$L.

If one wants to talk in terms of allocating the 1970 national budget of \$58,000,000 to \$L and \$C rather than allocating the average agency budget, one should spend 80 percent of the national budget on \$C and at least 10 percent of the national budget on \$L. The exact percentage to spend on \$L should equal the sum of the \$L figures calculated by the above four-step process for each agency, divided by \$58,000,000. The same above percentages could be applied to the 1971 national budget provided that the Legal

Services Program continued to set a minimum of about 80 percent on $C and about 10 percent on $L.

If in step 4 the value of $L for a given agency comes out to be less than 10 percent of the total budget (as might happen with an especially large budget per participant), then spend exactly 10 percent on $L. Doing so will satisfy the minimum $L constraint and at the same time satisfy the minimum benefit constraint, although the satisfaction level produced may be higher than 7.00. This is all right because the minimum benefit constraint does not require that *only* the minimum benefits be obtained, but rather that *at least* the minimum benefits be obtained.[31] If, however, in step 4 above the value of $L comes out to be more than 20 percent of the total budget (as might happen with an especially small budget), then one cannot spend exactly 20 percent on $L and still satisfy the 7.00 satisfaction level.[32] In other words, it is possible to devise a set of inconsistent constraints that cannot be satisfied simultaneously. Graphically, this means having a set of constraints that do not produce a closed feasible region in which the optimum allocation points can lie.

One especially interesting thing to note from figure 13-1, which is of value in minimizing costs below point A, is that we could further lower the costs without lowering the satisfaction if we could decrease only the minimum $C constraint line (which automatically decreases the minimum total cost line). For example, if we were to lower the $C from $54.67 to $46.00, we could still obtain a 7.00 satisfaction level by spending $46.00 for $C and $6.23 for $L or an optimum total cost of $52.23 which would be a saving of $16.11 from the maximum total cost of $68.34 per participant. The difference between what we do save by spending at point A and what we could save by spending at a point on the minimum satisfaction line to the left of point A represents opportunity cost or lost increased optimization. Regardless of the economics, for political reasons it is unlikely that a drastic reduction in case handling will be allowed by the Office of Economic Opportunity, if it means an increase in law reform under a relatively conservative presidential administration.

Likewise, if we were willing to lower our minimum satisfaction line, we could also save some additional money although at reduced satisfaction and less than we could save by lowering the minimum $C line. Whether the saved money would offset the reduced satisfaction would depend on how many dollars one satisfaction unit is worth to the consumer-evaluators, about which more will be said later. Both the minimum $C line and the minimum satisfaction line are referred to as binding constraints in this cost minimization problem because the optimum point is pushing against the intersection of the minimum $C line and the minimum satisfaction line. Binding constraints, and only binding constraints, raise the possibility of opportunity costs and of increased optimization by changing the constraints. Nonbinding constraints may become binding if the former binding constraints are changed, as would happen to the minimum $L if the minimum satisfaction line were substantially lowered.

An alternative way of interpreting the cost minimization in figure 13-1, which is related to production and consumption economics, is to say that the point of cost minimization is the point where a line running below and parallel to the maximum cost line will be exactly tangential to the feasible region. What we are then saying is that constraint 7 defines a family of parallel equal cost lines, one of which represents the optimum cost line. The optimum cost line, however, must be within or at least touching the feasible region where all the constraints are simultaneously satisfied. Such an optimum cost position exists only at point A. This point can be thought of as the point where the government producer of legal services minimizes its total costs in allocating its budget to two factors of production, namely law reform and case handling, analogous to labor and capital.[33]

Maximizing Benefits. Instead of minimizing costs at a given satisfaction level, figure 13-1 can be used to maximize benefits at a given total cost level. Thus, if one wants to keep total costs at or below the maximum cost level of $68.34 and yet maximize satisfaction, point B will involve the optimum allocation between law reform dollars and case handling dollars. This is the point where the maximum cost line intersects both the maximum $L line and the minimum $C line. At this point, $C equals $54.67, and $L equals $13.67, consuming the total $68.34 budget.[34] If one plugs those values of $C and $L into the regression equation given in constraint 10, those values would produce a satisfaction level of exactly 9.27.

The average level of satisfaction for the 49 agencies used from the Auerbach data was only 6.45 because the agencies were not optimally allocating their funds between law reform and case handling. With the above-described benefit-maximization allocation causing the satisfaction level to rise to 9.27, there would be a gain of 2.82 satisfaction units, or a 44 percent gain. To have the Legal Services Program or any governmental program produce 44 percent more satisfaction without spending additional money, by merely reallocating its expenditures, seems to be a change worth adopting, or at least worth looking into.

The reason point B represents the optimum cost maximization point is because it is the point on the maximum cost line that is farthest away from the minimum satisfaction line and yet not beyond either the maximum $L line or the minimum $C line. Any allocation point closer to the minimum satisfaction line would involve less satisfaction even though it would be within the feasible region where all the minimum and maximum constraints are satisfied. Likewise, any allocation point farther from the minimum satisfaction line would fail to satisfy the constraints on \$C, \$L, and possibly on S as well if one moves above the maximum S line.

Instead of saying the benefit maximization point is to spend \$54.67 on case handling per participant and \$13.67 for law reform, it would generally be more meaningful to state the proper allocation in terms of percentages. The optimum percentage of an agency's budget to allocate to \$C should be 80 percent since that is the minimum percentage that can be allocated. The remaining 20 percent of the budget should all be allocated to law reform if one wishes to maximize total satisfaction rather than to save some of the budget. These same percentages apply to the 1970 national budget of \$58,000,000 if one wants to talk in terms of allocating that national budget to \$L and \$C rather than allocating the average agency budget.

If allocating the remaining 20 percent of an agency's budget to \$L results in producing more than the maximum 12.00 possible satisfaction (as might happen with an especially large agency budget per participant), then only as much \$L as is needed to bring satisfaction up to the maximum S Level need be spent.[35] To determine this optimum \$L short of 20 percent, (1) calculate 80 percent of the budget available to satisfy the minimum \$C constraint, (2) plug that figure into the combined constraint 9 and 10 formula $12.00 = 6.29 + (.34 \cdot \$L) - (.03 \cdot \$C)$ in place of \$C, (3) solve for \$L, and (4) divide this solution of \$L by the total budget to determine the percentage of the total budget to allocate to \$L.

As the cost minimization analysis, figure 13-1 reveals the presence of opportunity costs that keep down benefit maximization. Note that if the maximum \$L line could be raised, substantially greater satisfaction benefits could be obtained at the same maximum cost level. Likewise, the minimum \$C line (which is the complement of the maximum \$L line) could be lowered to produce greater satisfaction benefits at the same maximum cost level. The maximum cost line also represents a binding constraint. However, if it is raised (unlike raising maximum \$L and lowering minimum \$C), the total costs will be raised. This means one would have to decide whether the additional units of satisfaction are worth the additional units of cost.

An alternative way of interpreting the benefit maximization in figure 13-1 that is related to consumption and production economics is to say that the point of benefit maximization is the point where a line running above and parallel to the minimum satisfaction line would be exactly tangential to the feasible region. What we are then saying is that constraint number 10 defines a family of parallel equal benefit lines, one of which represents the optimum benefit line. That optimum benefit line, however, must be within, or at least tangential to, the feasible region where all the constraints are simultaneously satisfied. Such as optimum benefit position exists only at point B. This point can be thought of as the point where the government, representing consumers of legal services, maximizes their total utility by allocating their collective budget to two consumer goods, namely law reform and case handling, analogous to food and clothing.[36]

Optimizing Other Goals. Perhaps there are other meaningful goals that could be optimized besides minimizing total costs or maximizing total benefits. One can of course change the constraints while keeping the same goals or objective functions. This was done between the Auerbach data and the Kettelle data with regard to changing the maximum percentage of the budget that could be devoted to law reform. Likewise, the equal benefit equation expressed in constraint 10 could be changed if empirical data were available on some of the intervening variables (like prior satisfaction and rising expectations) which may be interfering with the true relation between case handling and satisfaction.

Point C within the feasible region at first glance looks as if it might be an optimum point for something. More careful examination, however, indicates that it is the point where total costs are maximized at a minimum level of satisfaction or where total benefits are minimized at maximum total cost. No rational producer or consumer would have as a goal to maximize costs irrespective of satisfaction or to minimize satisfaction irrespective of costs. Likewise, it is not rational in terms of getting the most for one's money to seek to maximize $L or $C or to minimize $L or $C irrespective of the effect on total costs or total satisfaction. Thus, the only rational goal optimization involving a single variable is to minimize costs subject to the satisfaction constraints or to maximize satisfaction subject to the total cost constraints.

However, what about minimizing or maximizing some combination of variables? More specifically, what about maximizing total satisfaction minus total costs (which is the same thing as minimizing total costs minus total satisfaction). To maximize satisfaction minus costs sounds like maximizing profits since profits equal benefits or revenue minus costs. This also sounds like an ideal way to combine cost minimization and benefit maximization and thereby avoid having to choose between those two goals. So long as satisfaction and costs are measured on two different dimensions, however, one cannot subtract one from the other. To do so would be like subtracting hours from pounds or typewriters from miles. It is also like subtracting three oranges from two crates of oranges. To express the answer or the remainder in terms of oranges or crates, one has to know how many oranges are in a crate. To express the answer in money or in some other medium of exchange, one must translate both oranges and crates into dollars or other monetary units.

If benefits were measured in dollars instead of satisfaction units and costs were also measured in dollars, the problem would be quite simple and the optimum allocation of $L and $C to maximize satisfaction minus costs would be either at point A or at point B. It can be proved that, in any linear programming problem, the optimum solution must always be at a corner point within the feasible region, assuming there is a feasible region.[37] Corner point C can be eliminated as being irrational since it maximizes cost and minimizes satisfaction. This only leaves corner points A and B.

At corner point A the total satisfaction is 7.00, and the total cost is \$61.75. At corner point B the total satisfaction is 9.27, and the total cost is \$68.34. Corner point A rather than B maximizes satisfaction minus cost if each satisfaction unit is worth only \$1.00. This is so because \$7.00 in benefits minus \$61.75 in costs means a loss of only \$54.75 whereas \$9.27 in benefits minus \$68.34 in costs means a larger loss of \$59.07. On the other hand, if each satisfaction unit is worth \$10.00, then point B rather than A maximizes satisfaction minus cost, because \$70.00 minus \$61.75 means a profit of only \$8.25, whereas \$92.70 minus \$68.34 means a larger profit of \$24.36. Obviously, whether point A or point B is the point of minimum losses or maximum profits depends on how many dollars one satisfaction unit is worth.

Unfortunately, there is no meaningful way of determining how much one satisfaction unit is worth in terms of dollars from the data available. Methods have been suggested for converting nonmonetary consumer values into monetary ones, but they all involve rather sophisticated surveying of the evaluators, and this was not done when the evaluation studies were made by the Auerbach or Kettelle management consultant firms.[38] In the legal services problem, it is the benefits that are nonmonetary, while the costs are monetary. In environmental protection problems, by way of contrast, the social costs are partly nonmonetary aesthetic costs, and the benefits (such as electric power) are often capable of monetary measurement.[39] Perhaps in the future, governmental agencies in making evaluation studies will seek to use the methods available for determining the demand curve or indifference curve between nonmonetary units and dollars so as to facilitate subsequent policy analysis designed to maximize benefits minus costs.[40]

If one cannot combine cost minimization and benefit maximization by maximizing benefits minus costs, then one must choose between these conflicting goals. The main advantage of minimizing costs is to have some money left over from the budget which can be used for expansion of the program beyond what was originally contemplated. This may be especially important in legal services work since there are so many communities in the country which need a legal services agency, but there are virtually no funds available for expanding the number of agencies as contrasted to just maintaining the existing ones at their present levels of operation. It also seems wasteful to spend more than the number of dollars needed to obtain a minimum level of satisfaction, especially if additional spending produces diminishing returns or diminishing utility. If the government is mainly viewed as a producer of services, then the government should seek to minimize the cost of production by choosing the optimum combination of production factors the way a manufacturer does.

On the other hand, it may be quite unrealistic to expect local agencies to return the savings they obtained from a more rational allocation of dollars to law reform and case handling while maintaining the existing level of satisfaction. It is unrealistic because local agencies fear that if they save portions of their budget, next year's budget will be substantially reduced or at least not increased. It may also be unrealistic because agencies will tend to find a way of spending the savings on themselves rather than returning the savings for use by other less efficient agencies. The more meaningful approach may therefore be to allow each agency to spend all of its budget while trying to persuade it to divide it between law reform and case handling in such a way as to provide maximum satisfaction or benefits. One can also try to cut the potential savings out of agency budgets in advance and encourage them to use the remaining budget to maximum efficiency so as to maintain the same level of satisfaction as existed under the former higher budget. In addition, if the government is mainly viewed as a consumer of services, then the government should seek to maximize the utility of its purchases by choosing the optimum combination of products the way a rational consumer theoretically does.

Although one cannot (1) simultaneously minimize costs and maximize benefits or (2) maximize benefits minus costs, one can arrive at a compromise position between minimizing costs and maximizing benefits. Thus with the data from figure 13-1, one can choose an $L of $10.37 which is the midpoint between $7.07 (the cost minimization position) and $13.67 (the benefit maximization position). Doing so will mean a compromise $C of $54.67, TC of $65.04, and S of 8.18. The $C remains at minimum $C in this compromise; TC remains the sum of $L and $C; and the new S can be calculated accurately enough by interpolation between the S at the cost minimization position and the S at the benefit maximization position.

Ultimately, the choice between these two alternative strategies, or a compromise between them, depends on the nature of the problem and especially on the values of the evaluators or the policy makers who have hired the evaluators. One criticism that might be levied against the satisfaction ratings in the Auerbach and Kettelle data is that the evaluators there were not representative in their values of some group for which the critic has a high regard. The evaluators, however, were chosen, at least indirectly, by high level officials in the Office of Economic Opportunity, who were themselves appointed by the president and approved by congress, who are in turn chosen by the general electorate. Unfortunately, although those evaluators may reflect representative values as of 1969 when the

Table 13-1
The IBM Cards Showing the Constraints and Goals

$L	*$C*	*Total Cost*	*S*	*Relation*	*Constant*
1	0	0	0	GE	6.83
1	0	0	0	LE	13.67
0	1	0	0	GE	54.67
0	1	0	0	LE	61.50
0	0	1	0	GE	61.50
0	0	1	0	LE	68.34
1	1	−1	0	EQ	0.00
0	0	0	1	GE	7.00
0	0	0	1	LE	12.00
−.34	.03	0	1	EQ	6.29
0	0	1	0	MN	
0	0	0	1	MX	

evaluation began, those 1969 values may no longer prevail. Anyone seeking to make use of an evaluative policy analysis must of course consider by whom and when the evaluations were made.

Before leaving the section on choosing between legal activities while assuming a constant or linear return to dollars spent, it should be pointed out that no matter what goals one seeks to optimize in a linear programming problem, there are now canned or previously prepared computer programs available for doing the arithmetic work involved. The arithmetic was fairly simple for figure 13-1 and could be carried out by hand or with a desk calculator, but linear programming problems can be devised for which a computer is quite helpful. This is especially so if (1) the constraints establish numerous corner points in the feasible region or (2) there are more than two activity variables involved, thereby producing a three-dimensional or N-dimensional figure. However, a problem with N activity variables can be simplified by grouping the activities together to form two groups of M and N − M activities respectively. After allocating an optimum role to the M activity group and the N − M activity group, one can break each of those groups down into a pair of conflicting activities or into a pair of conflicting groups of activities.

With a canned linear programming routine, the ten constraints to satisfy and two goals to optimize are provided on twelve IBM data cards punched as shown in table 13-1.

These twelve IBM data cards are preceded by a format card informing the computer that the first four columns of data in this data matrix are (1) the first activity variable, (2) the second activity variable, (3) the total cost variable, and (4) the total benefit variable. The sixth column contains a positive number, and the fifth column shows the relation between the four variables and that number. The five possible relations are (1) greater than or equal to, (2) less than or equal to, (3) equal to, (4) minimize, or (5) maximize. The numbers in the first four columns are the coefficients of the variables in the relational equation. Card 10 is algebraically equivalent to the satisfaction-regression equation, but is written that way so that the "a" coefficient number can be on the right side of the relation term as a positive number. Preceding these twelve cards is the format card and a couple of cards identifying the user, the program call number, and the number of data cards. That's all there is to getting out of the computer the optimum values of $L, $C, total costs, and total benefits at points A and B (provided there is a feasible region), plus an analysis of the possible opportunity costs.

Unfortunately, these computer programs work only when there are solely linear or constant returns constraints in the problem in spite of the fact that diminishing returns may be more empirically realistic. How to handle a cost minimization or benefit maximization problem with diminishing returns relations between dollars spent and benefits obtained (particularly with regard to providing legal services to the poor) is the subject to which we now turn.

Choosing Among Legal Services Activities with Diminishing Returns and a Positively Sloped Equal Benefit Line

Constraints to Satisfy

Constraint 10 expresses the relationship between total benefits obtained and dollars spent for each activity. As initially stated, it produces a straight satisfaction line when graphed. Such a straight line relationship may accurately reflect empirical reality over a short distance of total expenditures like an increase from $30 to $40. Over a long distance of expenditures, however, like an increase from zero dollars to $100 or more, incremental expenditures may not produce equally incremental benefits. The principle of diminishing returns or diminishing utility is a common phenomenon in that, although incremental expenditures may produce incremental benefits, they may do so at a decreasing rate. In other words, each additional unit purchased tends to produce less additional satisfaction than the previous unit because there is a lessening need for each additional unit.[41]

In view of the fact that the constant returns or straight line assumption may be realistic for many situations, and in view of the greater complexity in dealing with diminishing returns or curved line relations, one may wish to

(1) skip this section, and the next, (2) not read them so thoroughly, or (3) delegate the reading of them to someone else. If, however, one has an understanding of basic algebra and a little patience, one can master the potentially useful policy analysis material contained in the rest of this chapter. What may seem difficult at first may be quickly clarified from the graphing or from the concrete examples which are interspersed within the more general discussion.

To adjust constraint 10 to reflect this diminishing returns phenomenon, one can simply rewrite the general formula to read total benefits = (benefits with a one dollar cost) · (Activity 1 raised to the power of weight 1) · (Activity 2 raised to the power of weight 2). In terms of the algebraic symbols used in the legal services problem, the formula would be $S = a \cdot \$L^{b}{}_{1} \cdot \$C^{b}{}_{2}$. If this equation is graphed, it produces a line relating S to \$L and/or \$C that rises but at a decreasing rate, eventually tapering off to almost a plateau, provided that the two weights are each decimals less than one. This equation or curve is referred to as an exponential curve with decimal exponents or sometimes as a Cobb-Douglas function.[42]

Constraint 7 expresses the relationship between total costs and dollars spent for each activity. Unlike the original constraint 10, it always accurately reflects reality since it is true by definition of total cost that the sum of the costs of the individual activities adds up to the total cost.

Values for "a," "b_1," and "b_2" in the above curved satisfaction-line formula can be determined in a manner similar to the way those values are determined in the straight satisfaction-line formula. To do so, however, requires transforming the curved formula into a straight line by changing the multiplication signs to addition and the power exponents to multiplication without changing the meaning of the formula. Fortunately, this can be done by taking the logarithm of both sides of the equation because the $\text{Log}(Y \cdot X) = \text{Log } Y + \text{Log } X$ and $\text{Log } Y^X = X \cdot \text{Log } Y$. Therefore, taking the log of both sides of the curved satisfaction equation results in the transformed logarithmic equation $\text{Log } S = \text{Log } a + (b_1 \cdot \text{Log } \$L) + (b_2 \cdot \text{Log } \$C)$. Taking the log of a number merely means finding in a logarithmic table an exponent for the base ten such that when ten is raised to the power of that exponent, the result will equal the number whose logarithm we are seeking.[43]

It is fortunate that canned computer programs are readily available for solving the value of "a," "b_1," and "b_2" in the above logarithmic equation. All that is needed is to inform the computer for each of the 49 legal services agencies in the Auerbach data (1) how much was spent for law reform or \$L, (2) how much was spent for case handling or \$C, and (3) what was the agency's overall satisfaction rating, as was done in determining constraint 10 before. One then informs the computer (1) to find the logs of \$L, \$C, and S; (2) to in effect plot dots representing the logs of \$L and \$C against the log of S; (3) to fit a straight line or plane to those dots that minimizes the squares of the vertical distances from those dots to the line; (4) to determine the slope of \$L to S (while statistically controlling for \$C), which equals b_1; (5) to determine the slope of \$C to S (while statistically controlling for \$L), which equals b_2; and (6) to determine where the line or plane crosses the S axis, which equals the log of "a." One can then determine the value of "a" by consulting a logarithmic table.

If this is done with the Auerbach data, then $b_1 = .30$, $b_2 = -.31$, and a = 14. This means that the exponential equation can now be read as $S = 14 \cdot \$L^{.30} \cdot \$C^{-.31}$. Because a number taken to a negative exponent means the same as the reciprocal of the number taken to the same exponent made positive, and since a decimal exponent close to .33 is the same as the cube root of the number to which the exponent is taken, this exponential equation simplifies to

$$S = 14 \cdot \sqrt[3]{\$L} / \sqrt[3]{\$C}.$$

Note that in this equation as \$L gets bigger, S gets bigger; and as \$C gets bigger, S gets smaller (just as in the constraint 10 linear equation). One should also note that the above exponential equation fits the Auerbach data better than the linear regression equation in constraint 10 in view of the fact that the sum of the squared deviations from the dots to the exponential line is slightly less than the sum of the squared deviations to the linear regression line.[44]

In order to better understand the problem involved in minimizing total costs and maximizing total benefits when dealing with a diminishing returns satisfaction curve, it is helpful to graph one or more satisfaction curves and one or more total cost lines. For the cost minimization problem, the most relevant satisfaction curve is the minimum satisfaction one. It is, however, difficult to draw a curve accurately because so many points must be determined, whereas the position of a straight line can be determined simply by finding two accurate points and then connecting them. Fortunately, an exponential curve can be easily and meaningfully converted to a straight line by finding two accurate points for the curve on logarithmic-interval (rather than equal-interval) graph paper and connecting these two points.

Figure 2 graphs on logarithmic paper the diminishing returns satisfaction line for a minimum satisfaction level of 7.00. If one expresses \$L in terms of in the simplified exponential equation, then $\$L = (7.00 \cdot \sqrt[3]{\$C} / 14)^3$ which easily reduces to $\$L = \$C/8$, or $\$C = 8 \cdot \$L$. Therefore, to draw the minimum satisfaction line, one can simply connect the point that corresponds to \$L = 1, \$C = 8 and the point that corresponds to \$L = 12, \$C = 96. In a similar manner, the maximum satisfaction line can be drawn where S = 12.00. It is even easier to draw the maximum and minimum \$L and \$C lines since they are unaffected by the fact that logarithmic paper is being used, although there is a change in the physical distances between those maximums and minimums from figure 13-1.

The minimum and maximum total cost lines which would be straight on equal-interval paper now become curves on log-interval paper. As before, any point on a total cost line involves the same total cost as any other point on the same line, just as any point on a benefit line involves the same total benefit as any other point on the same line. Plotting the minimum total cost line therefore simply involves plotting and connecting a number of points each one of which has a value for \$L and \$C such that the sum of those two values adds up to \$61.50 or up to \$68.34 for the maximum total cost line.

Goals to Optimize

One can see from figure 13-2 that point A is the point where total costs are minimized while still providing the minimum 7.00 satisfaction level, because that is the point within the shaded feasible region where all the constraints are simultaneously met which is farthest away from the maximum cost line and closest to the minimum cost line. To determine exactly where point A is and the value of \$L and \$C at that point, one must decide what lines or equations logically intersect at the point where total costs are minimized and where at least minimum satisfaction is obtained. This intersection is the point where the minimum \$C line intersects the minimum satisfaction line, provided that intersection does not occur below the minimum \$L line. It is wasteful to spend more than the minimum \$C in view of the fact that \$C correlates negatively with satisfaction, and thus extra spending on \$C means reduced satisfaction.

To find optimum \$L, plug minimum \$C which is \$54.67 into the minimum S formula, $7.00 = 14 \cdot \sqrt[3]{\$L}/\sqrt[3]{\$C}$, and solve for \$L. Doing so, however, will yield an \$L of \$6.80 which is less than the minimum \$L. This means the optimum \$L has to be the minimum \$L of \$6.83 in order to satisfy the minimum \$L constraint, even though an \$L of \$6.83 combined with a \$C of \$54.67 will produce an S of 7.02 which is higher than the minimum S of 7.00 but still satisfies the minimum S constraint.[45]

In comparing the figure 13-2 cost minimization solution with the one from figure 13-1, it should be noted that the optimum total cost in figure 13-2 is only \$61.50, a savings of \$6.84 per participant. This is even more than the savings of \$6.59 per participant in figure 13-1, and thus even more than the estimated \$6,000,000 national annual savings for the OEO Legal Services Program. As with figure 13-1, having a minimum \$C as high as \$54.67 produces a binding constraint and thereby creates opportunity costs and lost savings. Unlike figure 13-1, having a minimum \$L as high as \$6.83 is

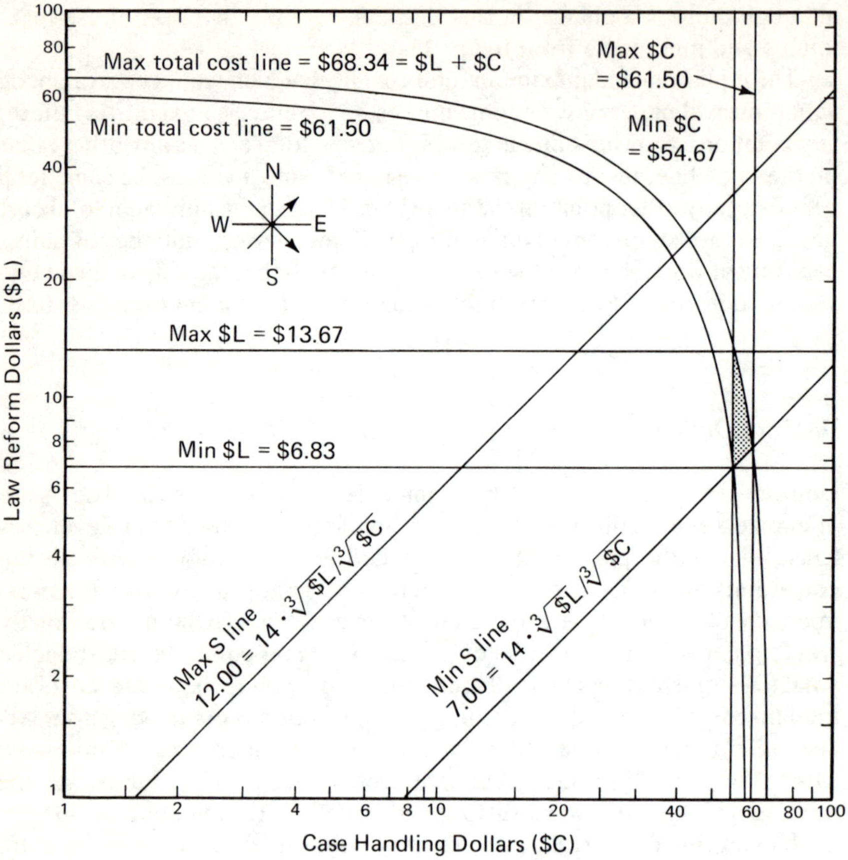

Point A is where total cost is minimized while providing at least 7.00 units of satisfaction.
$L = $6.83 $C = $54.67 TC = $61.50 S = 7.02

Point B is where satisfaction is maximized while not spending more than $68.34.
$L = $13.67 $C = $54.67 TC = $68.34 S = 8.83

Figure 13-2. Allocating $L and $C to Minimize Costs or Maximize Benefits (with diminishing returns and a positively sloped equal-benefit line)

also a binding constraint because less $L could still produce the minimum 7.00 S without changing the minimum $C.

It may be partly a coincidence of the example used that the diminishing returns solution for optimum $L and $C came out as close to the constant returns solution as it did since one might expect a greater difference. The similarity between the two solutions indicates that diminishing returns are not so great in the expenditure of dollars for law reform and case handling relative to the satisfaction obtained, at least within the range of expenditures that are currently being made. This may further indicate that substantial additional sums can be spent on legal services without soon incurring diminishing returns.

Point B is the point in figure 13-2 where benefits are maximized for the average agency below the \$68.34 per participant limit. This is the benefit maximization point because it is the point within the shaded feasible region where all the constraints are simultaneously met which is farthest away from the minimum satisfaction line and closest to the maximum satisfaction line. As with figure 13-1, point B is logically the point where the minimum \$C of \$54.67 is spent and the maximum \$L of \$13.67. At that point, the total cost will be the maximum cost of \$68.34. To calculate the satisfaction level at that point, simply plug the optimum \$L and \$C into the formula $S = .14 \cdot \sqrt[3]{\$L} / \sqrt[3]{\$C}$ and solve for S. Doing so yields an S of 8.83.

In comparing the figure 13-2 benefit maximization solution with the one for figure 13-1, it should be noted that the optimum total satisfaction in figure 13-1 is 9.27 as contrasted to 8.83 in figure 13-2. Both represent substantial percentage gains over the 6.45 satisfaction rating which the average agency had in the Auerbach data. To the extent that the diminishing returns relation more accurately fits the empirical data, the gain from 6.45 to 8.83 or 37 percent is the more realistic gain available by better allocation to \$L and \$C while still only spending \$68.34 per participant. As with figure 13-1, both the minimum \$C constraint and the maximum \$L constraint are preventing point B from rising higher toward the maximum satisfaction level, and they are thus creating opportunity costs which may or may not be politically justifiable.

Point C in figure 13-2 (like figure 13-1) is the irrational point where costs are maximized at the minimum satisfaction level and where benefits are minimized at the maximum cost level. As with figure 13-1, a compromise position can be arrived at between point A and point B wherein one can choose a midpoint \$L of \$10.25 which means a \$C of \$54.67, TC of \$64.92, and S of 8.01. Rather than interpolate to determine the compromise value of S, one can obtain greater accuracy by plugging the compromise values of \$L and \$C into the formula for relating S to \$L and \$C.

One important comparison between the figure 13-2 approach and the figure 13-1 approach is that all the cost minimization and benefit maximization (once the constraints have been determined) can be done for figure 13-1 by easy to use canned computer programs. The figure 13-2 curved line diminishing returns approach, however, generally requires graphing to arrive at approximate solutions, or the use of a desk calculator to arrive at exact solutions, since computer programs are not so available for handling optimizing problems with nonlinear constraints.

Choosing Among Legal Services Activities with Diminishing Returns and a Negatively Sloped Equal Benefit Line

Constraints to Satisfy

Although figure 13-2 complies with the empirical data gathered by both Auerbach and Kettelle, it is unusual to have benefit lines that are positively sloped from southeast to northwest rather than inversely sloped from northeast to southwest. In other words, it is more common for Activity 1 dollars and Activity 2 dollars to move in opposite directions in order to hold total benefits constant than for them to move in the same direction. A positively sloped equal benefit line has no effect on the procedures used in linear programming where all the relations are straight lines. Such a line, however, does affect the appropriate methodology for optimizing costs or benefits when diminishing returns are involved.

In order to demonstrate how one minimizes costs and maximizes benefits with a diminishing returns equal benefit line that is negatively sloped, as is more commonly the case, let us assume the constraint 10 relation is $S = .7 \cdot \sqrt[3]{\$L} \cdot \sqrt[3]{\$C}$, rather than $S = 14 \cdot \sqrt[3]{\$L}/\sqrt[3]{\$C}$. By changing the division sign to a multiplication sign, the relation between \$C and S is changed from negative to positive, and the relation between \$C and \$L is changed from positive to negative. By changing the value of "a" from 14 to .7, we create a minimum satisfaction line that falls between the minimum and maximum total cost lines. Figure 13-3 shows the minimum and maximum satisfaction lines corresponding to this new equal benefit equation.

To illustrate how to minimize costs at a minimum level of satisfaction or maximize satisfaction at a maximum level of costs using the total cost and total benefit lines of figure 13-3, it is necessary to ignore the minimum and maximum \$L and \$C constraint lines. This is so because if those lines are complied with, then there is no point on the minimum satisfaction line that is simultaneously between the minimum and maximum \$L lines and the minimum and maximum \$C lines. Let us make the reasonable assumption that the minimum \$L is zero dollars, and the maximum \$L is \$68.34, and that likewise the minimum \$C is zero dollars, and the maximum \$C is \$68.34. In other words, let us remove the minimum and maximum constraints on the separate activity variables as is often done in linear programming problems and see what happens. One obvious result is that the new feasible region is the shaded area between the minimum satisfaction line and the maximum total cost line. What is not so obvious is exactly what point within that shaded area is the optimum minimum cost point for allocating \$L and \$C, and what point is the optimum maximum benefit point.

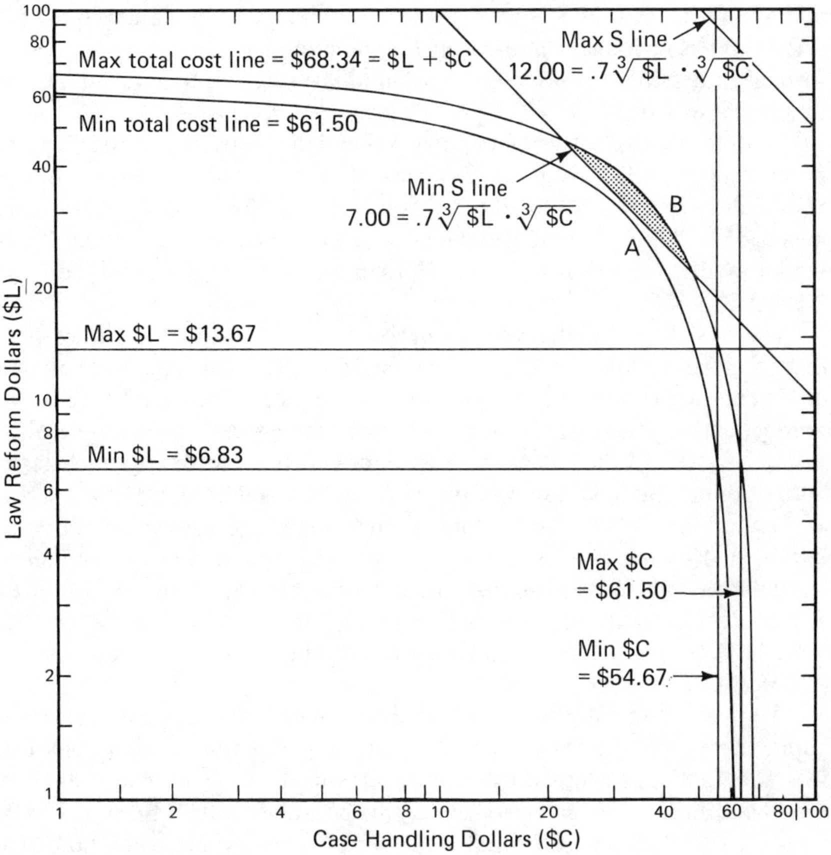

Point A is where total cost is minimized while providing at least 7.00 units of satisfaction.
$L = $31.62 $C = $31.62 TC = $63.24 S = 7.00

Point B is where satisfaction is maximized while not spending more than $68.34.
$L = $34.17 $C = $34.17 TC = $68.34 S = 7.37

Figure 13-3. Allocating $L and $C to Minimize Costs or Maximize Benefits (with diminishing returns and a negatively sloped equal-benefit line)

Goals to Optimize

The cost minimization point is at point A. Geometrically, this corresponds to a point on the minimum satisfaction line that is about midway between the two points where the minimum satisfaction line intersects the maximum total cost line, because that is the point within the new feasible region which is farthest away from the maximum total cost line and closest to the former minimum total cost line. Actually, there is no longer a minimum total cost line if there is no longer a minimum \$L or minimum \$C; therefore, what was formerly the minimum total cost line should be referred to as an equal cost line equal to \$61.50.

To determine exactly where point A is and the value of \$L and \$C at that point, one must first state \$L in terms of \$C in the latest version of the combined constraint 8 and 10 formula which is $7.00 = .7 \cdot \sqrt[3]{\$L} \cdot \sqrt[3]{\$C}$. This means $\$L = [7.00/(.7 \cdot \sqrt[3]{\$C})]^3$ which simplifies down to $\$L = 1000/\$C$. If we know that total cost = \$L + \$C, then we also know that total cost = $(1000/\$C) + \$C$.

We must next find the calculus derivative of the total cost with respect to \$C for the equation total cost = $(1000/\$C) + \$C$. The derivative of Y (a dependent variable) with respect to X (an independent variable) is the number corresponding to the ratio between a change in Y and a change in X when the value of the change in X becomes so small as to approach zero, but not quite reach it. A derivative can also be thought of as the algebraic expression for the slope of the tangent to a curve at any given point on the curve such as the point where the curve is at a minimum or maximum. Fortunately, tables are available whereby one can read off the derivative of any expression without fully understanding what a derivative is.[46] Such a table indicates that the derivative of the total cost with respect to \$C is $(-1000/\$C^2) + 1$.

We then set this derivative equal to zero which means we are now at a point where there is no slope, or a horizontal slope, between total costs and \$C, and total costs are thus at a minimum at the 7.00 given level of satisfaction. We then solve for \$C at this point. If $(-1000/\$C^2) + 1 = 0$, then C = \$31.62. For the final step, we plug this value of \$C into the equation $7.00 = .7\sqrt[3]{\$L} \cdot \sqrt[3]{\$C}$ and solve for \$L. Doing so reveals that the optimum \$L is also \$31.62.[47] Thus, at point A, the total cost is \$63.24 with a satisfaction level of 7.00.

In effect, what we have done through the above use of differential calculus is to find the value of \$L and \$C at the point where the lowest possible total cost line just barely touches the minimum satisfaction line. This lowest total cost line has a value of \$63.24 at any point along the line. A total cost line one penny less than \$63.24 (if the arithmetic is done accurately) would not quite touch up to or be tangent to the minimum S line, and thus would produce less than 7.00 satisfaction units. Likewise, a total cost line one penny more than \$63.24 wound intersect the minimum S line rather than just barely touch it, and thus would produce more than 7.00 satisfaction units.[48]

Note that the optimum solution involved spending some money for law reform and some money for case handling even though there was no minimum $L and no minimum $C, and thus, in terms of the constraints, all of the money could have been spent for $L. One reason some money was spent for $L and some for $C is that, in setting up the hypothetical constraint 10 which would show a negatively sloping equal benefit line, we gave $L and $C equal weight in determining S since the cube root is taken of both $L and $C in the formula. Doing so not only causes some $L and some $C to be spent in the optimum solution, but also causes equal amounts to be spent on $L and $C. However, even if the weight given to $L were substantially greater (as would be that obtained by taking only the square root of $L in constraint 10), some money would probably be spent on $C in the optimum solution, because although at lower expenditure levels it would be more efficient to spend on $L, the phenomenon of diminishing returns would cause continued spending on $L to become inefficient relative to spending on $C. This point of inefficiency might be reached before enough money could be spent on $L to produce a 7.00 minimum satisfaction level.

The only binding constraint in this cost minimization situation is the minimum satisfaction line. If it were lowered, additional savings could be had and opportunity costs avoided. As before, however, we cannot judge whether lowering the minimum S line would be worth the dollars saved without knowing how many dollars one satisfaction unit is worth. With a minimum S line of 7.00, there is a savings of $5.10 from the $68.34 available per participant. This savings, however, is as hypothetical as the slope and shape of the minimum benefit line.

The benefit maximization point is at point B. Geometrically, this corresponds to a point on the maximum total cost line that is about midway between the two points where the minimum satisfaction line intersects the maximum total cost line, because that is the point within the feasible region farthest away from the minimum S line of 7.00 and closest to the maximum S line of 12.00.

To determine exactly where point B is and the value of $L and $C at that point, one must first state $L in terms of $C in the combined constraint 6 and 7 formula which is $\$68.34 = \$L + \$C$. This means $\$L = \$68.34 - \$C$. If we know that satisfaction units obtained $= .7 \cdot \sqrt[3]{\$L} \cdot \sqrt[3]{\$C}$, then we also know that satisfaction $= .7 \cdot \sqrt[3]{\$68.34 - \$C} \cdot \sqrt[3]{\$C}$. We must next find the calculus derivative of satisfaction (as the dependent variable) with respect to $C (as the independent variable) for the equation $S = .7 \cdot \sqrt[3]{\$68.34 - \$C} \cdot \sqrt[3]{\$C}$. By consulting a table of derivatives as we did with the cost minimization problem, we find that the value of the simplified derivative of S with respect to $C is $(-.462 \cdot \$C + \$15.78654)/[\$C^{.67} \cdot (\$68.34 - \$C)^{.67}]$. We next set this derivative or slope equal to zero to be at the point where S is a maximum at a total cost of $68.34. We then solve for $C in this equation.

Doing so reveals that optimum \$C = $-15.78654/-.462$ = \$34.17. For the final step, we plug this value of \$C into the equation \$68.34 = \$L + \$C and solve for \$L. Doing so reveals that the optimum \$L is also \$34.17.[49]

To determine the satisfaction level at this point, we plug the above benefit maximization values of \$L and \$C into the formula $S = .7 \cdot \sqrt[3]{\$L} \cdot \sqrt[3]{\$C}$, and we find that S = 7.37. Considering that the average S for the 49 agencies in the Auerbach data was only 6.45 with an average total cost of \$68.34, this means that by properly allocating our total cost available to \$L and \$C, we can obtain an increase of .92 satisfaction units or 14 percent if the above satisfaction formula were real rather than hypothetical. The only binding constraint in this benefit maximization situation is the maximum total cost line. If it were raised, additional benefits could be had and opportunity costs avoided, but we do not know whether those additional satisfaction units would be worth the additional dollars.

In effect, what we have done through the above use of differential calculus is to find the value of \$L and \$C at the point where the highest possible satisfaction line just barely touches, or is tangent to, the maximum total cost line. As previously mentioned, this highest possible S line has a value of 7.37 at any point along the line. A satisfaction line .01 more than 7.37 (if the arithmetic is done accurately) would be beyond the capacity of a maximum total cost of \$68.34 to reach. Likewise, a satisfaction line .01 unit less than 7.37 would be needlessly below the capacity of a maximum total cost of \$68.34.[50]

One might question the need for finding a derivative, setting it equal to zero, and solving for \$C (as we just did) when in this example one could have found that \$C = \$34.17 by merely dividing the \$68.34 maximum cost by 2. This, however, is only true for this example because \$L and \$C are given the same cube root weights in the formula relating total benefits to \$L and \$C. In a less simple but more realistic example, \$L and \$C would have different weights, and the exact optimum \$L and \$C for maximizing benefits on the maximum total cost line in figure 13-3 could be derived only by consulting a table of derivatives and doing the algebra and arithmetic involved. One could, however, arrive at approximate optimums for \$L and \$C simply by observing where B seems to fall on a graph like figure 13-3.

If spending the maximum total cost results in achieving more than the maximum total possible satisfaction, then find the value of \$L and \$C at the point where total costs are minimized at the 12.00 rather than 7.00 level of satisfaction. This involves going through the same steps described earlier for finding the value of \$L and \$C at a cost minimization point by finding the derivative of the total cost with respect to \$C for the equation total cost = (5038/\$C) + \$C, setting this derivative equal to zero, solving for optimum \$C, and then plugging that value back into the equation $12.00 = .7 \cdot \sqrt[3]{\$L} \cdot \sqrt[3]{\$C}$ to solve for optimum \$L.

As mentioned in discussing optimization involving diminishing returns and a positively sloped equal benefit line, canned computer programs are not available for handling optimizing problems with nonlinear constraints. This is likewise so with diminishing returns and negatively sloped equal benefit lines. A desk calculator, however, can greatly facilitate the calculus arithmetic involved. If more than two activity or independent variables are present, one can, in effect, group the activity variables into conflicting groups by the calculus approach of partial differentiation or partial derivatives.[51]

The two point C's in figure 13-3 (like point C in figure 13-1 and figure 13-2) represent the irrational positions where costs are maximized at the minimum satisfaction level and where benefits are minimized at the maximum cost level. With the data from figure 13-3, and compromise optimum between points A and B is \$L = \$32.90 per participant, \$C = \$32.90, TC = \$65.80, and S = 7.19. By this stage in the development of the minimization and maximization methodology as applied to the Legal Services Program, one should be able to see that optimum points A, B, and C, as well as the ten constraints, are all present in one form or another in figures 13-1, 13-2 and 13-3 as explained in the accompanying text.

Some Conclusions

The most important *methodological* principles developed in more detail in this analysis are five in number. These principles all relate to how one can make better policy decisions by allocating scarce financial resources in order to obtain more for one's money.

First, in choosing between alternative activities or deciding how much to spend on each activity, it is helpful to both algebraically and geometrically determine (1) the minimum and maximum level desired for each activity, for total costs, and for total benefits, and (2) the relation between expenditure for each activity on the one hand and total costs and total benefits on the other hand.

Second, in determining the relation between the activities and the total benefits, it is helpful to gather data on specific instances of activity spending and benefits obtained and to feed these data into a canned computer program in order to obtain the coefficients for a linear or logarithmic regression line.

Third, in order to minimize total costs, find a point geometrically or algebraically representing the expenditure values for each activity which is farthest down from the maximum cost level but provides at least the minimum satisfaction level.

Fourth, in order to maximize total benefits, find a point representing the expenditure values for each activity that is farthest up from the minimum satisfaction level, but does not exceed the maximum cost level.

Fifth, seek to maximize benefits minus costs if both benefits and costs can be measured in terms of the same units. Otherwise, choose between cost minimization or benefit maximization on the basis of one's values or the values of some controlling group, or else compromise between cost minimization and benefit maximization.

The most important *substantive* principles developed in more detail in this analysis are four in number. These principles all relate to how the OEO Legal Services Program can allocate its scarce resources in order to obtain more for its money.

First, substantial reductions in total costs expended by the OEO Legal Services Program seem possible if linear or other optimizing programming techniques are used to more rationally allocate local agency budgets between law reform and case handling, without resulting in lowering the satisfaction level below the minimum desired and especially without resulting in lowering the satisfaction level below the currently prevailing low level.[52]

Second, substantial increases in satisfaction by the OEO Legal Services Program seem possible if linear or other optimizing programming techniques are used to more rationally allocate agency budgets between law reform and case handling, without raising currently prevailing agency budget levels.

Third, a dollar spent for law reform tends to produce substantially more satisfaction than a dollar spent for case handling. In fact, a dollar spent for case handling produces negative satisfaction at least to the extent it detracts from law reform dollars available.

Fourth, substantially more dollars can be spent on the OEO Legal Services Program before extra dollars produce significantly diminishing incremental returns.

The real value of all this analysis, however, is not in laying out a set of abstract principles as a kind of mathematical recreation. Nor is it to make the Legal Services Program more efficient. Instead, the real or broader value lies in the possibility that the general principles described here with a Legal Services application will be expanded by other researchers and used by policy makers and policy appliers in more efficiently allocating scarce governmental resources in a large variety of legal policy situations.[53]

Appendix

This appendix deals with some matters that cut across figures 13-1, 13-2,

13-3 in the text. These points were more clearly recognized by the author after completion of the chapter.

A "point D" could be shown in figures 13-2 and 13-3 (as it is shown in figure 13-1). This point represents the empirical position of the average agency as contrasted to optimum positions A and B (reflecting goals of minimum cost and maximum satisfaction respectively) and as contrasted to the "malimum" or worst position C (where costs are maximized and satisfaction is minimized within the feasible region). This empirical D point corresponds to a $L of $6.16 (or 9 percent of the average budget), a $C of $62.18 (or 91 percent of the average budget), a TC of $68.34, and an S of about 6.50 which is close to malimum point C.

One might ask for an explanation of the deviation between empirical point D and optimum points A and B. The answer, in general terms, is simply that the average agency budget is not being allocated efficiently between law reform and case handling in light of the relative evaluation of these two alternative activities by the OEO evaluators. More specifically, many agencies probably shy away from additional law reform work because it is more time consuming, more controversial, less frequently requested by individual clients, and more difficult to perform.

A "point E" might also be mentioned—where in figures 13-1 and 13-2 the maximum satisfaction line and the minimum total cost line intersect, thereby maximizing benefits and minimizing costs simultaneously. At that point in figure 13-1, $L = $20.41, $C = $41.09, TC = $61.50, and S = 12.00. (The values of $L and $C were found by solving for $L and $C in the pair of simultaneous equations $61.50 = $L + $C, and 12.00 − 6.29 = .34 $L − .03 $C). In figure 13-2, $L = $23.76, $C = $37.74, TC = $61.50, and S = 12.00 (These values of $L and $C were found by solving for $L and $C in the pair of simultaneous equations $61.50 = $L + $C, and $12.00/14 = \sqrt[3]{\$L}/\sqrt[3]{\$C}$.) The "super-optimum" point E, however, is to the left of the feasible region in that it allows for more than 20 percent $L and less than 80 percent $C. There is no such super-optimum intersection point in figure 13-3 given the negative relation in figure 13-3 between $L and $C in achieving a constant level of satisfaction.

An even greater super-optimum point F exists in figures 13-1 and 13-2 where nothing or $.01 is spent on $C, and just enough is spent on $L to provide 12.00 (or 7.00) units of satisfaction at a cost quite substantially below $61.50. The value of $L for such a point F can be found by solving for $L in the equations 12.00 = 6.29 + (.34 · $L) + (.03 · 0), and $12.00 = 14 \cdot \sqrt[3]{\$L}/\sqrt[3]{.01}$. The constraints, however, prevent such a solution because when the constraints are exceeded, the satisfaction equations no longer hold. To achieve 12.00 or 7.00 units while only spending .01 for $C in figure 13-3 would require spending far more than the maximum $68.34 for $L given the negative and curvilinear relation in figure 13-3 between \$L and \$C in achieving a constant level of satisfaction.

Where would the optimum points A and B be within the feasible region if the size or direction of the regression weights of \$L and \$C were to change in the satisfaction equation? So long as the regression weight of \$L is larger than the regression weight of \$C in the satisfaction equation, then the benefit maximization point will be on the minimum \$C line as high as one can go without going above the maximum \$L line or the maximum S line whichever comes first. Likewise the cost minimization line will also be on the minimum \$C line as low as one can go without going below the minimum \$L line or the minimum S line whichever comes first. On the other hand, if the regression weight of \$L is smaller than the regression weight of \$C, then the benefit maximization point will be on the minimum \$L line as far to the right as one can go without exceeding the maximum \$C line or the maximum S line whichever comes first. Likewise the cost minimization line will also be on the minimum \$L line—as far to the left as one can go without exceeding the minimum \$C line, or the minimum S line, whichever comes first.

Slight differences between the results shown in this chapter and the results obtainable from the quantities given herein, are due to the fact that the quantities given are generally rounded from the more precise original quantities from which the results shown are calculated.

Notes

The author thanks Roger Detweiler and Fred Baldwin of the Office of Economic Opportunity for access to data on the Legal Services Program and also Marian Neef, Secil Tuncalp, and Tony Champagne of the University of Illinois for their assistance in processing the data.

1. Robert Llewellyn, *Linear Programming* (Addison-Wesley, 1962); and S. Vajda, *Mathematical Programming* (Addison-Wesley, 1961).

2. William Baumol, *Economic Theory and Operations Analysis* (Prentice-Hall, 1965); Harvey M. Wagner, *Principles of Operations Research with Applications to Managerial Decisions* (Prentice-Hall, 1969); and Samuel Richmond, *Operations Research for Management Decisions* (Ronald Press, 1968).

3. Guy Black, *The Application of Systems Analysis to Government Operations* (Praeger, 1968); and Roland M. McKean, *Efficiency in Government through Systems Analysis* (Wiley, 1958).

4. One exception is Charles Laidlaw, *Linear Programming for Urban Development Plan Evaluation* (Praeger, 1972).

5. For a review of the literature of scientific legal-policy decision-making, see Louis Mayo and Ernest Jones, "Legal-Policy Decision Process: Alternative Thinking and the Predictive Function," 33 *George Washington Law Review* 318 (1964). Some more recent related material is included in Gordon Tullock, *The Logic of the Law* (Basic Books, 1971).

6. Harry Stumpf, *Lawyers and the Poor* (Sage Publications, 1973): "The O.E.O. and Legal Services: A Symposium," 14 *The Catholic Lawyer* 91-174 (Spring, 1968); U.S. Dept. of Health Education and Welfare, *The Extension of Legal Services to the Poor* (Govt. Printing Office, 1964); and John D. Kettelle Corporation, *Evaluation of Office of Economic Opportunity Legal Services Program–Final Report* (OEO Evaluation Division, 1971).

7. Fred Baldwin, *Evaluating the OEO Legal Services Program* (OEO Evaluation Division, 1972): Spiro Agnew, "What's Wrong with the Legal Services Program," 58 *American Bar Association Journal* 930 (1972): William Klaus, "Legal Services Program: Reply to Vice President Agnew," 58 *American Bar Association Journal* 1178 (1972): Eli Jarmel, "The Volume Problem," in *Legal Representation of the Poor,* pp. 3-1 through 3-19 (Matthew Bender, 1972); and Herbert Semmel, "Allocating Limited Resources: The Case Load Problem," in *Social Justice through Law,* pp. 56-69 (Foundation Press, 1970). The Jarmel and Semmel readings include excerpts from Gary Bellow, Edgar Cahn, Geoffrey Hazard, and others. For over 1,000 bibliographic items on legal services (most with long abstracts), see Chilton Research Services (1971).

8. Hugh Duffy et al., *Design of an On-Site Evaluation System for the Office of Legal Services of the Office of Fconomic Opportunity* (Urban Institute, 1970); Auerbach Corporation, *Office of Legal Services Individual Project Evaluations Final Report* (OEO Office of Legal Services, 1971); and Kettelle Corporation, *op. cit.* note 6.

9. According to the Kettelle report, *op. cit.* note 6, the on-site visits were conducted by teams typically composed of an attorney acting as team leader, two additional attorneys, and one community analyst. Criteria used in the selection of attorney members included empathy with the needs of the poor community and an understanding of and appreciation for the goals of the Office of Legal Services.

10. The quantity of law reform and related activities is given in three verbal categories in the Auerbach data rather than as a percentage, although it is given as a percentage in the Kettelle data. The first verbal category in the Auerbach data is "virtually no other activity [other than case handling]"; the second category is "some special activities in law reform and group representation"; and the third category is "considerable amount of other [than] case activity." These three verbal categories were

translated to 2 percent, 10 percent, and 20 percent respectively on the basis of observing that in the Kettelle data the average of the bottom third of the projects was about 2 percent, the middle third about 10 percent, and the top third about 20 percent. The translations also make sense in light of the common sense meaning of the verbalization used and statements made in the allocation-debate literature.

11. The number of dollars per participant was used rather than the raw number of dollars so as to provide comparability between agencies operating with different clientele sizes. The number of dollars per population within the geographical area of each agency would not be as accurate because two geographical areas of equal size may differ in the number of poor people and especially in the number of poor people who participate in the legal services program. Counting clients or counting cases produces approximately the same results in the optimizing solutions since agencies tend to rank the same on quantity of clients or cases. Some clients or participants have multiple cases, but some cases have multiple clients. Agencies do have more participants than cases even if participants only refer to immediate recipients of services, not those indirectly benefiting.

12. A rating of 1 through 3 means: "Project has critical deficiencies. Close down or cut back project." A rating of 4 through 6 means: "Project has internal problems. Requires technical assistance. Fund at project-in-place level." A 7 through 9 means: "Project operating efficiently. Could benefit from technical assistance. Fund at project-in-place level." A 10 through 12 means: "Project operating efficiently. A strong force in the War on Poverty. Expand if project can effectively handle additional resources."

13. The Kettelle data provides direct percentages on percent of law reform rather than percentages translated from verbal categories, and the Kettelle data provides the number of project participants rather than the number of planned project participants. The other variables are measured the same in both sets of data. Copies of the Kettelle final report, which contain the raw data, are available from the Evaluation Division of the Office of Economic Opportunity or from the National Technical Information Services of the U.S Department of Commerce. The Auerbach data are only available on computer tapes for special research from the OEO Office of Legal Services.

14. The especially deviant cases were also removed from the analysis because they have a tendency to distort the degree and even the direction of the relationship between (1) case handling and law reform dollars spent and (2) satisfaction obtained.

15. In the evaluation questionnaires, law reform and related activities (as contrasted to individual service cases) refer to (1) law reform (i.e., amending existing laws or changing regulations and practices thereby

benefiting others in addition to individual client); (2) economic development (includes technical assistance such as forming cooperatives, negotiating loans, small business counseling, and acting as a promoter, incorporator, and advisor to entrepreneurs); (3) community education (i.e., informing target community members of what the law can do for them); and (4) group representation. See Kettelle Corporation, *op. cit,* note 6, at 132-133.

16. One of the sixteen agencies was eliminated from the analysis of the Kettelle data. Without that deviant agency, the Kettelle agencies spent a total amount of $47.50 per participant, $39.22 (or 83 percent) on case handling, and $8.28 (or 17 percent) on law reform. The one deviant case spent a total amount of $270.08 per participant.

17. Policy-making problems that do not involve the allocation of scarce resources to two or more activities include such controversial issues as whether to pass legislation abolishing capital punishment, legalizing marijuana, prohibiting malapportioned legislatures, or legalizing medical abortions. For a generalized model for handling such policy problems, see Nagel, *The Legal Process from a Behavioral Perspective* (Dorsey, 1969), pp. 360-373.

18. As indicated in note 10, there are only three categories in which the agencies are placed with regard to percentage of effort devoted to law reform activities corresponding to 2 percent, 10 percent, and 20 percent. The verbal description of the 2 percent category as being "virtually no other activity [other than case handling]," and the general rejection in the debate literature of so low a level of law reform indicate that legal services agencies should seek to reach at least the next higher category.

19. The maximum allowable $L in working with the Kettelle data was considered to be 40 percent of the average budget rather than 20 percent as with the Auerbach data because (1) some of the existing agencies in the Kettelle data had indicated an average percent of attorney time on law reform at 35 and 36 percent, and (2) doing so allows for a broader range in which the optimum allocation of $L and $C can be positioned.

20. Instead of stating law reform and case handling in terms of monetary units, one could have stated those activities in terms of man hours spent. Information on dollars rather than hours, however, is more readily available. Dollars are also interchangeable, but hours of senior, more experienced lawyers are not generally interchangeable with hours of junior lawyers.

21. See note 12.

22. For additional detail on constructing a linear regression line to relate two variables, see Hubert Blalock, *Social Statistics* (McGraw-Hill, 1960), 273-285 and 326-329; and J.P. Guilford, *Fundamental Statistics in*

Psychology and Education (McGraw-Hill, 1956), 365-369 and 390-396. The reason law reform related activities and case handling are the only two independent variables used is because we are trying to decide an optimum balance to allocate to these two types of activities. For a discussion of other variables related to evaluator satisfaction (such as the nature of the agency personnel, the local bar, the poverty community, and the geographical region), see Anthony Champagne, "Legal Services: A Study of Program Implementation at the Local Level" (U. of Illinois dissertation, 1973).

23. The correlation coefficent between \$L and S is +.64, whereas the correlation coefficient between \$C and S is −.27.

24. In the Auerbach data there is a +.26 correlation between \$C and \$L. This means that when \$C is high, \$L also tends to be high and vice versa, but not necessarily as a causal relation. More likely \$C and \$L are both co-effects of how high the overall budget is. If the overall budget is held constant, then by definition additional case handling means a reduction in law reform since TC = \$C + \$L.

25. If budget amounts and satisfaction scores for each agency could be obtained over time, a linear programming routine could be applied to allocating funds among the approximately 300 legal services agencies so as to maximize national satisfaction from the program.

26. In the Kettelle data, the correlation between satisfaction and \$C was positive when \$L was ignored. However, when \$L was held constant, \$C had a negative weight in the regression equation. This means that among agencies that are approximately alike on \$L, those that are high on \$C have a lower S than those that are low on \$C.

27. The ten constraints for the Kettelle data calculated by methods similar to those used for the Auerbach data are as follows:

1. Minimum \$L = \$4.74 or 10% of maximum total cost.
2. Maximum \$L = \$19.00 or 40% of maximum total cost (see note 19).
3. Minimum \$C = \$28.50 or 60% of maximum total cost.
4. Maximum \$C = \$42.75 or 90% of maximum total cost.
5. Minimum total cost = \$33.24.
6. Maximum total cost = \$47.50.
7. Total cost = \$L + \$C.
8. Minimum benefits = 7.00.
9. Maximum benefits = 12.00.
10. Total benefits = 7.16 + (.42 · \$L) − (.06 · \$C).

28. For the Kettelle data, the cost minimization point (corresponding to the Kettelle constraints in note 27) is \$L = \$4.75, \$C = \$28.50, total cost = \$33.25, and S = 7.38. In this example, the minimum \$L and the minimum

$C turn out to be the optimum $L and optimum $C because by spending the minimum of each, one can obtain more than the 7.00 minimum satisfaction level.

29. To be exact, if one plugs a value for $L of $6.83 and a value for $C of $54.67 into the formula S = 6.29 + (.34 · $L) – (.03 · $C), then the value of S comes out to be only 6.97. The value of S by spending at the minimum total cost line would be substantially less than 7.00 if the minimum satisfaction line would have had either a steeper slope or would have begun at a point to the left of figure 13-1 further away from the minimum $L line. The difference between 6.97 and 7.00 is .03 satisfaction units, not .03 dollars. One satisfaction unit may be worth many dollars.

30. There were 265 legal services projects as of January 1969. 3 *Law in Action* 4 (Jan. 1969). The budget for 1970 was $58 million. 3 *Law in Action* 5 (April, 1969). Figures giving the number of legal services agencies at a given point in time vary depending on whether one counts the separate community agencies for multiple-community programs like the California Rural Legal Assistance or the downstate Illinois Land of Lincoln Legal Assistance Foundation.

31. If the total budget available per participant is higher than $71.00, then even by spending only the minimum 10 percent on $L, a satisfaction level greater than 7.00 will be obtained. This $71 figure was arrived at by solving for B in the equation 7.00 = 6.29 + (.34 · .1B) – (.03 · .8B).

32. If the total budget available per participant is as low as $16.14, then by spending the maximum 20 percent on $L, a satisfaction level of 7.00 can still be obtained (but not if the budget is lower than $16.14). This figure was arrived at by solving for B in the equation 7.00 = 6.29 + (.34 · .2B) – (.03 · .8B).

33. For additional detail on cost minimization and production economics, see Samuelson, *Economics: An Introductory Analysis* (McGraw-Hill, 1967), 523-529, and Baumol, *op. cit.* note 2, at 250-294.

34. For the Kettelle data, the benefit maximization point (corresponding to the Kettelle constraints in note 27) is $L = $15.73, $C = $28.50, total cost = $44.23, and S = 12.00. In this example, the maximum S level of 12.00 can be obtained without spending the total budget of $47.50. Instead, the minimum $C is spent and just enough $L above the minimum $L to bring S up to the 12.00 maximum.

35. If the total budget available per participant is $129.77, then exactly 12.00 units of satisfaction can be obtained by spending the maximum 20 percent on $L. This $129.77 figure was arrived at by solving for B in the equation 12.00 = 6.29 + (.34 · .2B) – (.03 · .8B). Therefore with a budget larger than $129.77, less than 20 percent should be spent on $L or else some of the $L will be wasted seeking theoretically non-existent additional

satisfaction. If, however, the total budget available per participant is higher than \$571.00, then even spending the minimum 10 percent on \$L will still result in exceeding the 12.00 maximum satisfaction level. This \$571 figure was arrived at by solving for B in the equation $12.00 = 6.29 + (.34 \cdot .1B) - (.03 \cdot .8B)$.

36. For additional detail on cost minimization and consumption economics, see Samuelson, *op. cit.* note 33, at 429-434, and Baumol, *op. cit.* note 2, at 169-249.

37. Kemeny, Snell, and Thompson, *Introduction to Finite Mathematics* (Prentice-Hall, 1959), 249-259; Baumol, *op. cit.* note 2, at 79-84.

38. Baumol, *op. cit.* note 2, at 211-217 and 512-528, and Miller and Starr, *Executive Decisions and Operations Research* (Prentice-Hall, 1960), 65-72.

39. On the measurement of non-monetary costs and benefits, see Black, *op. cit.* note 3, at 37-89; Dorfman, *Measuring Benefits in Government Investments* (Brookings, 1964); and Guilford, *Psychometric Methods* (McGraw-Hill, 1954), 154-301.

40. One cannot translate satisfaction units into dollars by determining the slope of the regression line between satisfaction obtained and total cost spent for each of the 49 Auerbach data agencies. This is so because such a line would represent the relation between quantity of legal service satisfaction units *supplied* and the price per unit, rather than the relation between the quantity of legal service satisfaction units *demanded* and the price per unit. A supply curve has a positive or direct relation between units supplied and the price paid, whereas a demand curve has a negative or inverse relation between units demanded and the price paid. These two curves or lines may also have different shapes as well as directions. This is basically a problem of identifying the proper equation in a simultaneous relationship. Baumol, *op. cit.* note 2, at 221-28; and Hubert Blalock, *Theory Construction: From Verbal to Mathematical Formulations* (Prentice-Hall, 1969), 48-59.

41. Samuelson, *op. cit.* note 33, at 23-26 and 417-419; and Baumol, *op. cit.* note 2, 185-188 and 253-255.

42. Guilford, *op. cit.* note 39, at 43-78; and Baumol, *op. cit.* note 2, 14-17 and 402-403.

43. For further detail on exponents and logarithms, see Baumol, *op. cit.* note 2, at 17-19; or any intermediate algebra test.

44. Stated in other terms, the multiple correlation is .84 between Log \$L and Log \$C as independent variables and Log S as the dependent variable, whereas the multiple correlation is only .64 between \$L and \$C as independent variables and S as the dependent variable.

45. Actually, the S level at point A in figure 13-2 is 7.15 if one does not round off the original b_1 and b_2 from .31 and −.31 respectively to .33, and if one does not round off the original "a" value from 13.9 to 14.

46. Virtually everything you always wanted to know about calculus applied to minimization and maximization problems but may have been afraid to ask can be found in Baumol, *op. cit.* note 2, at 42-69; Richmond, *op. cit.* note 2, at 40-66 and 577; and Blalock, *op. cit.* note 40, at 166-171.

47. If one finds the derivative of total cost with respect to one input variable in the diminishing returns relation using only algebraic symbols rather than numbers, then the optimum value of the input variable at minimum total costs equals b_2/b_1 times MIN S/"a" where b_2/b_1 is raised to the power of $b_1/(b_2 + b_1)$ and where the second element is raised to the power of $1(b_1b_2)$. If one considers \$C to be the input variable, substituting 1/3 for b_1, 1/3 for b_2, 7.00 for minimum satisfaction, and .7 for "a" yields an optimum \$C of \$31.62.

48. In light of the above tangential-curves conceptualization, as an alternative to finding the derivative of the total cost with respect to \$C or \$L, one could find: (1) the derivative or slope of \$C with respect to \$L in light of the fact that \$C = TC − \$L, and (2) the derivative or slope of \$C with respect to \$L in light of the fact that $\$C = [7.00/(.7 \cdot \sqrt[3]{\$L})]^3 = 1000 \cdot \$L^{-1}$ when S equals 7.00. The first derivative equals −1, and the second derivative equals $-1000/\$L^2$. If these two derivatives are set equal to each other (to show we are looking for the value of \$L at the point of minimum TC where the slopes of the two curves are equal or tangential), then $-1 = -1000/\$L^2$, and \$L = \$31.62. Plugging this value of \$L into the second equation above yields a value of \$31.62 for \$C. The value of \$C could also be found by setting the derivative of \$L with respect to \$C (where \$L = TC − \$C) equal to the derivative of \$L with respect to \$C (where \$L = 1000/\$C), and then solving for \$C.

49. If one finds the derivative of total satisfaction with respect to one input variable in the diminishing returns relation using only algebraic symbols rather than numbers, then the optimum value of the input variable at maximum satisfaction equals b_2 times $1/b_1$ times the value of the other input variable raised to a power equal to $2b_1 - 1$ with the product resulting from multiplying those three terms together raised to a power equal to $1/(2b_2 - 1)$. This equation formula thus gives us the ratio of optimum \$C to optimum \$L (or other pair of input variables) for any regression values. For example, if $b_1 = 1/3$, and $b_2 = 1/3$, then \$C = \$L. Further since \$L = TC − \$C, then \$C = TC/2 = \$34.17.

50. In light of the above tangential-curves conceptualization, as an alternative to finding the derivative of the total satisfaction with respect to \$C or \$L, one could find (1) the derivative or slope of \$C with respect to \$L

in light of the fact that \$C = \$68.34 − \$L, and (2) the derivative or slope of \$C with respect to \$L in light of the fact that $\$C = [S/(.7 \cdot \sqrt[3]{\$L})]^3 = 2.915\, S^3 \cdot \$L^{-1}$. If these two derivatives are set equal to each other (to show we are looking for the value of \$L at the point of maximum S where the slopes of the two curves are equal or tangential), then $-1 = -2.915\, S^3/\$L^2$, and thus $\$L = \sqrt[2]{2.915\, S^3}$. By substituting $.7 \cdot \sqrt[3]{\$L} \cdot \sqrt[3]{\$C}$ for the value of S in this last equation, we find that \$L = 1.00 · \$C. This means \$L = \$68.34 − \$L or \$L = \$34.17, and \$C = \$34.17. The value of \$C could also be found by setting the derivative of \$L with respect to \$C (where \$L = \$68.34 − \$C) equal to the derivative of \$L with respect to \$C (where $\$L = 2.915S^3/\$C$), and then solving for \$C.

51. Baumol, *op. cit.* note 2, at 57-59; and Richmond, *op. cit.* note 2, at 78-79.

52. "Low" prevailing level refers to the fact that the average agency now produces only 6.45 units of satisfaction, but the minimum desired is 7.00 since any agency below that level was considered by the evaluators to be a "project that has internal problems and requires technical assistance," whereas a project at that 7.00 level was considered to be a "project operating efficiently."

53. Some controversial issues involving the allocation of scarce governmental resources include allocating funds (1) between busing versus compensatory education in improving educational opportunities for poor children, (2) between subsidizing low-rental public housing versus home ownership for the poor and lower middle-class, (3) between anti-water pollution enforcement programs versus water clean-up facilities, and allocating funds between (4) fair employment enforcement activities versus manpower training to provide better employment opportunities to minorities, (5) between urban and rural legal services agencies, and allocating funds, (6) among the approximately 300 legal services agencies so as to maximize national satisfaction from the program.

14 Measuring Unnecessary Delay: The Actual Versus the Predicted

This chapter has two purposes. Its primary purpose is to discuss various ways of measuring unnecessary delay in administrative proceedings. Its secondary and broader purpose is to discuss various ways of measuring the difference between the ideal effects of a legal policy and the real effects, or the difference between normative measures and empirical measures.[1]

"Unnecessary administrative delay" in this context means, in a conceptual sense, consumption of more than the minimum time necessary to satisfy the relevant constitutional and statutory requirements to which each agency is subject. In terms of operational calculations, "unnecessary administrative delay" is the difference between (1) the time that is actually consumed and (2) the time that one would expect to be consumed in light of (a) the complexity of the cases and (b) certain objective time expectations.[2]

If the occurrence of unnecessary delay can be measured at the various *stages* in the *types* of administrative proceedings which are held before the quasi-judicial *agencies* which exist at all *levels* of government, then a big initial step will have been taken toward removing such delay. The next logical step is to determine to what extent various recommendations for reducing delay correlate with reduced or low delay, as indicated by making comparisons between agencies or types of proceedings which have, and those which have not, adopted the recommendations, and by making before-and-after comparisons within agencies and types of proceedings.[3]

Measuring Actual Time Consumed and Case Complexity

In order to measure the time actually consumed in a case one needs to know when the time begins to run and when it ends. "Start" can be defined as the

Thanks are owed to the following who played a part in the preparation of this chapter but who are not responsible for the results: (1) the U.S. Senate Subcommittee on Administrative Practice and Procedure for which the author was an assistant counsel when he conducted the research; (2) the Yale Law School—Russell Sage Program in which the author was a Law and Social Science Fellow when he wrote the article; (3) the 1971 Conference on Measuring Public Policy Impact at Florida State University where the article was initially presented; and (4) the National Science Foundation which partly financed the writing under grant GS-2875 as one of a series of policy science studies on measuring and achieving effects of alternative legal policies.

date when a proceeding is put on a list or given a number; so that in the normal course of events (barring withdrawal, settlement, or default), it will proceed through a hearing and decision. This, for example, is the date when a complaint is filed in a National Labor Relations Board (NLRB) or Federal Trade Commission (FTC) prosecution-type proceeding, or when an application is filed in a Federal Communications Commission (FCC) or Interstate Commerce Commission (ICC) licensing proceeding. This excludes administrative investigations prior to the complaint. "Finish" can be defined as the date when the final administrative decision sought is handed down. This excludes judicial review subsequent to administrative proceedings.

Knowing how much time is consumed from start to finish (i.e., total time) is helpful, but it would be even more helpful to know how much time is consumed at each stage of the administrative proceedings. The stages can be defined as follows:

1. The "pleading" stage goes from "start" until the last of the prehearing papers are submitted.

2. The "awaiting hearing" stage goes from the end of the pleadings until the first testimony is taken at the hearing.

3. The "total hearing" stage goes from the first testimony until the hearing record is closed. Total hearing time will generally be longer than actual hearing time since hearings are frequently broken by long recesses and time is often allowed after the last testimony before the hearing record is considered closed such that no further testimony can be taken.

4. The "proposed findings" stage goes from the closing of the record until the parties submit their proposed findings or the deadline for submitting them expires.

5. The "awaiting preliminary" stage goes from the proposed findings until the hearing examiner actually issues his preliminary decision which may be the last decision if there is no review by the agency itself.

6. The "briefs" stage goes from the preliminary decision until the parties submit their briefs designed to influence the agency decision if they do submit briefs.

7. The "awaiting final" stage goes from the briefs until the agency or commission issues its final decision. If stages 6 and 7 are skipped, then 4 and 5 must occur. Likewise if 4 and 5 are skipped, 6 and 7 must occur.

Some measure of complexity must be considered in calculating the time expected as contrasted to the time consumed because truly complex cases inherently take longer than simple cases regardless how efficient an agency might be in processing its caseload. Meaningful approximations of case complexity for a single case can be obtained by looking at its transcript length, number of exhibits, and number of parties. If one is dealing with a group of cases, he can look at their average transcript length, average number of exhibits, and average number of parties. Occasionally an individual case may be simple in spite of: (1) a long transcript if the transcript is filled with trivia; (2) many exhibits if they all relate to the same transaction; or (3) many parties if their interests are not divergent. Likewise an individual case may sometimes be complex in spite of being low on these indices. Nevertheless these three indices (especially transcript length) generally seem to be valid. Other complexity measures that could be suggested include the number of pages of pleadings filed prior to the hearing, the number of hearing hours, whether the decision was unanimous, and whether the decision was appealed. These alternative measures all are less available and have less validity.

The above information with regard to time consumed and case complexity could be compiled by the federal, state, and local administrative agencies which condct formal administrative proceedings, if they were required to do so. For the fiscal years of 1962 and 1963, the Senate Subcommittee on Administrative Practice and Procedure did require such data to be kept by the federal agencies for nearly all their cases.[4] To facilitate processing, the data was punched on IBM cards with one card per case.

The cases were grouped into statutory types within agencies. A type can be defined as a group of cases heard by a single agency under a specific statutory authorization and therefore similar in subject matter. Within the Federal Trade Commission, for example, one type of case can deal with deceptive advertising practices under the FTC Act, and another type can cover discrimatory prices by manufacturers to retailers under the Robinson-Patman Act. By thinking in terms of *stages* within *types* of cases within *agencies*, one can more readily pinpoint causes of unnecessary delay.

After one has determined the actual time consumed (by each stage of each case) and also case complexity (for each case), one should then determine expected time for each stage. Unnecessary delay then equals actual time minus expected time adjusted for case complexity. Expected time can be calculated in light of trend analysis, dispersion analysis, or comparative analysis. Each of these three approaches will now be explained.

Expected Time in Light of Trend Analysis

One way to define the time expected to be consumed in any given year is to look to see how much time was consumed in past years. Thus one might expect an average of 50 days to be consumed in a type of proceeding this year if the type of proceeding consumed (1) an average of 50 days in the immediately preceding year, or (2) an average of 50 days over the previous

5 years, or more scientifically, (3) if a trend line projected or extended from the previous year shows that this year should consume 50 days. If this year an average of 150 days is actually consumed, then one can say there is an average of 100 days of unnecessary delay, ignoring for the moment changes in complexity.

A simple way to consider complexity under the trend analysis approach would be to determine this year's average transcript length at the end of the year. If the change in complexity from last year to this year is +15%, then one would expect this year to consume 50 days plus 15% of 50 days or 58 days in all. If 150 days are actually consumed, then 92 days represent unnecessary delay.

The above method of considering complexity in the trend analysis has two major defects. First, it only considers one of the three indices of complexity. Second, it assumes there is a perfect relation between a change in complexity and a change in time consumed when in reality a 20% increase in complexity may tend to produce a less than, or greater than, 20% increase in time consumed. To remedy both these defects one can make use of a simple regression program which is available at nearly any computer installation where statistical calculations are made. To use it, one goes through the following six steps:

Step 1. For each of the types of proceedings, record on an IBM card four things: (1) the percentage change in time consumption, symbolized ΔT, which is pronounced "delta T"; (2) the percentage change in transcript length, symbolized ΔL; (3) the percentage change in the average number of exhibits, symbolized ΔE, and the percentage change in the average number of private parties, symbolized ΔP.

Step 2. These IBM cards can then be processed by the available regression program.

Step 3. The output of the computer run will mainly consist of four numbers which represent parts of an equation of the form $\Delta T = 2 + 0.8(\Delta L) + 0.2(\Delta E) + 0.3(\Delta P)$. These numerical parts of the equation (e.g. 0.8) are called regression coefficients or prediction weights. The weight given to each measure of complexity takes into consideration the overlap between the measures as well as the relation between each measure and the amount of time consumed.

Step 4. With a regression equation like this, we can calculate about as accurate an expectation of ΔT from ΔL, ΔE, and ΔP as is statistically possible. For example, if an X type of proceeding (1) increased its average transcript length by 15%, (2) decreased its average number of exhibits by 5%, and (3) increased its average number of parties by 20%, then one would predict from the above equation that the type of proceeding would probably increase its time consumed by approximately 19%, since $19 = 2 + 0.8(15) + 0.2(-5) + 0.3(20)$.

Table 14-1
Calculating an Expected Average via Trend Analysis

(1) What changed (all in type X proceedings)	(2) Base year average	(3) Present year average	(4) Difference (col. 3 minus col. 2)	(5) Percentage change (col. 4 divided by col. 2)
Days	50	150	100	200%
Transcript length	200	230	30	15%
Number of exhibits	20	19	−1	−5%
Number of private parties	5	6	1	20%

Trend Formulas for Calculating Average Time Expected for Type X Proceedings:

1. Expected Average, ignoring case complexity =
   Days in base year = 50 days.
2. Expected Average, considering transcript length =
   (Days in base year) + [(Percentage change in transcript length) ×
   (Days in base year)] 50+(15% of 50) = 58 days.
3. Expected Average, considering relation between three indices of case complexity and actual time consumed =
   (Days in base year) + [(Expected percentage change in days) ×
   (Days in base year)] = 50 + (19% of 50) = 60 days,
   where Expected percentage change in days =
   Sum of [(Computer-generated regression coefficients) ×
   (Percentage changes in complexity indices)] 2 + 0.8 (15) + 0.2 (−5) + 0.3 (20) = 19%.

Step 5. To calculate the expected time for this year, we then determine 19% of last year's figure and add this number to last year's figure. If last year consumed 50 days, we would thus expect this year to consume 60 days since 19% of 50 is approximately 10.

Step 6. The process of creating an equation like that produced in steps 1 through 3 for the total time should be repeated for each of the seven procedural *stages*. The seven equations should then be applied to each of the *types* of proceedings as was done in steps 4 and 5 for type *X*. All six steps can be quickly handled by the standard regression programs.[5]

Table 14-1 summarizes the basic trend analysis approaches that have been described above. Examining the table and the formulas beneath it, should help to clarify the calculations involved.

Instead of using last year's figure as a base year against which comparisons can be made, one could use a recent year in which the type of proceeding consumed the least amount of total time. This kind of trend analysis might be referred to as the golden base-year approach. A different golden base-year could be used for each type of proceeding or for each stage within each type of proceeding.

A more sophisticated approach than the single base-year approach is to use all the recent good and bad years for which data is available. Computer programs exist that can fit a straight or a curved line to the data points for multiple years so as to minimize the deviations from the points to the line, and they can also project the location of the next point.[6] Thus if a type or proceeding consumed an average of 50 days in 1968, 66 days in 1969, and 74 in 1970, the computer output would logically indicate that the expected average for 1971 is about 78, or else it would provide an equation from which one could derive the 78. The 78 days could then be adjusted upward or downward via regression analysis to take into consideration the percentage change from the previous years with regard to average transcript length, number of exhibits, and number of parties as was previously described.

Expected Time in Light of Dispersion Analysis

A second way to determine the time expected to be consumed by a given type of case is to look to the actual time consumed by the average case of that type. As an oversimplified example, if a type of proceeding like that in table 14-2 had three cases consuming 21, 9, and 6 days, respectively, then the *actual average* would be 12 days (i.e., 21+9+6 days divided by 3). If cases above the average were reduced to the average, the *expected average* would be 9 days (i.e., 12+ 9+6 days divided by 3). In this regard there is an unnecessary delay of 9 days in the first case and no unnecessary delay in the second and third cases. It is, however, more meaningful to talk about unnecessary delay in a set of cases or in a type of case rather than in individual cases. One would then say that in the above type of case, there is an *average unnecessary delay* of 3 days per case (i.e., 12 days actual average minus 9 days expected average). The average unnecessary delay per case as shown beneath table 14-2 is thus equal to the sum of the deviations (i.e., 9) above the actual average divided by the number of all cases (i.e., 3) which equals 3 days per case.[7]

Such a method of calculating unnecessary delay is used by the Interstate Commerce Commission to flag cases that may be consuming an excessive amount of time at a given stage. The ICC has a computer which prints out the docket numbers of the cases in each type of proceeding that have exceeded the average of their present stage. These docket numbers are called to the attention of those who are responsible for the types and stages involved. The target times are periodically adjusted to take changes in the legal rules and changes in the averages into consideration. Trying to hold unusually long cases down to the average of their type of proceeding not only tends to lower the average, but it also results in more uniformity of treatment. Lack of uniformity is undesirable even if the average time consumed is low if the lack of uniformity reflects the fact that some cases are receiving more favorable treatment than others.

Table 14-2
Calculating an Expected Average via Dispersion Analysis

		Time			*Complexity*			
(1)	(2)	(3)	(4)	(5)	(6)	(7)	(8)	(9)
Case number (all in type X proceedings)	*Time consumed*	*Deviation from avg. (col. 2 minus avg. time)*	*Percentage deviation (col. 3 divided by avg. time)*	*Transcript length*	*Deviation from avg. (col. 5 minus avg. complexity)*	*Percentage deviation (col. 6 divided by avg. complexity)*	*Percentage savable (col. 4 minus col. 7)*	*Days savable (col. 8 times col. 2)*
1	21	+9	+75%	36	+14	+64%	+11%	2.3
2	9	−3	−25%	12	−10	−45%	+20%	1.8
3	6	−6	−50%	18	−4	−18%	−22%	0
Average	12 = Avg. time			22 = Avg. complexity				1.4 = Avg. days savable = S_L

Dispersion Formulas for Calculating Average Time Expected for Type X Proceedings:

1. Expected avg. ignoring case complexity = (Actual avg. time) − $\left(\dfrac{\text{Sum of the deviation from average by just the above avg. cases}}{\text{Number of all cases}}\right)$ = 12 − 9/3 = 12 − 3 = 9 days.

2. Expected avg. considering transcript length = (Actual time avg.) − (Avg. days savable considering dispersion on transcript length) = 12 − 1.4 = 10 ½ days.

3. Expected avg. considering dispersion on all three indices of case complexity = (Actual time avg.) $-\left(\dfrac{S_L + S_E + S_P}{3}\right) = 12 - \left(\dfrac{1.4 + S_E + S_P}{3}\right)$

The main thing that is lacking in the above calculation of an expected average is the failure to take into consideration the fact that the cases which are above average on time consumed may be equally or even more above average on complexity, and thus not so readily reducible. In other words, if the spread on complexity were considered, then the actual average of 12 days in the hypothetical example mentioned above might be more realistically reducible to an expected average of only about 10 or 11 days rather than 9 days.

One meaningful way to consider complexity in determining the expected average is to feed into a computer the time consumed and the transcript length for each case in each type of proceeding. The computer can then be given instructions to make the simple calculations shown with the hypothetical data given in Table 14-2. For each case the computer should calculate:

(1) the percentage by which the case deviates from the time average of its type of proceeding as is done in column 4 of the table;

(2) the percentage by which the case deviates from the complexity average of its type of proceeding as in column 7;

(3) the difference between these two percentages as in column 8; and

(4) the product of this difference (where it is a positive difference) multiplied by the time consumed.

The computer should then average these products in order to determine the average days savable which in the hypothetical data is 1.4 days. By subtracting this figure from the actual average time, one arrives at the expected average time. In the hypothetical data, this would yield an expected average of 10 ½ days (i.e., 12 minus 1.4 days) rather than the 9 days arrived at when the complexity spread was ignored.

This method not only attempts to indicate the extent to which above-average cases can be reduced (as with case number 1 of the hypothetical data), but also the extent to which below-average cases can be even further reduced. Thus if a below average case is only 25% below the time average but is 45% below the complexity average, then it is still 20% improvable (as with case number 2 of the hypothetical data). On the other hand, if a case is above (or below) the time average but is even more above (or less below) the complexity average, then column 8 of the table will show a negative difference indicating the time consumed by that case is not readily improvable (as with case 3). In such a broadened method, deviant cases are in effect defined not as those that are above the average in time consumption, but as those that are more upwardly deviant on time consumption than they are on complexity.

For each type of proceeding, one could conceivably calculate three averages for the number of days savable. One figure would be based on transcript length as a measure of complexity as in table 14-2 and could be symbolized S_L. A second would use number of exhibits in a manner analogous to table 14-2 and be symbolized S_E. A third would use number of private parties and be symbolized S_P. To calculate the average expected time, one would subtract from the average actual time the sum (of $S_L + S_E + S_P$) divided by 3 for three indices.

Expected Time in Light of Comparative Analysis

A third way to get an expected time average is based on how well other types of proceedings do. The simplest form of this method would merely involve averaging the average time consumed for each of the types. In table 14-3, this calculation produces an overall average days consumed of 140 days. It is, however, obviously unrealistic to expect all types of proceedings to have the same expected average at a given stage in view of the fact that some types of proceedings are much more complex than others.

As a more sophisticated variation on the crude comparative analysis just described, one could divide the five types of proceedings in table 14-2 into separate complexity groups depending on their average transcript length. The types should be arranged from the one with the highest average transcript length to the one with the lowest. One can then examine this distribution for clusters and breaks in order to construct the groups, bearing in mind that there are more short-transcript cases than long-transcript cases. Doing this tends to reveal three discernible groups in column 3. The low complexity group contains types of proceedings with an average transcript length of less than 100 pages. The high complexity group contains types with averages of over 300 pages. The medium complexity group covers types that average 100-to-300-page transcripts.

If the average total time consumed of the high complexity group were 250 days, then all the types of proceedings that fell into the high complexity group would receive an expected time average of 250 days. Thus there would be three sets of expected time averages, one for each complexity group. This comparative method in effect only compares types of proceedings with other types of proceedings in their own complexity group. Nevertheless it is defective by virtue of the fact that it only considers one index of complexity. More important, it lumps many types of proceedings together into the high complexity group regardless of differences in their transcript length averages, and it lumps many together under medium complexity and many under low complexity.

The comparative method that is best for calculating the expected averages takes into consideration the exact scores that each type of proceeding

Table 14-3
Calculating an Expected Average via Comparative Analysis

(1) Type of proceeding	*(2)* Avg. days consumed	*(3)* Transcript length and group	*(4)* Number of exhibits	*(5)* Number of parties	*(6)* Avg. days per group
X	300	500 (high)	30	5	250 (high)
A	200	400 (high)	25	4	250 (high)
B	100	150 (med.)	20	3	100 (med.)
C	80	60 (low)	15	2	50 (low)
D	20	55 (low)	10	2	50 (low)
Average	140				

Comparative Analysis Formulas for Calculating Average Time Expected:

1. Expected avg. for type X, ignoring case complexity =
   Overall avg. days consumed = 140 days.
2. Expected avg. for type X, considering transcript length =
   Avg. days consumed by the types in the complexity group for type X = 250 days.
3. Expected avg. for type X, considering all three measures of complexity =
   Sum of [(computer-generated regression coefficients) × (complexity scores)] =
   − 54.8 + 0.3 (500) + 8.0 (30) − 10.7 (5) = 282 days.

received on all three measures of complexity. This method involves going through the following five steps which are related to those described under the trend analysis discussion:

Step 1. For each of the types of proceedings, record on an IBM card four things: (1) the average time consumed, symbolized T; (2) the average transcript length, symbolized L; (3) the average number of exhibits, symbolized E; and (4) the average number of private parties, symbolized P. The method cannot be applied to a type of proceeding which lacks any one of these four items of information unless a reasonable estimate is used for the missing information.

Step 2. These IBM cards can then be processed by a regression computer program as previously mentioned.

Step 3. The output of the computer run will mainly consist of four numbers called regression coefficients or prediction weights from an equation of the form $T = -54.8 + 0.3(L) + 8.0(E) - 10.7(P)$.

Step 4. With a regression equation like this, we can calculate about as accurate an expectation of T from L, E, and P as is statistically possible. For example, if a type of proceeding had 500 pages as an average transcript length, 30 as an average number of exhibits, and 5 as an average number of private parties, then we would predict from the above equation that the type of proceeding (in light of its scores on the three complexity indices) should consume 282 days, since $282 = -54.8 + 0.3(500) + 8.0(30) - 10.7(5)$.

Step 5. The process of creating an equation like that produced in steps 1 through 3 should be repeated for each of the seven procedural stages. The seven equations should then be applied to each of the types of proceedings as was done in step 4. All five steps can be executed by the regression program mentioned in step 2.

No two types of proceedings are likely to have exactly the same expected average time, unless by coincidence they had exactly the same average transcript length, number of exhibits, and number of parties. In other words the expected average of this approach takes into consideration all three indices of complexity about as much as it is statistically possible to do so. Thus if one type of proceeding has a bigger difference between its expected and actual time average than another type of proceeding does, then those responsible for the first type cannot readily complain that its complexity was not considered.

As an even more valid comparative approach, one could divide the types of proceedings into high, medium, and low complexity groups, as previously suggested, and then obtain a separate regression equation for each group of types at each of the seven stages. One would then have 21 rather than seven regression equations thereby providing more refined expected averages, but the additional regression work can be easily handled by standard computer programs.[8]

Presenting and Using the Unnecessary Delay Findings

Table 14-4 shows an example of one of the 61 administrative delay evaluation charts which were contained in a committee print done for the U.S. Senate Subcommittee on Administrative Practice entitled *Evaluation Charts on Delay in Administrative Proceedings*.[9] This one deals with NLRB proceedings involving charges against unions of unfair labor practices under the National Labor Relations Act, Section 8b. The chart shows the three measures of complexity and the *actual* time consumed at each of the seven stages plus the hearing days and total time. It also shows the time *expected* to be consumed in light of trend, dispersion, and comparative analysis.

Line VA provides the average days savable by adding the days-savable figures of lines IVA2, B2, and C2 and then dividing by three, or by two if one of the days-savable figures was incalcuable for lack of information. In calculating this average, all three evaluation approaches are given equal weight because they seem to be about equally meaningful, especially if case

Table 14-4
An Administrative Delay Evaluation Chart

I. Identification of the cases being evaluated
A. Agency = National Labor Relations Board
B. Type of Proceeding = Charges of union unfair labor practices section 8b
II. Complexity of the cases
A. Avg. transcript length = 261
B. Avg. number of exhibits = 20
C. Avg. number of private parties = 2

III. Time that was consumed									
A. Stage	*Total*	*Pleading*	*Awaiting hearing*	*Hearing total*	*Hearing days*	*Proposed findings*	*Awaiting prelim.*	*Briefs*	*Awaiting final*
B. Actual avg. days	343.	15.	53.	5.	2.	28.	42.	32.	179.
IV. Time expected to be consumed									
A. In light of past performance									
1. Expected avg.	372.	14.	29.	4.	2.	45.	49.	43.	183.
2. Days savable	–29.	1.	24.	1.	0.	–17.	–7.	–11.	–4.
B. In light of the possibility of reducing deviant cases									
1. Expected avg.	272.	12.	27.	2.	2.	25.	32.	28.	121.
2. Days savable	71.	3.	26.	3.	0.	3.	10.	4.	58.
C. In light of other types of proceedings									
1. Expected avg.	326.	46.	73.	47.	2.	11.	27.	32.	91.
2. Days savable	17.	–31.	–20.	–42.	0.	17.	15.	0.	88.
V. Overall evaluation									
A. Avg. days savable	20.	–9.	10.	–13.	0.	1.	6.	–2.	47.
B. Improvability rank out of 61 types of proceedings	26	31	21	52	14	20	20	31	12

complexity is considered in all three approaches. A minus-nine-days savable means that the type of proceeding consumed nine days less than expected, not that it went nine days too fast.

The last line of each evaluation chart gives an improvability rank for each type of proceeding at each stage relative to the other 61 types of proceedings. These ranks were determined by arranging the average days-savable figures for each stage for each type of proceeding, from the highest figure which received an improvability rank of 1 to the lowest figure which received a rank of 61. Thus the NLRB proceedings in table 14-4 ranked 26 out of 61 in improvable (or unnecessary) slowness of total time processing. The proceedings were faster rankwise at the hearing-total stage (52 out of 61), but slower rankwise at the awaiting-final-decision stage (12 out of 61).

What useful purposes can be served by evaluation charts like table 14-4 in general and the rankings in particular? One useful purpose is to encourage the administrative agencies which handle quasi-judicial and quasi-legislative proceedings to constantly re-examine their procedures and personnel in order to reduce the time that is needlessly consumed in light of past performance, in light of the possibility of reducing deviant cases, and in comparison with other types of proceedings. The rankings can serve as a particularly vigorous prod in view of the understandable desire of the agencies not to look bad when ranked against the other agencies. An example of this desire was displayed when a preliminary version of these evaluation charts was shown to the chairman of one of the regulatory commissions. His reaction to the fact that his agency had an improvability ranking close to number one (i.e., highly improvable) was that if things had not improved drastically since 1963 (the year on which the rankings were based) he would resign. Statistics compiled by his agency alone, without any attempt to compare agencies, would not have such a vigorous effect. The Administrative Conference of the United States or the Senate Subcommittee on Administrative Practice and Procedure is in a particularly good oversight position to provide such comparative statistics.

Another useful purpose that the evaluation charts can serve is to inform the agencies at which specific stages and in which types of proceedings a reduction in time may be most feasible. This purpose can be aided by the fact that the charts provide days-savable figures for each *stage* plus the total process rather than for just the total process. The points of occurrence and the causes of unnecessary time consumption can thereby be better located. Likewise for each agency the evaluation charts can be given for a few *types* of proceedings rather than have just one evaluation chart per agency. This further enables the agencies to isolate the occurrence and possibly the causes of unnecessary time consumption.

With regard to the causes and remedies of administrative delay the charts also provide scores, particularly on line VA, against which various suspected causes and partial remedies can be correlated. For example, it might be interesting to know what is the relation between (1) the use, or increased use, of prehearing conferences, and (2) the occurrence of improvement with regard to time spent from the opening to the closing of the hearing stage. Such a relation can be shown by dividing the 61 days-savable scores into about 5 intervals (corresponding to very low, low, medium, high, and very high), and doing likewise with the 61 scores giving the percentage of cases or the change in percentage of cases subjected to prehearing conferences within each type of proceeding. One can then tally the location of each type of proceeding in a 5-by-5 or 25-cell table to see if having a high or low percent of prehearing conferences corresponds to having a high or low days-savable score. As an alternative, one can determine the average hearing time consumed for the types of proceedings that fall into interval 1 on the prehearing percentages, and likewise for intervals 2, 3, 4, and 5.

One can also calculate a correlation coefficient that expresses the relationship as a number varying from −1.00 (completely opposite relationship) to 0 (no relationship) on up to +1.00 (completely concurrent relationship). In addition, the two scores of each type of proceeding can be plotted as a series of dots on a graph, and the linear or curvilinear relation which manifests itself can be expressed by an equation that enables one to predict the days-savable score of a type of proceeding from its percentage of prehearing conferences or vice versa.

Other relations that might be similarly determined could include: (1) the relation between (a) the frequency of oral argument and (b) improvability in the time spent waiting for a final decision; (2) the relation between (a) the continuity of hearings as measured by the ratio between hearing days and hearing total and (b) improvability in hearing time; (3) the relation between (a) backlog or quantity of relevant personnel and (b) various waiting times; and (4) the relation between (a) use of modified procedure or various forms of delegation and (b) days-savable in total time consumed.

Making such correlations with days-savable scores (rather than with raw time-consumption averages) enables one to come closer to determining the causes of and remedies for needless time consumption, rather than for mere time consumption. It also tends to statistically control for complexity since complexity can be considered in the days-savable scores. Therefore a finding that coverage by the Administrative Procedure Act correlates with substantially higher days-savable scores could not be so readily attributed to the fact that the APA applies to the more complex types of proceedings. For numerous hypotheses on the causes and remedies of delay in administrative proceedings in general and in specific agencies, see the committee print done for the U.S. Senate Subcommittee on Administrative Practice entitled *Questionnaire Survey on Delay in Administrative Proceedings*.[10]

In spite of the possible uses of evaluation charts like these particularly as a prod to increased efficiency, there will be those who will object to the idea of attempting a statistical evaluation of the work of administrative agencies with regard to unnecessary delay. On the other hand, one of the most frequent criticisms of the raw data formerly gathered by the Office of Administrative Procedure in the Department of Justice was that it failed to indicate how well the agencies were doing in light of their past performance, in light of the wide time variations of their cases, and in comparison with other agencies. Evaluation charts like table 14-4 and future improved versions are designed to fulfill that general purpose.

To the extent that such charts do encourage some reduction in unnecessary time consumption, they will be striking at what may be the most serious procedural problem in the work of the administrative agencies. The work of the agencies has an important impact on the economy as well as on the immediate parties. The stakes are, therefore, high and whatever this evaluation chart approach can contribute to solving the problem should be welcomed by those interested in reducing needless delay. It is hoped that it will become a routine part of the work of the Administrative Conference of United States or the Senate Subcommittee on Administrative Practice and Procedure, as well as their counterparts at the state and local levels of government.

Some Broader Implications

The measurement analysis in this chapter was conducted primarily to aid in reducing delay in administrative proceedings. It should be noted, however, that the trend, dispersion, and comparative analyses which were used here could be similarly applied to measuring the gap between any ideal or normative variable on the one hand and a related real or empirical variable on the other hand.[11]

For example, suppose we desire to test the effects of different techniques designed to eliminate discrimination in granting probation between black and white defendants convicted of the same crime. Different objectivity-promoting techniques might relate to such things as how probation officiers are recruited, how judges are trained, and whether the jury participates in sentencing. In order to make the test, it might be quite helpful to have a dependent or criterion variable which represents the difference between the real and the ideal in each of a number of different courts. The real could be measured by determining the difference between the percentage of blacks and whites who get probation for various crimes. The ideal could represent the best difference (i.e., the difference closest to zero) that was achieved in a previous year, which would be a form of trend analysis. The extent to which blacks versus whites had a prior criminal record could be taken into consideration in a matter analogous to the way case complexity was considered in the *trend* analysis discussed above.

Likewise each court, where different objectivity-promoting techniques are used, can be given a predicted discrimination score in light of the difference between the average prior record of blacks and whites who are convicted in that court. This predicted score could take into consideration the relation between prior record and the granting of probation across all the courts involved, analogous to the way case complexity was used to predict expected time consumed in the *comparative* regression analysis discussed above.

Dispersion analysis can be used if each case before a given court involving probation is given a score of one, and each case involving a prison sentence is given a score of zero. The average sentence before each court would then be a figure between one and zero which represents a rough ideal. One could then determine the extent to which black and white defendants deviate from this ideal. The dispersion would be even more meaningful if degrees of prison sentence were involved instead of merely using prison versus probation.

In addition to controlling for prior record, one could also control for various environmental variables that tend to measure the amount of non-judicial discrimination in the community at large or that measure socio-economic variables which might be hypothesized as underlying causes of general discrimination. Controlling for such environmental variables would be analogous to the study Matthews and Prothro made of the impact of techniques designed to increase black voter registration.[12] They gave each southern county a criterion score that represented the difference between the actual and predicted percentages of blacks registered where the predicted percentage was based on a comparative regression analysis that considered 28 environmental variables.[13]

Other examples could be given where a study of the impact of alternative legal policies could be made more meaningful by using a dependent criterion variable that measures the gap between actual and predicted using trend, dispersion, or comparative analysis.[14] It is hoped that this chapter will contribute to developing methods for measuring such impact variables as well as methods for reducing delay in administrative proceedings.

Notes

1. On measuring the ideal and real effects of legal policies, see E. SUCHMAN, EVALUATIVE RESEARCH: PRINCIPLES AND PRACTICE IN PUBLIC SERVICE AND SOCIAL ACTION PROGRAMS (New York: Russell Sage, 1967), at

115-131; and D. Campbell, *Reforms as Experiments*, AMERICAN PSYCHOLOGIST, 24 (1969), at 409-429.

2. On measuring delay (i.e., time consumed) in judicial proceedings, but generally not "unnecessary" delay, see H. ZEISEL, H. KALVEN, and B. BUCHHOLZ, DELAY IN THE COURT (Boston: Little Brown, 1959), at 43-57; M. Rosenberg, *Court Congestion, Status, Causes, and Proposed Remedies*, in H. JONES, ed., THE COURTS, THE PUBLIC, AND THE LAW EXPLOSION (Englewood Cliffs, N.J.: Prentice Hall, 1965), at 32-37; and J. Navarro, and J. Taylor, *Data Analyses and Simulation of a Court System for the Processing of Criminal Cases*, JURIMETRICS JOURNAL, 1968, at 101-126. Some of this material applies by analogy to measuring unnecessary delay in administrative proceedings, but no scholarly publication has as yet appeared dealing specifically with that matter.

3. On the problems involved in reducing delay in administrative proceedings, see A. J. G. PRIEST, ed., RECOMMENDED PROCEDURES FOR PROTRACTED HEARINGS BEFORE ADMINISTRATIVE AGENCIES (Washington, D.C.: Admin. Corp. of the U.S., 1963); and S. NAGEL, LEGAL PROCESS, at 46-58. By analogy some of the judicial delay literature also applies, such as ZEISEL *et al., op. cit. supra* note 2; and A. LEVIN, and E. WOOLEY, DISPATCH AND DELAY: A FIELD STUDY OF JUDICIAL ADMINISTRATION IN PENNSYLVANIA (Philadelphia: University of Pennsylvania Institute of Legal Research, 1961).

4. T. CHITTENDEN, JR., ed., STATISTICAL DATA RELATING TO ADMINISTRATIVE PROCEEDINGS CONDUCTED BY FEDERAL AGENCIES FOR FISCAL YEAR 1963 (Washington, D.C.: Government Printing Office, 1964); and STATISTICAL DATA RELATING TO ADMINISTRATIVE PROCEDINGS CONDUCTED BY FEDERAL AGENCIES (Washington, D.C.: Admin. Conf. of the U.S., 1962). Conf. of the U.S., 1962).

5. On regression analysis, see H. BLALOCK, SOCIAL STATISTICS (New York: McGraw-Hill, 1960), at 273-282; and BMD: BIOMEDICAL COMPUTER PROGRAMS (Berkeley: University of California Press, 1968), at 258-275. On the analysis of the differences between actual scores and scores predicted by regression analysis, see N. R. DRAPER, and H. SMITH, APPLIED REGRESSION ANALYSIS (New York: Wiley, 1966).

6. On projecting or extending trend lines, see M. HAGOOD, and D. PRICE, STATISTICS FOR SOCIOLOGISTS (New Sork: Holt, 1952), at 160-187.

7. On the analysis of deviations from an average, see J. P. GUILFORD, FUNDAMENTAL STATISTICS IN PSYCHOLOGY AND EDUCATION (New York: McGraw-Hill), 1956, at 82-85.

8. On some problems of making comparisons across entities rather than over time, see ADAM PRZEWORSKI and HENRY TEUNE, THE LOGIC OF COMPARATIVE SOCIAL INQUIRY (New York: Wiley-Interscience, 1970).

9. S. NAGEL, ed., EVALUATION CHARTS ON DELAY IN ADMINISTRATIVE PROCEEDINGS (Washington, D.C.: Government Printing Office, 1966).

10. S. NAGEL, ed., QUESTIONNAIRE SURVEY ON DELAY IN ADMINISTRATIVE PROCEEDINGS (Washington, D.C.: Government Printing Office, 1966).

11. Increased analysis of the differences between predicted and actual measurements is also advocated by E. R. Tufte, *Improving Data Analysis in Political Science*, WORLD POLITICS, at 641-654, (1969); and J. Tukey, and M. B. Wilk, *Data Analysis and Statistics: Techniques and Approaches*, PROCEEDINGS OF THE SYMPOSIUM ON INFORMATION PROCESSING OR SIGHT SENSORY SYSTEMS (Pasadena: California Tech. Press, 1965). Both these items are reproduced in E. R. TUFTE, THE QUANTITATIVE ANALYSIS OF SOCIAL PROBLEMS (Reading, Mass.: Addison-Wesley, 1970).

12. D. Matthews, and J. Prothro, *Political Factors and Negro Voter Registration in the South*, 57 AM. POL. SCI. REV. 355-367 (1963).

13. For much of the data needed to make the above described trend, dispersion and comparative analysis of black and white criminal sentencing treatment, see S. NAGEL, LEGAL PROCESS, at 81-112, and the American Bar Foundation data on which that chapter is based.

14. One could distinguish between (1) studies which compare actual scores with predicted scores from (2) studies that compare actual scores of empirical perception with actual scores of normative expectations. An example of the latter type of study is H. Jacob, *Black and White Perceptions [and Expectations] of Justice in the City*, 6 LAW & SOC'Y REV. at 68-89 (August 1971).

Part V
Increasing Compliance With the Law

The legal system is obviously not working well if its laws are not being complied with, regardless of the non-discrimination of the legal process, the competency of its personnel, or the efficiency of its procedures. This section of the book discusses the problems involved in increasing compliance with the law. The most important law to be complied with in terms of the hierarchy of the legal structure is constitutional law. Individuals may get hurt if criminal statutes or tort and contract rules are violated, but the whole legal system is in jeopardy if its basic constitutional principles are violated, particularly by governmental officials whose non-complying example may breed a general disrespect for the law.

Chapter 15 mainly deals with the causes of constitutional compliance and thus also the causes of non-compliance. Through a better understanding of the variables that correlate with compliance, one can better devise means for increasing compliance. The causal variables that are particularly emphasized in Chapter 15 relate to the types of laws involved, who the policymakers are, who the policy-appliers are, who the policy-recipients are, and the nature of the facilitating and inhibiting environmental conditions. These concepts are the the same basic concepts referred to back in the section of this book on basic concepts and methods. Chapter 15's reference to the effects of non-compliance ties in with viewing law or legal behavior as both a stimulus to subsequent effects and as a response to prior causes.

The traditional method for obtaining compliance with the law is through the negative sanctions of fines and jail sentences. Such a method, however, may not be as effective as various alternatives, or at least it may not be as effective by itself as it would be in combination with various alternatives. Chapter 16 discusses a variety of alternative means for obtaining legal compliance, particularly in the context of environmental law. It deals with (1) sliding fees that go down as a reward for high compliance and go up as a punishment for low compliance, (2) contingent injunctions that enjoin certain activities subject to the possibility of jailing for contempt if the non-complying behavior is not modified, and (3) the use of tax deductions, credits, exemptions, and subsidies to encourage increased compliance.

It also deals with other potentially powerful although somewhat less effective incentives such as (4) objective civil penalties whereby private individuals can bring lawsuits for damages caused by non-complying behavior and where the damages are mainly assessed by using a scientifically determined formula or statistical chart, (5) adversely publicizing wrongdoers and their non-complying behavior, and (6) the use of selective government buying power to reward high compliers and to thereby punish some non-compliers. The chapter also mentions (7) fines and jail sentences and (8) conference persuasion as often being the least effective compliance incentives generally because of their lack of use (as in the case of fines and jail sentences) or their lack of penalizing costs (as in the case of conference persuasion).

15 Causes and Effects of Constitutional Compliance

Setting of These Comments

The problem of legal or constitutional obligation may be approached in any of three ways. One approach is to seek a precise definition of the concept of obligation as John Ladd has done.[1] Another approach is concerned with when should the law be obeyed, which James Luther Adams has followed.[2] The third approach is concerned with what conditions are conducive to legal compliance. This is the viewpoint that is emphasized in Gray Dorsey's paper.[3]

Professor Dorsey finds four conditions to be particularly relevant to encouraging a felt or empirical constitutional law obligation, as contrasted to a mere formal or legalistic obligation. First the law should contain symbols that evoke a positive response based on generally held beliefs, such as the symbol of monarchy in England in 1688, but not the symbol of republicanism in China in 1912. Second, the law should be administered by a ruling party that advocates widely shared values, such as the value of natural equality as advocated by the American revolutionaries in the late 1700s, but not the value of mere pragmatism as advocated by the Chinese revolutionaries in 1912. Third, the law should contain constitutional principles whose detriments and benefits are foreseeable, such as the principle of territorial sovereignty in international law in the mid-1900s. Fourth, constitutional and other legal interpretations should conform to the social and economic conditions of the time, such as an interpretation of the American Constitution that allows minimum wage laws in the 1900s rather than prohibits such laws as interferences with freedom of contract.

Professor Dorsey's analysis is quite insightful and empirically valid so far as it goes. There seem, however, to be many more factors determining constitutional compliance than those which he has described. The general factors can possibly be grouped into five basic categories. These categories relate to (1) the nature of the specific laws involved, (2) the law makers, (3) the law appliers, (4) the law recipients, and (5) certain facilitating and inhibiting environmental factors.[4] Professor Dorsey possibly has also neglected to make use of relevant behavioral science data dealing with the empirical correlates of constitutional compliance.[5] Perhaps it might be useful to attempt to spell out the subcategories to which these general concepts refer and to tie them to relevant behavioral science data. First, however, the relation should be clarified between Dorsey's concept of felt obligation and the concept of compliance.

Relations between Compliance and Felt Obligation

One might say that just because Southern school administrators increased their compliance with *Brown v. Board of Education* does not mean they increased their felt obligation. The truth of such a statement depends partly on definitions and partly on empirical fact.

By definition, "compliance" means behaving in conformity with the law. "Obligation in the positive law sense" means having a legal duty as a citizen to behave in conformity with properly passed laws. "Obligation in the natural law sense" means having a moral duty as a human being to behave in conformity with what is considered inherently right. "Felt obligation" means feeling that one should behave in conformity with the law or principle involved.

One can have a positive law obligation or a natural law obligation and still not have a felt obligation if one is unaware of or in disagreement with the law or principle involved. But what about the relation between compliance and felt obligation? It is theoretically possible (situation 1) that a Southern school administrator could have a felt obligation toward Southern custom which is greater than his felt obligation toward the Supreme Court, and yet still comply with law by desegregating his school district because of the financial inducements of federal aid to education. It is also theoretically possible (situation 2) that a Southern school administrator could have a felt obligation toward *Brown v. Board of Education*, and yet still not comply by refusing to desegregate his school district because of adverse local customs and pressures.

Definitionally speaking, there is no conflict between compliance and felt obligation in either of the above two examples where the administrator thinks he should not comply but does, or where he thinks he should comply but does not. There is no conflict because the concept of felt obligation is broad enough to say that if an administrator feels he should comply because of financial benefits to the school for which he is responsible (situation 1), then that is just as much a felt obligation as where he feels he should comply because of respect for or agreement with the law. Likewise the concept of felt obligation is broad enough to say that if an administrator feels he should not comply because of local custom and pressures (situation 2), then it is appropriate to say he does not really have a felt obligation to comply and that his predominant feelings are not in conflict with his behavior, although he apparently has mixed feelings.

Empirically speaking, it is generally contrary to empirical fact (as studies of cognitive dissonance have shown)[6] for most people's attitudes and behaviors to remain in conflict for very long. In order to live with themselves, they generally change their attitudes to conform with their behavior or they change their behavior to conform with their attitudes. Thus external behavior is generally a good indicator of attitudes. Indeed if actions speak louder than words, then actions surely speak louder than conscious and subconscious thoughts.

One important aspect of the behavioral movement in social science is to emphasize the observable. One can observe compliance, but one cannot directly observe a felt obligation. However, one can observe responses to attitudinal questions that may reveal the presence or absence of a felt obligation. It is hoped that future studies of man's obligations will make more use of observation to determine what causes both external and internal compliance and what consequences flow from such compliance.

Causes of Compliance

With regard to the *types of laws* that are most likely to produce a felt obligation to comply, the key element seems to be the extent to which the law deviates from custom or habit.[7] For example, attitudinal and behavioral surveys show that there is a greater propensity on the part of school authorities to comply with Supreme Court decisions outlawing compulsory racial segregation in the public schools than there is to comply with decisions outlawing compulsory prayer and Bible reading in the public schools.[8] These differences in compliance rates are largely attributable to the fact that school segregation before the Supreme Court's ruling was customary only in the South, whereas religious activities in the public schools were more widespread throughout the country.[9] Likewise the University of Chicago jury studies show that juries are much less likely to comply with the letter of the law where the law deviates from customary values, as in the liquor laws or gambling laws as contrasted to laws against kidnapping and arson.[10]

A second key element built into the law itself is the clarity of the standards to be applied in determining whether the law has been violated. Thus when the standard of school segregation was "with all deliberate speed,"[11] there was very little speed. When, however, the Office of Education published its more precise Educational Guidelines,[12] this was a partial factor in accelerating desegregation. Likewise the American Bar Foundation studies of police behavior show that nonenforcement of the law is often due to ambiguity in defining crimes.[13]

With regard to who the *lawmakers* are, recent public opinion polls show that actions taken by Congress are more likely to produce favorable attitudes and compliance than actions taken by the President or the Supreme Court.[14] Likewise there is some polling evidence showing greater respect for federal policymakers than for state and local policymakers although this respect probably varies from region to region.[15] Disagreement among the lawmakers is also an empirical factor promoting resistance to their policies.[16]

With regard to the policy *administrators*, one key distinction seems to be whether the law is administered by the courts through injunctions and damage suits (as voting registration discrimination originally was) or, in the alternative, whether the law is administered by executive officials (like the federal registrars provided for by the Voting Rights Act of 1965). Clearly this change in administrative personnel and procedures made a big difference in the percentage of blacks registered to vote in the Southern states.[17] Executive officials have more time and expertise than judges do, and they can also take the initiative in sanctioning violators.

Another key element at the policy administration stage is the nature of the sanctions available to the administrators. Thus the felt obligation to conform was low when the only sanction against segregation in the public schools was the rare possibility of being held in contempt of court. But when the sanction became loss of important federal aid to education funds, the felt obligation became much higher.[18] Increased compliance here was a result of a change both in the severity and in the certainty of the sanctions involved.

In the context of constitutional obligation, *law recipients* or obligees (to use John Ladd's term) can vary on such relevant characteristics as region, occupation, and political party. As for region, one would expect more resistance to freedom of speech in the more conservative Southern states than in the North, as was shown in Berelson's civil liberties survey.[19] Likewise Arnold Rose finds more resistance to freedom of assembly among countries with a Latin background than among those with an Anglo-Saxon background due to a conservative fear of revolutionary associations combined with a liberal fear of business and church groups.[20] As for occupations, clearly a desegregation law directed toward members of the armed forces is easier to enforce than one directed toward real estate operators.[21] With regard to party affiliation, recent nationwide surveys show significant differences between Democrats and Republicans with regard to their respective support for the constitutional interpretations of the Supreme Court.[22]

The fifth general compliance determinant refers to the facilitating and inhibiting *environmental conditions*. The communications media and educational facilities are particularly important, since the degree of felt obligation may depend substantially on how the law is presented to those who are expected to comply with it. Thus Richard Schwartz in a recent systematic controlled experiment showed that appeals to conscience and to a sense of civic responsibility can produce greater compliance with the income tax laws than can threats to punishment.[23] Likewise a recent questionnaire study of numerous communities shows a high correlation between increased police education programs and increased police adherence to legality in the field of search and seizure.[24] Favorable or unfavorable economic, political, or other social conditions may also be quite important in producing compliance, which explains why periods of economic depression or unpopular war sometimes lead to constitutional upheavals.[25]

In tying this material together, the key question does not seem to be, "Why do people feel an obligation to obey the law?" Rather it is a series of five questions. First, why do people feel an obligation to obey some types of laws more than others? Second, why do people feel a greater obligation toward some lawmakers than others? Third, why are some law appliers more effective than others even when the content of the law is held constant? Fourth, why do some people feel a greater obligation to obey the law than others do? Fifth, why under certain social conditions is there more legal compliance than in the absence of those conditions?

Effects of Compliance

Moreover, instead of asking the question, "Should people obey the law?" it seems more meaningful to ask three analogous questions that relate to the specific laws, law recipients, and environmental conditions involved. First, what are the effects of noncompliance to certain specific laws like the selective service law as contrasted to laws against highway speeding? Resistance to the selective service law may save lives by encouraging the government to make a greater effort to seek peace, whereas resistance to speeding may jeopardize lives, not save them. Second, what are the effects of noncompliance by certain specific persons like an idealistic law student as contrasted to a Students for a Democratic Society activist who has been repeatedly convicted of various violations? The idealistic law student may by his noncompliance destroy his chances of passing the bar's character and fitness committee, thereby sacrificing the opportunity to become a social reform lawyer, whereas the SDS activist may advance his political career by his noncompliance. Third, what are the effects of noncompliance under certain specific conditions such as the presence of a foreign policy based on the destruction of fascism, as in World War II, versus a foreign policy based on the protection of fascism, as some say is involved in the Vietnam War? Clearly, one cannot say that the conditions under which a war is fought are irrelevant to the degree to which one should obey the selective service laws. In general, just as the likelihood of noncompliance varies with the nature of the law, the personnel, and the conditions, so also do the effects of noncompliance vary.

The effects of noncompliance have not been as much studied by social scientists as the causes of noncompliance. Nevertheless Joel Grossman of the University of Wisconsin's Law and Sociology program is conducting a study of the impact of civil rights civil disobedience activities,[26] and various social scientists are in the process of studying the effects of the race riots which constitute an extreme form of noncompliance with basic legal principles.[27] A few political scientists have touched on the effects upon certain segments of the public of compliance and noncompliance by various law administrators.[28] There are also studies of the effects of specific laws or judicial pronouncements rather than the effects of compliance and noncompliance in general.[29] The increased concern for impact studies in law and political science may yield numerous findings and theories in the future with regard to both the effects and causes of compliance.[30]

In closing I want to emphasize that constitutional compliance or obligation can be viewed as either a dependent or an independent variable. When viewed as a dependent variable or an effect, the problem is to determine what the independent variables or causes of compliance are. When viewed as an independent variable or cause, the problem then is to determine what are the dependent variables or effects of compliance or noncompliance. In addition to determining these cause and effect relations, it is important to define operationally the concept of compliance or manifested obligation so that it can be quantitatively correlated with other variables. What is especially encouraging is the fact that the tentative cause and effect answers offered by social theorists and philosophers are being increasingly tested by behavioral scientists. Thus the field of legal compliance and obligation is another area where philosophy and behavioral science are constructively working together.

Notes

This chapter is based on Nagel's comments regarding Gray Dorsey's paper on "Constitutional Obligation" presented at the 1967 annual meeting of the American Society for Political and Legal Philosophy and later reprinted in R. PENNOCK (ed.), POLITICAL AND LEGAL OBLIGATION: NOMOS XII (Atherton, 1970), (hereinafter referred to as PENNOCK).

1. John Ladd, *Legal and Moral Obligation,* in PENNOCK.

2. James Luther Adams, *Civil Disobedience: Its Occasions and Limits,* in PENNOCK.

3. Gray L. Dorsey, *Constitutional Obligation,* in PENNOCK.

4. For further detail on the use of these categories to generate empirical hypotheses, see Stuart Nagel, *A Conceptual Scheme of the Legal Process*, AMERICAN BEHAVIORAL SCIENTIST, at 1-10 (1963); and STUART NAGEL, THE LEGAL PROCESS FROM A BEHAVIORAL PERSPECTIVE (Homewood, Ill.: Dorsey Press, 1969).

5. Some of this recent literature is brought together in THEODORE BECKER, ed., THE IMPACT OF SUPREME COURT DECISIONS: EMPIRICAL STUDIES (New York: Oxford University Press, 1969). Many of the compliance factors are discussed in Samuel Krislov, *The Perimeters of Power: Patterns of Compliance and Opposition to Supreme Court Decisions*, paper presented at the 1963 meeting of the American Political Science Association.

6. LEON FESTINGER, A THEORY OF COGNITIVE DISSONANCE (New York: Harper & Row, 1957); JACK BREHAN and ARTHUR COHEN, EXPLORATIONS IN COGNITIVE DISSONANCE (New York: Wiley, 1962); and Robert Abelson, *Modes of Resolution of Belief Dilemmas*, JOURNAL OF CONFLICT RESOLUTION, III (1959), 343.

7. ROBERT MACIVER, THE WEB OF GOVERNMENT (New York: Macmillan, 1951), 73-81; Arnold Rose, *Sociological Factors in the Effectiveness of Projected Legislative Remedies*, 11 J. LEGAL ED. 470-81 (1959).

8. In a survey of 7,000 junior high school principals, 79 percent of the 4,500 respondents indicated agreement with the Supreme Court's racial segregation decisions, but only 45 percent indicated agreement with the Supreme Court's prayer and Bible-reading decisions. DONALD ROCK and JOHN HEMPHILL, REPORT OF THE JUNIOR HIGH SCHOOL PRINCIPALSHIP (National Association of Secondary School Principals, 1966). There is a high correlation between agreement with the Supreme Court and having a feeling of obligation to the Court's decisions, as is shown in Richard Johnson, *Compliance and Supreme Court Decision-Making*, 1967 WISC. L. REV., 170-85.

9. School segregation figures before and after *Brown v. Board of Education* are given in the publication of the Southern Education Reporting Service and the Civil Rights Commission. Analogous figures on disestablishment of prayers and Bible-reading in the public schools are reported in Donald Reich, *The Impact of Judicial Decision-Making: The School Prayer Cases*, paper presented at the 1967 meeting of the Midwest Political Science Association; and Ellis Katz, *Patterns of Compliance with the Schempp Decisions*, 14 J. PUB. LAW 396-408 (1966).

10. HARRY KALVEN and HANS ZEISEL, THE AMERICAN JURY (Boston: Little, Brown, 1966) at 286-97.

11. *Brown et al. v. Board of Education of Topeka*, 349 U.S. 294 (1954).

12. OFFICE OF EDUCATION, *General Statement of Policies under Title VI of the Civil Rights Act of 1964 Respecting Desegregation of Elementary and Secondary Schools*, March 1966.

13. Wayne LaFave, *The Police and Non-Enforcement of the Law*, 1962 WISC. L. REV. 104 and 188-91.

14. Kenneth Dolbeare, *The Public Views the Supreme Court*, in HERBERT JACOB, LAW, POLITICS, AND THE FEDERAL COURTS (Boston: Little, Brown, 1967), p. 197.

15. Even in Texas, attorneys are more favorable in their attitudes toward most federal judges below the United States Supreme Court level than they are toward most state judges below the state supreme court level. Bancroft Henderson and T. C. Sinclair, *The Impact of the Selection Process upon the Role of the Judge: An Explanatory Case Study*, paper presented at the 1962 meeting of the Midwest Political Science Association.

16. Stuart Nagel, *Political Parties and Judicial Review in American History*, 1962 J. PUB. LAW, 328-40, shows laws passed by a sharply divided Congress are more likely to be declared unconstitutional. Stuart Nagel, *Court Curbing Periods in American History*, 18 VAND. L. REV. 925-44 (1965), shows Supreme Court decisions with a percentage of dissents are more likely to generate court-curbing activities.

17. This increase in compliance was anticipated in Charles Hamilton, *The Impact of the Civil Rights Acts on Southern Federal Judges*, 1965 WISC. L. REV. 72-102.

18. Jim Leeson, *Faster Pace, Scarcer Records*, SOUTHERN EDUCATION REPORT (January 1966), 28-32.

19. SAMUEL STOUFFER, COMMUNISM, CONFORMITY, AND CIVIL LIBERTIES (Garden City, N.J.: Doubleday, 1955).

20. Arnold Rose, *On Individualism and Social Responsibility*, 2, ARCHIVES OF EUROPEAN SOCIOLOGY, 163-69, (1961).

21. Contrast ch. 11, *The Armed Forces* with ch. 8, *Housing and Real Property*, in JACK GREENBERG, RACE RELATIONS AND AMERICAN LAW (New York: Columbia University Press, 1960). For a national survey on how different occupations react to the Supreme Court in general as contrasted to specific Supreme Court decisions, see William Daniels, *Public Attitudes toward the Supreme Court*, paper presented at the 1967 meeting of the Midwest Political Science Association.

22. Walter Murphy and Joseph Tanenhaus, *Public Opinion and the United States Supreme Court: A Preliminary Mapping of Some Prerequisites for Court Legitimation of Regime Changes*, paper presented at the 1967 University of Iowa Shambaugh Conference, and Stuart Nagel, *Editorial Reaction to the Church and State Cases*, 30 PUBLIC OPINION QUARTERLY, 647-55, (1966).

23. Richard Schwartz and Sonya Orleans, *On Legal Sanctions*, 34 U. Chi. L. Rev. 274-300 (1967).

24. Stuart Nagel, *Testing the Effects of Excluding Illegally Seized Evidence*, 1965 Wisc. L. Rev. 283-310.

25. For a quantitative study of compliance to the school desegregation decision that places emphasis on environmental variables as well as the nature of the law administrators and the law recipients, see Sheldon Stoff, The Two-Way Street: Guideposts to Peaceful School Desegregation (Indianapolis, Ind.: David-Stewart Co., 1967).

26. Joel Grossman, *A Model for Judicial Policy Analysis: The Supreme Court's Response to the Sit-In Cases*, paper presented at the 1967 University of Iowa Shambaugh Conference.

27. Some preliminary discussion of the consequences of the 1967 race riots are given in the symposium issue of Transaction (September 1967).

28. Richard Johnson, The Dynamics of Compliance: Supreme Court Decision-Making from a New Perspective (Evanston, Ill.: Northwestern University Press, 1967); Jack Peltason, Fifty-Eight Lonely Men: Southern Federal Judges and School Desegregation (New York: Harcourt, Brace, 1961).

29. Theodore Becker, see note 2.

30. Arthur Miller, *On the Need for Impact Analysis of Supreme Court Decisions*, 53 Geo. L. J. 365-401 (1965). Ernest Jones, *Impact Research and Sociology of Law: Some Tentative Proposals*, 1966 Wisc. L. Rev. 331-39.

16 Incentives for Compliance with Environmental Law

Basic Concepts and Principles

Much has been written about means of increasing compliance with the standards set in various fields of law.[1] These studies tend to deal with either traditional criminal law where negative sanctions of jail and fines are emphasized, or civil law where negative sanctions of damage suits are emphasized.[2] These studies also cover such constitutional law fields as racial discrimination, school prayers, and illegal police practices where injunctions backed by threats of negative sanctions are frequent.[3] Some studies have also been made of the compliance problems of economic regulatory agencies, like the NLRB, SEC, and ICC where conference persuasion and economic incentives like adverse publicity and franchise awards are often used.[4]

The environmental law field provides an especially excellent laboratory area in which a variety of means can operate simultaneously for increasing compliance with environmental protection standards.[5] The compliance incentives discussed in this chapter include (1) discharge taxes or fees, (2) contingent injunctions, (3) tax rewards and subsidies, (4) objective civil penalties, (5) publicizing wrongdoers, (6) selective government buying power, (7) fines and jail sentences, and (8) conference persuasion.

Compliance with legal rules in general can be increased by means other than manipulating positive incentives and negative sanctions. For example, compliance has a positive correlation with the clarity of the standards, the prestige of the policy-makers and policy-appliers, the public support for the standards, and the lowness of the costs involved in complying with the standards.[6] These means, however, will not be discussed in this chapter. Instead, the emphasis will be on discussing the relative degree of compliance obtainable from a variety of rewards and punishments.

Some non-incentive factors that may substantially increase compliance with specific environmental law standards include (1) a combination of central and local governnental regulation; (2) a combination of administrative and court adjudications; (3) a combination of administrative and legislative rule-making; (4) environmental protection agencies that combine numerous governmental anti-pollution activities in an agency that is independent of the regular cabinet agencies with a head having fixed tenure; (5) advisory boards with representatives from industry, labor, consumers, and conservation groups; (6) a combination of inter-city, interstate, and international activities; (7) easier access of anti-polluters to the courts by relaxing jurisdictional requirements and providing attorneys; (8) a system of permits to begin or continue certain operations which are monitored by periodic inspection; (9) government research and grants to accelerate anti-pollution technology and compulsory licensing of existing patents; and (10) programs to educate the public concerning the detriments of pollution.

Although the emphasis here will be on the dependent or effect variable of compliance obtained or obtainable, it should be recognized that positive and negative incentives have other effects such as the degree of (1) cost to the government and thus the taxpayers, (2) cost to consumers especially those who can least afford to pay, (3) cost to the polluter and thus to his stockholders, and (4) cost to the employees of the polluter, and (5) cost to the general public in terms of reduction in fair procedure and respect for the legal system if the incentives are manipulated without adequate concern for separating the innocent from the guilty.[7] Likewise, political feasibility or likelihood of significant adoption and application should and will also be considered.[8]

The degree of compliance (which we might characterize as being high, medium, or low) depends in the case of negative incentives on the difference between: (1) the probability of the negative incentive occurring multiplied by the degree of punishment which the negative incentive brings measured in monetary terms, and (2) the degree of benefit which violating the standards provides also measured in monetary terms. This difference can be symbolized: \$(Prob. × Cost of Noncompliance) − \$(Benefit of Noncompliance). Likewise, the degree of compliance in the case of positive incentives depends on the difference between: (1) the degree of monetary reward which the positive incentive gives to compliance, and (2) the degree of benefit which violating the standards provides, where both are measured in monetary terms. This difference can be symbolized: \$(Benefit of Compliance) − \$(Benefit of Noncompliance). If element #1 in either formulation above is greater than element #2, compliance will be preferred over noncompliance. The greater the positive difference is between element #1 and element #2, the more compliance will be preferred.[9]

Incentives with Relatively High Compliance Potential

Discharge Taxes or Fees

Given the above notions with regard to the circumstances under which compliance is preferred over non-compliance, the most effective incentive is probably the discharge tax, provided it is accurately assessed. The discharge tax, fee, or charge is an assessment placed on a polluter which varies depending on the degree of his pollution. When accurately assessed, which may sometimes be quite difficult, it is high enough to cause all such polluters, or at least the average such polluter, to feel that it would be cheaper to institute changes in equipment or procedures than it would be to pay the assessment.[10]

Such assessments can be levied upon water polluters (effluent charges), air polluters (emission charges), or those engaged in other types of pollution. With water pollution, the assessments need not be high enough or accurate enough to stop the initial polluting, but they should be high enough so that the assessments collectively can pay to have the waterway involved cleaned to whatever level is desired. With air pollution, however, since there is no way to clean the ambient air outside buildings, the charges should be high enough to stop the initial polluting. Under either approach, competitive firms in the same industry will have an incentive to reduce pollution and thereby cut their discharge assessment in order to (1) be able to sell his product for less so as to capture a larger share of the market or (2) be able to hold constant his sale price and total income but increase the gap between income and expenses.

Water pollution taxes have been authorized and tried in the Ruhr region of Germany and in the state of Vermont. Air pollution taxes are being actively pushed by Congressman Aspin and the Coalition to Tax Pollution. The main advantage of such a tax is that it either reduces the initial pollution as far as desired or else it provides for funds to clean up the pollution which occurs in spite of the tax.

The main disadvantage of such a tax is that it will be passed on to the consumers of the products involved to the extent that it can be passed on without the consumers shifting to other products or simply reducing their use of the products involved. Poor consumers may be disproportionately affected because products that are likely to create pollution such as electricity generation may relate more to necessities than to luxury items, and because poor consumers have a higher propensity to consume their total income than rich consumers do.

As a further disadvantage, the polluter may also use this extra tax or retooling expense as an excuse for not meeting wage increase demands, or even as a trigger for investing his capital in another enterprise if the expense means the difference between profit and loss in his business firm. Under such circumstances, what appears to be a low-cost program to the government and the taxpayers may require substantial tax money to retrain and relocate displaced workers. To the extent that tax payments are correlated with income, burdening the taxpayer seems more related to ability to pay than burdening the consumer. Legislation can try to prohibit the passing of discharge taxes, fines, or other anti-pollution costs onto the consumer beyond a certain amount as California legislation has tried to do by limiting the cost of auto exhaust filters to $65.00 although detecting and prohibiting the passing of such costs is a difficult exercise in cost accounting and governmental control of business operations.

Discharge taxes or fees have been criticized as providing a license payment to pollute. In the case of water pollution, no harm is done if these "license payment fees" are at least high enough to clean up the water. In the case of air pollution, however, the discharge fees must be high enough to stop the initial pollution or else they will have little effect on pollution reduction although the fees could be used to pay for policing expenses. It may, however, be undesirable from the point of view of objective due process if a policing agency is too dependent on taxes or fines levied for wrong-doing which could thereby cause it to find wrong-doing present where it otherwise would not.[11]

Contingent Injunctions

Less oriented toward economics and more oriented toward traditional legal techniques is the contingent injunction. It involves a court order directed toward a polluter saying that *if* his pollution is not eliminated or decreased below a certain level within a certain time, then he will be ordered to cease operating. If he continues to operate after the time period for compliance has expired, the firm may be subjected to physical padlocking and the officers subjected to severe negative sanctions for contempt of court (including jail terms) until compliance is achieved. This approach includes removing operating licenses or permits or seriously threatening to do so. Contingent injunctions thus provide the positive incentive of continued operation for compliance (analogous to reduced charges with discharge taxes), and the negative incentive of forced closing for non-compliance (analogous to increased charges with discharge taxes).

The main advantages of contingent injunctions are (1) they allow flexibility to specify whatever threshold (if there is any above zero) the judge finds can be reasonably tolerated on the basis of the evidence presented, and (2) they can get the pollution stopped or substantially reduced if fully enforced. The main disadvantage is the difficulty of shutting down a polluter especially if (1) he is important to the economy, (2) his pollution is not clearly toxic, and (3) he is trying to comply. The contingent injunction also has the disadvantage that a more subjective value judgment is involved in determining the notion of "reasonable" threshold than is involved in determining the level of effective discharge fees which can be a relatively more empirical engineering and economics decision.[12]

Tax Rewards and Subsidies

Discharge taxes and contingent injunctions tend to emphasize negative sanctions for non-compliance. Tax rewards and subsidies, on the other hand, tend to emphasize positive incentives although the withdrawal of a tax reward to subsidy which a firm had been receiving can be thought of as a punishment, especially if the firm's competitors are continuing to receive the tax reward or subsidy.

If the government, and thus the taxpayers, were willing to pay the "full cost" of anti-pollution devices for business firms by way of a subsidy or tax credit, then virtually full compliance should be achievable by definition of full cost. Under such an abundant government support system, the businessman would have nothing to lose by changing his equipment and procedures, but might have something to lose by not doing so in view of the negative sanctions against polluters which simultaneously exist along with the government subsidies. This is especially true if the subsidy operates on a cost-plus basis, thereby paying more than just the costs of making changes.

The big drawback to such a system is that it is politically unrealistic to expect the government and the taxpayers to bear the complete burden for pollution control. Taxpayers feel that polluters, since they are basically the ones at fault, should bear more of the burden out of their profits especially where fault and costs are not so difficult to determine as they are in automobile accidents. To the taxpayer it probably seems outrageous to reward a polluter for not violating the law. The taxpayer is only willing to allow *some* tax depreciation, tax credits, and tax exemptions; and these often do not provide enough of an incentive for business firms to minimize pollution. Low-interest loans, for example, may be virtually no incentive if the businessman has to pay back the principal on a product which in no way (1) decreases the expenses of his firm, (2) increases the income, or (3) increases his profits.

Indeed, some tax laws may at least partially negate the effect of other tax laws with regard to encouraging pollution reduction. For example, the federal income tax provides accelerated depreciation for a smokestack filter, thereby allowing the firm to pay lower income taxes now and to invest the money saved into possibly profitable activities and thus earn more than enough to pay the higher tax later. At the same time, local governments may provide a much more valuable property tax exemption on the whole factory to get it to locate in their communities, regardless of its smokestacks.

Businessmen may even resist outright subsidies as looking too much like welfare. They would rather have a more subtle indirect subsidy via a tax saving if they could get the legislature to provide for large pollution-oriented tax reductions.[13]

Incentives with Medium Compliance Potential

Objective Civil Penalties

Allowing private individuals to bring damage suits may have some deterrent effect on the behavior against which damage suits can be brought, especially if the damages obtainable are large enough to offset the benefits received by the alleged wrongdoer. Normally, however, the subjectivity involved in establishing liability and in determining damages serves as more of a deterrent to the potential plaintiff's bringing the lawsuit than as a deterrent to the potential defendant's behavior.

Nevertheless, civil suit systems can be devised where liability and damages are objective enough to involve an almost automatic determination. This is so in workmen's compensation cases where a worker-plaintiff need only show that he was injured on the job in order to establish liability and then damages will be determined by consulting charts showing the value of different types of injuries. Employers have an incentive to prevent their workers from being injured in order to reduce the workmen's compensation awards and thus the employer's workmen's compensation insurance premiums. Injuries can also be disruptive in productivity even if the worker is replaced.

Workmen's compensation suits can be directly involved in pollution control when a worker is injured by on-the-job pollution such as noise pollution. Such suits can also serve as a model for creating a system whereby outsiders who are injured by a firm's pollution can successfully sue simply by showing the firm has exceeded the water effluent levels or air emission levels established in the water or air pollution regulations. The administrative tribunal or judge would then consult some charts in order to assess the damages which the polluter-defendant should pay to the citizen-plaintiff. The system would have an even stronger impact in changing behavior if it provided for automatic increases in the assessed damages for delay in stopping the pollution.

Such a system of objective civil penalties is *not* now provided for, but citizen suits to enforce the federal air pollution standards by injunction are now allowed, and private plaintiffs can sue polluters if they can show that (1) the polluter acted unreasonably and was thus negligent, (2) the polluter's behavior was the proximate cause of the plaintiff's injury, and (3) the plaintiff did not negligently contribute to his own injury. If a system of objective penalties were provided for, there would be at least as much deterrence of pollution as the workmen's compensation system produces against unsafe working conditions without the need for government prosecution and the concurrent costs to the taxpayer.[14]

On the other hand, such a system is weakened by (1) the difficulty in establishing the damage assessment charts in order to both compensate for and deter against the pollution behavior, (2) the lack of flexibility in such a system as compared to the contingent injunction, and (3) the dependency of such a system on suits brought by private individuals rather than better-financed government agencies as in some of the alternative incentive systems. The bringing of private suits can be facilitated by allowing private attorneys a 20 percent fee contingent on their winning the case, as is done in workmen's compensation cases. Like all the alternative incentive systems discussed which involve new anti-pollution legislation, there is the drawback present of the lobbying power of manufacturing and other polluting firms who possibly can collectively successfully resist such legislation especially by arguing it will lead to harrassment of legitimate businessmen.

Publicizing Wrongdoers

In small societies or communities, adversely publicizing wrongdoers can have a significant effect on changing their behavior where everyone tends to know each other. Such a system of social control normally would not work in an industrialized, urbanized society at least for individual misbehavior. Large firms selling widely known brand name products might, however, be substantially influenced by the threat of well-circulated adverse publicity.

Such a system of publicizing misbehavior is partly behind the information circulation of the Securities Exchange Commission, although the SEC merely provides potential stock purchasers with information on specific companies without evaluating the companies. The 1970 federal air pollution legislation (as contrasted to the earlier legislation) provides for making known to the public the extent to which each automobile manufacturer is complying with the auto emission standards of the Environmental Protection Agency. Quite often polluting business firms agree to cease-and-desist orders of administrative agencies or injunctions of courts out of fear of the consequences of adverse publicity.

On the other hand, many polluting firms do not sell a brand name product to the ultimate consumer, like the steel mills in the Gary, Indiana, area. Likewise, some firms like local electric companies have a monopoly on their product and are not so likely to be hurt by adverse publicity. In addition, the government is often reluctant to stigmatize business firms, especially when the government is in a period of high sensitivity to the interests of business. Stigmatizing wrongdoers may also spill over to complying business firms.

Furthermore, there is the possibility that overly strong publicity stigma may make an outlaw of a polluting firm and thereby increase its insensitivity to public opinion and decrease its likelihood of rehabilitation. Finally, there is some question of how much due process procedure must be given a firm before the government (as contrasted to a private consumer or environmental protection organization) can label it guilty of wrongdoing.[15]

Selective Government Buying Power

Another positive reward incentive and one that has a basis in economic thinking is the notion of selective government buying to (1) reward business firms that comply well with environmental law standards and (2) to punish business firms that don't by a withdrawal of the government as one of the firm's purchasers. The 1970 air pollution legislation does not provide for the federal government to rank its purchasing in terms of the pollution rank order of business firms selling a given product. The legislation does, however, prohibit the government from buying from non-complying firms until they are back in compliance analogous to withdrawing government buying power or grants from firms that racially discriminate.

A more positive portion of the 1970 legislation is the part that enables the federal government to purchase feasible electric or steam automobiles at 150 to 200 percent of the cost of similar internal combustion automobiles in order to provide a guaranteed market as a stimulant to the development of feasible non-polluting automobiles. Such a system should have a substantial impact on those business firms which have government contracts or potentially could have, especially if they are in a competitive field.

The major drawback to this interesting approach, however, is that many polluters and their competitors have no government contracts to compete for. In addition, government purchasing agents and legislators want products bought from sellers who can sell them most cheaply thereby saving the taxpayer money and encouraging cost-efficient business practices. Such purchasing agents and legislators possibly do not give adequate consideration to the costs to society of the continued air, water, and other pollution which could have been decreased through selective government buying especially if done on all levels of government.[16]

Incentives with Low Compliance Potential

Fines and Jail Sentences

The most common incentive to deter traditional criminal misbehavior is fines and jail sentences. If imposed in the pollution field, these negative sanctions could be a real deterrent to middle-class businessmen for whom jail would indeed by subjectively a severe punishment.

Realistically speaking, however, it is very difficult to get a criminal conviction in pollution cases in view of the high safeguards for protecting the innocent in criminal cases in general, and in view of the legal talent which businessmen in particular can muster to take full advantage of these safeguards. Furthermore, middle-class businessmen generate a great deal of sympathy from prosecutors, judges, and juries, especially if they are expansive entrepreneurs. In addition, fines (unless they are very high) are somewhat easily absorbed as a business expense; and jail sentences for polluting (even after conviction involving dangerous toxic pollution) are an extreme rarity.

These defects have all been found to be present in related businessman crimes such as violations of housing codes, rent control laws, and other economic regulatory legislation. In light of these defects, what might in theory be an effective deterrent in practice has a very low compliance potential.[17]

Conference Persuasion

The major tool for decreasing water pollution under the pre-1972 legislation was conference persuasion. In theory it serves the useful purpose of minimizing conflicts between the complainants and the polluter. It is especially useful where the complainants are employees of the polluter, as in union management negotiation over noise pollution standards within a factory. Such a system theoretically allows the pollution to be decreased to at least the partial satisfaction of both sides without the bitterness engendered by the adversary system operating in the courts.[18]

Experience with the early federal water pollution legislation, however, has shown that the conference persuasion method results in long delays with very little compliance since it has nothing to back it up except rational discussion or the ethics and good will of the polluter. It does not internalize the costs of pollution to the business firm unlike the prior incentives discussed such as discharge taxes, contingent injunctions, and objective civil penalties. Likewise, it does not significantly reward the business firm for compliance unlike the prior incentives such as tax rewards, subsidies, and selective government buying power. Nor does it provide the punishments associated with publicizing wrongdoers or with fines and jail sentences.

Finding an Optimum Mix among the Alternative Incentives

In spite of the rank order which has been given the above eight incentives, one should not see them as mutually exclusive alternatives or even as sequential alternatives. At least in theory, they can all operate simultaneously. They are not necessarily redundant to each other. In practice, however, given the reality of scarce available resources, each incentive cannot be simultaneously adopted to an infinite extent. Linear programming and indifference curve analysis provides one approach to determining an optimum mix of these incentives, or at least to providing insights into the problems involved in determining an optimum mix.[19]

One way we can obtain data to apply a linear programming model to the problem is by sending questionnaires to knowledgeable people in communities across the country asking them to indicate to what extent their communities make use of each of the eight incentives. A simple scale could provide for three categories as follows: (category 0) "this incentive is not used in our community"; (category 1) "this incentive is slightly used in our community"; and (category 2) "this incentive is greatly used in our community." The words "slightly" and "greatly" may not have precise meaning, but we are doing some discriminating by providing for three categories rather than just "present" and "absent." In other words, it is better to be able to do some distinguishing on degree of presence than none at all. A more precise scale or set of scales can be developed, but this simple scale can be used to illustrate what is involved.

While attempting to measure the presence of each of the eight incentives for say approximately 100 communities or political subdivisions, we should also seek to measure the degree of compliance with environmental law or environmental goals. A simple measure of compliance would be to determine the degree of water pollution, air pollution, and other kinds of pollution for a recent year or for an average of recent years on a scale from 0 to 100 developed by environmental scientists and engineers. Each kind of pollution can be treated as a separate dependent variable, or else an unweighted or weighted composite dependent variable can be created from the separate measures. Appropriate weights can be arrived at by surveying groups whose values are considered relevant. To make this composite variable more sophisticated, we can add in non-pollution variables like changes in the community's industrial output. We can then have a net benefit variable in which reduced pollution (assuming we measure pollution at two points in time) is treated as gross income, and reduced industrial output is treated as an expense to be deducted. For the sake of simplicity, however, let us just use a measure of water pollution in each community rather than a composite, net benefit, or over-time variable.

After arriving at eight incentive measures for each of 100 communities and one pollution measure, we can then have a computer perform a multiple regression analysis for us. Such an analysis will yield a prediction weight for each of the eight incentives treated as independent variables with pollution treated as the dependent variable to be predicted. With this multiple regression equation, we can now arrive at a series of indifference lines or indifference curves. Each line (or hyperplane since we are dealing with an eight dimensional surface) will show for a desired level of pollution what combination of incentive activity levels and their prediction weights will produce the desired level of pollution or net composite benefit. Desired levels for water pollution are mentioned in the Federal Water Pollution Control Act of 1972, and they are currently being operationalized by the National Water Commission.

For example, an indifference line for a pollution level of 30 on a 0 to 100 scale would be $30 = a + b_1X_1 + b_2X_2 + ... + b_8X_8$. Each X in this equation represents the amount of emphasis which could be placed on any one of the eight incentives on our simple three-point scale. The b-coefficients in this equation represent the prediction weights which the computer generates when we feed it eight independent variable scores and one dependent variable score for each of our 100 communities. The a-coefficient represents the probably high amount of pollution the computer indicates from the data that we would be likely to expect if we had a city that scored 0 on every one of the X variables. The prediction weights for some of the X's might be negative because calculating each prediction weight involves holding constant the other possibly more important incentives.

If one had the maximum amount of effort available to allocate to each of these eight incentive activities, that would be a maximum of twenty-four units since each incentive alone could be allocated a maximum of three units on our simple scale. To use this indifference analysis model in any given community, one needs to determine how much maximum effort or emphasis could realistically be expended on each incentive given existing economic and political constraints. For example, a given community might in effect say through its policy makers that the maximum effort available for X_1 is 1, for X_2 is 2, X_3 is 0, X_4 is 1, X_5 is 1, X_6 is 2, X_7 is 2, and X_8 is 0. For such a community the maximum total effort it is willing to expend is nine units which represents the sum of the maximum effort it is willing to expend for each incentive activity. For simplicity, let us assume the community is willing to expend a minimum total effect of zero. This assumes that its minimum constraint for each incentive activity is zero although in some communities for political, legal, or other reasons, the minimum on a given activity might have to be higher than zero.

With the above hypothetical data, we now have all the information we need in order to make use of the standard computer routines for doing linear programming. One way to use such a routine is to first inform the computer of the minimum and the maximum constraints on (1) each of our eight incentive activity variables, (2) our one dependent or goal variable, and (3) our one total cost or total effort variable. In the previous paragraph, we indicated the minimum and maximum constraints on the activity variables and the total cost variable for a hypothetical community or other political unit. The community policymakers can determine the maximum level of water pollution that they are willing to tolerate on our 0 to 100 scale in light of the damage that water pollution does. They can also determine the minimum level of water pollution below which they may not be willing to go since going below that level is predicted to mean too great a reduction in industrial output or unduly expensive prevention and cleanup costs.[20]

After informing the computer of the above constraints, we then inform the computer what the objective functions or goal variables are that we want the computer to maximize or minimize subject to the constraints. One goal variable would be to minimize pollution as low as possible or maximize water quality as high as possible without exceeding our total cost constraint and without going below our minimum pollution constraint and not violating the other constraints. That goal variable can be symbolized TB (for total benefits) $= a + b_1X_1 + \ldots + b_8X_8$ as described above. We could also use our more sophisticated goal variable of NB (for net benefits) which involves subtracting any industrialization reduction costs or other costs that we consider to be undesirable side effects of maintaining low pollution. Another goal variable would be to minimize our total incentive-activity costs without going below our minimum water quality level or our maximum water pollution level and not violating the other constraints. That goal variable can be symbolized TC (for total costs) $= X_1 + X_2 + \ldots + X_8$.

After informing the computer of the above constraints and alternative goals, the linear programming routine will then instruct the computer to inform us what the value of X_1 should be, X_2 should be, and so on through X_8 in order to optimize the TB, NB, or TC goals without violating the given constraints. With that information we have solved the problem of finding an optimum mix among the alternative incentives. We can find other solutions by making such changes as changing (1) the constraints, (2) how we define the goal variables, (3) what activity variables we include, (4) what communities we use in our sample, and (5) how precisely we categorize the activity variables.

Some Conclusions

In spite of the rank order which this chapter has given to the eight incentives, one should not see them as mutually exclusive alternatives as the optimum mix section of the chapter has emphasized. They can all operate simultaneously. They are not redundant to each other. Their enforcement is not likely to glamorize the wrongdoing as in liquor and marijuana prohibition where life styles more than societal jeopardy was the key issue. To the extent that any one incentive alone has a high compliance potential, that incentive plus any other (or set of others) have together an even higher compliance potential. What is needed is more legislation in diverse fields of pollution (like the 1970 federal air pollution legislation) which relies on multiple incentives to combat the extremely serious and growing problems which affect the environment of us all.

In one variation or another, all eight of the incentives for compliance with environmental law discussed in this chapter are also available for other kinds of law enforcement like school desegregation, illegal police practices, and banning religious indoctrination in the public schools. In situations other than environmental law compliance, however, the relative rank order of the effectiveness of the eight incentives might be different. The important thing is to get policymakers and policy-appliers to think of incentives for obtaining compliance in broader terms than just the traditional negative sanctions of fines and jail sentences.

Notes

1. S. KRISLOV et al., COMPLIANCE AND THE LAW: A MULTIDISCIPLINARY APPROACH (Sage, 1972); S. WASBY, THE IMPACT OF THE UNITED STATES SUPREME COURT: SOME PERSPECTIVES (Dorsey, 1970); and H. JONES, THE EFFICACY OF LAW (Northwestern U. Press, 1969).

2. F. ZIMRING, PERSPECTIVES ON DETERRENCE (Govt. Printing Office, 1971); and G. CALABRESI, THE COSTS OF ACCIDENTS: A LEGAL AND ECONOMIC ANALYSIS (Yale U. Press, 1970).

3. H. RODGERS AND C. BULLOCK, LAW AND SOCIAL CHANGE: CIVIL RIGHTS LAWS AND THEIR CONSEQUENCES (McGraw-Hill, 1972); R. JOHNSON, THE DYNAMICS OF COMPLIANCE: SUPREME COURT DECISION-MAKING FROM A NEW PERSPECTIVE (Northwestern U. Press, 1967); and S. NAGEL, THE RIGHTS OF THE ACCUSED IN LAW AND ACTION (Sage, 1972).

4. J. ANDERSON, POLITICS AND THE ECONOMY 65-101 (Little Brown, 1966); and M. BERNSTEIN, REGULATING BUSINESS BY INDEPENDENT COMMISSION 217-249 (Princeton U. Press, 1955).

5. F. GRAD, G. RATHJENS, & A. ROSENTHAL, ENVIRONMENTAL CONTROL: PRIORITIES, POLICIES, AND THE LAW 217-277 (Columbia U. Press, 1971); F. GRAD, ENVIRONMENTAL LAW 7-15 to 7-59 (Matthew Bender, 1971); and J. DAVIES, THE POLITICS OF POLLUTION 176-192 (Pegasus, 1970).

6. S. KRISLOV, THE SUPREME COURT IN THE POLITICAL PROCESS 134-155

(Macmillan, 1965); Nagel, *Causes and Effects of Constitutional Compliance,* in R. PENNOCK & J. CHAPMAN, POLITICAL AND LEGAL OBLIGATION 219-228 (Atherton, 1970).

7. COUNCIL ON ENVIRONMENTAL QUALITY, ENVIRONMENTAL QUALITY: THIRD ANNUAL REPORT 269-310 (Govt. Printing Office, 1972); and COUNCIL ON ENVIRONMENTAL QUALITY, ENVIRONMENTAL QUALITY: SECOND ANNUAL REPORT 99-154 (Govt. Printing Office, 1971). The above references refer to the economic costs. See footnote 15 with regard to the due process costs.

8. R. COOLEY AND G. WANDESFORD-SMITH, CONGRESS AND THE ENVIRONMENT (U. of Washington Press, 1970); and J. MITCHELL &. C. STALLINGS, ECOTACTICS: THE SIERRA CLUB HANDBOOK FOR ENVIRONMENT ACTIVISTS (Pocket Books, 1970).

9. Prest & Turvey, *Cost-Benefit Analysis: A Survey*, 75 ECONOMIC JOURNAL 683 (1965); G. BLACK, THE APPLICATION OF SYSTEMS ANALYSIS TO GOVERNMENT OPERATIONS (Praeger, 1968); and C. MYERS & A. D. TARLOCK, SELECTED LEGAL AND ECONOMIC ASPECTS OF ENVIRONMENTAL PROTECTION 1-58 (Foundation, 1971).

10. An oversimplified formula for calculating the discharge tax to a given firm might involve solving for X in the following equality of proportions:

$$\frac{X \text{ charges to given firm}}{\text{Cost to keep river segment at a given level}} = \frac{\text{The firm's quantity of pollution}}{\text{Total pollution in river segment}}$$

11. For further details on discharge taxes and fees, see Delogu, *Effluent Charges: A Method of Enforcing Stream Standards*, 19 MAINE LAW REV. 39 (1967); A. V. KNEESE & B. T. BOWER, MANAGING WATER QUALITY: ECONOMICS, TECHNOLOGY, AND INSTITUTIONS (1968); J. KRIER, ENVIRONMENTAL LAW AND POLICY 422-468 (Bobbs-Merrill, 1971); and R. ZERBE, BIBLIOGRAPHY ON THE LAW AND ECONOMICS OF POLLUTION CONTROL (U. of Chicago Press. 1973).

12. For further detail on injunctions, see J. KRIER, ENVIRONMENTAL LAW AND POLICY 177-206 (Bobbs-Merrill, 1971); L. JAFFE & L. TRIBE, ENVIRONMENTAL PROTECTION 594-618 (Bracton, 1971); V. YANNACONE & B. COHEN, ENVIRONMENTAL RIGHTS AND REMEDIES 82-142 (1971); and Note, *Injunctions*, 78 HARVARD LAW REVIEW 994 (1965).

13. For further detail on tax rewards and subsidies, see Gerhardt, *Incentives to Air Pollution Control,* 33 LAW AND CONTEMPORARY PROBLEMS 358 (1968); Reitze & Reitze, *Tax Incentives Don't Stop Pollution*, 57

AMERICAN BAR ASSOC. JOURNAL 127 (1971); and H. WOLOZIN, THE ECONOMICS OF AIR POLLUTION, (W. W. Norton, 1966).

14. For further detail on civil penalties see Kovel, *A Case for Civil Penalties: Air Pollution Control,* 45 J. URBAN LAW 153 (1969); Juergensmeyer, *Control of Air Pollution through the Assertion of Private Rights,* DUKE LAW JOURNAL 1126 (1967); Gribetz & Grad, *Housing Code Enforcement: Sanctions and Remedies,* 66 COLUMBIA LAW REVIEW 1254 (1966); and Note, *Private Remedies for Water Pollution,* 70 COLUMBIA LAW REVIEW 734 (1970).

15. On the use of publicity stigma as a sanction, see Schwartz, *Social Factors in the Development of Legal Control*, 63 YALE LAW JOURNAL 471 (1954); H. KOONTZ & R. GABLE, PUBLIC CONTROL OF ECONOMIC ENTERPRISE 445-463 (McGraw-Hill, 1956); and *Wisconsin v. Constantineau*, 400 U.S. 433 (1971). The *Constantineau* case held that posting notices about someone's drunkenness without providing a hearing with direct and cross-examination is unconstitutional. For some further detail on the due process aspects of alternative incentives for compliance with environmental law and other legal norms, see H. PACKER, THE LIMITS OF THE CRIMINAL SANCTION 149-248 (1968), and Nagel, *Environmental Policy and Constitutional Law,* 1 POLICY STUDIES JOURNAL 213 1973.

16. On selective government buying power, see L. MUSOLF, GOVERNMENT AND THE ECONOMY 98-122 (Scott Foresman, 1965); M. REAGAN, POLITICS, ECONOMICS, AND THE GENERAL WELFARE 95-114 (Scott Foresman, 1965); and COMMERCE CLEARINGHOUSE, GOVERNMENT CONTRACTS REPORTER (1970).

17. On criminal sanctions, see H. PACKER, THE LIMITS OF CRIMINAL SANCTIONS (Stanford U. Press, 1968); Ball & Friedman, *The Use of Criminal Sanctions in the Enforcement of Economic Legislation: A Sociological View,* 17 STANFORD LAW REVIEW 197 (1965); and R. LANE, THE REGULATION OF BUSINESSMEN (Yale U. Press, 1954).

18. On conference persuasion, see *United States v. Bishop Processing Co.,* 287 F. SUPP. 624 (1968), 423 F.2d 469 (1970), cert. denied 398 U.S. 904 (1970); and Cole, *Government in the Bargaining Process: The Role of Mediation,* 333 ANNALS OF THE AMERICAN ACADEMY OF POLITICAL AND SOCIAL SCIENCE 42 (1961).

19. For an elementary discussion of linear programming, see S. RICHMOND, OPERATIONS RESEARCH FOR MANAGEMENT DECISIONS 314-82 (Ronald Press, 1968). For an elementary discussion of indifference curve analysis see P. SAMUELSON, ECONOMICS 441-446 (McGraw-Hill, 1973). For a discussion that combines the two see W. BAUMOL, ECONOMIC THEORY AND OPERATIONS ANALYSIS 70-103 180-197 (Prentice-Hall, 1965) and S. NAGEL,

MINIMIZING COSTS AND MAXIMIZING BENEFITS IN PROVIDING LEGAL SERVICES TO THE POOR (Sage Publications, 1974).

20. For a discussion of the use of input-output analysis to predict the effects of pollution reduction on industrial output, see National Commission on Water Quality, *Assessment of Modelling and Indirect Benefit Indicators* (1973); B. MAR & W. NEWELL, ASSESSMENT OF SELECTED RANN ENVIRONMENTAL MODELLING EFFORTS (National Science Foundation, 1973); Herzog & Ridker, *The Model,* pp. 303-311 in R. RIDKER (ed.), POPULATION RESOURCES AND THE ENVIRONMENT (Government Printing Office, 1972). These materials are also useful in discussing the problems involved in measuring the monetary damage which pollution incurs.

Part VI
Some Needs of Legal Policy Research

The purpose of this section is not to discuss how some aspects of the legal process can be improved upon or made more effective in light of some given goals, but rather to discuss some trends and needs in legal policy research which may be useful in improving the legal process.

Chapter 17 brings out that the legal process field within political science has been moving within recent years toward applying the systematic inductive methods of behavioral research toward important legal policy problems. More specifically, there has been an increased concern for studying (1) the impact of Supreme Court decisions, (2) law in action at the grass roots trial court level, (3) law and poverty problems, (4) criminal justice problems, (5) law across cultures, and (6) law and social change.

The impact analysis trend seems to be undergoing some sub-trends which involve a shift (1) from an effects or compliance perspective to a goal optimizing perspective, (2) from impact on policy-appliers to impact on the ultimate policy-consumers, (3) from constitutional law to all fields of law, (4) from the Supreme Court to all sources of legal policy, (5) from citation analysis and anecdotal observation to experimental methodologies, and a shift (6) from theoretical concepts relating to legalistic structures or political groups to stimulus-response concepts.

In order to make legal policy research more effective in improving the legal process, the needs of such research include not only an acceleration of the above trends, but also the development of some new institutions in law research and teaching. Chapter 18 proposes three institutions which may be helpful in that regard. First is a legal data repository which would bring together for secondary analysis the empirical, machine-readable data which many legal researchers are now accumulating. Such a repository would involve clarifying the way in which the data are coded and preparing a catalog for potential users informing them what data are available. The repository could be part of a larger inter-university consortium which conducts other clearing-house, training, researching, and related functions for empirical legal research besides the archiving of data.

A second new institution for advancing legal policy research might be the establishment of a series of empirical readings to supplement traditional casebooks in basic law school courses like contracts, property, and torts. Such a partial re-orienting of those basic courses will aid in providing many forthcoming lawyers with an empirical perspective which may result in their doing, commissioning, or using empirical legal research as law scholars, legal policymakers, or practicing lawyers.

A third such institution might involve bringing a number of law professors who are interested in social science together with a number of social scientists who are interested in law to inventory what has been done and needs to be done of mutual interest on such social problems as pollution, poverty, crime, consumer protection, free speech, labor relations, and international peace. These, however, are substantive legal policy problems rather than the procedural ones which this book has emphasized. It is these important substantive problems toward which empirical legal policy research will probably now increasingly turn.

17 New Trends in Law and Politics Research

General Developments

Political science has generally been divided into the fields of political theory, comparative government, international relations, public administration, policy formation, state and local government, and public law. The public law or legal process field has also been called the law and politics field to emphasize that it is the study within political science of the judicial process, constitutional law, and related subjects. Law and politics research has changed greatly since 1955 in both methodology and substance. It is the purpose of the articles in the symposium of the autumn 1971 issue of the *Law and Society Review* to illustrate some of the more recent trends in law and politics research, particularly trends of interest to law professors, sociologists, and others in the broader area of law and society research.

The methodology of public law within political science as of 1955 consisted almost exclusively of the analysis and synthesis of Supreme Court opinions relating to cases in constitutional law (McCloskey 1957). In the following eight or so years, many political scientists supplemented this legalistic method with an anecdotal method emphasizing stories of what happened behind the scenes with regard to events preceding (Vose 1958, and Murphy 1964) or following (Peltason 1961) the Supreme Court opinions. This anecdotal analysis became the basis for new textbooks and courses in the *Judicial Process* (Murphy and Pritchett 1961). Likewise, other political scientists supplemented the legalistic method by using the same Supreme Court opinions to quantitatively measure differences among the judges (Schubert 1958 and 1965) or differences among the facts in the cases (Kort 1957 and 1968). This measurement analysis became the basis for other new textbooks and courses in *Judicial Behavior* (Schubert 1964).

Since approximately the early 1960s, there has been an attempt to go beyond legal synthesis, anecdotes, and mere measurement of variables and to apply systematic quantitative induction to determine (1) how social and psychological variables cause differences in legal policies and decisions and (2) how legal policies and decisions affect social and psychological variables (Becker 1964 and Nagel 1969). This inductive causal analysis is frequently referred to as the behavioral approach to public law, although the term is also used to include non-causal measurement of judicial voting differences.

In 1968 David Easton, in his inaugural address as President of the American Political Science Association, recognized the on-going development of the post-behavioral approach to political science. The essence of the post-behavioral approach involves applying the systematic inductive methods of behavioralism to important political party problems (Easton 1969). The public law field, like other fields of political science, has been showing increased scientific concern for being socially relevant, as the articles in this symposium illustrate. (All the articles were originally presented as papers at the 1970 annual meeting of the American Political Science Association on six different panels exemplifying six related trends in law and politics research.)

Specific Concerns

The main post-behavioral or policy-behavioral development within public law has been the increased concern for studying the impact of Supreme Court decisions. There is, however, already discernable an old and a new kind of impact analysis within public law, about which more will be said in the third section of this chapter. Martin Levin's article on "Policy Evaluation and Recidivism" (1971) particularly illustrates the new impact analysis. For other impact studies, see Wasby (1970) and Becker (1969). The impact analysis trend, if broadly defined, in effect leads to the other new concerns in legal process research.

A second trend is the increased concern for studying law in action at the grass-roots trial court level. A paper by Mendelsohn, Klonoski, and DeAngelia, on "Lay Participation in the Courts: A Study of the Willingness of Witnesses and Jurors to Serve Again," (1970) not only deals with trial courts rather than the Supreme Court, but also with witnesses and jurors rather than judges. Unfortunately, due to unforeseeable complications, this particular paper was not ready in time to be included in the symposium. For other grass-roots legal studies, see Klonoski and Mendelsohn (1970) and Dolbeare (1967).

Substantively public law political scientists have developed an increased concern for poverty problems. There is an increasing recognition that civil rights legislation under the equal protection clause can do little for the many blacks and others who are poor, as contrasted to direct anti-poverty legislation. Harry Stumpf's article on "The Legal Profession and Legal Services: Explorations in Local Bar Politics" (1971) brings a kind of Bentleyan pressure-group analysis to the field of poverty law. For other poverty law work by political scientists, see tenBroek (1966), Jacob (1969), and Hannon (1969).

The law and order problem has received considerable recent attention from public law political scientists who wish to study socially relevant policy problems. Herbert Jacob's article on "Black and White Perceptions of Justice in the City" (1971) was one of many papers dealing with an empirical approach to criminal justice which were submitted for presentation at the 1970 annual meeting of the American Political Science Association. For other criminal justice work by political scientists, see Summers and Barth (1970), Becker and Murray (1971), and Nagel (1972). Perhaps political scientists, like other social and natural scientists, will also soon turn some of their attention toward environmental law problems.

As part of the post-behavioral concern for policy problems, legal process research has also sought to study controversial legal issues simultaneously in a number of countries in order to perceive better the cause and effect relations. David Bayley's article, "The Police and Political Change in Comparative Perspective," (1971) draws upon the literature from many countries to explain how the political culture influences police development and vice versa. For other cross-cultural studies of judicial process and behavior, see Becker (1970) and Schubert and Danelski (1969).

Likewise, rather than just focusing on public law at one point in time or chronologically, increased attention is being given to the relation between law and social change. Michael Barkun's article dealing with the reciprocal relation of "Law and Social Revolution" (1971) is part of that new trend. For some other political science work on law and social change, see Grossman and Grossman (1971) and Nagel (1970). Law and social change was the theme of the public law panels coordinated by Herb Jacob for the 1971 annual meeting of the American Political Science Association. The way Barkun's article builds toward interdisciplinary theory seems a fitting finale to the Law and Politics Symposium.

Although each of the six articles (in the symposium on which these comments are based) has been used to illustrate only one of the six above-mentioned trends, each article could have been used as an example of more than one of the trends. At least a few of them are simultaneously impact studies, grass-roots studies, relevant to poverty problems, relevant to criminal justice, involved with comparisons over space, or involved with comparisons over time.

Old and New Impact Analysis

As previously mentioned, the main post-behavioral development within public law has been the increased concern for studying the impact of Supreme Court decisions. In spite of the recency of impact research, one can already discern an old and new impact analysis within public law. The new differs from the old on about six different dimensions.

First, one can classify impact studies in terms of whether the research proceeds from an effects perspective or an optimizing perspective. An effects perspective begins with one or more legal policies as independent variables (like Brown v. Board of Education or Miranda-Escobedo), and then one asks what effects these legal policies will have or have had. Usually only one legal policy is studied, and the only effect is compliance with the law. The effects perspective is present in most of the studies Steve Wasby (1970) cites in his review and synthesis of the older impact literature.

By contrast an optimizing perspective begins with one or more policy goals as dependent variables (like reducing criminal recidivism as in Martin Levin's 1971 article in the symposium), and then one asks what legal policies will most achieve these goals, such as probation versus incarceration. Both perspectives can yield causal propositions, but the optimizing perspective is more capable of generating policy ideas because it does not take policies as givens the way the effects perspective does.

A second important dimension for classifying old and new impact studies is in terms of whether they are concerned with impact on policy-appliers or impact on the ultimate policy-consumers. The older impact research almost always studied impact on lower judges, legislators, school administrators, or on police rather than the impact of legal policies on the total society, segments of the general public, or on other non-governmental personnel. Again Wasby's book illustrates the older analysis, whereas Martin Levin's article is concerned with the impact of criminal law not on police or governmental behavior, but on the criminal segment of the general public.

A third important way of classifying impact studies is in terms of the type of law involved. Steve Wasby, in the preface to his book, recognizes that nearly all political science impact studies have been in the field of constitutional law or civil liberties rather than more grass-roots legal fields like contracts, torts, property, poverty, and criminal law. Some of the newer impact studies, like Martin Levin's, are breaking out of the civil liberties confines into the impact of diverse laws and law in general.

A fourth dimension, partly related to the type of law, is the source of law. The old impact analysis, as illustrated by the title of Wasby's book (1970), dealt only with the Supreme Court as a policymaker. The source of policy in Martin Levin's article, on the other hand, is the grass-roots criminal court judge or state legislature. For too long within political science, there has been an artificial division of labor such that public-law people study courts and policy-formation people study legislatures, rather than study both kinds of policy makers and policy impact as part of the same total legal process.

The fifth dimension is a methodological one. The old studies more frequently used a legalistic methodology that partly involved using *Shepard's Citator* to determine the effects of Supreme Court decisions on lower courts, or doing a content analysis of state statutes or other legal materials subsequent to the legal policy whose impact was being studied. When the research got out of the law library into the field, its methodology was likely to consist of anecdotal observation. Recently, however, impact studies have been making more use of quasi-experimental techniques like those advocated by Donald Campbell (Campbell 1969; Campbell and Ross 1968; and Ross, Campbell, and Glass 1970). They have also involved the use of true experimental techniques as advocated by Richard Schwartz (1961 and 1967), where the experimenter determines randomly who will be subjected to the experimental stimulus. Martin Levin's random assignment of some convicted defendants to probation and some to incarceration illustrates this relatively new kind of impact analysis. Either a quasi-experimental or a true experimental methodology will probably involve comparisons of entities in different places or over time.

A sixth and final classification dimension relates to the theoretical perspective used. The older studies tended to view impact in terms of a legalistic hierarchy of court structure or in terms of intervening pressure groups. Two of Wasby's three frames of reference explicitly take these legal and group approaches (Wasby 1970, pp. 57-99). The new studies, however, are emphasizing stimulus-response theory and individual learning and conditioning, as illustrated by William Muir's (1967) study of prayer in the public schools or the work of James Levine (1970a and 1970b).

Perhaps the future will see a continuation of the old impact analysis and also an increase in impact studies (1) that take a goal-optimizing perspective rather than just an effects or compliance perspective, (2) that deal with impact on ultimate policy-consumers rather than just intermediate policy-appliers, (3) that go beyond civil liberties law into private and other fields of law, (4) that likewise go beyond the Supreme Court into legislative and other sources of legal policy, (5) that use experimental or at least quasi-experimental techniques, and (6) that often supplement a legal and group perspective with an individual stimulus-response perspective.

The above comparison between the old and new impact analysis could also be made to some extent between the old and new analysis of trial courts, poverty law, criminal justice, comparative law, and legal history. The general shift is toward less legalistic and anecdotal methods and toward more systematic quantitative induction.

At the broader level of public law research in general (rather than just impact research), the new trends do indicate increased research in: (1) law as a causal variable, (2) law at the basic trial and pre-trial level, (3) law and poverty, (4) law and crime control, (5) law viewed cross-culturally, and (6) law in the context of social change. These new trends, combined with the older public law research, should help to stimulate a further revitalizing of legal process research within political science.

References

BARKUN, Michael (1971) "Law and Social Revolution," 6 Law and Society Review 113.

BAYLEY, David (1971) "The Police and Political Change in Comparative Perspective," 6 Law and Society Review 91.

BECKER, Theodore L. (1970) Comparative Judicial Politics: The Political Functionings of Courts. Chicago: Rand McNally.

———. (1969) The Impact of Supreme Court Decisions. New York: Oxford University Press.

———. (1964) Political Behaviorism and Modern Jurisprudence: A Working Theory and Study in Judicial Decision-Making. Chicago: Rand McNally.

BECKER, Theodore L. and V. MURRAY (1971) Government Lawlessness in America. New York: Oxford University Press.

CAMPBELL, Donald T. (1969) "Reforms as Experiments," 24 American Psychologist 409.

CAMPBELL, Donald T. and H. Laurence ROSS (1968) "The Connecticut Crackdown on Speeding: Time-series Data in Quasi-experimental Analysis," 3 Law and Society Review 33.

DOLBEARE, Kenneth (1967) Trial Courts in Urban Politics: State Court Policy Impact and Functions in a Local Political System. New York: John Wiley.

EASTON, David (1969) "The New Revolution in Political Science," 63 American Political Science Review 1051.

GROSSMAN, Joel and Mary GROSSMAN (1971) Law and Change in Modern America. Pacific Palisades, Cal.: Goodyear.

HANNON, Philip J. (1969) "The Leadership Problem in the Legal Services Program," 4 Law and Society Review 235.

JACOB, Herbert (1971) "Black and White Perceptions of Justice in the City," 6 Law and Society Review 69.

———. (1969) Debtors in Court: The Consumption of Government Services. Chicago: Rand McNally.

KLONOSKI, James R. and Robert I. MENDELSOHN (1970) The Politics of Local Justice. Boston: Little, Brown.

KORT, Fred (1968) "A Nonlinear Model for the Analysis of Judicial Decisions," 62 American Political Science Review 546.

———. (1957) "Predicting Supreme Court Decisions Mathematically: A Quantitative Analysis of the 'Right to Counsel' Cases," 51 American Political Science Review 1.

LEVIN, Martin (1971) "Policy Evaluation and Recidivism," 6 Law and Society Review 17.

LEVINE, James P. (1970a) "Implementing Legal Policies Through Operant Conditioning: The Case of Police Practices." Presented at the meetings of the American Political Science Association, Los Angeles.

———. (1970b) "Methodological Concerns in Studying Supreme Court Efficacy," 4 Law and Society Review 583.

McCLOSKEY, Robert (1957) Essays in Constitutional Law. New York: Knopf.

MENDELSOHN, Robert and James KLONOSKI (1970) "Lay Participation in the Courts: A Study of the Willingness of Witnesses and Jurors to Serve Again," (paper presented at the 1970 annual meeting of the American Political Science Association convention).

MUIR, William K. (1967) Prayer in the Public Schools: Law and Attitude Change. Chicago: University of Chicago Press.

MURPHY, Walter (1964) Elements of Judicial Strategy. Chicago: University of Chicago Press.

MURPHY, Walter and C. Herman PRITCHETT (1961) Courts, Judges, and Politics. New York: Random House.

NAGEL, Stuart S. (1972) Rights of the Accused. Beverly Hills, Cal.: Sage Publications.

———, (ed.) (1971) Symposium on New Trends in Law and Politics Research. 6 Law and Society Review 9-141.

———. (1970) "Law and Social Change," 13 American Behavioral Scientist 483.

———. (1969) The Legal Process from a Behavioral Perspective. Homewood, Ill.: Dorsey Press.

PELTASON, Jack (1961) Fifty-Eight Lonely Men: Southern Federal Judges and School Desegregation. New York: Harcourt, Brace and World.

ROSS, H. Laurence, Donald T. CAMPBELL, and Gene V. GLASS (1970) "Determining the Social Effects of a Legal Reform: The British 'Breathalyser' Crackdown of 1967," 13 American Behavioral Scientist 493.

SCHUBERT, Glendon (1965) The Judicial Mind: The Attitudes and Methodologies of Supreme Court Justices, 1948-1963. Evanston, Ill.: Northwestern University Press.

______. (1964) Judicial Behavior: A Reader in Theory and Research. Chicago: Rand McNally.

______. (1958) "The Study of Judicial Decision-Making as an Aspect of Political Behavior," 52 American Political Science Review 1007.

SCHUBERT, Glendon and David J. DANELSKI (1969) Comparative Judicial Behavior: Cross-Cultural Studies of Political Decision-Making in the East and West. New York: Oxford University Press.

SCHWARTZ, Richard D. (1961) "Field Experimentation in Socio-legal Research," 13 Journal of Legal Education 401.

SCHWARTZ, Richard D. and Sonya ORLEANS (1967) "On Legal Sanctions," 34 University of Chicago Law Review 274.

STUMPF, Harry, Henry SCHROERLUKE, and Forrest DILL (1971) "The Legal Profession and Legal Services: Explorations in Local Bar Politics," 6 Law and Society Review 47.

SUMMERS, Marvin R. and Theodore BARTH (1970) Law and Order in a Democratic Society. Columbus, Ohio: Charles E. Merrill.

TenBROEK, J. (1966) The Law of the Poor. San Francisco: Chandler.

VOSE, Clement (1958) "Litigation as a Form of Pressure Group Activity," 319 Annals 20.

WASBY, Stephen L. (1970) The Impact of the United States Supreme Court: Some Perspectives. Homewood, Ill.: Dorsey Press.

18 Proposals to Facilitate Socio-Legal Teaching and Research

The purpose of this chapter is to describe three proposals for facilitating socio-legal teaching and research.[1] One proposal relates to establishing a repository and clearinghouse for machine-readable data relating to legal phenomena. The second proposal relates to establishing a law and society series of paperbound booklets designed to provide empirical readings to supplement traditional law school courses. The third relates to having a law and social problems conference designed to discuss what social science has already developed with regard to the effects of alternative legal policies in such controversial areas as pollution, poverty, crime, labor problems, consumer protection, international peace, and freedom of speech.

A Legal Data Repository

An institution which has greatly facilitated empirical political science research is the Inter-University Consortium for Political Research at Ann Arbor, Michigan. Its main function is to provide a repository or archive for IBM card data on a variety of subjects for use by political scientists and others in testing hypotheses about the occurrence, causes, and effects of various kinds of political attitudes and behavior. The data generally come from studies conducted by political scientists analyzing such entities as voters, legislators, administrators, countries, and states. These same data, however, can be used repeatedly to test hypotheses which the original researcher did not have in mind. To make the data reusable for this kind of secondary analysis requires carefully determining exactly how the original information was coded on the IBM cards. The Consortium gathers such data, checks them for consistency, catalogues it, distributes, indexes, and duplicates coding keys and data decks on request.

Within the last few years, many legal research projects have made use of questionnaires, docket analysis, surveys, and other research techniques which have generated machine-readable data which could be used for secondary analysis if the data were made more accessible. What is possibly needed is for some university or foundation to send out letters to law school deans, law professors, social scientists doing legal research, and other relevant persons asking which they might have and also asking them to indicate other collections of machine-readable data of which they are aware. After making consistency checks and distributing indexes, the university or foundation could then make these data decks and coding keys available at cost to researchers requesting them.

The need for such a legal data repository is illustrated by the developments relating to the data gathered by Lee Silverstein as part of his criminal docket analysis. He arranged to have data gathered with regard to numerous variables for approximately 11,000 criminal cases from all 50 states. He used these data as part of his research on providing attorneys to indigents in criminal cases.[2] In gathering the data, however, he had the foresight to include many variables that others might find helpful in testing hypotheses relating to the description and causes of various decisional outcomes and other occurrences in criminal cases. Other researchers have used his data for secondary research studies.[3] Unfortunately, Lee Silverstein died, and his data and coding keys were not completely preserved at the American Bar Foundation where his research had been conducted. Some of the data and his code, however, were preserved by the political consortium which will thereby enable further research with data that might otherwise have been lost.

The legal data repository project could be partially financed by government and private foundation money, especially in view of its potential payoff for testing hypotheses about the effect of alternative legal policies in different geographical areas, time periods, or fields of law. Perhaps the project could also be financed by member law schools the way the political consortium is financed by member universities.

In November, 1968, this writer mailed the questionnaire and cover letter shown in Appendix B to all law school deans who were members of the Association of American Law Schools, mainly to determine their interest in participating in such an inter-university consortium for empirical legal research. Sixty-one of the 116 law schools responded either by completing the questionnaire, by a letter, or both, constituting a 53 percent response. Of those responding to the questionnaire, their responses were overwhelmingly favorable. If a highly positive response is scored 5, a mildly positive response scored 4, undecided scored 3, mildly negative 2, and a strongly negative response scored 1, then the average response of the questionnaires to the eleven questions was 4.1.

The average response per question when the questions are arranged in rank order of favorableness is as follows:

Question	*Avg. Response*
2. Having an annual index of data and research	4.8
3. Conducting nationwide or regional surveys	4.4
1. Maintaining a data archive	4.3

Question	*Avg. Response*
5. Summer training institute	4.3
4. Providing consultation	4.2
7. Having occasional conferences	4.1
6. Year-long training program	4.0
8. Publishing newsletter or journal	3.9

The questionnaire also asked the law school deans to indicate their willingness to pay approximately $500 to $1,500 per year to receive the above-mentioned services. Using the same 5, 4, 3, 2, 1 favorableness scale, this question produced an average 3.8 response. When the deans were asked if they would be willing to send a representative to an organizing meeting in conjunction with the December, 1968, AALS meeting, the average response was 4.1; and it was 3.6 with regard to a spring, 1969, meeting at the American Bar Center. A chart showing how each law school responded to each questionnaire item is available on request from this writer.

It was decided by the president and the board of trustees of the Law and Society Association that it was premature to hold an organizing meeting at the 1968 AALS convention. Instead, they decided to establish a consortium committee to plan appropriate future strategy. The committee consisted of Alfred Conard, Geoffrey Hazard, and Stuart Nagel, with Gresham Sykes as chairman. Unfortunately, the committee has been largely dormant, although subject to revival if renewed interest can be shown.

The latest development in the creation of this legal data repository or inter-university consortium for empirical legal research is the establishment of some new agencies and personnel within the National Science Foundation who have expressed an interest in seeing the idea furthered. These people include Melvin Day of the Office of Science Information Service, Frederick Huszagh of the Law and Social Science Program, and Frank Hersman of the RANN program. In letters from Howard Hines of the NSF Social Science Division dated March 14, 1969, and from Melvin Day, dated February 13, 1971, encouraging statements were made. Their feeling, however, seems to be that there is a need at the present time for more legal research which will generate new data which can later be incorporated into a repository for secondary analysis. In the meantime, the political consortium at Ann Arbor can temporarily serve as a repository for some of the legal data that is being gathered.

Supplementary Empirical Readings

Another proposal for facilitating socio-legal teaching and research is to try to get published a series of short, inexpensive paperbound supplements which would provide empirical readings to supplement traditional casebooks in the basic law school fields like contracts, property, and torts.

Traditional law school casebooks contain little social science material and law professors find it difficult to ferret out relevant items from the widespread literature for assignment to their students. Many law professors, however, would possibly like to use such materials if they were more conveniently available.

Many writers commenting on the need for law school curriculum reform have called for greater inputs of empirical materials, such as Harry Kalven, David Cavers, and Abraham Goldstein writing in Geoffrey Hazard, Jr., Law in a Changing America (Prentice Hall, 1968). Practicing lawyers have also indicated more empirical social-science study would have been valuable to their law practice. For example, in a Report on Legal Education prepared in 1969 for the Illinois Board of Higher Education by a committee headed by Robert Underwood of the Illinois Supreme Court, 55 percent of a random sample of Illinois lawyers agreed with the statement, "I would be better able to serve my clients or employer if, while in law school, I had more contact with other academic disciplines as they relate to law." Eighty-six percent of the lawyers who had interdisciplinary training agreed with the statement, "The curriculum which I followed in law school prepared me to properly serve my clients or my employer," whereas only 64 percent of the lawyers who just had traditional case study training agreed with the statement.

It is fairly easy to develop a set of empirical readings in constitutional law, given the work of political scientists and others in the field.[4] Likewise, it is relatively easy to develop a set of empirical readings in criminal law, given the work of sociologists and others in that field.[5] With extensive searching, however, it is also not so difficult to come up with a set of relevant empirical readings for courses which have no social science counterpart like contracts, property, and torts. For example, an empirical contracts supplement running approximately 150 to 200 pages might include items like the following:

I. Applying Empirical Methods to Contract Law

1. Richard E. Speidel, "Contract Law: Some Reflections upon Commercial Context and the Judicial Process," 1967 Wisconsin Law Review 822 (1967). Use pages 822-832.

2. Philip Schuchman, "Empirical Studies in Commercial Law," 23 Journal of Legal Education 181 (1971). Use pages 181-188.

II. Social Forces as Determinants of Contract

1. Harold Havighurst, "The Legal Enforcement of Promises," The Nature of Private Contract (Northwestern University Press, 1961). Use pages 59-63 and 90-92.
2. Lawrence Friedman, Contract Law in America, (University of Wisconsin Press, 1965). Use pages 184-194.
3. Stewart Macaulay, Law and the Balance of Power, (Russell Sage Foundation, 1966). Use pages 197-202.

III. Meaning of Contracts to the Participants

1. Stewart Macaulay, "Non-Contractual Relations in Business: A Preliminary Study," 28 American Sociological Review 55 (1963). Use pages 55-69.
2. Franklin M. Schultz, "The Firm Offer Puzzle: A Study of Business Practice in the Construction Industry," 19 University of Chicago Law Review 237 (1952). Use pages 237-40 and 282-285.
3. Comment, "The Statute of Frauds and the Business Community: A Re-Appraisal in Light of Prevailing Practices," 66 Yale Law Journal 1038 (1957). Use pages 1038-1040 and 1062-1068.
4. Stewart Macaulay, "Private Legislation and the Duty to Read—Business Run by IBM Machine, the Law of Contracts and Credit Cards," 19 Vanderbilt Law Review 1051, (1966). Use pages 1051-1052 and 1118-1121.

IV. Contracts of the Poor

1. Federal Trade Commission, Economic Report on Installment Credit and Retail Sales Practices of District of Columbia Retailers, (Government Printing Office, 1968). Use the six pages reproduced in Dodyk, Poverty Law at 833-839.

2. David Caplovitz, The Poor Pay More (Free Press, 1967). Use pages 170-192.

V. Consumer Protection Legislation

1. William C. Whitford, ''Law and the Consumer Transaction: A Case Study of the Automobile Warranty,'' 1968 Wisconsin Law Review 1006, (1968). Use pages 1006-1013 and 1094-1098.
2. Comment, ''An Empirical Study of the Arkansas Usury Law: 'With Friends Like That . . .',\'' 1968 University of Illinois Law Forum 544, (1968). Use pages 545-546 and 586-588.
3. John Hicinbothem and Mitchell Sikora, ''A Survey of Experience under the Massachusetts Retail Installment Sales Act,'' 9 Boston College Industrial and Commercial Law Review 1020 (1968). Use pages 1020-1031.
4. Monroe P. Friedman, ''Using Simulation Techniques to Predict the Behavioral Effects of New Laws: The Case of Truth-in-Lending Legislation and the Consumer,'' 54 Journal of Applied Psychology 297 (1970). Use pages 297-301.
5. Comment, ''A Case Study of the Impact of Consumer Legislation: The Elimination of Negotiability and the Cooling-Off Period,'' 78 Yale Law Journal 618 (1969). Use pages 618-623, 628-630, and 655-656.
6. Robert Shay, ''The Impact of the Uniform Consumer Credit Code Upon the Market for Consumer Installment Credit,'' 33 Law and Contemporary Problems 752 (1968). Use pages 752 and 763-764.

VI. Contract Enforcement

1. John Frank and John Endicott, ''Defenses in Equity and 'Legal Rights',\'' 14 Louisiana Law Review 380 (1954). Use pages 380-390.
2. Sally Grant, ''Resort to the Legal Process in Collecting Debts from High Risk Credit Buyers in Los Angeles—Alternative Methods for Allocating Present Costs,'' 14 UCLA Law Review 879 (1967). Use pages 879-880 and 896-905.
3. George Brunn, ''Wage Garnishments in California: A Study and Recommendations'' 53 California Law Review 1214 (1965). Use pages 1234-1243 and 1248-1249.

4. David Caplovitz, Debtors in Default (temp. ed. 1970). Use pages 39-42 of Chapter 10 and 73-75 of Chapter 11.
5. Philip Shuchman, "Profit on Default: An Archival Study of Automobile Repossession and Resale," 22 Stanford Law Review 20 (1969). Use pages 20-22 and 53-57.
6. Herbert Jacob, "Winners and Losers: Garnishment and Bankruptcy in Wisconsin," 7 Trans-Action 24 (1969). Use pages 24-31.

Likewise, Appendix B provides a rough outline for a set of empirical readings in tort law and an outline for a set in property law. These outlines are not as edited as the one for contract law, but they illustrate some of the richness of the available socio-legal literature. A fully edited set of readings would not only indicate how each item is to be excerpted, but would also provide introductory and transitional text material as well as further bibliographic references. Additional empirical references on torts and property from readers of this article will be greatly welcomed by this author.

Some interest in publishing such a series has been expressed by Foundation Press, Bobbs-Merrill, and West. The main drawback seems to be a feeling that law school teaching is not yet sufficiently empirical-oriented to make such a series commercially feasible. The costs of publishing, however, can be kept down by making each volume short, paperbound, and printed via offset printing rather than typesetting. Readings like the Selected Essays on Constitutional Law (West, 1963) were commercially unsuccessful possibly because they were long, hardbound, and typeset. They also tended simply to duplicate traditional law review articles without editing and without transitional material, rather than to provide a mixture of edited law library and non-law library materials.

A Law and Social Problems Conference

A third proposal for facilitating socio-legal teaching and research is to have an interdisciplinary conference on law and social problems. The conference would not be devoted to speeches on methodology or on the general need for empirical legal research. Instead, the conference would discuss what social science has already developed and needs to develop with regard to the effects of specific legal policies in such controversial areas as pollution, poverty, crime, consumer protection, freedom of speech, labor problems, and international peace.

A top law professor and social scientist could co-chair a panel or series of panels on each of the seven problem areas. Example persons include the following:

Social Problem	*Law Professor*	*Social Scientist*
1. Pollution	Frank Grad Columbia Law School	Clarence Davies Poli. Sci. Dept. Princeton University
2. Race and Poverty	Joel Handler Wisconsin Law School	Duane Lockhard Poli. Sci. Dept. Princeton University
3. Crime	Abraham Goldstein Yale Law School	William Chambliss Sociology Dept. U. of Calif., Santa Barbara
4. Consumer Protection	Philip Shuchman U. of Conn., Law School	David Caplovitz Sociology Dept. City Univ. of New York
5. Free Speech	Norman Dorsen N.Y.U. Law School	Samuel Krislov Poli. Sci. Dept. Univ. of Minnesota
6. Labor Problems	Alfred Blumrosen Rutgers Law School	Karl DeSchweinitz Economics Dept. Northwestern Univ.
7. International Peace	Myres McDougal Yale Law School	Michael Barkun Poli. Sci. Dept. Syracuse Univ.

All of the above law professors have shown an interest in the application of social science to their respective fields of law. Likewise all of the above social scientists have shown an interest in the impact of law on behavior in their respective fields of social science.

An additional panel or set of panels could deal in a general way with law and social problems and be co-chaired by a general interdisciplinary social scientist (like Victor Rosenblum of Northwestern or Richard Schwartz of Buffalo) and an interdisciplinary law professor (like Maurice Rosenberg of Columbia or Harry Kalven of the University of Chicago).

Frank Hersman of the Office of Intergovernmental Science Programs of the National Science Foundation expressed an interest in encouraging such a conference in a paper he presented at the 1970 AALS meeting on "Legal Research and the Federal Government." There has not, however, been any significant follow-up. This proposal, could potentially be financed by the National Science Foundation if more interest were shown by the law teaching profession.

These three proposals all seem relevant to advancing socio-legal teaching and research. To some extent they may have been premature when they originated. As of now, however, they do seem to be ideas whose time has come. If more interest can be expressed by law teachers to the relevant governmental agencies, the private foundations, and the commercial publishers, then perhaps the needed implementation will be forthcoming.

Appendix A: Survey Materials on Having an Inter-University Consortium for Empirical Legal Research

Part One: The Cover Letter

UNIVERSITY OF ILLINOIS
Urbana, Illinois 61801

Department of Political Science
Dean John Doe
The Law School
University of Whiteacre
City, State Zip

Dear Dean Doe:

I am writing to inquire as to the interest of your university or law school in participating in an Inter-University Consortium for Empirical Legal Research.

The main purpose of such an entity is to muster some of the collective resources of member universities toward retrieving, generating, processing, and disseminating behavioral legal data which would generally be too expensive to be done by an individual researcher or even a member university. Such a legal consortium would possibly be modeled in part after the highly successful Inter-University Consortium for Political Research. For illustrative purposes I am enclosing a brochure and an organization memo on the political consortium.

The legal consortium idea already has the mild to strong endorsement of various officers and members of the Law and Society Association, the AALS Jurimetrics Committee, and the AALS Research Committee although a systematic survey of these groups has not yet been made. Additional support can possibly be obtained from the National Law Foundation or the National Social Science Foundation if those bills are passed by Congress.

Before proceeding further with the organization of such an entity, it seems appropriate to determine the attitudes of the deans of the AALS law schools toward the possible benefits to be received from an Inter-University Consortium for Empirical Legal Research and toward their willingness to participate. To aid in making this determination, I am enclosing a one-page questionnaire that should take less than five minutes to complete, although you may make any comments you wish between the lines of the questionnaire or on a separate sheet. A stamped, self-addressed envelope is enclosed for your convenience in mailing it back. I shall be happy to send you the results of the questionnaire when the returns have been processed. The results may also be published in the Law and Society Review and in the AALS Reports of Committees.

If enough of the responding law schools indicate a favorable interest in the basic idea, perhaps an organizing meeting can be held in conjunction with the ABA convention at Philadelphia this August or in conjunction with the AALS convention in New Orleans this December. I look forward to receiving your response.

Very sincerely yours,
Stuart S. Nagel
Associate Professor

SN:jn
Enclosures (4)

Part Two: The Questionnaire

Questionnaire on Having an Inter-University
Consortium for Empirical Legal Research

I. Possible Benefits to Be Received from Consortium-Type Functions

For each of the following functions, please indicate your opinion as to the degree of benefit you feel empirical legal research would receive from having these functions performed by a consortium-type organization. Please use the following symbols on the lines provided:

++ Great benefit to empirical legal research
\+ Beneficial but not greatly
0 Undecided or indifferent
− Harmful to legal research

1. Bringing together IBM card data, questionnaires, and coding keys for immediate availability to legal researchers other than the original compilers. ____
2. Preparing and disseminating an annual index of available data and on-going research. ____
3. Conducting nationwide or regional surveys of attitudes and behavior relevant to law for a number of legal researchers simultaneously. ____

4. Providing consultation on matters relating to sampling, measurement, statistical analysis, programming, and computer runs. ____
5. Summer training institutes on research design and statistical inference for law professors and graduate law students. ____
6. A program whereby law professors can spend an academic year learning quantitative research methodology in the social science departments of a major university the way social scientists spend an academic year attending Harvard Law School. ____
7. Having occasional conferences on subjects relevant to empirical legal research especially inter-disciplinary conferences. ____
8. Publishing a journal describing the consortium's activities and publishing articles that apply empirical or behavioral research techniques to legal matters. ____

II. Willingness to Participate

For each of the following statements, please indicate your attitudes using the following symbols:

++ Agree strongly
\+ Agree but not strongly
0 Undecided
– Disagree but not strongly
– – Disagree strongly

1. My university or law school would probably be willing to pay from approximately $500 to $1,500 a year to receive the above-mentioned services. (The exact amount will be based on (1) ability to pay, (2) the use made by researchers from each member university, and (3) funds available from government and foundation grants.) ____
2. My university or law school would be willing to choose a representative to send to an organizing meeting in conjunction with:
   a. The December, 1968, conventicn of the Association of American Law Schools in New Orleans. ____
   b. A special organizing meeting at the American Bar Center in Chicago sometime in spring, 1969. ____

Signed ________________________________

School ________________________________

Appendix B: Some Items for Empirical Readings in Torts and Property

Part One: Tort Law

I. What *Causes* the Tort System to Be What It Is

1. Robert Rabin, "Some Thought on Tort Law from a Socio-political Perspective," 1969 Wisconsin Law Review 51 (1969).
2. Albert Ehrenzweig, "Civil Liability: A Neglected Area of Psychoanalytical Research," 10 The American Image 15 (1953).
3. Martin Shapiro, "Decentralized Decision-Making in the Law of Torts," in S. Sidney Ulmer (ed.), Political Decision Making 44 (Van Nostrand, 1970).

II. *Personnel* in the Tort System

A. Plaintiffs

1. Roger Hunting, "Payment for Accident Victims: The Claimant's Eye View," 33 New York State Bar Journal 81 (1961).
2. Stuart Nagel and Lenore Weitzman, "Women as Litigants," 23 Hastings Law Journal 171 (1971).

B. Lawyers

1. Murray Schwartz and Daniel Mitchell, "An Economic Analysis of the Contingent Fee in Personal Injury Litigation", 22 Stanford Law Review 1125 (1970).
2. Jerome Carlin, Lawyers on Their Own (Rutgers U. Press, 1962).

C. Jurors

1. Harry Kalven, Jr., "The Jury, the Law and the Personal Injury Damage Award," 19 Ohio State Law Journal 158 (1958).

III. Essential *Legal Elements*

A. Negligence

1. Edward Green, "The Reasonable Man: Legal Fiction or Psychosocial Reality?" 2 Law and Society Review 241 (1968).
2. Hirsch Silverman and Bernard Seidler, "A Psychological Evaluation of the Law of Torts," 47 ABA Journal 180 (1961).

B. Damages

1. Marc A. Franklin, et al., "Accidents, Money and the Law: A

Study of the Economics of Personal Injury Litigation," 61 Columbia Law Review 1 (1961).

2. R. A. Holmes "On the Economic Welfare of Victims of Automobile Accidents," 60 American Economic Review 143 (1970).
3. Alfred Conard, et al., Automobile Accident Costs and Payments (1964).
4. U. S. Dept. of Transportation, 1 Automobile Personal Injury Claims (1970).

IV. *Reform* From Contributory Negligence to No Fault

1. Maurice Rosenberg, "Comparative Negligence in Arkansas: 'A Before and After' Survey," 13 Arkansas Law Review 89 (1959).
2. William C. Whitford, "Strict Products Liability and the Automobile Industry: Much Ado About Nothing," 1968 Wisconsin Law Review 83 (1968).
3. Robert Keeton and Jeffrey O'Connell, Basic Protection for the Traffic Victim—A Blueprint for Reforming Auto Insurance (Little Brown, 1965).
4. P. S. Atiyah, Accidents, Compensation and the Law (Fred Rothman, 1970).
5. Guido Calabresi, The Costs of Accidents: A Legal and Economic Analysis (Yale U. Press, 1970).

Part Two: Property Law

I. The *Need* for Empirical Research on Property Law

Jacob Beuscher, "Law-in-Action Research in Rural Areas of the United States," 1969 Wisconsin Law Review 757 (1969).

II. Real Estate Sales Transactions and Ownership

1. John Payne, "Ancillary Costs in the Purchase of Homes," 35 Missouri Law Review 455 (1970).
2. Marshall Harris & William Hines, *Installment Land Contracts in Iowa* (1965).
3. William Hines, "Real Property Joint Tenancies: Law, Fact and Fancy," 51 Iowa L. Rev. 582 (1966).

4. William Hines, ''Personal Property Joint Tenancies: More Law, Fact and Fancy,'' 54 Minnesota L. Rev. 509 (1970).

III. *Landlord-Tenant* Relations

1. Comment, ''Housing the Poor: A Study of the Landlord-Tenant Relationship,'' 41 U. of Columbia Law Review 541 (1969).
2. Warren Mueller, ''Residential Tenants and their Leases: An Empirical Study,'' 69 Michigan Law Review 247 (1970).
3. Ted Vaughan, ''The Landlord-Tenant Relation in a Low-Income Area,'' 16 Social Problems 208 (1968).
4. Richard Lempert and Kiyoski Ikeda, ''Evictions from Public Housing: Effects of Independent Review,'' 35 American Sociological Review 852)1970).
5. George Sternlieb, *The Tenement Landlord* (Rutgers U. Press, 1966).
6. Chester Rapkin, *The Private Rental Housing Market in New York City* (N.Y.C. Plan Commission, 1965).

IV. *Land Use* Law

1. Curtis Berger and Patrick Rohan, ''The Nassau County Study: An Empirical Look into the Practices of Condemnation,'' 67 Columbia Law Review 430 (1967).
2. K. H. Connell, ''The Land Legislation and Irish Social Life,'' 11 Economic History Review 1 (1958).
3. Norman Williams, Jr. and Edward Wacks, ''Segregation of Residential Areas Along Economic Lines: Lionshead Lake Revisited,'' 1969 Wisconsin Law Review 827 (1969).
4. Sheldon Plager and Joel Handler, ''The Politics of Planning for Urban Redevelopment: Strategies in the Manipulation of the Public Law,'' 1966 Wisconsin Law Review 724 (1966).
5. David Levin, ''New Directions in Land Acquisition and Land Use,'' 1969 Wisconsin Law Review 848 (1969).
6. Jesse Dukeminier and Clyde Stapleton, ''The Zoning Board of Adjustment: A Case Study in Misrule,'' 50 Kentucky Law Journal 27, 310 (1962).

V. Wills and *Inheritance*

1. Lawrence Friedman, ''The Law of the Living, the Law of the Dead: Property, Succession, and Society,'' 1966 Wisconsin Law Review 340 (1966).
2. Allison Dunham, ''The Method, Process and Frequency of Wealth Transmission,'' 30 Chicago Law Review 241 (1962).

3. Thomas Shaffer, ''Death, Property, and Lawyers: A Behavioral Approach (U. Press of Cambridge, Mass., 1971).
4. Marvin Sussman, et al., The Family and Inheritance (Russell Sage Foundation, 1970).

Notes

1. The author acknowledges the suggestive ideas of: Lawrence Friedman, Arthur Leff, Philip Shuchman, Richard Speidel and George Wallace with regard to empirical reference in contract law; Harry Kalven and Jeffrey O'Connell in tort law; William Hines, Quintin Johnstone, Myres McDougal and Sheldon Plager in property law. Ernest Jones was helpful with regard to all sections of this chapter.

2. L. SILVERSTEIN, DEFENSE OF THE POOR IN CRIMINAL CASES IN AMERICAN STATE COURTS (1965).

3. Gerard & Terry, *Discrimination Against Negroes in the Administration of Criminal Law in Missouri,* 1970 WASH. U.L.Q. 415; Nagel, *Disparities in Criminal Procedure,* 14 UCLA L.REV. 1272 (1967).

4. F. WIRT & W. HAWLEY (eds.), NEW DIMENSIONS OF FREEDOM IN AMERICA (1969) and T. BECKER (ed.), THE IMPACT OF SUPREME COURT DECISIONS (1969).

5. R. QUINNEY, CRIME AND JUSTICE IN SOCIETY (1969); W. CHAMBLISS & R. SEIDMAN, CRIME AND THE LEGAL PROCESS (1969); and A. GOLDSTEIN & J. GOLDSTEIN, CRIME, LAW AND SOCIETY (1971).

Index of Names

Index of Subjects

About the Author

Stuart S. Nagel is a professor of political science at the University of Illinois and a member of the Illinois bar. He is the author or editor of *The Legal Process from a Behavioral Perspective* (Dorsey, 1969), *The Rights of the Accused in Law and Action* (Sage, 1972), *Environmental Politics* (Praeger, 1974), *Policy Studies in America and Elsewhere* (Lexington Books, 1975), and *Policy Studies and the Social Sciences* (Lexington Books, 1975). He has held fellowships from the LEAA National Institute, Yale Law and Social Science Program, National Science Foundation, Center for Advanced Study in the Behavioral Sciences, Social Science Research Council, and the East-West Center. Dr. Nagel has been an attorney to the U.S. Senate Judiciary Committee, Office of Economic Opportunity, Lawyer's Constitutional Defense Committee in Mississippi, and the National Labor Relations Board.